REALIST CRIMINOLOGY

Crime Control and Policing in

In the 1980s in Britain a new school of critical criminology arose to challenge the political and philosophical idealism that characterized its critical predecessors, and to offer an alternative to the crime control policies of the 'New Right.' Arguing that by overemphasizing the crimes of the powerful, much of critical criminology had virtually ignored the impact of street crime on its victims, a 'left realism' emerged to reassert the centrality of the victim in the development of a progressive criminology. Critical realism recognizes the seriousness of street crime for those people victimized by it (particularly women), acknowledges that a consensus as to the desirability of a core group of laws does exist, and advocates various kinds of criminal justice reform and crime prevention strategies. In this respect, there are important parallels with debates in feminism concerning the role of the state in the problem of violence against women. One of the most important contributions critical realism has made to criminological research is the development of local crime surveys which attempt to measure patterns of victimization and policing and how these are perceived by the general public. Such research remains largely undeveloped in North America, and it is the purpose of this book to begin to take stock of these developments, and examine their relevance for North America. This is the first text to include a critical examination of left realism, examine its relationship to feminism, and comment on its relevance outside Britain.

John Lowman is a professor at Simon Fraser University and Associate Director of the School of Criminology.

Brian D. MacLean teaches criminology at Kwantlen College and is an associate research fellow at the Centre for Criminology at Middlesex University.

Realist Criminology:
Crime Control and Policing
in the 1990s

Edited by
John Lowman
Brian D. MacLean

University of Toronto Press
Toronto Buffalo London

© University of Toronto Press Incorporated 1992
Toronto Buffalo London
Printed in Canada

ISBN 0-8020-2828-4 (cloth)
ISBN 0-8020-7702-1 (paper)

⊚

Printed on acid-free paper

Canadian Cataloguing in Publication Data

Main entry under title:

Realist criminology: crime control and policing
in the 1990s

ISBN 0-8020-2828-4 (bound)   ISBN 0-8020-7702-1 (pbk.)

1. Criminology. I. Lowman, John, 1950-
II. MacLean, Brian, 1950-

HV6025.R43 1992   384   C92-095006-X

for Dawn and Laura

Contents

Foreword:
The Criminology That Came in
Out of the Cold

Some fifteen years ago, before the first big crime surveys in Britain and Canada, radical criminology tended to follow Gramsci and Althusser to present crime as an ideological distraction from the real, driving contradictions of class; Hobsbawm and Thompson to present crime as primitive, inchoate protest; and Bonger and Rusche and Kirchheimer to present crime as the product of a rampant individualism spawned by capitalism. There was no talk of the pains of crime or of victims and victimization. Neither was there talk about crime control and policing unless it was to despatch them as the works of a repressive capitalist state. The politics of radical criminology ignored the criminal justice policies and programs of prerevolutionary society either as ephemeral or as wilfully calling for the impossible with the result that the fabric of the state might be stretched beyond endurance. To do otherwise would have exposed the criminologist to charges of co-optation, correctionalism, and reformism. 'Bourgeois' criminology was itself dismissed as almost wholly administrative, positivist, empiricist, and ideologically compromised.

There was little public criticism of radical criminologist by radical criminologist in the late 1960s and early 1970s. It was as if debate were framed by a set of implicit political imperatives that discouraged division in the face of a common enemy. And when dissent *did* come, it appeared from without (although not from what were called '*bourgeois*' criminologists; so segmented was the discipline of criminology that different groups could coexist in their own parallel universes. 'Bourgeois' criminologists seemed to hope merely that radical criminology would go away).

The critical assault took two guises. First, in the later 1970s, was a feminism that was as much practical and campaigning as cerebral, as much sited in rape crisis centres, transition houses, and refuges as in the study and the library. It was a feminism that rediscovered and then championed the assaulted and abused woman. Feminist criminologists protested that male violence to women was indeed significant, that women's fears about crime were neither irrational nor mystified, and that the scholarly examination of the victimization and deviance of women was not a political distraction at all (Heidensohn 1968; Smart 1976). Radicals conceded that some part of their enterprise did require re-examination. There was, wrote Jones, MacLean, and Young (1986: 2-3), 'a general tendency in radical thought to idealize their historical subject (in this case the working class) and to play down intra-group conflict, blemishes and social disorganization. But the power of the feminist case resulted in a sort of cognitive schizophrenia amongst radicals ...' The response to that first assault was to trim. It became commonplace for radical argument to hedge itself about with special clauses that treated rape and domestic violence as empirical cases apart.

The second assault stemmed from the brute world of empirical data that so many radicals had dismissed or neglected in the past. The national and local crime surveys of the early 1980s came literally and symbolically to redefine the terrain of criminology, crime, and social control. It became apparent that the fear of crime was no mere artefact of false consciousness; that crime inflicted real distress; and that those most vulnerable to victimization were the very groups that radical criminology had adopted as its own: women, Blacks, Asians, and the working class. It was tacitly acknowledged that perhaps, after all, there was some substance to the 'bourgeois' preoccupation with control (although it must also be said that 'bourgeois' criminology had been just as remiss in its neglect of the victim and victimization).

Those who were to evolve into left realists did not protest, as Durkheim once protested, that the new facts must be wrong. They did not wriggle, as so many do, in the throes of cognitive dissonance. They did not evade the implications of a new form of knowledge. They publicly recanted, and for that they deserve praise. It is never easy to recant, particularly in a world where existing publications confront their authors as an indelible record of inconsistency and where colleagues hover like carrion birds for opportunities to expose contradiction. After the first crime surveys, John Lea and Jock Young (1984: 262) asserted baldly that 'there was a belief that property offences are directed solely against the bourgeoisie and that violence against the person is carried out by amateur Robin Hoods in the course of their righteous attempts to redistribute wealth. All of this is, alas, untrue.' Lea and Young proclaimed what was, in effect, a pure and simple paradigm shift in the face of anomaly (although one might remark that criminology undergoes a scientific revolution *every* time Jock Young changes his mind).

Where once there had been an increasingly sterile argument about what Marx and Engels *really* meant to say about crime and control – argument that had long since fallen prey to the law of diminishing marginal returns – left realists reinvigorated radical criminology. They have coupled a succession of new and significant questions to new methods of exploring the empirical world and, above all, to local crime surveys (this book is, as much as anything, a celebration of the local crime survey that Brian MacLean and his colleagues pioneered in Islington). *Realist Criminology: Crime Control and Policing in the 1990s* documents how left realists are newly and importantly self-critical, no longer unquestioningly loyal to one another in the service of class warfare. They are now more eclectic and open, no longer self-enclosed, no longer refusing 'bourgeois' criminology and its works as irredeemably corrupted. They have embraced a pragmatism where once there was only a trust in an unspecified revolutionary future (Downes 1979). They no longer claim to 'know best' (Cohen 1975) but take the common-sense knowledge of lay people very seriously indeed. And the effect has been that they have galvanized large tracts of criminology.

The most ferocious debates left to left realism are with the ghosts of left criminology and with those still farther on the left who refuse to be impressed by the new facts of crime surveys. There is a silence towards the right, and I wonder what unbridgeable differences can now be said to remain between left realism and the more theoretically informed and catholic remnants of what used to be disparaged as 'bourgeois' criminology, between left realism, on the one hand, and Skogan, Reiner, Ericson, Downes, Morgan, Pease, Bottoms, and Wiles, on the other; between the administrative criminology of the left and the administrative criminology of the not-so-left or the politically unaligned. Indeed, there are contributors to *Realist Criminology* itself who cannot comfortably be named left realists at all. It may be the case that very similar substantive problems are now being pursued by criminologists who differ only in their use of descriptive language and sense of a past. In all this, the book may perhaps celebrate another welcome event: an end to the criminological cold war and the facile ideological oppositions of the 1970s and early 1980s.

References

Cohen, S. 1975. 'It's All Right for You to Talk,' in R. Bailey and M. Brake, eds., *Radical Social Work*, 76-95. London: Edward Arnold

Downes, D. 1979. 'Praxis Makes Perfect,' in D. Downes and P. Rock, eds., *Deviant Interpretations*, 1-16. Oxford: Martin Robertson

Heidensohn, F. 1968. 'The Deviance of Women: A Critique and an Enquiry.' *British Journal of Sociology*, 19 (June): 160-173

Jones, T., B. MacLean, and J. Young. 1986. *The Islington Crime Survey: Crime, Victimization and Policing in Inner-City London.* Aldershot: Gower

Lea, J., and J. Young. 1984. *What Is to Be Done about Law and Order?* Harmondsworth: Penguin

Smart, C. 1976. *Women, Crime and Criminology.* London: Routledge and Kegan Paul

Paul Rock
London

Preface

In these days of shrinking university budgets and the considerable expense required to bring visiting scholars to British Columbia, we do not have the frequent opportunity to interact with our colleagues from abroad. And even if, as professional academics, we are able to travel to a few national and international conferences, students rarely enjoy such opportunities. We have found that one way of overcoming these geographic difficulties has been to organize conferences in Vancouver – thereby bringing the Mohammeds to the mountains, so to speak. The conference format allows funding to be attracted from outside the university, and has the added advantage for visitors that they get to meet colleagues with kindred interests, and visit Vancouver, surely one of the most spectacular cities in North America. Over the past fifteen years, the School of Criminology at Simon Fraser University has convened a series of conferences and symposia on key issues in criminology. The most recent of these, 'Realist Criminology in the 1990s,' was co-sponsored with the University of British Columbia and the Social Sciences and Humanities Research Council of Canada (SSHRC).

The seeds for a conference on left realism were sown in July 1989 at the British Criminology Conference in Bristol. We realized that, whether it was being denigrated or saluted, left realism found a place in most of the panels: love it or hate it, most presenters felt it necessary to address the realist project. Yet many of these debates have hardly found their way into the literature on the other side of the Atlantic; when they have, left realism has often been caricatured. There is yet to be a good idea in criminology which did not originate in pub discussions, and it was in the pub with Jock Young that the idea of an international conference on left realism was first proposed. Planning began immediately upon our return to Canada, and the conference was held in Vancouver in May 1990. This book presents a series of essays which further develop some of the key ideas discussed at the conference. Thus, without the conference to stimulate critical debate, it is unlikely that this book would have germinated. Bringing the project to fruition would not have been possible without the kind assistance of numerous individuals and organizations.

We would like to acknowledge the financial assistance provided to the conference by the Social Sciences and Humanities Research Council of Canada; the Office of the Vice-President, Research, University of British Columbia; the Office of the Dean of Arts, University of British Columbia; the Faculty of Arts Conference Fund, Simon Fraser University; the School of Criminology, Simon Fraser University; the Vancouver Bar Association; the Solicitor General Canada; and the British Columbia Ministry of the Attorney General.

We would also like to thank Mimi Ajzenstadt, Tom Daoust, Kimberly Daum, Catherine Gibson, Carol Hui, Maria Koroneous, Marion Sewell, Mojdeh Shariari, Manisha Singh, and Suzanne Stacy for their volunteer assistance. Wendelin Fraser and the staff at Simon Fraser University Harbour Center Downtown Campus; Leanna Hayes and the catering staff at the Hotel Georgia; Sandy Ingram at the Sands Hotel; Florida Town, Media and Public Relations, Simon Fraser University; Gavin Wilson, Community Relations, University of British Columbia all contributed to making the conference a success. We would also like to especially thank all of the conference participants: Seema Ahluwalia, Daniel Birch, Jack Blaney, Benjamin Bowling, Neil Boyd, Pat Carlen, Dorothy Chunn, Claire Culhane, Dawn Currie, Elliot Currie, Nanette Davis, Walter DeKeseredy, Karlene Faith, Ezzat Fattah, Paul Havemann, Marlee Kline, Roger Matthews, Rob McQueen, Bob Menzies, Ray Michalowski, Kate Painter, Frank Pearce, Ken Pease, Tony Platt, Chuck Reasons, Herman Schwendinger, Julia Schwendinger, Ken Stoddart, Simon Verdun-Jones, Sandra Walklate, and Jock Young, as well as Bonnie Quan for her invaluable typing assistance.

While the conference may have served as the initial spark for this project, no book is completed without a good deal of work by its publisher. Staff at the University of Toronto Press have been especially helpful. We would like to thank Beverley Beetham Endersby and Lorraine Ourom, editorial department, and Virgil Duff, Managing Editor. Their unique combination of personal and professional approaches made working on the manuscript a pleasurable, painless experience. We would also like to thank our anonymous reviewers for their helpful suggestions on earlier versions of the manuscript.

Finally, we would especially like to thank our contributing authors for their patience, professionalism, and assistance in making this book a reality.

John Lowman and Brian MacLean
July 1992

INTRODUCTION
Realist Criminology in the 1990s

1 Introduction: Left Realism, Crime Control, and Policing in the 1990s

John Lowman and Brian D. MacLean

Social-scientific discourse has developed rapidly in the last three decades, and there are few disciplines in which such development is more readily observable than criminology. The emergence of new paradigms coupled with the scathing criticism of older ones has characterized criminological discourse since the mid 1950s. The once-dominant biological, psychological, and subcultural explanations for criminal behaviour had set the tone for a correctionalist criminology which located as the cause of crime some kind of pathology in the individual. By the mid 1950s such thinking had given way to the anomie tradition, which, while a much more fully social theory of crime causation, was also informed by a correctionalist ideology. Thus crime was still seen as being carried out by individuals who lacked something, which distinguished them from conforming, law-abiding citizens. Whether biological, psychological, or social in its orientation, criminology at this time was a positivistic or functionalist science and thus was ahistorical, empiricist, and reductionist.

During the 1950s, in particular with the writings of Edwin Lemert, a new paradigm began to develop in which crime was no longer seen as the product of pathological individuals, and a whole new set of questions began to emerge. Studies of norm violation gave way to studies of norm construction. Whereas criminology had previously accepted norms as both absolute and universal, this new investigation began to conceptualize norms as relative and as being culturally, spatially, and temporally specific. Thus central questions for criminologists shifted from 'who is criminal' to 'who is designated as criminal' and from 'what are the characteristics of a criminal' to 'what are the characteristics of the audience which labels individuals as criminal.'

This new paradigm ushered in forms of inquiry which radically departed from more conventional approaches to studying crime. <u>Once it was conceded that crime was socially constructed, the study of crime changed focus, analysing the process of that construction rather than incidents of norm violation.</u> Concomitant with this ontological shift came an appreciation of the social relations of inequality and the power relations that underlie the process by which certain elements of the population come to be defined as criminal and treated accordingly by the criminal justice apparatus. The fact that the less powerful segments of society were consistently overrepresented in criminal justice statistics became evidence that the administration of justice was unfair. Criminology tended to devolve into two main camps, each diametrically opposed to the other. On the positive side of this antithesis, criminologists were employed by the state to manage the 'crime problem.' Practitioners of this criminology have come to be known as 'administrative criminologists' (Young 1986). This 'state-sponsored' criminology has been increasingly seen by progressive criminologists as a science of social control in which the criminal justice apparatus serves to facilitate the process by which inequality is reproduced socially.

On the negative side of the antithesis, certain writers began to take an oppositional stance against state-sponsored criminology, and sometimes criminology itself. Advocates of this perspective have come to be known as 'radical,' 'critical,' or 'progressive.' Some do not believe that criminology is an inevitable vehicle of social reproduction, and instead view the discipline as a way by which social inequality can be transcended. For some constituencies of this group, criminology is to be seen as liberatory, a discourse and practice which does not seek to preserve existing social relations but to transform them into more equitable arrangements. Thus, at this level, a central debate in criminology is one characterized by the conservative elements coming into conflict with the progressive elements. If we were to remain at this level of investigation, however, it might seem as if both sides of this antithesis were somehow homogeneous. Our purpose here is to make explicit some nuances of progressive criminology.

If progressive criminology is seen by its various practitioners as playing a role in the transformation of relations of social inequality, that is where their similarities end. How such a transformation is to be brought about is hotly contested, as is the nature of such inequality, and the question of whether or not criminology has a role to play in such a transformation is now the subject of much controversy.

This book is about left realism, a type of criminology that claims to be progressive and committed to the transformation of social inequality. Whether or not it has such potential is the subject of much debate. On the progressive side, various proponents of Marxism, post-modernism, feminism, and ethnic criminology have criticized left realism for a variety of reasons. Some Marxists contend that realism is just another form of state-sponsored criminology and cite the survey research which informs realist criminology as an example of a right-wing technology. Some post-modernists argue that left-realist discourse has not moved beyond the categories employed by the 'law-and-order lobby.' Some feminists claim that left realism is yet another version of male-dominated criminological discourse, which is gender blind, and some ethnic criminologists would claim that left realism has not moved beyond the racist categories employed by a white middle-class, male-dominated criminology.

Our purpose in this book is to explore these debates in detail and to excavate carefully the strengths and limitations of realist criminology. In short, does realist criminology have the potential to play a role in social transformation or is it simply another variation of the conservative side of the criminological antithesis? Before undertaking this investigation, it will be useful to describe briefly how realist criminology emerged on the margins of criminological inquiry and quickly gravitated towards the centre.

The Emergence of Realist Criminology

In his 'Left Idealism, Reformism and Beyond,' Jock Young (1979) advances the concept of 'left idealism.' By this he means that while a critical criminological discourse based upon Marxist concepts had been developing in Britain in the 1970s, much of this literature was based primarily upon a philosophical idealism which, ironically, is not Marxist at all. Concepts such as 'free will,' 'social equality,' and 'human rights,' which are central to this line of inquiry, were used as if they were absolute truths when, in fact, they are specific to bourgeois political economy. Marx himself devoted much of his intellectual life to pointing out that any inquiry which uses such concepts as a starting-point must be idealistic and must serve to reinterpret history in such a way as to make the current social formation the only one ideologically possible.

Margaret Thatcher's rise to power on a law-and-order platform placed progressive intellectuals in the unenviable position of trying to determine the most appropriate way to combat the Conservative success at the polls. Thatcher was quick to launch an assault against the labour movement, education, and inner-city labour-controlled local governments. The result of this assault was further fragmentation of the British left. With regard to crime-control policy, the Thatcher government introduced a variety of authoritarian legislation that included reorganization of the police forces in England and Wales and the introduction of new and broader police powers to deal with the 'crime problem.' Criminologists were left in a quandary, and different divisions among them began to crystallize. In particular, the more Marxist elements of progressive criminology, those dubbed by Young 'left idealists,' rapidly came into conflict with the newly emerging 'left realists.'

Aside from the Conservative victory at the polls, racial unrest in the British inner city served to exacerbate the divisiveness that was already rapidly occurring in the progressive criminological community. In particular, the Brixton riots of 1981 led to a major division among criminologists. In their *Policing the Riots* (Cowell, Jones, and Young 1982), writers such as Jock Young, John Lea, Richard Kinsey, and David Cowell began to frame loosely a criminological discourse of left realism. This book elicited an immediate and negative reaction from a variety of academics and from researchers at different levels within the local government structure. The substance of the critique was that the realists were being co-opted by state-sponsored criminology, that as white researchers they really had no idea about the experiences of racial minorities in Britain (indeed, they were often depicted as racists), that their political position in relation to police accountability was conservative, and that their characterization of all who opposed them as idealists was unnecessarily fragmentary.

With the publication of *What Is to Be Done about Law and Order?* (Lea and Young 1984), a more formal account of the left-realist position was articulated. One important point made in this book was that, in their zeal to expose the state as an entity which acts in the interests of capital by criminalizing disenfranchised populations such as working-class and racial minorities, left idealists ignored the fact that crime really was a problem for the working class. The book proposed that the frequency of crime was at an all-time high, and that crime was disproportionately distributed among the working class, women, and racial minorities. The book goes on to consider the importance of undertaking surveys that would allow criminologists to map out the patterns of victimization in which the disenfranchised figured more prominently than did more privileged sectors of society. Some reaction to this book was also negative, and critics were quick to point out that realists had departed from a progressive agenda to the extent that they had been virtually co-opted. In examining the kinds of arguments advanced by realists, Martin Kettle, the crime reporter for the *Guardian*, comments about such reaction: 'For their pains, the [realists] have been denounced with extraordinary ferocity from the left, sometimes in an almost paranoid manner. To take crime seriously, to take fear of crime seriously, and worst of all to take police reform seriously, is seen by the fundamentalists as the ultimate betrayal and deviation' (1984: 367).

Attempts at launching the kind of surveys advanced by Lea and Young (1984) were thwarted by local councils parroting the critics of realist criminology. Despite the intensity of such debate, two crime surveys were finally initiated by realists. The Merseyside Crime Survey (MCS; Kinsey 1984, 1985; Kinsey, Lea, and Young 1986) commenced in 1984, and the Islington Crime Survey (ICS; Jones, MacLean, and Young 1986) began field-work operations in the spring of 1985. While both surveys can be seen as products of realist criminology, the ICS received considerable attention both in Britain and abroad. So much attention was received by this survey that many of the other inner-city London boroughs began to recognize that political mileage was to be gained from such studies and reversed their earlier decisions not to support such research. A spate of inner-city left-realist crime surveys followed, such as the Broadwater Farm Survey (Gifford 1986), the Newham Crime Survey (Harris and Associates 1987), the Hammersmith and Fulham Survey (Painter et al. 1989), and the Second Islington Crime Survey (Crawford et al. 1990). The impact of this latter research has been considerable. In his review of the ICS, Ken Bottomley notes: 'The Islington Crime Survey ... has a special significance, in the context of interpreting data from the national surveys, not only from its substantive findings, but because an increasing number of local authorities are commissioning similar surveys which will eventually comprise a rich source of comparative data on the impact of crime and attitudes to the police in particular localities' (1988: 51-52).

In addition to publications emanating from the surveys, the initial realist criminologists have produced a spate of literature since the mid 1980s on subjects ranging from police accountability to the prison-abolition movement. There is virtually no criminological ground that has not received some attention from these writers, and contributions to the left-realist literature have been made by criminologists from almost every country in the Western world. In commenting on the proliferation of this literature, Jock Young notes: 'Although having roots in the debates of the 1970s, left realist criminology has only really emerged in the post-1985 period. In that short time it has created considerable debate; the realist bibliography, with which we have been trying to keep pace at the Centre for Criminology, now stretches to eighteen pages and is in its seventh update' (1991: 15). This rapid acceleration of ideas resulted in an international conference on realist criminology in Vancouver, Canada, attended by approximately two hundred delegates. Funded in part by Simon Fraser University, the University of British Columbia, and the Social Sciences and Humanities Research Council of Canada, the conference served as a forum at which important aspects of the realist project were opened up for intellectual scrutiny and debate. Four aspects of this debate are summarized in this anthology.

Four Aspects of the Debate

This book has been organized so as to produce discussions in what we feel represent four key areas of contemporary debate surrounding the realist project. As noted above, much energy has been expended of late by realist criminologists coming to terms with the wide-ranging criticism of their work. For this reason we feel it is appropriate to begin the book with the case for realism made by some of its key figures from two continents juxtaposed with some of the key criticisms by a variety of authors. In Part One, 'The Case for Left Realism,' the proponents of realist criminology advance what they see as the key principles of realism and, where possible, rebuttals to some of the major criticisms which have been made of their work. Part Two, 'A Critical Assessment of Left Realism,' consists of a set of essays which critically evaluate the collective work of realist criminology and in some cases attempt to consider how realism might benefit from the intellectual developments in other areas of inquiry. Some of the essays consider how relevant a discourse specific to Britain might be to other countries, and some attempts are made to assess the transformative capacity of the realist project.

Realist criminologists argue that the survey, as employed by them, is sensitive to the experiences of the disenfranchised. In particular, this means that realist survey techniques have had to be informed by advances in the feminist literature. On the one hand, some feminists such as Gelsthorpe and Morris (1988), have argued that the ICS was tokenistic in its treatment of women. Such critique seems misplaced, however, since even a cursory reading of Jones, MacLean, and Young (1986) reveals that rather than receiving token consideration, gender was the central category of analysis in the ICS. Clearly, the pervasive nature of violence against women, both as analysed by feminist scholars and as illustrated by surveys such as the ICS, demands that any criminology which claims to be progressive must recognize the importance of gender inequality in the structuring of people's differential experiences and treatment, particularly within the apparatus of social control. Two questions immediately arise from this recognition as it pertains to left realism's claim to be sensitive to gender: to what extent has the realist project been informed by feminist analysis (or, said differently, to what extent does realist research remain true to feminist concerns), and to what extent have the practitioners of realism reorganized their division of labour to account for gender inequality? These questions are explored in Part Three: 'Left Realism and Feminism.'

By now it should be clear that the main empirical thrust of the realist project has been data collected from large-scale localized crime surveys. In his review of left-realist crime surveys, Victor Jupp observes that 'there is a certain irony that the social survey is the central pillar of new left realism. In another context and at another time surveys could easily have been cast aside as tools of state-sponsored, positivist criminology' (1989: 106). Much has been written on this subject, and the essays in Part Four, 'Left Realism and Victimology,' review that literature. The major issues which need to be explored here are: to what extent local surveys are sufficiently different from national surveys to merit special consideration; whether or not these surveys capture the experiences of racial minorities and women; and whether or not the categories of research are sufficiently different from those of state-sponsored criminology to merit their being distinguished as realist survey research.

Below is a summary of the key arguments advanced in each of the essays included in this book, organized by part title and author's name.

The Case for Left Realism

Jock Young

In 'Realist Research as a Basis for Local Criminal Justice Policy,' Jock Young discusses the central principles of left realism. Realism asserts that crime rates are a product of four interacting factors: (1) the police and other agencies of social control, (2) the public, (3) the offender, and (4) the victim. It treats as axiomatic the principle that analyses should be specific – that is, about specific crimes and specific police practices. In opposition to the notion of an 'average victim' emanating from national crime surveys, realism focuses on the unequal distribution of crime along the dimensions of age, race, class, and gender. Young opposes the sort of objectivism that has characterized the reporting of results from national crime surveys, especially the tendency to treat subjects' fears as being 'irrational.' In particular, a realist approach treats women's fear of crime as a rational response not just to criminal victimization, but to a whole range of incivilities (particularly various kinds of non-criminal harassment) to which men are not subjected.

While it is empirical, realism is not empiricist. It integrates theory and observation. Young argues that too much stress has been placed on opportunity and not enough on aetiology. Consequently, realism attempts to reverse the retreat from causality that has characterized much modern criminology. Young argues that inner-city crime is best conceptualized as rational behaviour rooted in material circumstances.

As well as pursuing empirical and theoretical goals, realism sets out to be practical. The local survey is designed to be a 'democratic instrument' – a way of giving people a voice when it comes to demands for police services and assessing police performance. In this respect, realism offers an alternative to

Fabianism because it resists relying on experts to define the 'true' nature of other people's suffering. But, in so doing, realism is not crass populism. Young rejects the kind of subjectivism which holds that the only problems that exist are those defined by research subjects.

If part of the practice of realism is to give people an opportunity to articulate their own problems rather than having their problems defined by experts, it is also practical in its desire to discover the principles by which crime-control measures succeed or fail. Realism is thus an attempt to link demand and supply – after discovering which crimes the public prioritize in terms of community safety, the task is to ascertain the effectiveness of various anti-crime initiatives. In this respect, Young argues that there appears to be a consensus that there should be a 'multi-agency' approach to crime control characterized by a coordination of intervention strategies.

Young concludes by suggesting that four tasks currently face progressive criminology: (1) we need to put money into the task of tackling the causes of crime; (2) we need to protect victims; (3) we need to develop more effective crime prevention schemes; and (4) we need to restrict the role of the police to crime fighting. And, above all, we need multiple strategies for social intervention.

Roger Matthews

In 'Developing a Realist Approach to Penal Reform,' Roger Matthews offers an alternative to both neoconservative prison-expansion rhetoric and to the currently available progressive alternatives to it, 'abolitionism' and 'reductionism.'

Abolitionism, as developed particularly in the work of Thomas Mathiesen (1973, 1986), issues from the argument that prisons are anachronistic institutions which cause more problems than they solve. The only way to overcome the perceived failures of liberal prison reform is to get rid of prisons altogether.

Reductionist arguments are based on much the same vision of the prison, but the abolitionist impulse is tempered by the argument that, no matter how destructive they might be, prisons remain necessary for a small number of violent offenders. The aim of reductionism is thus to reduce the prison population to a minimum.

Matthews argues that although each is based on a compelling critique of the prison, neither abolitionism nor reductionism is politically viable. Consequently, while he draws on these two models in articulating a radical and realizable progressive alternative, he argues against their 'impossibilism.' He cautions against the 'nothing works' trap and, in opposition to the 'get tough' policies of the New Right, reaffirms the rehabilitative potential of incarceration.

Nevertheless, he forcefully reasserts the desirability of creating alternatives to imprisonment and argues that alternatives do not necessarily have to end up widening the net of social control. The problem with the 'alternatives' put forward to date is that they do not offer programs that 'compete' with imprisonment (compete in the sense that they can be seen as an equivalent form of punishment) and that they are not realistic. To be realistic, Matthews argues, alternative modes of punishment should: express the level of public disapproval of crime; be directed at specific offender populations; fit with the existing structure of sanctions; protect the public; be educational, reintegrative, and socially relevant; and be subject to systematic monitoring and evaluation. Matthews favours the development of informal mechanisms, where possible.

Matthews's realist penal policy is minimalist: only those who cannot be reasonably dealt with in any other way should be incarcerated, and incarceration should be for the shortest possible period. He also suggests that the intensity of confinement be reduced since many prisoners are subject to a level of custodial security quite out of proportion to the risk they present.

Elliott Currie

Elliott Currie examines American left realism in his essay 'Retreatism, Minimalism, Realism: Three Styles of Reasoning on Crime and Drugs in the United States.' He believes that the United States is facing a social and political crisis of unprecedented proportions. Indeed, things are so bad that now there is a new willingness to try to reverse the damage done by ten years of neoconservative politics. But Currie laments that neither species of US progressivism – he calls these 'progressive minimalism' and 'progressive retreatism' – has been able to mount an effective challenge to neoconservatism.

Progressive retreatism, the stance of middle-of-the-road Democrats, has, for the sake of expediency, simply appropriated part of the conservative model of crime control, particularly its reliance on incarceration. It is a retreat to a punitive model of criminal justice.

Minimalism is characterized by two tendencies: (1) minimizing the seriousness of crime and/or drug problems by saying that they are vastly overstated; and (2) minimizing the potential of the state for dealing with such problems. Currie portrays this desire to limit state power as classic 1960s' thinking carried over to today. As part of the 'great denial,' minimalism has very little to say about what we should do about crime itself. Thus Currie argues that, even if the war on illegal drugs is silly, we still have to take seriously the carnage wrought by such substances: 'Too many well-meaning progressives simply do not get it when it comes to the trauma of drugs in the cities.' By not taking seriously this carnage,

Currie argues that minimalism relinquished the terrain to the New Right.

Given the problems that he sees with minimalism and retreatism, Currie's purpose is to offer an alternative to them: this he terms 'progressive realism' (noting that, in a political culture dominated by the centre and the right, a 'left' realism is not even feasible at this time).

Currie identifies two versions of progressive realism: a service model and a reconstructive model. The service model suggests that more services – training in effective parenting, prenatal care, mentoring, remedial education, etc. – are needed to deal with the ills of the inner city. But Currie is troubled by the narrowness of vision of this model because it does not deal with larger issues, especially those associated with labour-market processes. It is for this reason that he favours the reconstructive version of progressive realism: as well as services, we also need enrichment of the labour market, major reallocation of resources for low-income housing, public-works revitalization, and so on. Pouring money into human capital will not work if not supplemented by other measures in a holistic framework designed to facilitate large-scale community reconstruction and a new era of economic citizenship.

A Critical Assessment of Left Realism

Paul Havemann

What is the relevance of British left realism for Canadian 'justice studies'? This question is explored by Paul Havemann in his essay 'Canadian Realist Criminology in the 1990s: Some Reflections on the Quest for Social Justice.'

Given the specific historical circumstances of the emergence of a left realism – helping to recapture for the Labour Party the working-class, ethnic, and female vote from the clutches of Tory authoritarian populism – Havemann wonders how relevant left realism is in Canada. Relevant though some of it might be, he doubts that left realism, emerging as it does in what Thatcher once called 'post-socialist' Britain, signals a paradigm shift in the way its architects have implied. Thus the purpose of his essay is to offer Canadian progressives a somewhat different agenda for the 1990s – a conservatory model of capitalist democracy.

Havemann suggests that the main challenge for progressives is to uncouple social justice from economic growth and to struggle against the authoritarian-state minimalism that now prevails in many Canadian provinces and at the federal level.

When it comes to the academy, Havemann parts company with left realists to the extent that he is against criminology as a discipline: even if we are to take crime seriously, 'criminology' should be nothing more than what he calls a 'flag of convenience.' Criminology cannot, Havemann asserts, serve as a signifier for a progressive political project. On this score, Havemann believes that the concept of 'justice studies' provides a much better disciplinary vehicle for progressives, one that will not only allow the development of a political economy of criminal justice and the welfare state, but also provide a sound platform for public-policy advocacy.

When it comes to the practice of the justice perspective, Havemann urges that it be organized around the goal of creating a minimalist and non-coercive system of criminal justice. In this manifesto for justice studies, Havemann stands against such things as the erosion of welfare provisions, prisons, nuclear facilities, and waste dumps. By contrast, he stands in favour of community corrections, environmental and social impact studies, public committee memberships, and any other kind of involvement that comes to mind. Havemann's rallying cry is simple enough – progressives must become politically active whenever and wherever possible. For Havemann, this activism extends into the classroom, where justice studies offer a critical pedagogy to counter the hegemony of administrative criminology in research and in the academy.

In summary, Havemann suggests that justice studies be built around notions of social rights and democratic process: 'The justice studies project aims to create the vocabulary for rewriting the terms of the relationship between the people and the state so as to secure an ecologically sound socialist and feminist future.'

Raymond J. Michalowski

Realism has often been accused of being 'idealistic' itself because its advocates tend to romanticize socialism. Many political commentaries have observed that twentieth-century socialist and communist political orders are not really 'socialist' or 'communist.' In 'Crime and Justice in Socialist Cuba: What Can Left Realists Learn?' Raymond J. Michalowski argues that whatever labels these societies might be given, they are the only national political systems that are not organized around private-production economies. According to him, we need to take existing socialism seriously, but not necessarily approvingly, if we want to understand how to develop a realistic left politics and crime-control policy. To this end he examines three aspects of Cuban crime-control policy: (1) relationships between socio-economic inequality and crime; (2) the Cuban public culture of self-worth; and (3) community-based crime control. He then goes on to discuss the implications of Cuban crime policies and Cuban criminology for the left-realist strategies of localism, community prevention, and the fight against social inequality.

Michalowski suggests that Cuban criminology can be reduced to three main propositions: (1) the nature of lawbreaking is historically specific; (2) the principal cause of crime is the inequality that arises from the mode of production; and (3) crime can be reduced by reducing inequality. When it comes to theorizing crime causation there is a recognition that inequalities still occur under a socialist regime; however, there is more to crime causation than social inequality. Cuban criminologists also argue that bourgeois sentiment still influences ways of thinking, and that family breakdown is criminogenic.

In examining official and unofficial portraits of Cuban crime problems, Michalowski concludes that crime is much less of a problem in Cuba than it is in the United States. Cubans do not feel they are besieged by crime in the way that many Americans do. In accounting for the vastly different crime rates in Cuba and the United States, criminologists in Cuba would argue that there is less crime there because of a lower level of material inequality. In Cuba, an individual's worth is measured less in material terms than in terms of the level of social participation. Michalowski believes that there is a high level of local neighbourhood cohesion in Cuba, with the community playing an important role in a dynamic and ongoing revolutionary process. Political organizations are structured to maintain direct lines of communication between the central government and local communities.

In discussing the implications of Cuban political organization and criminal justice policy, Michalowski warns against the sort of localism that has become axiomatic in left realism. The Cuban approach stresses general social interests, not just local concerns. Realists should not restrict their thinking to the lowest level of analysis – the local day-to-day reality.

If community control seems to work quite effectively in Cuba, Michalowski argues that its success rests on a different conception of the individual's social responsibilities than one finds in liberal democracies. It might be difficult to achieve this same effect in liberal democracies where a different premium is put on privacy and individual liberty. Also, the formation of communities with binding social relations, as opposed to unconnected residential groupings, requires a widespread commitment to a set of overarching political principles, the likes of which are not discussed by left realists. Michalowski argues that the sort of singular concern about crime control that characterizes left realism is probably not sufficient to create a broader sense of community. He thus questions the extent to which localism can help to achieve socialist goals.

For Michalowski, the main problem with left realism is that it seems to treat as idealistic any attempt to restructure society fundamentally. But the question remains, can crime be reduced without a political program that aims to reduce substantially the inequalities around which liberal-democratic societies are organized? Given that left realism does not even address such broader questions, Michalowski concludes that it ends up looking more liberal and social democratic than socialist.

Robert Menzies

If critical criminology made progress in the 1970s and 1980s, it now finds itself in a defensive posture, caught in the crossfire emanating from the reaction to the demise of Eastern European and Soviet communism on one side, and from the deconstructionist onslaught of post-modernism on the other. It is in the space between New Right politics and post-modernism that the realist revival has occurred. Bob Menzies's purpose in 'Beyond Realist Criminology' is to reflect on this revival.

For Menzies, left realism presents a familiar rhetoric. Constructed around the familiar couples, cause and effect and action and outcome, it is a rationalist project with a progressive politic. And it is the retrenchment of criminology – old categories prevail, pragmatism holds sway. This is not a reconstructionist or deconstructionist program, but an exercise in the here and now.

Menzies sees the realist quest for engagement as both necessary and revitalizing. In that left realism contains the seeds of a people's criminology, it is to be applauded. But, for Menzies, it also harbours some dangerous implications, not the least of which concerns its reaffirmation of 'criminology.' The problem with this retrenchment is that realism sacrifices much that is critical in 'critical' criminology, particularly its deconstructionist edge. For Menzies, realism represents a one-sided and uncritical acceptance of the core discipline. He thus worries about the way realism scales down critical aspirations. He is critical of any program that concentrates activism at a local level, and asks what form and content the relationship between central state and proximal government should take. How is a social-democratic local state to articulate with a central state that is not? Menzies is also suspicious of realism's reliance on the 'community' and suggests that it confounds populism and democracy: state, political economy, law, ideology, and culture ought not to be so conveniently bracketed away.

In reasserting the importance of the victim, Menzies suggests that the offender has been lost. He also urges realists to not accept uncritically the victim's experience as primal: we should not reify the victim.

When it comes to progressive criminological programs, Menzies argues that analysis and action ought to remain open. Any progressive politic must retain a certain level of idealism: heads cannot entirely replace hearts. Consequently, for Menzies, we do not face a choice between realism and idealism. Rather, the challenge is to create a dialectic between the two. To the question of whether this can be done in a discipline called 'criminology' Menzies offers a clear and resounding 'no.' He concludes that as a form of *criminology*, realism cannot hope to maintain a progressive edge.

John Lowman

In his commentary 'The Left Regulation of Prostitution: Reconciling Individual Rights and Collective Interests,' John Lowman examines the model of prostitution control described by Roger Matthews (1986) in his critique of arguments favouring the 'decriminalization' or 'legalization' of prostitution. Although opposed to criminalizing either the buyer or the seller of sexual services, Matthews believes that both legalization (brothels, red-light districts, and/or licensing) and decriminalization (repealing all laws relating to adult prostitution) would entrench the idea that women are objects to be bought and sold by men and would hasten the development of the sex market. He argues that prostitution is more opportunistic than has usually been supposed and opposes the 'impossibilism' that he claims is at the root of arguments for legalization and decriminalization.

Matthews treats decriminalization as if it is tantamount to delegalization – i.e., no control whatsoever – and suggests that it is based on a liberal-pluralist model of society in which free-willed individuals should be allowed to make contracts with each other. Some of its advocates may well have such a model in mind, but Lowman holds that others do not.

Lowman offers an alternative rationale for decriminalization: the state should not have the power to criminalize a person for taking money for something that would otherwise be perfectly legal. By the same token, he questions the criminalization of purchasing a 'service' that would be legal were money not changing hands.

While Matthews is opposed to criminalizing either the buyer or the seller of sexual services, he nevertheless wants to retain criminal-law sanctions to deter prostitution. On this score, Lowman suggests that Matthews ends up talking not about deterring prostitution, but about controlling the circumstances in which it takes place. In this respect, Lowman suggests that Matthews does not consider all the relevant arguments when it comes to making decisions about the type of regulatory system that should be put in place. He argues that if criminal law is going to prohibit the public nuisances attributed to prostitutes and their customers or to limit the exploitation of prostitutes, it should do so with criminal laws relating to generic nuisances and general exploitation rather than with status offences.

Lowman identifies several objectives that a regulatory system ought to pursue. In particular, regulation should ensure that if prostitution is going to occur, either it should be on a self-employed basis, or there should be worker ownership of any business (such as advertising) that might be involved with bringing customers and prostitutes together; however, Lowman argues that this should become a goal for the organization of *all* wage labour, not just prostitution.

Rob McQueen

One observation often raised by leftist critics of left realism is that, by focusing on street crime, realist research tends to ignore crimes of the powerful generally, and corporate crime in particular. In his essay 'Why Company Law Is Important to Left Realists,' Rob McQueen discusses strategies for regulating corporations and strategies for transforming the corporate form in order to make corporations more accountable. McQueen argues that rather than representing a particular class or faction of capital, company law is the meeting-point of various class interests. As such, it is an important site of political action for anyone interested in how to balance community interests with those of private capital. It is in this respect that McQueen extends left-realist demands for police accountability to propose the creation of a democratically accountable corporation.

In considering different normative conceptions of corporate form, McQueen believes that, in certain cases, limited liability encourages corporate irresponsibility. By making the company a legal individual, decision makers are often absolved of responsibility. He thus suggests much stricter controls on the granting of limited liability. McQueen believes that limited liability should be a privilege extended only to certain kinds of companies – and one that can be revoked – not a right of every company wishing to incorporate. For McQueen, other key issues for company law involve where to draw the line between the careless and the criminal, and how to punish or restrict illegitimate practices without interfering with legitimate business practices.

In suggesting changes in what we expect of companies, McQueen argues that companies have to do more than serve the interests of their investors. They also have to serve the interests of the communities in which they function – and without which they would not exist.

The challenge for left realism is to help understand and change community attitudes to corporate malfeasance and what should be done about it. In this respect, McQueen describes the kinds of sanctions that could be applied to corporations if they were required to take community interests into consideration when conducting their business. McQueen modifies the insights of Foucault and Donzelot to suggest ways in which the normative structure of corporate activity could be transformed. He suggests that surveillance by external regulatory bodies and the beefing-up of sanctions and levels of enforcement are not effective ways of dealing with such crimes as insider trading and unauthorized dealing in securities. Instead, various kinds of 'self-regulation' might help to make corporations more accountable. McQueen's image of self-regulation, however, is an unusual one. Self-regulation would occur by building into the corporate structure a system of accountability involving members of the outside community. McQueen concludes by considering the potential effectiveness of various punishments, such as equity fines and probation.

Left Realism and Feminism

Pat Carlen

What benefits can be gleaned by feminists from the left-realist political agenda? In 'Women, Crime, Feminism, and Realism,' Pat Carlen examines the potential that realist criminology has to inform analyses of women's crime and to facilitate campaigns and policies aimed at redressing the discriminatory wrongs that women presently suffer in the courts and prisons. She also examines some contributions and limitations of feminism in understanding women, crime, and criminology.

Reflecting on Carol Smart's (1989) warning that feminists should avoid 'the siren call of law,' Carlen agrees that feminists should be involved in the deconstruction of criminal law to show how it oppresses women. But, she argues, such a project should not preclude developing a feminist jurisprudence (including talk about 'equality' and 'rights') to guide reform of criminal justice and penal systems. Carlen goes on to make the same point about criminology itself: there is no reason why we should not take crime seriously *and* question and work against its material and ideological effects. Doing the one does not preclude doing the other.

As much as Carlen sees value in feminist projects in criminology, she also believes that they have limitations. In particular, she is concerned that images of a distinct and taken-for-granted female criminality are essentialist and reductionist. Consequently, she argues that theorists should abandon stable reference to 'male' and 'female.'

For Carlen, feminism is a politics, not a guarantor of theoretical truth, and so she rejects the notion that there is a distinct feminist method. Also, she disagrees with feminists who call for a non-interventionist stance on women's lawbreaking and criminalization since such a stance further disadvantages the very women who are already the most seriously victimized by gender inequalities and the poverty trap.

Given that Carlen believes that we can take crime seriously without necessarily compromising certain deconstructionist ideals, one of the main potentials she sees in left realism is its insistence that criminal justice is a relevant site of political action. Nevertheless, she laments the way that realists have downplayed deconstruction – they offer little in the way of an analysis that might subvert the common-sense meaning of crime.

It is in realism's strategy of democratization that Carlen sees the main point of convergence with feminism. Realists take both lawbreaking and victimization seriously: 'Indeed, the realists' work on women as victims of crime has been one of their major contributions to both feminist struggle and criminology.' What they have taken less seriously, she says, is people's experiences as suspects, lawbreakers, defendants, and prisoners.

In reacting to simplistic 'social conditions cause crime' formulas, realists have insisted that crime is a choice. But in so doing, Carlen argues, they have downplayed issues relating to substantive equality and justice and have not always thought through the implications of some of their conclusions. Thus she asks, 'is it either logical or justifiable for realists to use the anti-socialist rhetoric of individualism in the furtherance of socialist political ends?'

Carlen concludes the essay by advocating a principled commitment to an open-ended deconstructionist program and a political commitment to collectivist (feminist and socialist) ideals and aspirations.

Dawn H. Currie

Many feminists have abandoned criminological inquiry altogether because, they claim, it is a discourse by men, for men, and about men. In her critique of realist criminology, Carol Smart (1989) claims that, because of its empiricism and commitment to etiology, realism has missed the boat altogether. In her essay 'Feminism and Realism in the Canadian Context,' Dawn Currie first reflects on the post-modernist critique of realism, particularly as developed in the work of Carol Smart. She then considers ways in which other feminist concerns coincide with and are taken up by realism.

In contrast to realism, post-modern feminism has abandoned the quest to discover some undistorted truth about crime, turning instead to the process by which 'truths' are created. While Currie believes that Carol Smart's (1989) deconstructive feminism does make a powerful contribution to our understanding of legal processes, she doubts that post-modernism will spell the end of 'science' in criminology or an abandoning of questions about 'causation.' Currie is suspicious of the localized and fragmented politics of diversity and resistance that post-modernist deconstruction gives rise to, since she believes that it is much more compatible with the liberalism of democratic societies than it is with the sort of political impetus that might give rise to a more profound social transformation, be it one involving race, class, and/or gender. It is one thing to deconstruct patriarchal social relations in the world of discourse, but quite another to change the material experience of women. Currie argues that only through mutual experience and collective action can an effective politics of resistance be forged.

In examining the connections between feminism and realism, Currie notes that they are both about reclaiming the discourse on crime and women's safety. Realism devotes a considerable amount of energy to estimating the frequency, distribution, and impact of violence and other crimes against women. To read this as *empiricist* or a new search for 'Truth,' Currie argues, is to misread the project.

For Currie, the most promising features of realism are its rejection of philosophical idealism; its consideration of race, class, and gender; and its insistence on taking seriously the point of view of victims and other respondents to crime surveys. Most importantly, realism attempts to be accountable *outside the academy*, not just within it. At least some feminism aspires to a similar sort of accountability. Indeed, Currie notes that second-wave feminism, unlike realism, took root outside the academy.

In opposition to Smart, Currie does not want to abandon the concepts of cause and effect. For Currie, the problem with post-modern deconstructionism is that it seems to locate domination and oppression in discourse without realizing that real material practices exist beyond the text. To suggest that we should not be concerned with cause is to forsake that material reality. Nevertheless, Currie says, to take this position is not to deny that post-modern critiques ought to transform the way in which we think about 'scientific' study.

Seema Ahluwalia

The potential connection between radical feminism and left realism is the subject of Seema Ahluwalia's 'Counting What Counts: The Study of Women's Fear of Crime.' Ahluwalia explores such connections by comparing the survey research in Britain carried out by both left realists and feminists on women's victimization and women's fear of crime.

Ahluwalia suggests that feminist and left-realist surveys share several features that distinguish them from conventional victimization survey research and victimology. Conventional perspectives have portrayed women's fear of crime as being 'irrational' – as overblown in terms of the 'objective' threat of victimization. In contrast, feminists and left realists have argued that women's fear is based on an accurate assessment of risk. The problem with conventional research on crime victimization is that, by focusing on the criminal event, it has not produced an accurate measure of risk. In particular, it has paid little attention to the non-criminal 'incivilities' (harassment, etc.) that contribute to female fear of men; the threat of violence to which women are generally exposed; and, in turn, the fear of crime that such experiences create.

In conducting local surveys, left realists have prioritized victim-centred definitions of crime, policing, and public-safety needs. In this respect they have been particularly sensitive to issues surrounding the criminal victimization of women.

Feminists have proceeded from the observation that women's lives are controlled by the threat and reality of male violence: the threat is ever present. The purpose of feminist survey research has been not so much to count instances of such violence as to demonstrate ways that conventional criminology and victimology have constructed, and in the process distorted, women's experience of criminal victimization. Most conventional surveys cannot hope to capture this experience because, in order to avoid 'telescoping' events through time, they usually ask only about recent experiences (e.g., over the past year). But women's fear reflects a lifetime of exposure to the threat of male violence. Also, in talking about an abstract 'average victim' conventional surveys do not pay enough attention to the geographic variation of victimization or its differentiation in terms of race, class, and gender. Using comparable data, local crime surveys have shown that working-class women really are victimized more than national surveys indicate.

If feminist and realist surveys are to be applauded for providing an alternative to conventional portraits of women's fear of crime, Ahluwalia faults them for not paying enough attention to the racial dimensions of victimization, for romanticizing the 'community,' and for not recognizing the variation of different people's experiences within communities.

Walter S. DeKeseredy

The purpose of Walter DeKeseredy's 'Confronting Woman Abuse in Canada: A Left-Realist Approach' is threefold: (1) to evaluate critically left-realist research on the abuse of women; (2) to assess critically Canadian survey research on female victimization; and (3) to show how left-realist survey technology can help to advance research on abuse of women in Canada.

When it comes to understanding victimization of women, DeKeseredy considers the Islington Crime Survey to be a considerable advance on national surveys such as the British Crime Survey. But he also believes that some important issues have been overlooked by left-realist accounts of violence against women:

a Left realism does not provide an analysis of patriarchal social relations.

b Female victimization is not class specific. Because left realism focuses on working-class experience, it does not address the independent importance of sexual inequalities across class lines.

c Survey research does not (cannot?) capture the experience of violence from the victim's perspective.

d Local surveys have ignored significant types of violence against women, such as commercial crimes, accidents and injuries in the workplace, and consumer victimization.

e Left-realist analyses have generally ignored the influence of marital status on violence against women.

f Left realists have not set out to answer the question 'why the abuse?' In this respect, their work on violence against women is largely atheoretical.

When it comes to the utility of the Canadian Urban Victimization Survey (CUVS) for understanding violence against women, DeKeseredy concludes that because it never set out to, it simply does not provide a comprehensive sociological understanding of female victimization.

In suggesting ways of enhancing research on violence against women, DeKeseredy discusses the Conflict Tactics Scale (CTS), the most frequently used measure of non-sexual violence. DeKeseredy argues that local surveys can help to overcome the disadvantages of both the CTS and the CUVS because they include measures of three phenomena largely ignored by these other types of research: (1) subcriminal sexual harassment on the street (DeKeseredy notes that, from the point of view of the women, only in retrospect can such incidents be considered 'minor'); (2) differences among racial and age groups (thereby countering the 'fallacy of homogeneity' that characterizes talk about 'average' crime victims); and (3) the psychological and financial impact of victimization on women.

Left Realism and Victimology

Sandra Walklate

Since the empirical referent for left realism has been data collected by surveys of victims, the distinction between a more traditional victimology and a more progressive victimology has increasingly gained analytical importance. In 'Researching Victims of Crime: Critical Victimology,' Walklate argues in favour of a critical victimology in opposition to 'conventional' or 'positivist' victimology. Positivist victimology is characterized by four themes: (1) identification of victims who contribute to their own victimization; (2) analysis of interpersonal crimes of violence; (3) identification of factors explaining why victimization is non-random; and (4) analysis of crime as it is conventionally understood. Generally in conventional victimology, and particularly when it comes to victim precipitation perspectives, there is too much emphasis on the 'culpable' victim.

While Walklate is largely in agreement with Miers's (1989) recent critique of positivist victimology, she differs in her interpretation of what a critical victimology ought to entail. For Miers, critical victimology is restricted to an interactionist level of analysis. For Walklate, a critical victimology ought also to include an analysis of the material and structural circumstances of victimization. It is for this reason that she believes that feminism and left realism – perspectives that Miers scarcely mentions – are particularly relevant to the construction of a critical victimology.

Walklate proceeds by examining the relative merits of left-realist and feminist perspectives. While left realists have claimed to be inspired by feminist issues, Walklate wonders to what extent they really have embraced a feminist problematic. Male class analysis remains the paramount feature of left realism. Measuring amounts of female victimization is not, in itself, sufficient to address feminist concerns. And, she asks, what aspect of whose reality does survey research tap into? In focusing on the victimized subject, such research tends to downplay the objective circumstances of female victimization. Surveys tend to gloss over the objective circumstances in which subjects' responses are constructed.

Left realism's main achievement, Walklate argues, has been an empirical one. It forcefully reminds policy makers that victimization is not distributed evenly, either geographically or socially. But it is difficult to see what it has contributed beyond a more thoroughly documented socio–structural-ecological view of crime. At a philosophical level, the contribution of left realism is questionable: that is because left realists have not paid enough attention to the question *what constitutes the real?* In tackling this question, Walklate suggests constructing a critical victimology around the philosophical realism of such writers as Giddens (1984) who are interested in the dynamic and dialectical relationship between social structure and human agency. Walklate claims that neither positivist nor realist surveys have been able to capture this dialectic.

Using a discussion of fear of crime as an example, Walklate suggests that the search for various 'generative mechanisms' (as opposed to 'causes') should guide critical research, so that concepts, hypotheses, and variables are more meaningfully linked. To do this, a variety of quite different research techniques would have to be employed in an attempt to unravel different layers of social reality.

Ultimately Walklate argues that the research agenda should be shifted away from measuring patterns of victimization towards a more complete understanding of the deeper order that produces and changes those patterns, and gives rise to the strategies people use to survive them.

Ken Pease

In his 'The Local Crime Survey: Pitfalls and Possibilities,' Ken Pease talks about the pros and cons of both local and national crime surveys based on his experience with the second sweep of the British Crime Survey and his role in the design and execution of a local survey in a large public-housing area north of Manchester, England.

In enumerating the advantages of local surveys, Pease suggests that: (1) they provide an alternative to official images of crime; (2) they can be an instrument of empowerment; (3) when repeated through time, they provide an alternative measure of change independent of the official crime-processing system; and (4) they are able to trace hard-to-capture crimes, especially those that require substantial rapport between interviewer and interviewee.

Although local surveys are more informative and persuasive at a local level, Pease believes that, in selling these advantages, the proponents of local surveys have denigrated national surveys with too broad a brush. He argues that because national and local surveys throw light on different issues, they should be used to complement each other rather than being seen as mutually exclusive alternatives. To make this point, Pease outlines some of the weaknesses of local surveys.

The basic problem with the local survey is that the number of people surveyed is so small that no interpretation other than at a most general level is possible. Local surveys are never local enough to capture small-scale variations in victimization. No matter what level of survey one is dealing with, there is considerable variation in victimization. At every level, repeat victimization accounts for much of the variation that we see.

Because most respondents are not crime victims, a variety of 'filler' questions allow non-victim respondents to provide information and result in an greater overall cost-effectiveness of the research. Pease contends that none of these questions belongs in a victimization survey, and he raises several reservations about such questions:

a Filler questions are ideologically driven, to date by the agenda of the left. They could just as easily be driven by some other ideological agenda with very different results.

b Information about lifestyle can quickly devolve into victim blaming.
c Linking rates of victimization and judgments about police adequacy may have unintended consequences, particularly the erosion of due process, as police effectiveness comes to be seen primarily as a matter of crime control.
d Through the 1980s there has been a shift from examining crime as a problem to examining the joint problems of crime and fear of crime. In the process, fear of crime has taken on a life of its own.

The main thrust of Pease's argument is that the opposition between local and national surveys is largely illusory: 'The victimization survey is too useful an instrument in giving crime victims a voice for its potential to be restricted by the independent development of, and sniping between, proponents of national and local surveys.'

While local surveys may capture important crimes which national surveys do not, some crimes are captured quite well by national surveys. National data can inform local issues and provide baseline data for local surveys. As a result, there is now an attempt to design national surveys as a series of local surveys.

Frank Pearce

In their attempt to respond to criticisms about their narrow focus on street crimes, realist criminologists explored some patterns of commercial victimization in the second sweep of the Islington Crime Survey. Some of the findings of this exploratory research are discussed by Frank Pearce in 'The Contribution of "Left Realism" to the Study of Commercial Crime.'

Pearce argues that left realism's commitment to empirical work is its major strength. While acknowledging the importance of white-collar and commercial crime, realists have nevertheless concentrated mostly on *crime between subjects* in a way that does not adequately describe the anonymous relationships between offenders and victims, such as the manufacturer and consumer in the case of a faulty product. Nor does it capture the extent to which acts of omission cause harm, as in the case of pollution or employers who do not fulfil their statutory obligations in bringing about workplace safety. The emphasis on crimes between subjects does not hold out much promise for controlling corporate crime. To take corporate and white-collar crime more seriously thus requires a modification of realism's conceptual categories and a broadening of its field of interest.

One difficulty encountered in talking about the feasibility of extending survey research to include white-collar and corporate crime is that of knowing who is victimized and who is responsible. Also there is the question of exactly what to include as 'crime.' Pearce argues that there is no intrinsic difference between criminal and civil offences – but there is an important ideological one. For this reason, he suggests that any kind of demonstrable wrong should be treated as a crime. Our focus should be on *illegalities* generally, not just on crimes and incivilities. Consequently, in the Second Islington Crime Survey, a strategic decision was made to call a wide range of illegalities 'crimes.'

Conducted in 1988, the Second Islington Survey asked a subset of respondents about commercial crimes, including safety at work, unlawful trading practices, and the victimization of housing tenants. In reviewing the findings of the survey, Pearce notes that very few of the offences that were uncovered were reported to any kind of agency. A greater percentage of respondents were victimized by commercial crime than by street crime: 29 per cent had been victims of a conventional crime (burglary, vehicle theft, theft from vehicle, vehicle deliberately damaged, theft, assault) whereas 39 per cent had suffered from deliberate overcharging and faulty goods and services and/or their misrepresentation.

Pearce concludes that crime and a very rational fear of crime play a very important role in downgrading the quality of people's lives in Islington. But if street crime is a massive problem, we should not forget that quality of life in this inner-city London borough is also under attack from commercial crime.

Brian D. MacLean

If victimization research is the major empirical thrust of left realism, then the historiography of crime survey research based on interviews with victims of crime is essential in understanding both the potential and limitations that such research has to offer. In 'A Program of Local Crime Survey Research for Canada,' Brian MacLean examines the evolution of crime survey methodology and assesses the ability of surveys to accurately measure crime and yield information about policing.

MacLean argues that, although victimization surveys have provided useful information about patterns of victimization, their major thrust has been political rather than academic. And he suggests that, although victim surveys and victimology have common origins, their objectives differ. It is mainly the victimization survey, he argues, that is of central interest to left-realist criminology.

Victimology is a supposedly 'scientific' discipline, with the crime victim as its object of inquiry. The predominant thrust of victimology has been to examine the extent to which victims precipitate their own misfortune. In contrast, victimization surveys, even if they have been a primary source of victimological data, were conceived primarily as a method for estimating the frequency and distribution of unreported crime.

MacLean identifies three phases in the development of victim surveys. He suggests that the first two generations were characterized by methodological difficulties which the third generation, local crime surveys, must address. The first-generation surveys, most carried out in the United States and some in England, were exploratory in nature. They produced estimates of the amount of unrecorded crime and allowed for the refining of survey methodology. They showed that victimization was spatially and socially clustered, and that samples had to be huge if they were to generate reliable estimates of criminal victimization.

Second-generation surveys differed from their predecessors in two important respects: they were more sophisticated methodologically and their theoretical trajectory was guided by a concept of victim precipitation. MacLean calls this development 'neopositivist' – a shift from the question that occupied conventional positivist criminology – 'what are the characteristics of a person who violates norms?' – to a different concern – 'what are the characteristics of a person who is victimized?' If second-generation victim surveys followed a theoretical mandate, they also fulfilled a political purpose by rescuing positive-administrative criminology from social constructionism, particularly its attack on the meaning of crimes known to the police. Furthermore, the second-generation survey served to rescue the law-and-order lobby from the assault of left-wing criminology and allowed crime control and policing to pass from the police to their employers (i.e., to departments of justice and other government agencies).

Third-generation surveys – local crime surveys funded by local councils – were developed in England to overcome the biases of police statistics, to provide an alternative to government knowledge about crime, to counter one-sided investigations into victim precipitation, and to fill the gap in our knowledge about community attitudes towards crime and policing.

In proposing a program of local crime survey research for Canada, MacLean notes that, while all sorts of criticisms have been made of left realism and of local crime surveys, virtually all of the critics suggest that local surveys do yield useful information about crime victimization and policing, both academically and politically. MacLean suggests that local surveys would facilitate important developments in Canadian criminology. In making the case for a program of local crime research, MacLean argues that surveys: (1) should be local, not national; (2) must be based on preparatory qualitative research; (3) must be longitudinal; (4) must be independent; (5) must be funded by different levels of government in partnership with each other; and (6) must be sensitive to the experiences of the disenfranchised.

Conclusion

Whatever strengths and limitations one accords to left-realist criminology, its importance to criminological discourse since the mid 1980s is not easily ignored. The publication of the Islington Crime Survey was at least successful in opening up a new line of debate in contemporary criminology. Since that time, realist criminology has received considerable scrutiny in two different ways. First, critics of realism have been keen to point out the perceived weaknesses – realism is populist, realism is another form of state-sponsored criminology, realism is class biased, realism is gender blind, realism is insensitive to the experience of racial inequality, and the advocates of realism are opportunistic. So vast has been the critique that virtually every major important publication in recent criminological debate has found it necessary to undertake some discussion about the kinds of arguments advanced by realist criminologists.

The second way that realism has received scrutiny has been by its own advocates in response to their critics. In this way, realism has been critically reflexive and has taken heed of such critique. In some ways the arguments for and against realist criminology have come to dominate the discussion advanced by its proponents, and the contribution to novel thinking has waned somewhat since the first wave of realist publication. The result has been a considerable impact upon criminological thinking. The positive aspect of this contribution can be recognized in the new information, data collected by surveys, and crime-control policy advocated by realist criminologists. The negative aspect of this contribution has been the resistance to some of these contributions by a variety of criminologists writing within a variety of intellectual traditions that range from the extreme left to the extreme right of the political spectrum. In short, realism has been a central feature in criminological debate. We can now commence with an investigation into both sides of this debate by examining the case made for realist criminology in Part One of this book. Jock Young begins chapter 2 by discussing the central principles of realist criminology.

References

Bottomley, K. 1988. 'Review Article: Victims of Crime.' *International Journal of Sociology and Social Policy*, 8 (5): 51-54

Cowell, D., T. Jones, and J. Young, eds. 1982. *Policing the Riots*. London: Junction Books

Crawford, A., T. Jones, T. Woodhouse, and J. Young. 1990. *The Second Islington Crime Survey*. London: Middlesex Polytechnic, Centre for Criminology

Gelsthorpe, L., and A. Morris. 1988. 'Feminism and Criminology in Britain,' in P. Rock, ed., *A History of British Criminology*, 93-110. Oxford: Clarendon Press

Giddens, A. 1984. *The Constitution of Society*. Cambridge: Polity Press

Gifford, Lord. 1986. *The Broadwater Farm Inquiry*. London: Borough of Harringey

Harris and Associates. 1987. *Crime in Newham: The Survey*. London: Borough of Newham

Jones, T., B. MacLean, and J. Young. 1986. *The Islington Crime Survey: Crime, Victimization and Policing in Inner-City London*. Aldershot: Gower

Jupp, V. 1989. *Methods of Criminological Research*. Contemporary Social Research no. 19. London: Unwin Hyman

Kettle, M. 1984. 'The Police and the Left.' *New Society*, 70: 366-367

Kinsey, R. 1984. *The Merseyside Crime Survey*, First Report. Liverpool: Merseyside Metropolitan Council

– 1985. *The Survey of Merseyside Police Officers*. Liverpool: Merseyside Metropolitan Council

Kinsey, R., J. Lea, and J. Young. 1986. *Losing the Fight against Crime*. Oxford: Basil Blackwell

Lea, J., and J. Young. 1984. *What Is to Be Done about Law and Order?* Harmondsworth: Penguin

Mathieson, T. 1973. *The Politics of Abolition*. London: Martin Robertson

– 1986. 'The Politics of Abolition.' *Contemporary Crises*, 10 (1): 81-94

Matthews, R. 1986. *Policing Prostitution: A Multi-Agency Approach*, Paper 1. London: Middlesex Polytechnic, Centre for Criminology

Miers, D. 1989. 'Positivist Victimology: A Critique.' *International Review of Victimology*, 1: 3-22

Painter, K., J. Lea, T. Woodhouse, and J. Young. 1989. *The Hammersmith and Fulham Crime and Policing Survey*. London: Middlesex Polytechnic, Centre for Criminology

Smart, C. 1989. *Feminism and the Power of Law*. London: Routledge

Young, J. 1979. 'Left Idealism, Reformism and Beyond: From New Criminology to Marxism,' in B. Fine, R. Kinsey, J. Lea, S. Picciotto, and J. Young, eds., *Capitalism and the Rule of Law: From Deviancy Theory to Marxism*, 11-28. London: Hutchinson

– 1986. 'The Failure of Criminology: The Need for a Radical Realism,' in R. Matthews and J. Young, eds., *Confronting Crime*, 4-30. London: Sage

– 1991. 'Asking Questions of Left Realism,' in B.D. MacLean and D. Milovanovic, eds., *New Directions in Critical Criminology: Left Realism, Feminism, Peacemaking and Postmodernism*, 15-18. Vancouver: Collective Press

PART ONE

The Case for Left Realism

2 Realist Research as a Basis for Local Criminal Justice Policy

Jock Young

The Problem of Crime

The crime rate is not a marginal concern but in many ways the moral barometer of our society, a key indicator as to whether we are getting things right, achieving the sort of society in which people can live with dignity and without fear. The control of crime is a project which severely stretches human imagination and ingenuity. Like most advanced industrial countries, Britain has faced a seemingly inexorable rise in crime in the postwar period. This rise has occurred despite a considerable improvement in living standards and a vast increase in expenditure on the police, the judiciary, and the prisons. If the former conjuncture shattered conventional wisdoms of those on the left of the political spectrum, the latter coincidence has been cold comfort to those who have accepted the dogma of the right.

I am not arguing that 'nothing works' – the crime-control lament of the 1970s – but rather that some commonly used measures undoubtedly do work, while some do not and others are actually counterproductive. However, precious little research is available to assist in sorting out the wheat from the chaff: this is an extraordinary situation, given the vast amount of money spent every year on crime-control measures. In 1988, for example, £3,500 million was spent on the police force, £698 million on the prisons, and a further £1,000 million on the criminal justice system in England and Wales. In the private sector £1,000 million was spent on security equipment alone, while as much again was spent by local authorities on crime-related matters. Yet the tide of crime is unabated. More research is urgently needed, but we must, for the moment, base our policies on the bedrock of substantiated research that has been built up over the last fifteen years. And this research must be utilized, and not merely a shopping list of crime-control measures to be ticked or crossed off as successes or failures. Some measures, neighbourhood watch, for example, which have failed for one purpose may, as I argue elsewhere, be of great use in other areas of crime control. And other measures, such as the improved lighting of estates, may well prove extremely successful in certain areas (see Painter 1988), but may, in fact, be of more limited use when applied to other types of estates or other parts of the city. What we need from research is not just a list of empirical findings, but the establishment of the principles of how crime-control measures succeed or fail. With this knowledge we can know how to refine existing effective institutions so that they work better, when to discard institutions that have negligible or counterproductive effects on the crime rate, and how to devise new interventions.

There is a consensus as to the need for a multi-agency approach to crime control. In part, it is based on the recognition of the obvious fact that crime has always been controlled by a multiplicity of agencies, from the family, through schools, to the police. More important, such concern for a multi-agency approach is about the coordination of society's interventions against crime; that is, we must concern ourselves not only with how effective each agency is with regard to crime control, but with how these various agencies can be welded into an effective, mutually supporting intervention. In order to be an effective strategy, each agency requires support from other institutions; we can judge the effectiveness of an innovation in practice in one area only when the requisite support occurs elsewhere.

The institutions designated to tackle the crime problem must, therefore, be scrutinized closely in terms of their effectiveness. But to do this demands that we have a clear notion of input, public demand, output, and what exactly constitutes a measure of success. Input, the gauging of public demand and priorities with regards to community safety, cannot simply be read off from the level of public requests for police assistance. First, community safety is a result of the actions of many agencies, the police being only one strand in the system of crime control. Second, even if the police were the only agency in the fight against crime, there are many reasons why the public should be reluctant to make demands upon them. As has been repeatedly shown, there are very considerable doubts among the citizens of inner-city areas about the ability of the police to tackle crimes that the public regard as serious. Many crimes are simply not reported because the public believes that reporting them is a waste of time. But effectiveness is only one part of the problem. Sections of the population are wary of contacting the police because they fear that their cases will not be dealt with sympathetically. Victims of racist attack may not report because they have encountered racist attitudes among police officers. Female victims of sexual assault may feel that they themselves are likely to be put on trial, both in the police station and in the courts. This problem of secondary victimization deters many of those most at need from seeking police assistance. Coupled with doubts about police effectiveness, it makes it impossible to garner input from the existing demand for police services. The social survey allows us to provide more accurate figures, but, as we shall see, survey data require a considerable amount of interpretation before we can ascertain from them what a rational input would look like.

Let us now turn to output. At first, the desired outcome would seem obvious: the *modus vivendi* of crime control is to control crime. But we must ask what crimes are being controlled and at what cost, and where these crimes figure in public priorities. That is, we must connect up demand with supply: what crimes do the public prioritize in terms of community safety and how effective are the various agencies and initiatives at controlling them on a cost-effective basis. But efficiency alone is an insufficient indicator of success. It is quite possible to pour resources into a particular estate or area to good result, but the reduction of crime at a particular point in the city may have little effect on the overall crime rate. At the extreme, the individual citizen may turn his or her home into a veritable fortress of locks, bolts, and guard dogs, which will undoubtedly reduce the chances of crime at a particular point in a street, but may not reduce – or, indeed, may increase – the incidence of crime in adjacent properties. On a larger scale, residents of a private estate may employ their own security guards and, by environmental means, isolate their housing from the neighbourhood. Such social sanitization may greatly reduce the incidence of crime in such privatized areas. Within the public realm, a local authority may select an estate and implement a considerable degree of target hardening, securing doors and windows or installing an expensive concierge system. Such 'showcasing' of one estate may produce good particular results, but have little effect on the more general incidence of crime in the area. The task of an effective crime policy is to reduce crime in general. In this it is like a community health project; success is not measured by the extent to which the well-off can purchase vaccines, private health care, and medicines, but the degree to which such indicators as reduced levels of infectious diseases and infant mortality and increased overall lifespan are present.

Crime, like illness, is a universal problem. It affects men and women of all classes, ages, and races. For this reason, being a prevalent and universal phenomenon, it rates very high in people's assessment of problems that figure in their area. More people, for example, see crime in Islington as a problem than they do unemployment, inadequate housing, or poor education standards. These latter problems, however serious, affect, most directly, only parts of the population: those who are unemployed, those inadequately housed, those with children at school. But, however universal a crime problem is, crime affects particular parts of the population to a greater extent than it does others. In part, such is the case because, as we have shown, the incidence of crime focuses on certain parts of the population rather than others, but also, most importantly, because the impact of identical crimes varies considerably with the vulnerability of those who are the targets. To this extent, we must seek not only to reduce the crime rate universally, but to allocate greater resources to those who suffer greatest. Once again, community health provides a model. Ill health is a universal human problem, but ill health focuses on some sectors of the population more than on others. Therefore, in order to reduce the general rate of crime, we must selectively target our resources. Unfortunately – and this has been a general problem of welfare provision – resources are distributed not so much to those in greatest need as to those with the greater political muscle and social persuasion. The history of the National Health Service and of state educational provisions has adequately displayed this inequity.

I have outlined the background problems of crime-control intervention, and pinpointed problems of research, of the need for validated principles of intervention, of the necessity of a coordinated multi-agency approach, of the need to scrutinize problems of input, and of the notion of universal versus particular successes in the crime-control field. It is these issues that I intend to unravel in a systematic fashion.

Taking People Seriously: The Problem of Input

The public pays for community safety and ultimately empowers the police and the local authority to make provisions for a safe environment. There is much talk at the moment of the quality of life and the emergence of green issues as priorities in the platforms of all political parties. Quite correctly, considerable focus is given to architecture, consumer satisfaction, creating a city environment in which it is a pleasure to live. But what can be more central to the quality of life than the ability to walk down the street at night without fear, to feel safe in one's home, to be free from harassment and incivilities in the day-to-day experience of urban life?

The social survey is a democratic instrument: it provides an accurate appraisal of people's fears, of their experience of victimization; it enables the public to express their assessment of police and public-authority effectiveness and their doubts as to the extent to which the police stay within the boundaries of the rule of law. If we are to view the public as a consumer, as Sir Peter Imbert (1989) most usefully suggests, then the social survey provides a detailed picture of consumer demand and satisfaction. Other measures are far from satisfactory: only a small proportion of crimes are reported to the police, so statistics of crimes known to the police, as an indicator both of the distribution of crime and of crime-rate fluctuation, are notoriously unreliable. Only the social survey can reveal the actual public demand for different kinds of police service and public assessment of police performance. And if the dark figure of crime makes official figures problematic, then the official statistics which present us with a picture of police-public encounters and the level of public grievances with police behaviour are even more flawed. To take one instance: the statistics on complaints against the police are virtually worthless.

The local survey of an inner-city area further allows us to go beyond the abstraction of the aggregate statistics of England and Wales as a whole. Crime is extremely geographically focused, and policing varies widely between the suburbs and the inner city. To add the crime rates for, say, a suburban area such as High Street, Farnham, to that of inner-city Holloway Road, Islington, produces a mélange of figures that are of little use to anyone. More invidiously, it allows politicians to 'show' that the fear of crime is irrational by alluding to the actual risk rate of the 'average' citizen. The 1982 British Crime Survey showed that the incidence rate of risk of experiencing a robbery in England and Wales was once every five centuries; an assault resulting in injury, once every century; a family car stolen, once every sixty years; and a burglary, once every fifty years (Hough and Mayhew 1983). But crime is geographically focused, and 'irrational' fears become more rational once we focus on the inner city. And the often-made assertion that certain groups have an irrational fear of crime because of their supposedly low risk rates often disappears on closer examination. The suggestion that women are irrational, for example, requires ignoring the fact that much crime against women, such as domestic violence, is concealed in the official figures; that women are less able to tolerate violence than are men; and that women experience harassment on a level which is unknown to most men. The last point, particularly, is important for public policing. Women experience a wider spectrum of crime than do men. Their range of victimization extends from harassment to serious crime. Men are much more likely to experience crimes only at the more serious end of the spectrum. As a result, men find it difficult to comprehend women's fears. The equivalent experience of sexual harassment for men would occur if every time they walked out of doors they were met with catcalls inviting them to fight. And the spectrum that women experience is all the more troublesome in that each of the minor incivilities could escalate to more serious violence. Sexual harassment could be a prelude to attempted rape; domestic quarrels could trigger wife battery; burglary is a possible precursor to sexual assault. If crime causes the quality of life to deteriorate for men, it has a much more dramatic impact on the lives of women in the inner city.

As we shall see, such considerations have bearing on key policy decisions, such as the role of beat policing and the potential of neighbourhood watch.

Social surveys, therefore, allow us to give voice to the experience of people, and they enable us to differentiate the safety needs of different sectors of the community. In this they often make reasonable the supposedly irrational. But it must not be thought that irrationality does not occur with regards to crime and the means of its control. Crime is a prime site of social anxiety, and the mass media provide the citizen with an extraordinary everyday diet of spectacular crimes, often of the most statistically atypical kind. It is, perhaps, not surprising that the news value of the most unusually garish offences is higher than that of the more mundane crimes that daily plague the lives of the inner-city dweller. And in a free society, there is little that can, or should, be done about such media predilections. For, in a real sense, the most unusual example of inhumanity tells us something of the extremes of moral depravity that are possible in today's society. The trouble occurs when the citizen comes to believe that what is typical on television is typical in his or her neighbourhood. The debate on the effects of the mass media on public attitudes is long and, in part, unresolved (see Cohen and Young 1981). A useful rule of thumb, however, is that the mass media have greatest influence on opinion where people have little direct knowledge of the matter in question, and the least where they have direct experience. Applying this rule to our findings, we would expect that there is little chance of inner-city dwellers being particularly irrational about most of the common serious crimes. A high rate of burglary, for example, would mean that most people would have been burglarized, or would know someone who had been, in the last five years. And their realistic understanding that the typical burglar is a lad from the area rather than a professional thief substantiates our rule of thumb. In the case of cannabis use, a surprisingly high percentage of people (31 per cent in Islington) have smoked the drug at least once in their lifetime. Their view of cannabis possession as one of the lowest policing priorities accords well with the general scientific assessment of the drug as being, on the whole, innocuous. Difficulties, however, arise as to the public's placement of tackling cocaine dealing among the top five policing priorities. Very few people (4 per cent) have used any hard drug, including cocaine and heroin. Thus, although cocaine use is a serious problem in itself, it is not a widespread phenomenon. There has, however, been considerable publicity of cocaine use in the mass media. This is a *prima facie* case for the existence of conditions necessary for the generation of a moral panic. Contrast it with drunken driving, another example of substance abuse – albeit a legal substance – which is also among the public's top five policing priorities. Alcohol abuse is well known to the public, as are the dangers of drunken driving. Here the response is rational and flies in the face of the conventional wisdom that police action against drunken driving is unpopular.

When we turn to crime control, the possibility of public irrationality is considerably greater. For, although members of the public may have experienced victimization, they have, on the whole, little knowledge of how effective crime control occurs. It comes as a surprise, for example, that a large proportion of serious crime is solved by the public rather than by police investigation. Neighbourhood watch is seen as a panacea against burglary, although one of our recent surveys showed that the average citizen would have to be on watch for forty-two years to see a burglary (Painter et al. 1989); their lace curtains would tear and their eyeballs would ache before they witnessed a break-in.

Social surveys can, therefore, provide us with a democratic input into the direction and prioritization of crime control. But they cannot provide us with a blueprint. You cannot read policy directives from social surveys, but neither can you provide directives without real consumer input. The process of moving from input to policing involves four stages: (1) identification of problems, (2) assessment of priorities, (3) application of principles, and (4) consideration of possibilities. Let us examine each of these items.

Identification of Problems

The victimization survey accurately provides a map of the problems of an area. Although based on public input, it delivers what any individual member of the public is ignorant of: that is, how private problems are publicly distributed. In this task, it pinpoints which social groups within the population face the greatest risk and in which geographical areas crime most frequently happens. In this it directs crime-intervention initiatives towards those people and places most at risk. Therefore, it reveals the concealed crime rate and it ascertains its social and spatial focus. But it goes beyond this, for risk rates alone, however delineated, do not measure the true impact of crime, and hence do not describe the actual patterning of crime as a social problem. To do this we must advance beyond the one-dimensional approach of aggregate risk rates and place crime in its social context. The myth of the universal victim underscores much of conventional victimology with its notion that victims are, as it were, identical billiard balls. Calculating the risk rate merely involves calculating the changes that result from an offending billiard ball's impacting upon them. People are, of course, not equal; they are more or less vulnerable, depending on their place in society. First of all, at certain parts of the social structure, we have a compounding of social problems. If we were to draw separate maps of the city, outlining areas of high infant mortality, bad housing, unemployment, poor nutrition, and so forth, we would find that all of our maps overlapped and, further, that the area shown would correspond to that for high criminal victimization (Clark 1970). And those suffering from street crime would also suffer most from white-collar and corporate crime (Lea and Young 1984). Further, this compounding of social problems occurs in the case of those who are more or less vulnerable because of their position in the social structure. That is, people who have the least power socially suffer most from crime. Most relevant here are the social relationships of age, class, gender, and race. By focusing on the combination of these fundamental social relationships, realist analysis allows us to note the extraordinary differences between social groups as to both the impact of crime and the focus of policing.

Let me make this position clear. There are two tendencies within contemporary victimology, both of them premised on fallacies, albeit opposing ones. The 'objectivists' conduct surveys which calculate the risk of crime and contrast it with public fear of crime. Thus, they are in a position to assign degrees of rationality to various groups. In particular, women and the elderly have been conventionally designated as irrational in that their levels of fear are higher than their supposed risk rates. More generally, the fear of crime in the population as a whole is seen to be greater than the average risk rates. As a corollary, fear of crime is seen as a problem separate from that of crime itself; indeed, taken to extremes, fear of crime is seen to be more of a problem than crime itself. Such a position has resonance among more radical writers, who will readily talk of moral panics regarding crime, for example, with regards to mugging and juvenile delinquency. The causes of fear of crime are thus, to a degree, separated from the experience of crime. The mass media, in particular, are seen as a potent influence on public ideas about crime across the board.

The 'subjectivists,' in contrast, believe that public perceptions of crime are *ipso facto* the problem of crime. They make no distinction between fear of crime and actual criminal victimization, and if one requires a rational input into the crime-control policing machine, then public opinion itself is the prime yardstick. Policing can be read off the computer printout of public opinion. In this measure, the task of 'subjectivists' is to show that public opinion is rational. And there is no doubt that by employing more sympathetic interviewers and exploring the 'dark' figure of crime, they have shown that much of what is seemingly 'irrational' has a rational basis. Both feminist research and the earlier work in this decade of radical victimologists have exhibited this tendency.

I have already indicated how a realist position differs from both objectivism and subjectivism. Objectivism, with its use of aggregate crime rates and its unwillingness to focus on the way in which crime affects particular subgroups of the population, is too prone to portraying fear of crime as irrational. It belongs to the old social-policy tradition of Fabianism, where experts readily bestow problems on a population supposedly ignorant of the true nature of their own suffering (see Corrigan et al. 1988). Subjectivism, on the other hand, is only too ready to believe that what people subjectively experience as their problem is the problem. It grants too much rationality to the citizens surveyed.

In contrast to both these perspectives:

a Realism notes that rationality and irrationality relate to the experience of crime and crime control. In the majority of serious crimes, inner-city dwellers, and their neighbours and friends, have a surfeit of experience: irrationality is unlikely here. For a minority of crimes, the lack of direct experience may well generate irrational responses. In terms of crime control, lack of knowledge of what goes on in either police or local authority intervention can generate incorrect evaluations.

b Realism points out that individual respondents are aware of the crime experienced by themselves or their acquaintances, but have only a rudimentary knowledge of the overall picture.

c Realism emphasizes that the nature of crime involves behaviour and evaluation: an objective action and a subjective assessment of this action as criminal. Over time, among different groups of people and in different countries, the evaluative element varies. All societies stigmatize violence, but intolerance of violence varies. What was considered normal, perhaps necessary, chastisement of children in Victorian times would be considered child abuse today. What is permissible physical punishment of children in Britain would be illegal in Scandinavia. This essential dyad of criminology – behaviour and the differential reaction against it – is ignored by most victimologists. Thus, although everyone condemns violence, different sections of the population identify different points on the continuum of violence as intolerable. Women are undoubtedly less tolerant of violence than are men, and there are significant indications that upper-middle-class women are less tolerant than are lower-working-class women. The latter is shown in the well-known 'education effect,' where educated women report greater levels of violence than do the less educated (see Young 1988b; Hough 1986). Victimization studies rely on the assessment of victims. They reflect differences in experienced behaviour, coupled with differential evaluations of that behaviour. Differences in victimization rates do not, therefore, merely reflect differences in criminal behaviour. They should not be interpreted this way, although such interpretations are made by both tendencies in victimology. Realists recognize that differences in evaluation have to be taken into account. Women and old people may, for example, have higher levels of fear of crime than do young men who experience high risk rates. Yet to term the former 'irrational' and oddly take the fear rate of men as being the standard for rationality denies the fact that people have the right to exhibit different levels of willingness to tolerate violence.

This is not to give carte blanche to relativism: to suggest that each section of society has an uncriticizable right to its own standards of rationality. Particularly where there is little contact with crime, enormous possibilities exist for the gross overestimation of risk rates, and distorted views as to what constitutes a typical crime. But it is not appropriate for the social scientist to inform the public as to what level of tolerance they should have about crime or what standards they should demand with regards to the quality of life in their area. Thus, while the cognitive component of fear of crime may be critically examined, the tolerance component should remain outside the orbit of the expert.

d Realism indicates that the individual may be unaware of the real impact of crime on his or her life. A middle-class woman, for example, may have evolved or inherited a series of avoidance patterns that minimizes the risk of crime to the extent that the pressures of crime on her everyday life may not be apparent. She might, for instance, scarcely confront harassment in public space because she moves from her house, to her car, to friends' houses, or meets people publicly in a 'protected' area, together with friends in a tranquil wine bar or restaurant. The working-class youth who experiences the intransigence of the street may well be part of a subculture which, by its bravado and toughness, never admits to worrying about crime. The lower-working-class woman, trapped in a scenario of domestic violence, may see her predicament as an individualized experience, with no notion of the generalized vulnerability of the patriarchal relations in which she is trapped. All of these people – and many more in different situations – will reply to a questionnaire on the level of their everyday taking care of the business of life experience without an understanding of why or how they are trapped in these situations. All of them will be either unconscious or falsely conscious of the reality of their predicament (see Walklate 1989).

e All of this being said, we must start from the premise of people's actual grievances in the world. To bestow problems on people is to commit the errors of the objectivists, to take people's understanding of their grievances as the be-all and end-all of analysis is to enter the arena of subjectivism.

f The expert, the social analyst, therefore, has a vital role in contextualizing the problem of crime by mapping the problems and then putting them into context. In short, the analyst uncovers problems and then gives weight to their severity. This is the basis for a rational input into the system of crime control. This brings us to the next stage, prioritization.

Assessment of Priorities

A survey can ask the public about their crime-control priorities but, as I have outlined above, its designers cannot be sure that these priorities realistically reflect the actual problems of a community. To do so with some assurance requires the weighting of three inputs: public priorities, the prevalence of each particular crime, and an assessment of each crime's impact.

Let us start with the first two inputs. Here we need to combine public priorities with the actual prevalence of a problem. In this way we are able to distinguish those problems which the public rightly see as grave, yet are comparatively restricted (e.g., cocaine) from those which are widespread (e.g., burglary, drunken driving). But we must go farther than this, for – as I have outlined above – we must take cognizance of the impact of problems. That is, although burglary, for example, is a universal problem throughout the community, its effect on the poor is incommensurably greater than on those who are better off; that is, although tackling burglary by any standard is a top priority of crime control, burglary against certain groups would be a particular priority. Special attention to the policing of poorer estates, and the provision of local-authority insurance schemes for those groups who are frequently uninsured, would thus be relevant policy initiatives.

Application of Principles

To deal adequately with the problem of crime we must be able to ground our interventions in empirical research which uncovers both the actual nature of crime and crime control and the underlying processes by which crime control could or actually does succeed. Realist method insists on the following principles.

1. Focusing on Lived Realities

The experiences of the public with regards to crime and policing cannot be reduced to global figures of the average risk rates of particular crimes or the 'normal' citizen's experience of policing. All evidence indicates that the impact of crime and policing is geographically and socially focused: it varies enormously by area and by the social group concerned. The reason for selecting an inner-city area is to enable us to detail such experiences at the sharp end of policing, while comparing these data to those derived from wider-based surveys of total cities and the country as a whole. The reason for the use of extremely concentrated sampling is to be able to break down the impact of crime and policing in terms of its social focus, that is, on social groups defined by the combination of age, class, gender, and race. Such a concentrated social focus corresponds more closely to the lived realities of different groups and subcultures of the population. Thus, just as it is inaccurate to generalize about crime and policing from gross figures based on large geographical areas, it is incorrect, even within particular areas, to talk in terms of 'all' young people, 'all' women, 'all' Blacks, 'all' working-class people, and so forth. Generalizations which remain on such global levels frequently obfuscate quite contradictory experiences, generating statistics which often conceal vital differences of crime impact. We have shown, for example, how the introduction of age into the analysis of fear of crime by gender changes the usual generality of fear of crime being low among men and high among women. In fact, older women and men in the middle age group have a similar fear of crime, as do younger women and older men. And, in the case of foot-stops by the police, it becomes evident that differentials based on race are much more complicated than the abstraction that Blacks are more likely to be stopped than are Whites. No older Black women in our sample were stopped. Young, White women were over three times more likely to be stopped than were older Black men. And even the differential between young Black men and young White men becomes remarkably narrowed when class is introduced into the equation. Such an approach in realist method is termed an awareness of the specificity of generalization, the need to ground analysis firmly in specific areas and social groups. This approach is in marked contrast to those that try to explain differences in experience in terms of only one of the major social distinctions: age, class, gender, or race. Such reductionism, as exemplified by radical feminism or fundamentalist class analysis, simply does not fit the reality of social experience. This approach enables us to be more discriminating about generalization with regards to changes in modes of policing and methods of crime control. For example, with regards to the debate about shifts from consensual to more coercive forms of policing (Lea and Young 1984), it allows us to ascertain whether or not contradictory forces are at work, involving consensual policing of certain areas and groups and more coercive methods with others. Similarly, the likely efficacy of crime-control measures such as beat policing or neighbour-hood watch must be related to specific community experience and to particular locations.

2. Corresponding to the Reality of Crime and Policing

The most simple equation in crime control is that which envisages the police directly controlling crime rates. This equation, enshrined in conventional wisdom, is, in the face of the last twenty years of research, palpably untrue. It is incorrect because it is too abstract; because it embraces only part of the process, missing out essential variables; and because it is phrased in terms of quantities and not relationships. It simply puts too much onus on the police: to congratulate the police on a decline in the crime rate or to criticize them for an increase is as foolish as holding doctors responsible for the sickness rate of the nation.

At heart, realism points to the fact that crime rates are a product of four interacting factors: the police and other agencies of social control, the public, the offender, and the victim. Any changes in one of these factors will affect the crime rate, and the police are only one factor in the equation. The point here is that crime rates cannot be explained simply in terms of crime-control agencies, and that many more agencies are involved in crime control than just the criminal justice system. Changes in the demographic composition of the population (particularly the number of adolescent males) can remarkably affect the crime rate by altering the number of possible offenders. Changes in the lifestyle of the public – for example, if people go out more at night, thus putting themselves at risk – can increase the number of potential victims and thus greatly affect the rate of crime (Felson and Cohen 1981). In recent years, criminology has begun to incorporate both these factors – witness the debate on age structure and crime (see Greenberg 1984) and the development of lifestyle analysis (see Felson 1987).

But, turning to the control agencies themselves, it has become apparent that the simple equation of police affecting the crime rate is a gross oversimplification. Probably the most dramatic innovations in recent criminology involve the new emphasis on the powerful role of the public and informal processes in the control of crime and the delineation and advocacy of a multi-agency approach to crime control.

Thus there is a tendency within the field of crime control to overemphasize the role of the police, criminal courts, criminal law, and the prisons. Commentators of all political persuasions, both of the right and the left, have elevated the crime-control function of the police to a paramount position. The involvement of other institutions is played down; resources are allocated in accordance with this belief; and the whole discussion about crime control revolves around the success or failure of beat policing, numbers of police, police technology, and so on, in the fight against crime.

In his pioneering study of the London police, David Smith correctly points to the limited role of the police in the overall system of social control:

Another example of the limited, yet decisive, role of the police is in the control of disruptive behaviour in schools. The example is particularly interesting because such a high proportion of the incidents that the police deal with concern children and young people. Many fights and scuffles take place in schools, which might in other circumstances be interpreted as minor assaults. There is also a considerable amount of damage to school property (most of it minor damage) and a fair number of thefts. The schools have their own systems of rewards and punishments for trying to prevent this kind of behaviour and dealing with it when it does occur. They also have links with parents through which they try to use the family to reinforce the codes of conduct applied at school. The vast majority of fights, thefts and incidents involving deliberate damage to property are dealt with by the school procedures and within the family. There is always, implicitly, a threat that a matter may be reported to the police if the offender does not step into line, but in practice the police are informed in a very small proportion of cases (though we do not know what the proportion is). Even when they are informed, they will not take action unless the school or other loser decides to press a charge. Thus, schools and families not only bear the main responsibility for controlling the behaviour of children, but they also largely decide when the police shall be involved and whether or not formal proceedings shall be started.

Examples of this kind show that it is mostly not the police, but other agencies and individuals that 'set the agenda' for law enforcement. (1983: 12)

His example is particularly relevant, as, of course, a very large proportion of what are conventionally defined as crime and incivilities are, in fact, committed by adolescent boys who are members of both schools and families. Indeed, these are the two social institutions which form the major rubric of their lives. Immediately upon such a simple insight being brought to light we are forced to ask: How do these institutions coordinate together in terms of crime control (i.e., police, education, and the family)? The answer to this question is, of course, that, although social control is *de facto* multi-agency, there is nowhere near any coherent notion of their coordination, let alone a planned distribution of resources.

The discourse centring around crime control is replete with reference to police, criminal law, and prisons. Even when multi-agency approaches are advocated, as in multi-agency policing, such approaches cast the police as the pivotal organization which coordinates, initiates, and sets the agenda for crime control. Yet, in fact, the initiatives for crime control are largely external to the police. At the most simple level, it is the public that informs the police of the existence of crime in 95 per cent of instances (Jones, MacLean, and Young 1986). Further, as Smith points out:

Although there is some truth in the platitude that 'the police are dependent on the support of the public', the formulation is too simple and does not go far enough. The police are not, for the most part, the prime movers, the initiators of the societal processes that control deviant behaviour; on the contrary, they work, for the most part, at the margins, where the usual processes of control have broken down. Most of the time they are responding to direct requests from individuals or other agencies, and even then they can only act effectively where the assumptions and values that govern their actions are more generally shared. Even within that small proportion of their total activity in which they appear to be taking the initiative, the police act as a continuation and development (by specialists) of more general efforts by the mass of people and institutions to maintain order, control and coherence. In other words, the police are a small but extremely important element within a much larger complex of inter-related systems of control. They require support, though not uncritical support of unthinking obedience; for they themselves are only supporting (not initiating or directing) the wider forms of social control. (1983: 10)

But, once again, although crime control involves many agencies and is predominantly not police initiated, there is little coordination of and principles guiding such initiation. At least one-half of serious crime is not reported to the police – the so-called dark figure of crime (see Hough and Mayhew 1983; Jones, MacLean, and Young 1986). This dark figure occurs for various reasons: because the public think the police are ineffective at controlling a particular crime, because they deem them an inappropriate agency, because they fear the police, or because they fear further victimization from the criminal. The relationship, then, between police and public is central to the success or failure of policing. The effectiveness of the multi-agencies themselves is dependent on the relationship among them.

The degree of impact of a crime intervention by one agency is dependent on the other agencies. To take a simple example: no amount of propagation by the police of crime-prevention advice in terms of better locks and bolts will be effective on estates if the council does not simultaneously strengthen the door-frames of its tenants' houses. Or, of greater significance, police effectiveness is almost totally predicated on public support: it cannot function without the information flow from the informal system of social control. And the same is true of deterrence: the effect of police cautioning or the sentences of the courts relates closely to the degree of public stigma.

The simple equation of police fighting crime therefore needs to be totally rewritten. Most anti-social behaviour is controlled directly by the public; multiple non-policing agencies are involved in crime control, and the policing function itself is profoundly predicated on public support.

Realism, then, points to a square of crime (see figure 2.1), involving the internal understanding between police and the other agencies of social control, the public, the offender, and the victim. The relationship between the four corners of this square determine crime rates (Young 1987, 1992).

I have pointed to the relationship of the police and the public as being of

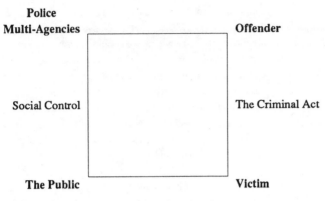

FIGURE 2.1. The 'square of crime'

primary importance. Indeed, that relationship is central to the study of crime. But the interaction between all components is important. For example, the police and agency response to victims greatly affects the actual impact of victimization and, in certain instances such as rape and sexual assault, can even involve what has been termed 'secondary victimization,' that is, where the victim becomes further stigmatized by police and courts. All of this, particularly in terms of willingness to report crime to the police, affects the official crime rate and the possibilities of clear up. Similar relationships occur between the offender and the public. In the case of burglary, for example, the close relationships of certain sections of the public to the purchase of stolen goods creates an illegal hidden economy which greatly succours and encourages the crime. These last two relationships are not of primary focus in this present essay: the relationship between public and police is, as is the relationship between police and offender. In this case the effect of illegal policing on groups prone to crime – many members of which are innocent at the time of arrest or stops in the street – may well create subcultures alienated from the public. It can trigger the metamorphosis of potential into full-blown offenders.

3. Social Control and Relevant Publics

The agencies involved in the control of crime depend upon public support. They cannot bestow social harmony on the public; such harmony is achievable only through cooperative effort. To take the police as an example: as we have seen, most crime is made known to the police by the public. But, more than this, most crime is solved by the public, and offenders are not detected directly by the police. Furthermore, the process of giving evidence in court extends this need for public cooperation throughout the judicial system. While a substantial section of the public is unwilling to cooperate with the police, a majority are only too willing to do so and to give testimony in court. Is public cooperation, then, a matter of only marginal concern? In fact, it is a crucial weakness because of the simple fact that those who are willing to cooperate have the least knowledge of crime and those who are alienated from the police and courts – the relevant public – are much more knowledgeable. If, of course, the latter group consisted only of the small number of offenders, then such wariness of the police would be understandable. But the majority of those alienated are, in fact, honest, law-abiding people, who have, ironically, high victimization rates and on whom, because of their poverty, crime has its greatest impact. The people who need a police service most are those who suffer the greatest level of injustice from the police in terms of experiences of both excessive policing, such as stop and search, and police illegalities, such as excessive use of force upon arrest. It must be a priority of policing to ensure what I have termed the relevant public are treated strictly within the limits of the rule of law.

4. Open and Closed Systems

The distinction between open and closed systems is a fundamental one made in the recent realist philosophy of science (Bhaskar 1980). Most scientific laws are predicated on research carried out *in vitro*, that is, in closed systems where all extraneous factors are held at constant values. Here the matter of tracing causality is quite simple. But in the actual natural world – for example, in sciences such as meteorology – the multiplicity of uncontrolled extraneous factors present in an open system makes statements of cause and effect extremely difficult. Y follows X, depending on the contingency of circumstance: it is better, therefore, to speak of 'causal powers' which may or may not be enacted, depending on circumstance. The social world is an 'open system' *par excellence*, influenced by extraneous factors of great importance. Thus, one of the avowed aims of the Police and Criminal Evidence Act (PACE) – that of providing the police with powers to tackle crime – presents us with considerable problems in delineating causality and judging whether the legislation has been effective.

To hold that police intervention or other forms of crime control would be instrumental in changing the crime rate in such an open system requires a series of assumptions: namely, that the number of possible victims and offenders, and public reaction to crime are constant. But changes in the social structure of the area affect all of these factors. For example:

a increased gentrification of an area would affect the number of victims and, by increasing relative deprivation, the number of possible offenders;

b increased population mobility would affect the social solidarity of an area, and hence the strength of public control of crime;

c changes in the age structure of the area, particularly increases in numbers of young males, would affect the number of putative offenders;

d changes in employment and economic marginalization in an area would affect the number of offenders;

e changes in lifestyle, for example, increases in the number of evenings out, would affect the victimization rate, in terms of both risks in public space and risks of homes unattended.

We can attempt to control for some of these variables, but over any reasonable length of time an open system will exhibit changes in many of them.

What I am pointing to is that the process which gives rise to crime rates is a system of relationships, and what is more, it is an open system (see figure 2.2). With the exception of short-term experiments, where a social intervention, such as improvements in lighting, is introduced and the effects measured (see Painter 1988), it is extremely difficult to pinpoint cause and effect in such an open system. For example, what effects has PACE had on the crime rate over a three-year period, where multiple changes have occurred in Islington? Or, as we have examined elsewhere, how can we construct a police performance indicator in terms of clear-up rates, given that the amount of crime known to the police, which forms the denominator, is dependent on many factors on which policing has only a partial influence (Crawford et al. 1990)?

5. Realism Focuses on Specific Police Practices and Specific Crimes

Turning once more to our 'simple equation' which suggests that more policing results in less crime, we must clearly state and analyse what types of policing are likely to be effective against what types of crime.

In the 1970s, faced with the continuing rise in the crime rate and a fiscal crisis in the cost of police and prisons, politicians in the United States became increasingly interested in the most effective ways to use resources. The main focus of research was directed to police work, particularly the work of the RAND organization and the Police Foundation. Their findings were to have a devastating effect on subsequent criminology. For they pointed out, among other things, that:

– increased policing does not necessarily reduce crime rates or increase clear-up rates;

– saturation policing does not reduce crime, but only increases displacement;

– improving response times to emergency calls does not affect the likelihood of arresting criminals;

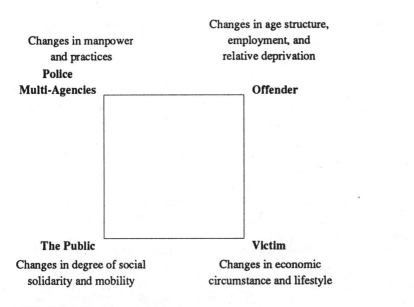

FIGURE 2.2. The 'square of crime' as an open system

- crimes are not solved by criminal investigations, but largely by public witnessing;
- the kinds of crime of which the public are most fearful are rarely encountered by the police on patrol; and
- neither random motor patrols nor foot patrols have any effect on the crime rate.

This summary of findings I have culled from Jerome Skolnick and David Bayley's incisive book, *The New Blue Line*. They write:

Those findings are devastating. They mean that the primary strategies followed by American police departments are neither reducing crime nor reassuring the public. Like other public institutions – schools, the Defense Department, prisons – the police often devote resources to traditional but bureaucratically safe approaches that no longer work – if they ever did. That probably explains why additions of money or personnel have slight measurable effects on security. How could they, when existing strategies seem largely bankrupt? The studies clearly imply that protection needs to be provided by citizens themselves, and that their assistance is essential in capturing and prosecuting the people who victimize them. The job for the police, therefore, is to work with the public so as to ensure that those things happen, to develop specific and articulate approaches that can achieve results. (1986: 5-6)

It has become a conventional wisdom in criminological and policing circles that extra beat policing will have little effect on the crime rate. Thus, Clarke and Hough write in their summary of the literature: 'There is little evidence that increasing the number or frequency of foot patrols actually reduces crime – although this may achieve other important objectives in terms of public satisfaction and feelings of security' (1984: 6; see also the assessments in Morris and Heal 1981, ch. 5; Wilson 1985, ch. 4). The expert consensus is that the public are misguided in their nearly universal demand for more foot patrols as a method of controlling crime, as indicated in repeated surveys on both sides of the Atlantic. What is granted, however, is that such patrols make them less fearful, but the overall impression is of a public which, on this score, is viewed as being irrational. This conventional wisdom of modern criminology is translated in policy terms into a considerable opposition to any increase in foot patrols and to a more technologically sophisticated and mobile police force.

There are many problems with the equation that more beat policing is not cost effective in controlling crime. They exist on the level of input (what sort of beat policing, doing what, about what?), output (what sort of crime?), and general problems of objective, independent measurement. Such problems beset all assessments of crime control, although, in fact, studies of beat policing are relatively more sophisticated than those in most other areas.

Let us briefly outline a critique of the literature.

a. What Is Beat Policing? The major problem of input is the fact that beat policing can involve a variety of practices. It can involve aggressive policing, which alienates a community, or cooperative policing, which enhances the flow of information from the public to the police (see Kinsey, Lea, and Young 1986). The first style of policing would tend to increase crime, the second to decrease it; thus it makes no sense whatsoever to generalize from such contradictory inputs. What is necessary is generalization based upon the impact of precisely delineated types of beat policing.

b. What Crime Is to Be Controlled? The most frequent output to have been measured is burglary. Thus Clarke and Hough continue:

Set in temporal and geographical context, crimes are rare events, and are committed stealthily – as often as not in places out of reach of patrols. The chances of patrols catching offenders red-handed are therefore small, and even if these are somewhat increased, lawbreakers may not notice or may not care. An average foot beat in a large British city covers a square half-mile, with 4-5 miles of public roadway and a population of about 4,000. Thus, given present burglary rates and evenly distributed patrol coverage, a patrolling policeman in London could expect to pass within 100 yards of a burglary in progress roughly once every eight years – but not necessarily to catch the burglar or even know that the crime was taking place. Research interviews with habitual burglars and other offenders have confirmed that they realise that the risks of being caught red-handed are low, and it is questionable whether they would be sensitive to changes in the level of risk brought about by changes in conventional foot patrol. (1984: 6-7)

This is absolutely correct, of course, as burglary is a particularly hard crime to observe, and all evidence suggests that the numbering of expensive items, and action against fences are likely to be more effective than beat policing (see Lea et al. 1988: 14-15). And, anyway, as the British Crime Survey shows, one-half of offences do not occur in public places. So it is plausible to eliminate both private crimes and publicly concealed crimes from the output likely to be affected by beat policing and concentrate on publicly visible crimes. By these I refer to crimes such as street fights, hooliganism, drunk-and-disorderly behaviour, and harassment. These visible crimes are widely experienced and cause the public considerable distress and fear. They are not the top public priorities with regards to policing, but rather occupy the middle range. Importantly, they are linked to all the major offences on a continuum ranging from sexual pestering to actual sexual assault, threatening behaviour to actual physical attack, vandalism of a vehicle to taking a vehicle and driving it away. It is my contention that beat policing may well prevent precisely such behaviour and that this is the rational basis for the decreased public fear of crime evidenced in many of the experiments.

Furthermore, as I have argued, the problem of public incivilities has particular relevance for women, in that they experience a much wider spectrum of crimes than do men.

A major part of the problem, therefore, is deciding what sorts of crimes beat policing could conceivably decrease and measuring the effect of such policing on this part of the spectrum of criminality. At root this involves a redefinition of crime as a problem that includes minor offences. It means widening the focus from major crime (which surely must be included) to crimes which the police themselves often regard not as 'real' but as 'rubbish' crimes (see Smith and Gray 1983).

c. Order Maintenance or Crime Control? In the literature, it is often conceded that foot patrols can have an effect on minor crimes. The strange twist, however, is that such minor illegalities are not seen as crimes, but as disorderly behaviour. The subsequent debate occurs between those on the right – the most articulate exponent being James Q. Wilson, who argues that the police are justified in acting against disorder even when a crime has not been committed – and libertarians who see the policing of order as a dangerous extension of state power.

More than this, it is frequently suggested that the primary focus of policing is, in fact, the maintenance of order rather than the control of crime. Thus, Reiner writes in his authoritative *The Politics of the Police*:

The historical and sociological evidence should have made clear that crime fighting has never been, is not, and could not be the prime activity of the police. To see it as such is a part of the mythology of media images and cop culture, but presents a stumbling-block to sensible discussion or policy-making. The core mandate of policing, historically and in terms of concrete demands placed upon the police, is the more diffuse one of order maintenance. Only if this is recognised can the problems of police powers and accountability really be confronted in all their complexity, and perhaps intractability. In this light, the vaguely defined 'public order' offences like breach of the peace or the vagrancy acts (which are such a scandalous embarrassment from either a crime control or due process approach) speak to the very heart of the police function. (1985: 171-172)

The presentation of policing as largely a symbolic order-maintaining activity rather than an instrumental crime-controlling activity also derives from the work of James Q. Wilson (1985). As we have noted elsewhere, this conventional distinction between order maintenance and crime control is, in terms of actual legality, largely illusory. For much of the problems of order, in fact, are criminal or potential criminal offences (Kinsey, Lea, and Young 1986: 77-87).

I have argued previously that a policing strategy must have as its core, crime control. This aim reflects the demands of the public and is also held to be of highest value within the ranks of police officers themselves. The alternatives of crime control or order control are false. Thus, the fact that the public prioritize as police tasks both the investigation of crime and a deterrent presence on the street (Kinsey, Lea, and Young 1986; Jones, MacLean, and Young 1986) is not a contradiction, as has often been suggested. These tasks are merely different parts of the same continuum.

What has occurred is that the distinction made by the patrolling officers between 'unimportant/uninteresting' offences and 'real crime' has been enshrined in this false theoretical distinction between order and crime. For it does not, in practice, largely correspond to that of the non-criminal versus the criminal. But this belief has allowed civil libertarians to argue that all order intervention is illegitimate, while those on the right concur in that they regard crime control alone as the rightful focus of policing. The public demand for more beat policing, which is evident in all surveys and among all groups, may well, then, have a rational core. Thus demand emerges from the recognition that minor levels of anti-social behaviour are a problem, are indicative of more serious crime, and can be controlled by beat policing. James Q. Wilson and G.L. Kelling half grasp this in their classic article 'Broken Windows' (1982), where they posit that such patrols, by reducing disturbing behaviour, allow the community to revitalize itself and stem the spiral of increasing criminality which befalls an area, publicly seen as having 'tipped' into disreputability. Wilson and Kelling are in all probability correct in their surmise that the foot patrol may control minor crime and that this can stop a spiral of disorganization within a neighbourhood. But they are wrong when they hint that this should permit the police to act beyond the bounds of law. We must aim to maintain the delicate balance between intervention within the rule of law and intervention beyond it, between productive and counterproductive policing. This point is clearly recognized by the public who both condemn police illegalities and demand the effective policing of both minor and serious crime.

6. The Specific Reality of Crime

As I have noted, a term like 'beat policing' can mean many things. But policing is only one side of the equation. The other side is crime itself. It is essential that we look at the specific reality of different crimes. For it has to be stressed that policing must fit the crime – that it must be adapted to a particular crime's shape, content, and spatial presence. I hinted at this in discussing the public versus the private dimension of burglary and crimes of disorder. Let me elaborate.

a. Shape. Each type of crime presents a different network of relationships; if we compare illegal drug use, burglary, and assault with offensive weapons – three of the crimes that the PACE legislation was devised to deal with – we note markedly different structures (see figure 2.3). Drug dealing has a well-known pyramidal shape; burglary involves numerous victims and regular fences; assault may well be a one-off case of victimization.

b. Content. Crime involves both cooperation and coercion. In the case of drug use, every step of the pyramid is consensual; in the case of burglary, dealing in stolen goods is consensual and the actual act of stealing coercive; in the case of assault, the act is purely coercive.

c. Spatial Presence. All crime has a spatial dimension, and the geography of crime varies widely according to the specific crime. Drug dealing has an international dimension, a national distribution, and a focus on specific areas of the city. Dealing in cannabis stretches spatially from, say, Pakistan to All Saints

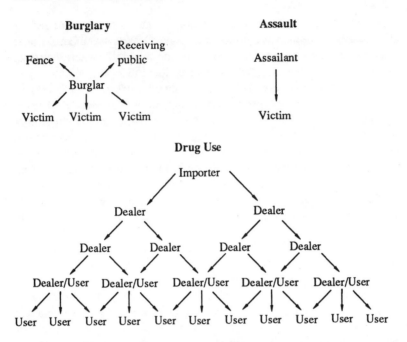

FIGURE 2.3. The different 'shapes' of three crimes

Road, Notting Hill. Burglary occurs widely across a locality and is part of a hidden, locally based economy. Assault has no wider spatial dimension. However, it occurs frequently in specific areas. In the case of assault by a stranger, for example, the crime has a pronounced geographical focus which is made manifest, both in the incidence of assault and in the fear of victimization expressed in the avoidance of certain areas. Just as specific crimes involve differing structures of relationships, they involve particular structures in space.

Crime occurs privately and publicly, and specific crimes are private at certain points of their structure and public at others. In the case of drug dealing, all aspects of the crime, apart from those occurring at street level, are extremely private transactions. At the level of the opportunistic user, it is quasi-public; people must know the dealers and, like any other 'shopkeepers,' they must be relatively open to the public. In the case of burglary, apart from the brief, circumspect act of breaking in, the act itself is private: it occurs usually when the owner is absent and neighbours can see no suspicious activities. Subsequently, the sale of stolen goods is quasi-public: it occurs publicly when a fence wittingly or unwittingly sells stolen goods or when direct public purchase occurs in the public areas of the pub or workplace. Assault in a public place is, by its very nature, an open event. Unlike domestic violence, it is coercion in the street, in a public house, or in some other public venue. Given these fundamental dimensions of specific crimes, it is evident that there must be a match between specific crimes and the particular practices of crime control.

It is obvious from this analysis that certain crimes are more difficult to police than others (particularly if they are consensual and take place in private) and that particular points of intervention in the specific reality of the crime present greater difficulties than others. There are resistant points and there are weak spots. One of the fundamental axioms of policing must be that police practice fit the nature of the crime. Sadly this is not the case. It is a long-known secret – Colquhon made this point in the nineteenth century – that the weak point of burglary is fencing (see Lea et al. 1988: 14-15). The detection of burglary by the usual deployment of beat police is largely doomed to failure. As we have seen, Clarke and Hough (1984) estimate that patrolling police officers come within one hundred yards of a burglary only once every eight years; our own study shows that the average citizen sees a burglary once every forty-two years, giving little hope for neighbourhood watch as being effective in this area. Our major initiatives against burglary traditionally have been directed at precisely those points where they have very little chance of effect.

7. Putting Behaviour into Context

Realism involves the invocation of rationality that is rooted in material circumstances; that is, it places the behaviour of the offender, the police officer, the victim, and the public at large in the actual material circumstances that each individual experiences (Lea and Young 1984). This is not to say that people do not make mistakes in understanding the world, whether it is the behaviour of the police officer involved in a stop and search or the fear of crime of the citizen. Indeed, to err is *ipso facto* the very nature of rational behaviour. Rather, realism sets itself against an idealism which analyses people's beliefs and behaviour primarily as a product of free-floating ideas and prejudices, whether they are the product of outside influences, such as the mass media, socially detached group values, or personal psychological attributes.

Realist method relates attitudes and beliefs to actually lived experience in specific material circumstances. For example, it attempts to explain police behaviour, not in terms of a group of people acting in accordance with, say, authoritarian personalities, a macho-culture, or rigid 'them' and 'us' attitudes engendered at training school. All of these things may or may not apply, but they are not the primary determinants of police behaviour. To take a police patrol as an example, it is the actual nature of the police task, the experiences confronted in attempting to achieve objectives in the face of the opportunities and difficulties encountered on the job, that is central to understanding the behaviour of patrolling officers. In the specific instance of PACE legislation, I would argue that police practice can be deduced neither from legal rules nor from a free-floating cop culture or the autonomous prejudices of individual police officers. Realism attempts to put police practice, the interpretation of rules, the generation of an occupational culture, and the attitudes of individual officers in context. The stop-and-search procedures are largely ineffective in dealing with the crimes to which the legislation was directed: burglary, hard-drug use, and carrying weapons. Direct information, gleaned either from the public or by detective work, would be needed in order to gain a high yield from such a procedure. In the absence of such information, patrolling officers equipped with stop-and-search powers, and wishing to have at least some yield from their work, will, of necessity, target those groups which have high offending rates, particularly young, working-class males – Black and White. As most people stopped will be perfectly innocent, such a trawling of a particular social group will inevitably create a counterproductive hostility in the target groups and accusations of unfairness, selectivity, and prejudice. But it is the inadequate tools for the job and an ill-thought-out piece of legislation which create the working context for the police, not merely the enactment of personal and cultural prejudice.

8. Realism about Cost-effectiveness in Tackling Crime

Realism states that any intervention has its costs. Different crime control measures have to be measured in the following terms: how effective they are compared to each other; how effective the marginal increase in resources is in one area rather than another; and what the cost of the measure is in terms of other desiderata, for example, the quality of life or the exercise of civil liberties.

Consideration of Possibilities

What are the possible means of controlling crime? Crime can be regulated by attacking the causes which give rise to offending; it can be deterred by policing and sentencing the offender; and it can be prevented by target-hardening.

Over the last fifteen years, conventional wisdoms have been overturned, both by the seemingly intractable nature of the crime problem and by a series of abrasive research findings which have fundamentally altered our way of looking at crime. And the shift in the focus of control has moved from tackling causes to more police and greater deterrence, to crime prevention – largely in the form of target-hardening.

In the immediate postwar period there was a consensus stretching across a large section of informed opinion that the major cause of crime was impoverished social conditions. Anti-social conditions led to anti-social behaviour; political intervention and economic reconstruction which improved conditions would, therefore, inevitably lead to a drop in the crime rate. Yet precisely the opposite happened. Slums were demolished, educational standards improved, full employment advanced, and welfare spending increased: the highest affluence in the history of humanity was achieved, yet crime increased. In Britain, for example, between 1951 and 1971 the real disposable income per person increased by 64 per cent, while the crime rate more than doubled, with a rise of 172 per cent (Young 1988a).

It is important to remember the dismay that this crime rate caused, particularly in those countries with a developed welfare state. As R.A. Butler, the home secretary for much of this period, noted, the rise came 'after years of the most massive social and educational reform for a century' (cited in Fyvel 1962: 14). And if lay opinion was disturbed, criminology was in tatters.

There has always been an uneasy balance in criminological thinking between those who believe that improving social conditions will reduce the crime rate and those who advocate quicker and surer punishment. The first option was summarily dismissed; more police, more prisons, and longer sentences became the order of the day. But, as I have mentioned, a series of devastating research findings began to emerge from the United States in the late 1970s with regard to the effectiveness of policing; extra police did not reduce the clear-up rate; police patrol was not effective in dealing with most of the crimes that the public feared; it was the public, not detective work, that solved crime; improved response times did not increase the likelihood of arrest (Skolnick and Bayley 1986). And all of this was underscored by the crisis in the prisons, with their riots, overcrowding, and chronic recidivism.

So, if the 'better conditions equals less crime' equation had broken down, so had the 'more police equals less crime' equation. It was the failure of both these conventional responses to crime that directly gave rise to the present orthodoxy of target-hardening, which attempts neither to eliminate the causes of crime by social amelioration nor to deter crime by punishment. Such an approach finds ready political resonance: better locks and bolts and more effective informal surveillance are sufficiently non-punitive to satisfy liberal sentiment, while advocating the privatization of community safety fits well with government policy. A new bipartisan approach to crime emerged, with both the establishment and radicals stressing that crime was a greatly exaggerated problem and that the fear of crime was sometimes more of a problem than crime itself. Both had grave doubts about the 'crime wave.' Both believed that the police could do little about crime and, most important, both deemed that it was unnecessary to understand causes.

Causes are no longer seen to be relevant to policy. Thus, Ron Clarke (1987), former head of the Home Office Research and Planning Unit, invoked the metaphor of 'humps in the road': these simply impede speeding; we do not need to know the causes of fast driving. Melanie Phillips, in a perceptive article (1989) in the *Guardian*, sums up this approach:

A short while ago, I asked a senior civil servant why the government seemed reluctant to commission research which tried to explain why certain anti-social activities took place. Was it not a little short-sighted to formulate policies on, say, crime prevention without trying to establish why young men of a certain age were given to acts of violence?

He reacted as if this was an outlandish suggestion. There was no point in asking why things happened, he explained patiently, because the only thing that mattered was that they were happening, and would undoubtedly continue to happen, probably in ever greater volume. Young men had always been violent, since the beginning of time, had they not? They would always be violent, whatever we did with them, would they not? So what was the point of trying to understand their behaviour?

His responsibility was not to ask why, but to work out how best to contain it all with the minimum of social inconvenience. It was the classic response from within a political culture that plays a never-ending game of crisis management, a culture that is essentially reactive, putting out fires when they explode, building more and more prisons, employing more and more police officers, drafting stiffer and stiffer penalties, introducing identity cards, but paying little attention to any explanations which might just possibly enable us to step in and prevent the explosion in the first place: prevent the football fan from becoming the hooligan, prevent the father from torturing the child.

This political unwillingness to seek explanations, particularly those which might conflict with ideological preconceptions, has found in recent years an echo in the social science research community itself. Researchers here appear to have lost a degree of confidence in their ability to identify causes, preferring to concentrate on what is happening rather than why people behave in certain ways.

A major database for the new administrative criminology was the British Crime Survey carried out in three sweeps in the period from 1982 to 1988. The results were presented in terms of the risk rates of the average citizen's being victimized. Since we have already fully criticized the concept of aggregate rates, let us examine the policy implications of this flight from aetiology. The format for the presentation of crime data as average risk rates is part of a wider process referred to by the rather Orwellian phrase the 'normalization' of crime. The policy formula, widely accepted in Home Office and policing circles, is that risk of crime is much lower than the public suspect – serious crimes of violence are comparatively rare – and that the mass media have contributed to irrational fears, particularly among women and the elderly. Crime is a normal part of everyday life, the role of the police should be restricted to that of high-profile serious crimes and crime-prevention advice, the local authority should become responsible for 'designing out' crime, and the 'active citizen' becomes the major player in crime control by making his or her home more secure and by becoming involved in neighbourhood watch (Newman 1984). The normalization of crime is accompanied by the privatization of community safety. The core slogan 'the fear of crime is as much a problem as crime itself,' borrowed strangely enough from Ramsey Clark (the Democratic attorney general in the United States in the 1960s) became the conventional wisdom of Britain in the 1990s. And such a slogan is bipartisan: while the right tells of 'irrational fears,' the left talks of 'moral panic.'

The breach in this consensus was a series of studies which focused on crime in the inner city, against women in particular. Feminists, such as Jalna Hanmer and Sheila Saunders (1984), found more rape and attempted rape in a survey of seven adjacent streets in Leeds than did the whole of the British Crime Survey (see also Hall 1985), while a series of local surveys financed by radical councils in Merseyside, Islington, and Hammersmith found alarming levels of crime, with one in two households suffering a serious crime every year, and a virtual curfew of 40 per cent of women in their homes because of fear of crime (Kinsey, Lea, and Young 1986; Jones, MacLean, and Young 1986; Painter et al. 1989). The calculation of general risk rates for the whole country overlooked the fact that crime was extremely focused, both geographically and socially, and, as we have seen, the notion that women were irrational in their fears began to look very suspect when the research lens was turned upon the inner city. Furthermore, widespread dissatisfaction with police performance was revealed, with over 50 per cent of the public judging the police to be unsuccessful in tackling burglary, street robbery, sexual assault, and hard-drug trafficking.

Nor was the attempted devolution of crime prevention to the public very successful. Despite its phenomenal success as a social movement, neighbourhood watch was an abject failure in tackling crime. In retrospect, it was difficult to imagine how the watch schemes were supposed to work. Designing out crime was the most effective strategy, but the point is reached where there are diminishing marginal returns in crime reduction and a deleterious impact on the quality of life.

It is of vital importance that we face up to the problem of crime in our inner cities. To do this will involve social crime prevention, better design, public involvement, and more effective policing. Successive governments have produced one part of the jigsaw of crime prevention at the expense of all others. Ironically we now have experience of all parts of the jigsaw puzzle: what we do not have is the wit to put them together.

Four tasks face us: our first is to put money into tackling the causes of crime. We must reopen the question of the causes of crime. Common sense tells us that the reality of crime involves offenders and victims. Therefore, intervention can occur at two points: that of protecting the victim and that of preventing offences. Present government policy has focused too exclusively on the victim: it seeks, through target-hardening and the increasing privatization of security, to make the public responsible for their own safety, while dealing with offenders with a strong police force and in the courts only after the offence has been committed. But to prevent offending before it occurs by removing the causes of crime itself has become an anathema. What is needed are resources directed at the likely offenders, frequently adolescent boys, in terms of anti-crime education in schools, massively greater youth employment possibilities, and better leisure facilities. The French government has given a lead in its energetic social crime-prevention policies (see King 1988). The social-democratic consensus of the 1950s that better conditions would reduce crime led to attempts to reduce absolute deprivation. But it is not absolute, but relative deprivation which causes crime (Lea and Young 1984). It is not the absolute level of wealth, but the perception that resources are unfairly distributed that affects the crime rate. The structural unemployment of youth cheek by jowl with a wealthy middle class as now occurs within our gentrified inner cities is a recipe for a high crime rate (Lea, Matthews, and Young 1987). To reduce crime we must reduce relative deprivation by ensuring that meaningful work is provided at fair wages, by providing decent housing in which people are proud to live, by ensuring that leisure facilities are available on a universal basis, and by insisting that policing is equally within the rule of law, for working class and middle class, for Blacks and for Whites (Currie 1985).

For political rather than cost-effective reasons, the government has set itself against such social intervention. Its focus on one-half of the crime equation is misguided, since to put funds solely into one side of intervention produces declining marginal returns. Intervention should occur at both levels.

We must also stress that the role of the police is to fight crime, not to act as traffic cops – a separate force, as in most of Europe, should do that – not to act as lost-property agents, and not to act as secret social-service agents. And, in order to fight crime, they must gain public support, for this is the lifeline of effective policing. In over 90 per cent of cases, the police depend on the public to identify the culprit, provide evidence, and give testimony in court. Without public support, policing either fails or lapses into a desultory authoritarianism. The goal must be to bring policing priorities into line with the public that pays for it (Kinsey, Lea, and Young 1986). Last year we spent £3.5 billion on the police force. It is important to consider whether we are getting value for our money. Of the 3.7 million crimes reported to the police, one-third were cleared up: some two million crimes every year are not solved. As the clear-up rate has fallen by about one percentage point per year during the tenure of the present government, the figure of unresolved crime has risen faster than the crime rate itself. All of this is exacerbated in the inner city, where crime is highest. In London, the general clear-up rate is 16 per cent, falling to 9 per cent for crimes such as burglary.

The crux of the problem is the extremely low rate of productivity per police officer. In all, 1.25 million crimes were cleared up: about ten crimes per police officer every year. Of course, the police do other things than attempt to control crime – this, indeed, is perhaps the crux of the matter – but even so, such a performance is scarcely reassuring. And in the metropolitan areas, where crime hits hardest, performance is lowest. Just 4.5 crimes are cleared up per police officer in London in a year. Indeed, if the sizeable civilian back-up were to be taken into consideration, the true figure would be fewer than 3 (Lea, Matthews, and Young 1987).

It should be thought neither that the level of public criticism of the police is extraordinary nor that the police are an exceptional public body. Indeed, our Hammersmith survey showed public assessment of the police ability to reduce burglary to be on par with their evaluation of the council's ability to keep the streets clean, and police are perceived to be as unsuccessful in tackling heroin dealing as the local authority is in its efforts at council house repairs (Painter et al. 1989). The key problem is how one manages to make any bureaucracy accountable to public demand and how to stop the goals of the organization from taking precedence over the priorities of the public (Corrigan et al. 1988).

Reversing the Retreat from Causality

Our point should now be clear. A realist policy acknowledges that there are various methods which, if properly tested, monitored, and costed, can reduce crime. But any one method, however effective, will have declining marginal returns if taken too far and too exclusively. Furthermore, any one method, be it public surveillance through neighbourhood watch, extra police on the streets, or target-hardening, will have costs that impact on the quality of life and the freedom of citizens. By putting too great an emphasis on target-hardening and ignoring the conditions which give rise to crime, present government policy has created an imbalance in intervention. It has focused on reducing the opportunities for crime, not on its causes. It has focused on one-half of the equation rather than on both of its sides.

I have considered the possibilities of intervention in the control of crime. I would like to conclude by looking at the institutions involved.

Multi-Agency Control

My strategy continues to reflect the fact that the Force alone cannot provide tidy solutions to the many problems that confront Londoners and impair their quality of life. Indeed, it would be a monstrous deceit for anyone to attempt to sustain such a fiction. The major resources for crime reduction are to be found in the community itself and in other public and voluntary agencies. (Newman 1987: 7)

Thus, the former commissioner of police, in his 1987 strategy statement, detailed his commitment to a multi-agency approach to crime control. Let us briefly note the reasons for the emergence of such an approach.

The Existing System of Crime Control

Multi-agency intervention is the planned, coordinated response of the major social agencies to problems of crime and incivilities. The central reason for multi-agency social intervention is that of realism: it corresponds to the realities of both crime and social control. Social control in industrial societies is, by its very nature, a multi-agency task. The problem is that social control is not coordinated and represents a series of other disparate policy initiatives, with little overall rationale for the allocation of resources, and includes institutions which are often at loggerheads with each other. Yet, as I have discussed, the various agencies are mutually dependent on each other, and each agency is dependent on public support, whether it is an agency dealing with domestic violence, child abuse, or juvenile delinquency. In this section, I wish to deal with the relationship between: the agencies and particular forms of crime; the agencies and the public; and the agencies themselves.

a. The Agencies and Crime. Different agencies are involved for different crimes and at different stages in the process of tackling offenders. If we compare burglary to child abuse we see immediately the differences between the involvement of the various agencies. In general, burglary will have a high police involvement in terms of the apprehension of the criminal. The local council will

TABLE 2.1
Agencies involved in crime control

Stages in the development of crime	Factors	Agencies
Causes of crime	Unemployment Housing Leisure	Local authority Central government Business
The moral context	Peer group values Community cohesion	Schools Family Public Mass media
The situation of commission	Physical environment Lighting Home security	Local authority Public Police
The detection of crime	Public reporting Detective work	Public Police
The response to offenders	Punishment Rehabilitation	Courts Police Social services Probation
The response to the victim	Insurance Public support	Local authority Victim support groups Public Social services

have the greatest role in the 'target-hardening' of the local estate. If the culprit is an adult, social services will be unlikely to be involved, but they will, of course, do so if the offender is a juvenile. In contrast, social services will play a major role in child abuse; the schools will be major institutions of detection, and the medical profession will play an important role in terms of corroboration. And in terms of the different stages of tackling offenders, one can see how the police role as a back-up agency for providing coercive intervention where necessary and legal evidence in the courts occurs at different times in the procedure from the long-term process of social-work intervention. One glance at table 2.1 demonstrates the multiplicity of agencies involved in this process and underlines the contrasts with the traditional approach, which highlights the police and the courts and focuses on only one part of the process.

Different agencies are involved at different points in the biographic trajectory of the offender. A realist approach to offenders is interested in the development of criminal behaviour over time. It breaks down this trajectory of offending into its component parts and notes how different agencies can and should be operative at different stages. Thus we can talk of: the *background causes* of crime, the *moral context* of opting for criminal behaviour, the *situation of committing* crime, the *detection of crime*, the *response to the offender*, the *response to the victim*. Let us examine each of these in turn, noting the factors involved and the agencies with the power to intervene.

1 *Background causes*: These lie in relative deprivation as witnessed in poverty and unemployment, in overcrowded housing conditions, in poor leisure facilities, and in inadequately funded families (particularly single-parent families). Here central government, the local authorities, and local business have responsibility.

2 *The moral context*: Here we have the family, the education system, the mass media, youth organizations, and religious organizations playing particular roles. The public themselves; the councils, in their provision of education and youth facilities; media professionals; adolescents; and local religious and youth leaders all have roles to fulfil.

3 *The situation of commission*: Here target-hardening, lighting, public willingness to intervene, and police patrols are important. The important agencies are the council, the police, and the public themselves.

4 *The detection of crime*: Here, as discussed above, the cooperation of police and public is paramount, in terms of the public both informing the police of crime and acting as witnesses in the courts.

5 *The response to the offender*: Here the police and the courts are paramount in their dual role of punishment and rehabilitation. A rehabilitated offender, of course, should not be a recidivist. In such cases, social services are prominent, not only in their role of caring for young people, but also in terms of their arranging for possibilities of employment and shoring-up of unstable family situations.

6 *The response to the victim*: Up until now we have discussed the whole process of multi-agency social intervention as if it were simply concerned with dealing with offenders and preventing offences. We must never forget, however, the other half of the dyad of crime: the victim. Here again, it is obvious that various agencies must be involved in tackling the problem of criminal victimization. Social services, for example, may have to deal with the after-effects of a mugging of an elderly person, the council has to repair doors after a burglary, battered women's refuges have to deal with domestic violence, the police have to deal with the victims' fears on the spot. Victim support has a vital role to play throughout. Thus our measurement of success – or of failure, for that matter – must be made not solely in terms of the levels of offending (i.e., crime), but also in the levels of victim support provided.

I have discussed the wide range of tasks which influence crime control, involve different agencies, and are influential at different times in the trajectory of offending. It is important to note how these agencies have different material possibilities of intervening and act within given political limitations. We have to choose, then, what agencies are involved and what factors can feasibly be manipulated.

Our approach views crime as a developing system, from its initial causes to the impact on the victim. In doing this it places the responsibility for crime control on a wide range of agencies and on members of the public themselves.

b. Multi-Agencies and the Public. The literature on multi-agency intervention is dominated by a discussion of the relationship among the institutions involved. Quite correctly, this analysis focuses on the possibilities of cooperation and likely conflicts among the agencies. However, it omits a crucial link in the scheme, namely, the relationship between the agencies and the public. We have noted the vital role the public plays in policing. If anything, this recognition is a major aspect of modern criminological thinking. And we must not restrict our attention to police-public relations, but the relationships between the public and the various agencies concerned with crime control. For social services, education, probation, and the local council, no less than the police, are dependent on public cooperation.

There is a widespread commitment to the multi-agency control of crime (Lea, Matthews, and Young 1989); however, the agencies from which the public would ask assistance varies with the specific crime involved. The public has different expectations of the various agencies, in terms of both the initial problem of dealing with crime and the subsequent intervention deemed necessary after the offender has been apprehended. This corresponds closely to our initial analysis of crime control as, of necessity, involving many agencies and creating demands on particular agencies at different points of the process of dealing with crime, from the initial background context which gives rise to crime to the actual point of commission of an offence, to the provision of support for the victim. In a sense the argument about whether the public want coercive (e.g., police) or non-coercive intervention (e.g., social-service intervention) is based on false alternatives. Both policing and social-service interventions are demanded by the public for different crimes and at different times. The general reaction to juvenile delinquency, for example, is far less coercive than that concerning crimes against women.

As far as different parts of the community are concerned, we find a fairly high degree of consensus in public attitude, whether one is talking of differences in age, gender, or race. This invalidates the notion that, for example, men and women have greatly different responses to crime in terms of the use of coercive or social-service measures.

What emerges clearly from the data is the role of the police as the leading agency of first referral. This is not, of course, identical with a view that the police should be the dominant agency in a multi-agency set-up, but merely that they are seen as an essential element in intervention. Indeed, in areas such as crime prevention, the local authority in particular is seen, perhaps, as having a more important role than the police. In tackling juvenile offences, social services are given a prominent role.

A crucial element in the discussion of the relationship between agencies and the public is accountability. Discussion in this area has been overwhelmingly dominated by the topic of police accountability. Of course, this must be extended to all agencies, with performance indicators based on public demand being devised for the array of crime-control institutions. As we have seen, the public are as critical of local authority provision as they are of police performance. Sir Peter Imbert, while correctly noting the need for a democratization of the relationship between the police and other agencies, argues that such a process must be accompanied by such a spreading of accountability.

If police openness and access are problematic, then power sharing is likely to be even more difficult to achieve. Early efforts to become involved in multi-agency approaches to crime and associated topics were painful but worthwhile experiences. But again we wanted to maintain the lead in every forum, to be the gatekeepers to power and to have the right of veto if decisions were made which did not suit us. Some of those attitudes still linger, and some for very good reasons, but there is in the main a real understanding of the advantages of working in partnership. The changes can be seen at every level from joint training with other agencies, to a better level of trust with elected representatives and community groups. I do not pretend that it is an easy path to tread for power sharing does not mean a surrender of power; rather it involves sharing of the knowledge which allows different interpretations and constructions to be placed on that information and which in turn can lead to different conclusions and different solutions.

With power sharing comes the sharing of responsibility ... [But] some do not want to share power when it is realised that a measure of accountability is attracted to whatever decision is made. It should also be noted that on occasion there may have been a deliberate ploy to involve others in unpopular decisions. Unfortunately some still choose to stand on the sidelines, criticising us for our actions but refusing the offer of participation until all their prior conditions have been met. Such a purist approach is very convenient to them as it allows the maximum of comment with the minimum of risk. The opposite side of the coin of power sharing is the acceptance of responsibility and a degree of accountability. (1989: 10-11)

c. The Relationship between Agencies: The Need for Multi-Social Intervention. We have delineated three dimensions of multi-agency intervention: (1) the relationship among the agencies and particular crimes; (2).the relationship between the agencies and the public; and (3) the relationship among the agencies.

Most of the discussion with regards to the multi-agency approach to crime has been in terms of the last area. Here we have delineated the need for multi-agency social intervention, where all agencies are involved in their clearly delineated roles, coming together in a forum where they relate to each other in a democratic fashion. This notion is in contrast to that of multi-agency policing, where the agencies meet together in a platform dominated by the police, in which the latter have the central coordinating role. Elsewhere we have argued for a conception of minimal policing which incorporates the following features:

1 a restriction of police intervention solely to crime control activities;
2 a restriction to only certain parts of the criminal justice process (e.g., in the case of child abuse to only those limited times and occasions where coercive force is necessary: all else is social work);
3 a clear delimitation of spheres between the various parts of the control apparatus (social work is social work and policing is policing, and so on);
4 the giving of priority, because of the different foci of points of the control apparatus, to conflict and debate among different sectors over any overreaching corporate agreement. (Kinsey, Lea, and Young 1986; Young 1987)

The democratic relationship among agencies must be based on their specialized knowledge about particular crimes and the relevance of particular crimes to the mandate of each agency, that is a division of labour predicated on the specific segment of the crime process in which the agency specializes. For example, at what point along the continuum of the development of crime outlined above is a particular agency's involvement paramount and what perspective does the agency represent? In the latter instance, a juvenile delinquent, for example, may be regarded from the point of view of guilt or innocence by the police, within the context of a family with problems by the social services, and as part of a family which causes problems for others in the estate by the housing officers. There has to be pre-established consensus as to specialization, although in some cases more than one agency will be involved at the same point. For example, lighting will be under the auspices of both the local authority's architect's department and its housing officers. Of course, different crimes will involve different types of multi-agency cooperation. Child abuse will involve a strong medical involvement as well as police and social services. Domestic violence will involve the voluntary agencies as well as the more usual constituents. Having brought together these agencies there will be a necessary conflict of interests, despite an agreement on acknowledged specializations. In child abuse, for example, social work, by necessity, has a brief focus on the general welfare of the child within the family; the police, more on the actual issues of culpability; the pediatrician, on the extent of physical contact and harm. What is necessary in the coordination of such expertise is that, in the final analysis, a corporate decision must be made, after listening to the contributions of each agency, and backed with sufficient executive power in order to come to an agreed decision. As it is, the agencies confer with each other, but then too often proceed upon their own paths with their own agendas. Such imbalances are dramatically seen where, in the case of child abuse, either medical or social services plays too dominant a role, or, in the case of crime prevention, where the police take too prominent a role. It is the task of local authorities to provide this coordinating role. It is the ultimate task of national government to ascertain how the provision of resources to each agency is based on the actual cost-effective contribution of each part, rather than, as at present, to allow resources to be decided by the separate agencies themselves. Such a conception of minimal policing in the context of multi-social intervention has clear implications for the second dimension of our analysis. We have seen that there is widespread community support for such a proposal. It does not involve a domination by the police of the other agencies, and, while advocating cooperation among the agencies, it does not suggest a corporatism involving a cosy level of agreement. Rather, because of the different approaches and priorities of each agency, room has to be made for a healthy debate and conflict of perspectives within a consensus delineated by public demands for the control of specific areas. Finally, in terms of the third dimension, the public accountability of agencies – a concern hitherto largely omitted in discussion of multi-agency intervention – the priority is to ensure efficiency and the need for public bodies to fall in line with the demands of the public whose support is necessary for their effectiveness and who, out of their rates and taxes, pay these bodies to perform the task of achieving a reasonable level of community safety.

All of this, with due regard to the three dimensions of multi-agency intervention, suggests the basis for a restructuring of these institutions so as to ensure a maximum level of service delivery in this area, while protecting the rights and dignity of the offender.

References

Bhaskar, R. 1980. *A Realist Theory of Science.* Brighton: Harvester

Clark, R. 1970. *Crime in America.* London: Cassell

Clarke, R. 1987. 'Situational Crime Prevention.' *British Journal of Criminology*, 20 (2): 136-147

Clarke, R., and M. Hough. 1984. *Crime and Police Effectiveness.* Home Office Research Study no. 79. London: HMSO

Cohen, S., and J. Young. 1981. *The Manufacture of News.* London: Sage

Corrigan, P., T. Jones, J. Lloyd, and J. Young. 1988. *Socialism, Merit and Efficiency.* London: Fabian Society

Crawford, A., T. Jones, T. Woodhouse, and J. Young. 1990. *The Second Islington Crime Survey.* London: Middlesex Polytechnic, Centre for Criminology

Currie, E. 1985. *Confronting Crime.* New York: Pantheon

Felson, M. 1987. 'Routine Activities and Crime in the Developing Metropolis.' *Criminology,* 25: 911-931

Felson, M., and L. Cohen. 1981. 'Modeling Crime Rates: A Criminal Opportunity Perspective.' *Research in Crime and Delinquency,* 18: 138-164

Fyvel, T.R. 1962. *The Insecure Offenders.* Harmondsworth: Penguin

Greenberg, D. 1984. 'Age and Crime: In Search of Sociology.' Mimeo

Hall, R. 1985. *Ask Any Woman.* Bristol: Falling Wall Press

Hanmer, J., and S. Saunders. 1984. *Well-Founded Fear.* London: Macmillan

Hough, M. 1986. 'Victims of Violence and Crime: Findings from the British Crime Survey,' in E. Fattah, ed., *From Crime Policy to Victim Policy,* 117-132. London: Macmillan

Hough, M., and P. Mayhew. 1983. *The British Crime Survey.* London: HMSO

Imbert, P. 1989. 'Preparing Police to Deal with a Multi-cultural Society.' Paper delivered at the International Police Exhibition and Conference, London, 2 September

Jones, T., B. MacLean, and J. Young. 1986. *The Islington Crime Survey: Crime, Victimization and Policing in Inner-City London.* Aldershot: Gower

King, M. 1988. *How to Make Social Crime Prevention Work: The French Experience.* London: NACRO

Kinsey, R., J. Lea, and J. Young. 1986. *Losing the Fight against Crime.* Oxford: Basil Blackwell

Lea, J., T. Jones, T. Woodhouse, and J. Young. 1988. *Preventing Crime: The Hilldrop Project.* London: Middlesex Polytechnic, Centre for Criminology

Lea, J., R. Matthews, and J. Young. 1987. *Law and Order: Five Years On.* London: Middlesex Polytechnic, Centre for Criminology

– 1989. *The State, Multi-agency Approaches and Crime Control.* London: Middlesex Polytechnic, Centre for Criminology

Lea, J., and J. Young. 1984. *What Is to Be Done about Law and Order?* Harmondsworth: Penguin

Morris, P., and K. Heal. 1981. *Crime Control and the Police.* London: HMSO

Newman, K. 1984, 1987. *Strategy Statement of the Commissioner of Police of the Metropolis.* London: Scotland Yard

Painter, K. 1988. *Lighting and Crime: The Edmonton Project.* London: Middlesex Polytechnic, Centre for Criminology

Painter, K., J. Lea, T. Woodhouse, and J. Young. 1989. *The Hammersmith and Fulham Crime and Policing Survey.* London: Middlesex Polytechnic, Centre for Criminology

Phillips, M. 1989. 'New Light on the Way We Live Today.' *The Guardian*, 10 February

Reiner, R. 1985. *The Politics of the Police*. Brighton: Harvester

Skolnick, J., and D. Bayley. 1986. *The New Blue Line*. New York: The Free Press

Smith, D. 1983. *Police and People in London*. London: PSI

Smith, D., and J. Gray. 1983. *The Police in Action*, vol. 4. London: PSI

Walklate, S. 1989. *Victimology: The Victim and the Criminal Justice Process*. London: Unwin Hyman

Wilson, J.Q. 1985. *Thinking about Crime*, 2d ed. New York: Vintage Books

Wilson, J.Q., and G.L. Kelling. 1982. 'Broken Windows.' *The Atlantic Monthly*, March: 29-38

Young, J. 1987. 'The Tasks Facing a Realist Criminology.' *Contemporary Crises*, 11: 337-356

– 1988a. 'Recent Developments in Criminology,' in M. Haralambos, ed., *Developments in Sociology*, vol. 4, 137-165. Ormskirk: Causeway Press

– 1988b. 'Risk of Crime and Fear of Crime: The Politics of Victimization Studies,' in M. Maguire and J. Pointing, eds., *Victims of Crime: A New Deal*, 164-176. Milton Keynes: Open University Press

– 1992. 'The Ten Principles of Realism,' in R. Matthews and J. Young, eds., *Issues in Realist Criminology*, 24-68. London: Sage

3 Developing a Realist Approach to Penal Reform

Roger Matthews

Much of the penal reform debate has been conducted within a framework constructed around the two leading positions – reductionism and abolitionism. Standing in opposition to the expansionist policies which have surfaced in a number of Western countries in the postwar period, these two positions have provided much of the intellectual ammunition for keeping the size of the prison system within existing limits. Although unified in their rejection of expansionist policies, reductionism and abolitionism express deeply opposed views about the appropriate forms of intervention. In one sense, they replicate in a particular form the classic political debates about reform versus revolution. On another level, they can be seen to embody some of the attributes of what has been termed, 'idealist' and 'administrative' criminologies (Young 1986).

The abolitionist position on penal reform arose in the early 1970s and was principally associated with the work of Thomas Mathieson (1973), who attempted to develop a response which went beyond the limitations and perceived failures of liberal reforms. In principle, abolitionism starts from the assumption that prisons are anachronistic institutions which create more problems than they solve, and that the aim ought to be to remove rather than improve them. Conversely, reductionism maintains that prisons remain necessary, in the foreseeable future at least, for certain categories of serious and violent offenders. The aim is to reduce the penal population to the minimum. Reductionists vary in the amount of reduction they perceive as desirable, while abolitionists vary in the degree to which the abolition of prisons is seen as an ideal or practical objective (de Haan 1990).

In this essay the abolitionist and reductionist positions will necessarily be caricatured. I will focus predominantly on those forms of reductionism which might more properly be referred to as *administrative reductionism*, concerned with the more effective management of the penal system, and the elimination of overcrowding. References to abolitionism will largely refer to those 'first-generation' abolitionists such as Mathieson, Christie, Hulsman, and Bianchi.

It should be said that I do not adopt these caricatured positions in order to provide an easy target or to denigrate them. Rather, the aim is to provide an accessible point of reference for working through the issues and to develop an alternative approach. From a realist perspective, these two dominant positions can be seen as offering a partial, one-sided approach; however, it is not the task of realism to synthesize them. At a number of points there may be a significant degree of overlap between the approach developed here and that of these two dominant positions. At other points differences may involve merely a shift of emphasis or priorities. However, in attempting to establish an alternative approach to penal reform, which is at once radical and realizable, it becomes necessary to develop a penal politics which draws ultimately upon a different theoretical and political tradition than that which informs abolitionism and administrative reductionism.

I have outlined some of the major differences between realism, reductionism, and abolitionism elsewhere (Matthews 1988). In doing so, however, it becomes apparent that realism, abolitionism, and reductionism do not, as yet, represent distinct theoretical positions, but rather offer a range of strategic approaches which are organized around a number of central propositions. Each draws upon a range of theoretical traditions and diverse philosophies. Providing a systematic critique of any of these positions, therefore, is extremely difficult. The major propositions held by each position may be different, but they are, in many cases, not incompatible. Some of the points of overlap and difference are exemplified in their respective approaches to the problem of generating alternatives to custody.

Developing Alternatives to Custody

Although reductionists and abolitionists agree that one of the central aims of penal reform ought to be to reduce the reliance upon custodial sanctions, there has been some reticence in both camps about developing alternatives. Thomas Mathieson, for example, argues that developing alternatives can inadvertently serve to reinforce the dominance of the prison, if they are built alongside, rather than instead of custodial institutions:

experience over the past decade or so has indicated quite clearly how dangerous planned and structured 'alternatives' to prison may be if the goal is decreased reliance upon prison.

Over the past ten or fifteen years, a number of such 'alternatives' have been implemented, under general names such as 'diversion' and 'decarceration'. Today, we have, in many countries, community service orders, halfway houses, various institutions of alternative conflict resolution, and so on. Study after study in the U.S., Canada and England, very strongly suggest that such 'alternatives' do not become true alternatives to prison. Rather they become 'add ons' to prison, either by simply increasing the number of people under formal social control, or at least, by adding more to the total formal control system than what is subtracted from it. (1986: 86)

Certain reductionists, too, have expressed considerable scepticism over the introduction and expansion of alternatives. Particularly in its more radical version, it is claimed that introducing alternatives tends to 'widen the net' of social control and ultimately lead to the expansion of both 'inclusive' and 'exclusive' forms of control (Blomberg 1980; Austin and Kinsberg 1982; Cohen 1985).

Although some of this scepticism over the use of alternatives was not without some justification, by the end of the 1970s there was a deep-seated pessimism or impossibilism, which claimed that 'nothing worked' and that alternatives would inevitably act in ways which were neither anticipated or desired. Among a significant group of penal reformers there was an emphasis upon non-interventionism and 'doing less good rather than more harm.' During the 1980s, however, a growing volume of evidence suggested that certain alternatives seemed to work for certain types of offenders under certain conditions. Evidence from Holland, Australia, Italy, Germany, and even England indicated that it was possible to reduce these prison populations and to implement more cost-effective community-based alternatives (Downes 1988; Hulsman 1982; Biles 1983).

It became evident that many of the alternatives developed in the 1960s and 1970s lacked credibility – particularly among the judiciary – as an alternative sanction to imprisonment. It also became evident that, if a substantial decrease in the prison population was to be achieved, then alternatives would have to be relevant for middle-range and some of the more serious offenders (Harris 1983/4). Thus, while noting that designing and implementing alternatives to custody is a difficult task, a realist position would stress that alternatives to custody have to be *competing* and *realistic*. By 'competing' it is meant that the sanction will be widely seen as being equivalent or more appropriate. By 'realistic' is meant that:

a the particular sanction adequately expresses the level of public disapproval of the offence, but that such alternatives should not be personally or socially more intrusive and burdensome than incarceration;

b alternatives are designed and directed at specific populations, and that clear guidelines are laid down for their implementation. Alternatives in the past have all too often been introduced without any clear indication of when and where they should be used. As a result, they were often used in ways which were inappropriate;

c the alternative has to be designed to fit into the existing structure of sanctions. Introducing new alternatives can have a profound effect upon existing sanctions, and policy makers must take this into account;

d the sanction should provide adequate protection for the public. People are understandably nervous about supporting diversion or decarceration policies if they feel that it might increase their level of victimization;

e there should be a preference for alternatives which have an educational, reintegrative, and socially relevant role; and

f alternatives, like incarceration, should be subject to systematic monitoring and evaluation. It cannot be assumed that because these sanctions are in the 'community' that they are necessarily benign or effective.

A realist position begins from the recognition that an effective decarceration policy will not be achieved simply by creating more and more alternatives. Rather, alternatives need to be carefully tailored and rigorously implemented if they are to have a significant impact upon the existing prison population. The debate around alternatives has encouraged a rethinking of the relationship between crime and punishment and between varieties of formal and informal control.

Punishment and Incarceration

One of the most positive strands of thought which has developed among abolitionists is the exploration of a range of possible sanctions. In particular, they have been critical of the crime/punishment couplet, and equally critical of the notion that punishment must inevitably lead to incarceration. However, it is the case that incarceration has the unique attribute among punishments that – in the absence of the death penalty – it is the only essentially coercive form of punishment.

Since abolitionists are generally very sceptical about the concept of crime, it follows that they see coercive intervention – which is designed to reduce crime – as being illegitimate (Steinart 1985). They do, however, concede that there are 'problematic situations' and a range of social conflicts (Hulsman 1986; Lea 1987). In most, if not all cases, the criminal law is seen as an inappropriate instrument for dealing with these problems. While critiques of the operation of the criminal law are important, at a certain point the abolitionists tend to slip into an anarchistic position which often becomes anti-state and anti-law. This is not a position which radical realists would support. On the contrary, law and state are seen as an essential element in a just social order, while crimes and conflicts, it would be argued, have important social and individual attributes which cannot be left to the offender and the victim to resolve. The development of state intervention into many of these areas of social life was intended historically to limit personal vengeance and to mediate the inequalities of power (Hirst 1986).

Although certain strands of abolitionist thought may be seen as theoretically and politically untenable, the exploration of the adoption of more informal sanctions is welcome. This focus upon the diverse mechanisms through which social control is accomplished serves as a constant reminder that the vast majority of problems and conflicts are resolved informally. In recent years, attention has shifted to the pivotal roles played by the family and the school in terms of regulating misbehaviour. Increasingly, it has become recognized, even by self-confessed 'hard-liners,' that incarceration is difficult to justify except for an extremely small number of offenders. For example, the degree to which a range of European administrations have adopted a formal position of using prison as a last resort, only when all other options have been tried, is testimony to the growing disenchantment with incarceration in many Western countries. The reasons for this disenchantment are many and include financial and pragmatic considerations as well as humanistic motives. But even among some conservatives, who see imprisonment as a way of avoiding the moral responsibility of crimes, incarceration has a diminishing appeal. Ironically, in some cases, incarceration offers a mechanism for individuals to avoid responsibility while the real impact of imprisonment falls upon family and friends.

When allowed to operate, informal sanctions are undoubtedly powerful. Sanctions which call upon conscience and morality are normally a great deal stronger than formal punishment, which can serve to further marginalize and alienate those whose stake in society might already be minimal (Braithwaite 1989). The emphasis upon developing informal sanctions provides a useful antidote to the punitive obsession which is evident in many countries and the reliance on 'get tough' policies by policy makers and politicians who are unable to generate more imaginative and constructive responses.

The problem is that at some point the reliance on formal solutions arises from the inadequacy or erosion of informal mechanisms. It is also the case that the effectiveness of informal sanctions is often dependent upon the often silent, but ultimately available, formal controls. Thus the question is not so much whether one is in favour of formal or informal controls, but of developing a more adequate relation between them. While it should be recognized that informalism is not necessarily as positive as some of the abolitionists believe, in most Western countries there is an overreliance on imprisonment. Reducing this reliance may involve being more sensitive to other ways of dealing with offenders. Like the more radical forms of reductionism and the more practical forms of abolitionism, realism would argue for minimalism in two senses: first, that only those who cannot be reasonably dealt with in any other way are incarcerated; and, second, that these recalcitrants should be kept in confinement for only the shortest possible period.

In terms of pursuing these goals, it is necessary to bear in mind the relation between crime and imprisonment and to avoid the now fashionable stance which seeks to divorce crime from control. On one side, it needs to be remembered that the level of incarceration in any country is partly a function of the level of serious crime, and that reducing the penal population is not only an administrative problem, but also involves addressing the question of crime. The relation may be mediated on a number of levels, and the judiciary, in particular, play a major role in transforming the crime rate into rates of imprisonment; however, crime still plays a basic and determinate role in this relationship (Box and Hale 1986). Furthermore, the level and organization of punishment not only has a profound effect upon the crime rate, but it also influences social norms. It is for this reason that it is necessary to take punishment seriously.

Justifications for Punishment

While there has been considerable debate over what is or what ought to be the primary purpose of punishment, I shall not elaborate them here; however, it is clear that four major justifications – retribution, deterrence (both specific and general), incapacitation, and rehabilitation – play some role in current sentencing practices and would no doubt share the honours in most conceivable systems of punishment. The issue is really the prioritization of these respective rationales, and of deciding in which type of cases each ought to predominate.

It is clear that retribution is a central element in many sentencing decisions. However, there are problems about the scale of retribution and differences in the perceived seriousness of offences among different social groups. But the disturbing aspect of the retributionist argument forwarded by its advocates is that incarceration is promoted not only *as* punishment, but also *for* punishment. Retributionism is a narrow and short-sighted justification which expresses little concern for recidivism and the potentially negative effects of various forms of incarceration.

Similarly, general deterrence undoubtedly has an effect through punishments like incarceration. It is difficult, however, to gain any precise data on the deterrent effect of any particular type of punishment. Such is the case primarily because deterrence is learned through a complex process of informal controls which make it difficult to assess the specific effect of any particular formal controls. The evidence on specific deterrence is more readily available. Normally measured as a function of recidivism rates or reoffending rates, the specific deterrent effect of incarceration is relatively low. Universally high reconviction rates for ex-prisoners suggest that, whatever the specific deterrent effect might be for a period of incarceration, it is rarely enough to keep ex-prisoners out of trouble. Most of the research also shows that increasing the intensity or duration of incarceration has relatively little effect upon recidivism rates.

Using imprisonment as a means of incapacitation has gained considerable support over the past decade or so (Van den Haag 1975). Among the supporters of incapacitation are some of the 'new realists' who are attracted by the notion that, if incarceration is used to keep certain categories of offenders out of circulation for a specified period, it could have a considerable impact upon the crime rate. According to James Q. Wilson: '[More accurately], it works provided at least three conditions are met; some offenders must be repeaters, offenders taken off the streets must not be immediately and completely replaced by new recruits, and prison must not increase the post-release criminal activity of those who have been incarcerated sufficiently to off-set the crimes prevented by their stay in prison' (1983: 146). Wilson believes that these conditions are, in fact, met and that the main issue which remains is determining precisely how much crime could be reduced through incapacitation. However, if we examine these conditions, it appears that they do not always operate in the way that Wilson suggests. First, evidence on the 'schools of crime' hypothesis is far from conclusive. Autobiographical accounts and other data do suggest that, for some groups of prisoners at least, the experience of incarceration encourages them to become involved in quite serious crime. While it is obviously difficult to estimate precisely the magnitude of this relationship, two observations can be drawn from the practice of continually recycling the same offenders. It indicates, first, that incarceration does little to reduce criminal activity, and, second, that many countries currently operate a policy of selective incapacitation. In other words, the repeated incarceration of this select group suggests that we are already pursuing the type of policy which writers like Wilson advocate. The problem is that such a policy seems to have little overall effect upon the crime rate.

There is also some uncertainty about Wilson's second condition concerning the replacement of offenders by new recruits. To some extent such replacement will vary from offence to offence. For the offences with which Wilson is mostly concerned – burglary and robbery – there may be little in the way of automatic replacements. In other areas where criminal activity is more organized, such as drug dealing, taking low-level offenders out of circulation will have little impact on the trade.

It would seem, then, that if incapacitation works, it is likely to be relevant only in the case of a limited range of criminal activity. It is unlikely to make much impact on organized crime or on the majority of violent crime. Even if we accept, for the moment, that incapacitation might have some level of impact upon certain categories of crime such as burglary and robbery, there are a number of problems in pursuing this approach:

a Introducing long and, in some cases, mandatory prison sentences on specific types of offenders would contravene deeply held notions of equal punishment and 'just deserts.'

b The evidence suggests that, in order to reduce the levels of these predatory crimes, an extremely large number of people would have to be locked up.

c Incapacitation would be effective only for those crimes which involved a small number of offenders being responsible for a large proportion of the crimes.

d There are problems of prediction and of instigating self-fulfilling prophesies. Although we know roughly from which groups and from which areas persistent property offenders are likely to be drawn, it is much more precarious to make predictions about individuals.

In the light of these qualifications it would seem that, although a strategy of selective incapacitation may prevent a small amount of crime, the costs and disadvantages of extending its usage seems unjustified. Rather, it would seem to be more profitable to place a greater emphasis upon rehabilitation.

The concept of rehabilitation has suffered badly in the hands of criminologists. The decline of the rehabilitation ideal was rapidly accelerated by the widely referenced Martinson report in the early 1970s, which claimed that 'nothing works.' This conclusion proved very useful for prison administrators who were looking for ways of reducing prison expenditure and resources. However, it was unjustified not only in terms of the findings of the report, but also in terms of the vast literature indicating that different forms of punishment and different modes of incarceration produced a wide range of 'successes' (Gendrau and Ross 1987; Palmer 1975).

As opposed to pursuing a policy of incapacitation, it would seem to make more sense to try, where possible, to rehabilitate persistent offenders, and thereby, reduce crime. As Elliot Currie puts it: 'The point seems obvious. If we can predict criminality through characteristics that are amenable to change, then there is no *logical* reason why we should lock up certain individuals on the basis of these characteristics rather than trying to change them' (1985: 97). This does seem strikingly obvious. But in order 'rehabilitate' the notion of rehabilitation into a more realistic policy, at least three points need to be recognized:

a We need to provide a broader and more social concept of rehabilitation. Too often the notion is conceived of in narrow psychological terms and is used as if it were synonymous with individual treatment.

b Relatedly, we need to develop more relevant measures of rehabilitation. The normal measure, recidivism, is imprecise and inadequate. Rehabilitation needs to be assessed not only in terms of recidivism, but also in relation to the development of a prisoner's social skills, well-being, and competence.

c Within the relatively short period of incarceration, the potential for change is often extremely limited. This, however, does not preclude the possibilities for constructive intervention. Although it will rarely be possible within a few months to have a transformative effect on twenty or thirty years of socialization, some beneficial interventions can be developed.

As Cullen and Gilbert (1982) argue, an emphasis on rehabilitation provides an important counterbalance to conservative 'get tough' policies. The emphasis on rehabilitation is a continual reminder that different offenders experience different personal and social circumstances and differential pressures to commit crime. As they also stress, the demise of the rehabilitative ideal was one of the reasons why it became difficult for critics to oppose conservative calls for tougher and longer punishments.

A further and no less important reason for reaffirming rehabilitation is that there is a strong and widespread support for rehabilitative policies among the public. The public's interest in rehabilitation is not difficult to understand. Most people have a vested interest in offenders leaving prison as less of a threat and nuisance than when they were sent to prison. People who leave prison more committed to crime, more marginalized, more debilitated, and less competent than they were when they arrived provide both a burden and a threat to the communities and families in which they reside. Public opinion is an important reference point in this debate. After all, the prison is supposed to serve the community. At present the public gets little value for its money. While public opinion remains a crucial element, it is all too often forgotten or ignored.

The Role of Public Opinion

In realist criminology, the four variables – the offender, the victim, the state, and the community (the 'square of crime') – are seen as the key elements in the 'construction' of crime (Lea 1992). Although stressed in relation to various forms of crime prevention, the role of the community has received relatively little attention when it comes to the penal sphere. It is often assumed that the state is the prime mover in the process of punishment, since it organizes and assumes responsibility for penal policies. However, public opinion can have a profound effect upon penal policy, although not always in visible ways.

Clearly, if we are interested in developing a democratic, responsive, and accountable penal system, then the attitudes and interests of the public need to be taken seriously. Indications that public opinion is being awarded some significance can be seen from the various public-opinion surveys which have been carried out in various countries. Although the different styles and methods employed by these surveys make comparisons difficult, the picture which emerges indicates that members of the public, by and large, are a great deal less punitive and a great deal more concerned with social protection, compensation, and strategies which make offenders less of a threat or a burden than has often been thought (Flanagan and Caulfield 1984).

According to the British Crime Survey (BCS), the British public, often presented as very punitive, surprisingly expressed a great deal of support for non-custodial sentences. Sixty-nine per cent of respondents also supported giving shorter sentences to non-violent offenders, 51 per cent supported extending the parole system, and 58 per cent were in favour of introducing weekend imprisonment (Hough and Mayhew 1983).

These findings should give encouragement to penal reformers who want to develop more constructive community-based sanctions. However, we cannot adopt public-opinion surveys uncritically. Instead, there is a need to engage with public opinion and stimulate public debate on these issues. Public-opinion surveys can provide the basis for comparing opinions both among different sectors of the population and between the public and policy makers. In this way, they can provide both an educative and an informative function. They may also provide a basis for encouraging wider public participation and for the mobilization of reforms (Matthews 1990a).

The role of public opinion in penal reform is often underestimated. Too often penal reformers blame high rates of incarceration on sentencing policy. But, recent evidence from Holland and Germany has shown that public opinion, however vaguely conceived, can play a crucial role in creating the climate of penal reform. In both of these countries and, to some extent, in England as well, there has been a growing public dissatisfaction with the use of incarceration (Feest 1988). Such changes in interest and concern can be influenced by a number of factors, two of the most important of which are the perceived level of serious crime and the fear of victimization. There appears to have been a marked change in these countries in attitudes towards to juvenile and female offenders. John Graham examines some of the effects of the changing penal climate in West Germany. In rejecting some of the usual explanations for the decrease in the juvenile custodial population he concludes that: 'a more likely explanation is that the change in the practice of prosecutors reflects a more general change in the climate of opinion concerning how best to respond to crime, particularly crime committed by young people ... this change in climate which is now also apparent in the U.K. for juvenile offenders, may be due in part to the psychological effects of a declining young population: fewer young people means fewer crimes, which means that crime is less threatening which, in turn, undermines the need for punitive sentencing based on the principle of general deterrence' (1989: 156). Also, Graham charts the way in which this less punitive attitude towards juveniles affects the treatment of other categories of offenders. There is a ripple effect as the confidence in the use of non-custodial policies expands and the benefits of a declining prison population are generally appreciated. Recognizing the important role which public opinion can play in penal reform may encourage penal reformers to engage more in public debate, develop more informative and reliable surveys, and clarify the term 'public opinion' itself.

Much of the interest in penal reform, as has been indicated, is focused on developing alternatives to custody. But for the large number of people who experience imprisonment, there is an urgent need to re-examine the structure of these penal fortresses.

Changing the Intensity of Incarceration

Prisons have been variously described in the literature as 'fortresses,' 'dustbins,' and 'warehouses.' Each of these terms conveys an essential component of the prison estate – in Britain at least. In this country, the preoccupation with security and containment means that many prisoners are subject to levels of restriction which are out of all proportion to the level of risk they pose or the seriousness of their offence. As John Conrad has suggested, there are definite advantages in balancing the intensity of confinement with the length of imprisonment: 'From appropriate restraint it follows that prison, or the system of prisons, must allow for different security requirements for all those who are imprisoned. Not only does it make no sense to maintain a peaceable cheque writer in maximum security, but it is also a prodigal waste of a scarce and costly resource. No prisoner should be assigned to more security than the safety of the public and the system require' (1985: 127). Different countries employ differential levels of restraint. The adoption of more open prisons, weekend visits, pre-release visits, and the like have provided some variation in the level of confinement. However, the level of segregation and confinement experienced by many prisoners is far greater than is reasonably required. This intensity has been compounded in many British jails by the practice of keeping prisoners locked in cells for a depressingly large proportion of the day.

While there have been attempts to introduce weekend imprisonment in Britain, a positive step in the direction of reducing the intensity of confinement, this was actively resisted by some penal reformers. Resistance of this type is an expression of some of the limitaions of penal reform in this country and how 'radical' intervention can work to maintain the status quo.

Experimentation with different levels and styles of confinement is required.

There should be an attempt to reduce the barriers between prisoners and the community and, at the same time, to encourage much more community involvement in the prison itself. The expansion of training, educational, and social programs within prisons may help to re-establish links between the prison and the community.

The final issue which requires serious consideration is the question of strategy. Often there has been a considerable agreement over objectives, but little appreciation of how these objectives might be realized. Within the criminal justice system as a whole, there has been a growing recognition of the importance of interagency cooperation in achieving stated objectives.

Multi-Agency Approaches

One of the most important aspects of the work of Thomas Mathieson is his concern with the problems of developing a penal strategy. Through the experience of his practical involvement in the struggle for penal reform, Mathieson has recognized the importance of establishing alliances. He has distinguished between making 'horizontal' and 'vertical' alliances, that is, a distinction between making alliances between penal-reform groups and organizations in the wider community, as well as alliances between the relevant agencies within the criminal justice system itself.

It has become apparent to many of those who have become involved in penal reform that, within the peculiar structure of the criminal justice system, agencies can effectively block reforms which they do not support. Implementing effective reforms necessarily involves gaining at least the tacit agreement of the agencies concerned. By the same token, it has also become evident that there is a considerable difference between the formal and informal activities of the agencies within the criminal justice system. In many cases where there is formal compliance with directives, other informal practices are sustained and endorsed by each of the agencies. It is for this reason that effective reform often comes from 'below,' thus making it extremely difficult for policy makers to impose unwanted policies. The recent history of penal reform in Britain is replete with examples of how policies have been resisted and undermined – particularly by powerful groups such as the judiciary and the probation service.

Interagency cooperation, however, has proved very effective in implementing non-custodial penalties for juveniles during the 1980s. The adoption of what has been termed a 'corporatist' approach to juvenile justice has encouraged the use of cautioning and other forms of diversion while reducing the use of custody (Pratt 1989). As noted above, the improved penal climate and the declining level of serious juvenile crime no doubt played a critical role in providing the background conditions for this policy; but, without a coordinated intervention, this objective may not have been achieved.

There are, of course, problems of accountability and continuity connected with multi-agency initiatives (Sampson et al. 1988; Lea, Matthews, and Young 1989). But there can be no doubt that when there is a broad agreement about the objectives of penal reform, it is important to involve all the relevant agencies in the development of the policy and the organizing of its implementation.

Conclusion

Recent experiences in a number of different countries have indicated that diversion and decarceration are, in fact, possible. As a consequence, there is a renewed interest in penal reform. This has been fueled by interest in privatization in the field of incarceration, an interest which has also conveyed the powerful message to penal reformers that radical change is both possible and necessary (Matthews 1990b). But at the moment, although significant changes have occurred, the decreases in prison populations remain relatively small, or tend to be limited to one particular section of the custodial population. The current task before us is to broaden the scope of these initiatives and develop strategies which will be effective for middle-term and some long-term prisoners. To do this will involve the development of competing and realistic alternatives to prison. It will also involve developing better crime-prevention techniques, constructing more effective modes of informal control, rethinking the policy of rehabilitation, and developing penal policies which may reduce both the level and the seriousness of offending.

Penal reform is primarily neither an administrative nor a narrowly political matter. It is an issue which is deeply influenced by public demands, levels of public tolerance, and the response to threat of real or anticipated victimization. Much progressive penal reform appears to come from 'below.' Imposing penal policies on reluctant or hostile agencies is extremely difficult. The organization of multi-agency initiatives requires further exploration. There still remains a great deal of confusion over strategy, and penal reformers continue to make claims which are unrealistic or often socially undesirable or imply that prison reform is principally an administrative matter. The tide of penal reform is starting to turn in many countries. Prison populations are declining in some countries for the first time in the postwar period. But, there is still a long way to go.

This is a revised version of a paper presented to the annual meeting of Canadian Law and Society, Learned Societies, University of Victoria, 30 May 1990.

References

Austin, J., and B. Krisberg. 1982. 'Unmet Promises of Alternatives to Incarceration.' *Crime and Delinquency*, 28: 374-409

Biles, D. 1983. 'Crime and Imprisonment: A Two Decade Comparison between England and Wales and Australia.' *British Journal of Criminology*, 23 (2): 167-172

Blomberg, T. 1980. 'Widening the Net: An Anomaly in the Evaluation of Diversion Programs,' in M. Klein and K. Teilman, eds., *Handbook in Criminal Justice Evaluation*, 572-592. Beverly Hills: Sage

Box, S., and C. Hale. 1986. 'Unemployment, Crime and Imprisonment and the Enduring Problem of Prison Overcrowding,' in R. Matthews and J. Young, eds., *Confronting Crime*, 72-97. London: Sage

Braithwaite, J. 1989. *Crime, Shame and Reintegration.* Cambridge: Cambridge University Press

Cohen, S. 1985. *Visions of Social Control.* Cambridge: Polity Press

Conrad, J. 1985. 'Charting a Course for Imprisonment Policy.' *The Annals of the American Academy of Political and Social Science*, March: 123-135

Cullen, F., and K. Gilbert. 1982. *Reaffirming Rehabilitation.* Cincinnati: Anderson Publishing

Currie, E. 1985. *Confronting Crime: An American Challenge.* New York: Pantheon

de Haan, W. 1990. *The Politics of Redress: Crime, Punishment, and Penal Abolition.* London: Unwin Hyman

Downes, D. 1988. *Contrasts in Tolerance.* Oxford: Clarendon Press

Feest, J. 1988. *Reducing the Prison Population: Lessons from the West German Experience.* London: NACRO

Flanagan, J., and S. Caulfield. 1984. 'Public Opinion and Prison Policy: A Review.' *Prison Journal*, 64: 31-46

Gendrau, P., and R. Ross. 1987. 'Revivification of Rehabilitation: Evidence from the 1980's.' *Justice Quarterly*, 4: 349-407

Graham, J. 1989. *Decarceration in the Federal Republic of Germany: How the Practitioners Are Succeeding Where the Policy Makers Have Failed.* London: HMSO

Harris, K. 1983/4. 'Strategies, Values and the Emerging Generation of Alternatives to Incarceration.' *New York University Review of Law and Social Change*, 12 (1): 141-170

Hirst, P. 1986. *Law, Socialism and Democracy.* London: Allen and Unwin

Hough, M., and P. Mayhew. 1983. *British Crime Survey.* London: HMSO

Hulsman, L. 1982. 'Penal Reform in The Netherlands.' *Howard Journal*, 21 (1): 35-47

– 1986. 'Critical Criminology and the Concept of Crime,' in H. Bianchi and R. Van Swaaningen, eds., *Abolitionism: Towards a Non-Repressive Approach to Crime*, 63-80. Amsterdam: Free University Press

Lea. J. 1987. 'Left Realism: A Defence.' *Contemporary Crises*, 11: 357-370

– 1992. 'The Analysis of Crime,' in J. Young and R. Matthews, eds., *Rethinking Criminology: The Realist Debate*, 69-94. London: Sage

Lea, J., R. Matthews, and J. Young. 1989. 'The State, Multi-Agency Approaches and Crime Control.' London: Middlesex Polytechnic, Centre for Criminology. Mimeo

Mathieson, T. 1973. *The Politics of Abolition*. London: Martin Robertson

– 1986. 'The Politics of Abolition.' *Contemporary Crisis*, 10 (1): 81-94

Matthews, R. 1988. 'Abolitionism, Reductionism and Realism.' Paper presented at the ASC, Chicago, November

– 1990a. 'Alternatives To and In Prisons: A Realist Approach,' in P. Carlen and D. Cook, eds., *Paying for Crime*, 128-150. Milton Keynes: Open University Press

– 1990b. *Privatizing Criminal Justice*. London: Sage

Palmer, T. 1975. 'Martinson Revisited.' *Journal of Research in Crime and Delinquency*, July: 133-152

Pratt, J. 1989. Corporatism: The Third Model of Juvenile Justice.' *British Journal of Criminology*, 29 (3): 236-255

Sampson, A., P. Stubbs, G. Pearson, and H. Blagg. 1988. 'Crime, Localities and the Multi-Agency Approach.' *British Journal of Criminology*, 28 (4): 478-493

Steinert, H. 1985. 'The Amazing New Left Law and Order Campaign.' *Contemporary Crises*, 9 (4): 21-38

Van den Haag, E. 1975. *Punishing Criminals*. New York: Basic Books

Wilson, J.Q. 1983. *Thinking about Crime*, rev. ed. New York: Vintage Books

Young, J. 1986. 'The Failure of Criminology: The Need for Radical Realism,' in R. Matthews and J. Young, eds., *Confronting Crime*, 4-30. London: Sage

4 Retreatism, Minimalism, Realism: Three Styles of Reasoning on Crime and Drugs in the United States

Elliott Currie

In this essay I talk about the political and intellectual climate in which the problems of crime and illicit drugs are now being discussed in the United States. I focus here on the recent trajectory of public discourse on crime and drugs more than on theory in academic criminology. I want to do this, in part, because I think what is taking place in the United States may, unfortunately, have increasing relevance for other countries – especially for those countries where, as in the United States, the systematic application of free-market policies has rapidly increased social dislocation and disintegration and where, as a consequence, the problems of urban violence and hard-drug abuse are rising.

The way these issues are defined in the United States by progressives and others, however, is not quite the same as it is in England or in Canada, partly because US crime and drug problems continue to be much worse. Since the debate takes parallel but distinct forms in different countries, I examine 'realism' from the US perspective.

Make no mistake, we are in a terrible mess in the United States today. In the considerably calmer environs of Canada and other English-speaking countries, it is easy to forget that, in the United States, we are facing a social crisis of unprecedented depth, severity, and complexity. Our cities are routinely wracked by high levels of violence, hard-drug abuse, and general social disintegration that are unrivalled outside the Third World and show no signs of abating.

So much for the bad news. If there is good news, it is that things have become sufficiently bad that there may be a new willingness on the part of a fairly broad spectrum of Americans to question the social and economic policies that have helped bring us to this state. As a result, there is now a political opportunity for progressives, if they are capable of seizing it.

The worsening of the US crisis has much to do with the damage wrought by ten years of neoconservative social policy. But it has also been exacerbated by the failure of progressives to mount an effective challenge to conservative policies – and that is the issue I wish to discuss.

I do not think there is a remote possibility that the crisis will be usefully addressed by the current administration in Washington, or by a continuation of more of the same policies and strategies that have gotten us to where we are. It will be addressed only through a strategy rooted in what I will call *progressive realism*.

I speak of 'progressive' rather than 'left' realism because, in the United States, the relative absence of a strong or influential left has traditionally skewed the crime debate towards the centre and the right. Consequently, much of the most useful thinking on crime has come from liberals and others who do not really fit a European (or even a Canadian) conception of the left – in addition to the smaller but determined band of those who do.

The tradition of progressive realism is flawed and in many ways incomplete. It is currently in disarray. But it is, nevertheless, creative and humane, and will be vital to any progressive strategy on crime control if it is to fit the hard realities of the United States in the 1990s. But it is not the only tradition to be found among US progressives. It competes with two others, which I will call *progressive retreatism* and *progressive minimalism*. As these rather pejorative terms imply, I think realism has much more to offer us than either retreatism or minimalism. In fact, the latter two represent pitfalls into which US progressives recurrently sink. In the process, they have repeatedly stymied prospects for developing a response to crime and drugs that is both effective *and* progressive.

Moreover, at least two distinct strands of thinking and practice coexist uneasily in progressive realism. One of them has resurfaced in the past few years, and is fast becoming the staple of liberal dialogue on these issues. I will argue below that, on the whole, this resurgence is all to the good – but by itself it is not enough.

I would stress that sorting out these paths is not merely an academic issue; it is extremely urgent in the United States today. The harsh reality is that, under the current conservative hegemony, many people are dying. In the state of California, a Black male born today has a better chance of being murdered than he does of attending the University of California. In Harlem, the Black 'excess mortality ratio' from drug-related illness – that is, the ratio of a Black man's chances of dying from the consequences of drug abuse as compared to those of a White man – is 283 to 1. These are just some of the realities that a progressive crime strategy must address, and which, I believe, only a progressive realism can address effectively.

What distinguishes progressive realism from minimalism and retreatism? As I use the term, 'retreatism' refers to the all-too-common tendency of many liberals and progressives – in the face of the apparent intractability of the crime problem and the success of the right in capturing it as a political issue – to simply appropriate parts of the conservative model of crime control, especially its heavy reliance on incarceration.

Retreatism is now the dominant and, indeed, official stance of the centre of the Democratic party in the United States. The Democratic Leadership Council, the quasi-official voice of that centre, recently issued a manifesto which, among other things (including coming out firmly in favour of the 'accumulation of wealth rather than its distribution' [New York Times, 12 March 1990]), committed the party to cease 'explaining away' crime and begin seriously punishing criminals. Begin? In California, to take but one example, we have quadrupled the prison population in less than ten years!

But retreatism is not confined only to middle-of-the-road Democrats. It has also been embraced by some progressives who believe that they can win back those White working Americans who they think have been alienated from progressive politics, at least in part because progressives are 'soft' on crime.

Lastly, there is a subtler form of retreatism. It involves defining policy priorities according to what is believed to be a politically 'hot' issue, rather than in terms of what is most destructive to ordinary people; that is, political expediency subordinates social need. I recently spoke on these issues to a conference of American liberals. Among other things, I urged them to think about making the prevention of domestic violence against women and children a major part of the liberal platform on crime. Some agreed; others were put off. It was not that they did not, deep down, comprehend the significance of these crimes, or the human suffering they represent – but they did not regard them as politically lucrative issues, capable of winning votes against the right. I think they were wrong about this, even in their own terms; a serious campaign against domestic violence could reach to the heart of the daily concerns of many working women in the United States. But, more important, in the name of a hollow and rudderless political pragmatism, this attitude represents a profound and corrupting retreat from confronting the problems that hurt people the most.

I do not think I need to dwell on what is wrong with this approach. Suffice it to say that progressive retreatism is, at best, spectacularly mistimed. It comes just when the failure of the conservative model of crime control – which it self-consciously mimics – has become ever more dramatically apparent in the streets of American cities. Nevertheless, the conservative model has remained extraordinarily tenacious, in large part because of the absence of effective opposition on its left. Since the end of the 1960s, the most articulate opposition to conservatism and liberal retreatism has come from what I am calling 'liberal minimalism.' But minimalism has not been up to the task.

By progressive minimalism I mean the twin tendencies to minimize the seriousness of the crime and/or drug problem and to seek to minimize the role of the state in dealing with it. This is akin to 'left idealism' (Young 1979) and has sometimes been buttressed by left-idealist scholarship. But, as I use it here, minimalism is basically a home-grown American product with specific historical roots.

Minimalism originated in the 1960s at a time when the defence of the powerless against abuses of authority was uppermost in the minds of many, if not most, progressives. There were good reasons for this emphasis, and minimalists fought hard, and sometimes successfully, for much-needed restraints on police power, for alternatives to imprisonment, and for protection of prisoners against abuse by prison staff.

These were important goals, and they remain so. But minimalism had little to say about what we should do about crime itself; indeed, it sought to discourage that discussion. But, by failing to offer remedies for the violence that besieged ordinary Americans, minimalism opted out of the real political debate.

Twenty or so years later, under considerably changed conditions, minimalism is still probably the dominant voice of American progressives on these issues, a fact that has helped keep progressives on the fringes of public debate. Part of the problem is that minimalism, in its desire to downplay the severity of the crime problem, is often just plain wrong in its empirical understanding of serious crime and drug abuse in the United States today. At the extreme, it is mind-bogglingly wrong.

Jock Young and his colleagues (cf. Lea and Young 1984) have spoken of the left's 'great denial' of the reality of street crime. That denial is central to progressive minimalism in the United States. In the past year or so I have heard the following statements of 'fact': that violence among inner-city youth in the United States is 'plummeting'; that Americans are ten times more likely to die in car accidents than be murdered; and that urban crime was much worse in the 1960s than it is today.

Not one of these statements is true. All of them spring from the lips of well-known criminologists. And they no doubt represent an earnest desire to counter the right's often successful efforts at whipping up public sentiment in the service of repressive measures against crime. But all of these statements are dead wrong, thus helping to destroy liberal credibility on crime. They all help to perpetuate an image of progressives as being both fuzzy-minded and, much worse, unconcerned about the realities of life for those ordinary Americans who are understandably frightened and enraged by the suffering and fear crime brings to their communities and families.

On the issue of drug abuse, the main thrust of liberal minimalism has been to portray fear and outrage about hard drugs as hysteria or manipulation; to argue that the real threat is not drugs themselves, but the war against drugs; and to downplay or reject evidence about the social and personal costs of hard-drug abuse, emphasizing instead the horrendous costs of drug law enforcement. In so doing liberal minimalists have raised important issues. But, in the process, they have glossed over the drug problem itself. No one in his or her right mind, to be sure, can support the silly and repressive measures undertaken by the Reagan and Bush administrations in the name of the war on drugs. But neither should we sidestep the responsibility for coming up with alternatives which acknowledge the seriousness of drug problems, particularly among the poor. Here we see the main problem with minimalism. By ignoring or slighting popular fear about the carnage wrought by drugs among the ranks of US have-nots, minimalism has appeared to align itself against working-class and poor Americans, and perhaps even to side with the forces that threaten their communities, families, and friends.

Minimalists have approached the genuinely tough and scary problems of crack, PCP, and methamphetamine abuse with the same intellectual and political reflexes brought to the marijuana issue in the 1960s and 1970s. But these reflexes are sadly inadequate as responses to the very real destruction that harder drugs are causing in our most vulnerable communities, and especially in the case of women and children. Many times I have listened patiently to good progressives telling me that the impact of, say, crack on the newborn or on the inner-city family is nothing but media hype. This is the kind of blindness – grounded, in part, in the strong individualist, libertarian strain which characterizes US progressivism – that helps to explain the curious alliance on drug policy that is emerging between some staunch civil-libertarian progressives, on the one hand, and ultra-conservative thinkers like Milton Friedman, on the other. It also reflects a kind of structural myopia resulting from the growing social distance between largely academic and professional progressives and the increasingly distressed bottom third of the US population which is undergoing a sort of crisis of invisibility as its living standard deteriorates.

In short, too many well-meaning progressives simply do not get it when it comes to the trauma of drugs in the cities. A world-view that cannot even acknowledge the seriousness of a social problem is necessarily unable to come up with anything approaching a credible remedy for it; in the absence of any effort to provide a remedy, there are plenty of other takers. Minimalism has thus effectively ceded the political terrain on illicit drugs and violent crime to the political right.

But there is a chink in the right's armor: things have now gotten so bad in many US cities that those charged with governing or doing business in them, as well as most of the people who live in them, have become alarmed and dismayed over the long-range and steady descent of our cities into something approaching a state of chaos. There is thus a real opening for political change in a way there was not five years ago. Can we seize this opportunity? Maybe. But to do so we will have to reappropriate the best of the tradition of progressive realism.

Progressive realism was actually the dominant outlook on crime in the United States, in theory if less so in practice, throughout most of the 1960s. Some of its best expressions can be found in the series of major reports produced under the auspices of various Democratic administrations in the 1960s – most notably the Crime Commission of 1967 and the Kerner Report (1968) on urban riots (President's Commission 1968; National Advisory Commission on Civil Disorders 1968).

This form of realism did portray crime and urban violence as very real and unusually virulent problems in the United States. But it also suggested that these were problems that could be dealt with only by a reformed, more equitable, and more rational justice system. Moreover, it was also emphatic in suggesting that crime was not just a criminal justice problem, but a *social* problem, the solution to which would require us to rethink our most fundamental social priorities. Viewed this way, the most critical need was for a comprehensive rebuilding – or, as it was often put in the 1960s, a 'reconstruction' – of the inner cities. The urban young, it was argued, needed to be provided with a real stake in social life; long-neglected basic human needs related to socialization, education, and nurturance had to be provided for. Such a reconstruction could not come about simply by the expansion of the conventional private economy, but would require considerable public expenditure targeted at the most disadvantaged groups, including a much-expanded public sector of useful employment and efficient, accessible social services. A recurrent theme in this realist progressive writing of the 1960s was that, if we did not do these things, all hell would break loose and we would be in for still worse trouble down the road (National Advisory Commission on Civil Disorders 1968: chs. 16 and 17).

We are now a generation farther down that road and we are, indeed, in worse trouble. So it is already past the time to put the half-forgotten realist agenda back in the centre of public debate. That is slowly beginning to happen now – slowly, and also unevenly. Two versions of progressive realism are emerging today, one more strongly, so far, than the other. For lack of better terms let me call them the *service model* and the *reconstructive model*.

The most visible alternative today to both the conservative model and progressive minimalism is the *service model*. This model is reminiscent of what in the 1960s was often called a 'service strategy' for the ills of the cities. It emphasizes the need for more preventive services for inner-city children and families – early-childhood education, training in effective parenting, prenatal care, mentoring, remedial education, and so forth – strategies that, to use the language of the 1960s, are mainly devoted to reducing crime and drug abuse by increasing the human capital of those individuals most 'at risk.'

These are all good aims, and ones I have often argued for. But I am troubled by a certain narrowness in this version of progressive realism. Behind the service model of realism is a genuinely humane concern for the plight of 'high-risk' populations, especially children. But there is also a pronounced blind spot when it comes to the importance of larger institutions, especially the labour market, that profoundly constrain what we can do, even with the best of intentions (and the best of funding), to improve their lot in life or decrease their risk of delinquency, crime, and drug abuse. It is that blind spot that leads me to think of this as a partial or incomplete version of realism.

The service model also rests on what one might call a 'deficiency model' of delinquency and crime. The assumption is that troublesome behaviour arises from some lack in the child or youth 'at risk' or in their family and, accordingly, the task is to deliver services that will overcome that lack; to fill the lacunae in the child's development. Sometimes, to be sure, this is an accurate diagnosis, even if US progressives have too often glossed over that hard fact. Many 'high-risk' children and families do need serious help – medical, psychological, educational. But the deficiency model tends to exaggerate individual incapacities and inabilities, thereby inflating the importance of services aimed at the individual while ignoring the possibility that, in many cases, it may be less the child that is incompetent than the institutional environment in which he or she is raised, especially the schools and the labour market. The point is that, even if all the 'at-risk' children in the inner city did have preschool programs, parenting programs, 'mentors,' or 'remedial reading' programs, could they be assured of security when they grow up? Of a challenging role in the US economy and society?

I think that to put the question is to know the answer. Short of simultaneous enrichment of the job market, changes in the direction of public investment, major shifts in the allocation of resources for such things as low-income housing development, public works revitalization, and community-level public services, there will be too few places for them to go – even if they turned out to be much better prepared than most young adults are today.

Another way of putting this is to say that in the liberal service model there is at least an implicit assumption of the infinite resilience and absorbative capacity of the US economy. If young people are given sufficient socialization and training, they will become like 'us' – part of that fat and sassy 'mainstream' that is always counterposed to the floundering urban 'under class.' The trouble is that there is not a shred of serious empirical research on trends in the US economy to support this happy view. Rather, the US economy is bifurcating, with massive strata of the poor and near-poor at one end and a smaller, truly affluent stratum at the other (Currie 1990). Given that the 'mainstream' is shrinking, measures to give the poor a 'hand up' into it, as the predecessors of these realists used to put it in the 1960s, are intrinsically limited.

This is a depressingly old debate. It permeated discussion of the War on Poverty in the United States in the 1960s and has progressed remarkably little since then. The limitations of the service model have become ever more apparent, given changes in the US economy in the intervening years. In 1962 it was possible to imagine, on the basis of then recent economic performance, that the economy would be able to absorb everyone in the advance towards ever-greater affluence. But instead of increasing affluence, a precipitous international economic decline has occasioned a massive 'restructuring' of the US economy. In the light of this restructuring, the weaknesses of a strategy limited mainly to preparation of the 'disadvantaged' for a hoped-for economic citizenship are more salient today than they were in the 1960s. The same caveat holds for the frequent emphasis on 'treatment on demand' as the chief liberal-realist alternative to the current war on drugs.

The 'soft' realist response to the Bush-Bennett drug war has been to counterpose a 'medical' to a 'law enforcement' model of the drug crisis and to argue for the expansion of treatment rather than an expansion of law enforcement. There is an important truth here: there really is not enough drug treatment available to low-income addicts. But some liberals have overstated the ability of treatment to deal with the drug crisis. And they have not been very clear about what treatment might actually consist of. The difficulty is that drug abuse is not a 'medical problem' in the same way that, say, a kidney infection is a medical problem. You do not cure it by giving the addict some medicine. Addiction is a social problem, and to cope with it you need to address a much broader range of issues and needs in an addict's life. If you do not, you will too often simply perpetuate the revolving-door syndrome we have today, in which addicts – if they enter treatment programs at all – are sent out the other end into precisely the same environmental conditions that drove them to drugs in the first place. Without altering social conditions we may 'save' some addicts, but we will not do much about the drug problem. We will not be able to treat our way out of the urban drug crisis, just as we will not educate or 'mentor' our way out of the crisis of urban youth violence and alienation.

What I would call the *reconstructive* version of progressive realism takes it for granted that we will need enhanced social services – early education, drug treatment, prenatal care – especially where those services have been most devastated by regressive budget policies. But the reconstructive version also insists that these 'human capital' or 'individual treatment' measures, while necessary, do not, by themselves, amount to a comprehensive crime strategy. Indeed, even to work well on their own terms, they must be integrated into a plan for what, in the glory days of liberal realism, was called 'community reconstruction.' And it would go a step farther to insist that the reconstruction of devastated communities can not occur only on a self-help basis – needless to say, the current administration is very fond of the notion of self-help, as are some progressives – but has to include substantial changes in national policy.

I can not here get into much detail about what reconstructive strategy would entail. In shorthand, I believe that we in the United States must move towards a version of the 'basic needs' strategy promoted by some progressive theorists of Third World development. I choose that imagery deliberately because I believe that US social structure is, in many respects, becoming more and more like that of a Third World nation – our policies on crime and urban disintegration must, therefore, face up to what we may describe as the 'Brazilianization' of the United States.

If you think that the Third World analogy is overwrought, consider that a recent study in the staid *New England Journal of Medicine* found that the life expectancy of Black men in Harlem is now lower than it is for men in Bangladesh (McCord and Freeman 1990). Infant mortality rates at the Martin Luther King general hospital in South-Central Los Angeles, home of the 'Crips' and 'Bloods,' are higher than on the island of Jamaica (US Congress 1988). Step one in a strategy of community reconstruction is to begin to turn these grim trends around.

Increasingly, in our cities and rural areas, the most basic needs of the bottom quarter of the population for medical care, housing, public education, and even basic public facilities are routinely not met. The most fundamental economic and social institutions in many communities have eroded or even collapsed. The possibility of such a collapse was already recognized by the progressive realists of the 1960s; it has gone much farther today. It lies at the heart of our escalating crises of urban violence and drug abuse. We do not have a hope of dealing with these problems in an enduring way, short of rebuilding those basic social institutions.

Just as in Brazil or Bangladesh, we also know (unless we are ideologically stupefied) that this rebuilding process cannot be accomplished by private market-driven economic growth alone. It requires a substantial foundation created by key public-sector investment designed to restore basic medical care, schooling, housing, and social services in these communities.

The overarching goal of this strategy is to begin to pull the bottom up by supplying new kinds of livelihoods while simultaneously addressing basic human needs. That strategy of raising the bottom – of pulling up rather than 'trickling down' – would allow us to narrow the highly criminogenic spread of social and economic inequality, to reverse the spreading of subemployment in the cities, and to provide the basic social infrastructure without which no community can survive for long. It fits well with what we know about the roots of violence and drug abuse in US cities today; and it should be a central theme in a revitalized progressive realism in the United States.

References

Currie, E. 1990. 'Heavy with Human Tears: Free Market Policy, Inequality, and Social Provision in the United States,' in I. Taylor, ed., *The Social Effects of Free Market Policies*, 299-317. London: Harvester-Wheatsheaf

Lea, J., and J. Young. 1984. *What Is to Be Done about Law and Order?* Harmondsworth: Penguin

McCord, C., and H.P. Freeman. 1990. 'Excess Mortality in Harlem.' *New England Journal of Medicine*, 322: 173-177

National Advisory Commission on Civil Disorders. 1968. *Report*. Washington, DC: USGPO

President's Commission on Law Enforcement and the Administration of Justice. 1968. *The Challenge of Crime in a Free Society*. Washington, DC: USGPO

US Congress, Select Committee on Children, Youth, and Families. 1988. *Young People in Crisis*. Washington, DC: USGPO

Young, J. 1979. 'Left Idealism, Reformism and Beyond: From New Criminology to Marxism,' in B. Fine, R. Kinsey, J. Lea, Sol Picciotto, and J. Young, eds., *Capitalism and the Rule of Law: From Deviancy Theory to Marxism*, 11-28. London: Hutchinson

PART TWO
A Critical Assessment of Left Realism

5 Canadian Realist Criminology in the 1990s: Some Reflections on the Quest for Social Justice

Paul Havemann

This essay is an attempt to assert a post-colonial posture from which to view British realism and realist trends in Canada. The post-colonial position involves a hybridization of perspectives arising from a dialectical relationship between Euro-American hegemonic systems and peripheral subversions of them which none the less reflect an independent identity. Contemporaneously and independently of the development of British realist criminology, a critical 'realism' has also evolved in North America. The Middlesex/Edinburgh realists have much to offer this North American development by way of comparison – although, in the process, we must always bear in mind the problems of overgeneralization, intellectual colonization, and the need for cultural and historical specificity in developing local strategies and models. In Canada a justice studies perspective and a social rights strategy, and in the United States a minimal reformism such as that offered by the Crime and Social Justice collective stand as examples of a practice of idealism which integrates a focus on cultural and ideological components of social life with a practice within and outside the academy (Michalowski 1991) and cautious reaffirmation of decentralized community control. These British and North American perspectives share a commitment to (a) avoid romanticizing or pathologizing crime and (b) develop an accurate victimology and alternative 'database,' and recognize the material basis for the fear of crime.

The specific characteristics of the Canadian context are crucial to framing a Canadian agenda for the 1990s. British realism evolved in the context of a dialectic among male labourism, Thatcherite economic libertarianism, and moral authoritarianism. In contrast, liberalism, corporatism, continentalism, ethnic separatism, and the New Right form the ideological terrain of Canadian practice. While Britain reluctantly attaches to Europe, Canada hovers on the periphery of America and the Pacific Basin (Kennedy 1988; Albo and Jenson 1989). Canada is a settler society where racism occurs primarily in the context of indigenous/settler relations. In the Euro-American core, racism is linked primarily to the international division of labour in a post-imperial and deindustrializing economy. In the United States and now in Canada, the 'judicialization or legalization of politics' through the Charter of Rights (Mandel 1989) erodes democracy and yet tantalizes British reformers (for example, the Charter 88 group, which includes Lord Scarman and calls for twelve major constitutional reforms, such as a Bill of Rights, proportional representation, political devolution, the incorporation of the European Convention on Human Rights into UK law, and a written constitution). In both Britain and Canada, democracy is undermined by assaults on localism, trade unionism, and universalism. For Canadians, the Canada–United States Free Trade Agreement will gradually usher in the demise of the welfare state's universalist approach to health, education, and pension benefits and the rise of selectivity and user-pays. Misogyny, the sexual division of labour, and both public and private patriarchal regulation abound in different forms.

Generally then, we must question the relevance of certain British realist assumptions to Canada. For example: has Canadian policing ever taken a form other than what Kinsey, Lea, and Young (1986) describe as 'military'? Has aetiological criminology ever been privileged in Canada in the way that it was in Britain and the United States?

Also, we should guard against certain portrayals of Canada. Too easily Eurocentric observers see Canada as the 'quintessentially bourgeois state' (Taylor 1987). This is a label conferred from the vantage point of someone blinkered by the nostalgia for a quintessentially British, male-labourist utopia. Ironically Taylor correctly observes that this nostalgia is also an impediment to realist thought about Britain (Taylor 1988).

Having said this, it should also be recognized that Canadians share with Europeans a range of questions about how to decentralize power, promote democratic accountability, counter the disempowering and disinforming discourses of the right, promote offender rights, and reaffirm rehabilitation and due process and the social responsibility of the collectivity.

Canadian justice studies must evolve a holistic critique of the impact of economic growth, of hierarchy, of ecological vandalism, of crimes against the poor and crimes by the powerful. It must overcome demarcation disputes about what is properly considered critical criminology, critical legal studies, critical social policy, realism or idealism; as well as atomization and political abstentionism within the academy, and academic obscurantism about the world outside it. All this is where First and Fourth worlds collide (Turpel 1989).

Missing in much of the writing by and about British realism is the attempt to contextualize the realist project socio-politically. For me British realism is a theoretical and empirical project addressing what Young (1986) has called an 'aetiological' crisis. More importantly it appears that it is also a political project addressing an ideological crisis. The theoretical and empirical project takes the form it does because of the political context in which it evolved. For example, British left realists tend to define their project in terms of its theoretical assumptions, but especially by its antagonism to elements of the (perhaps Trotskyite?) left active in local urban politics, and to fellow academic progressives who have been described as ultra-leftist, utopian, idealist, middle-class, armchair academics, and so on. The left realists' failure to articulate the political context of their project makes this sectarianism hard for outsiders to understand, and in the minds of many progressives renders their project suspect (e.g., Taylor 1988; Scraton 1987).

The political dimension of the realist project, it seems, is about 'recapturing' for the Labour Party the working-class, female and ethnic minority electorate from the clutches of pro-Tory 'law and order' authoritarian populism. The pursuit of this quarry takes place at both local government and parliamentary levels. In Britain, municipal government has been a bastion of a democratic socialism whose welfare-state social safety net has been under continuous and frequently successful assault from Thatcher (and Callaghan prior to 1978). Realists presumably attribute this to the left's, and especially Labour's, failure to take 'crime' seriously. This failure to take crime seriously has contributed to the Labour Party's political failure in what Thatcher has described as the world's first 'post-socialist society' (Brown and Sparks 1989).

It is against this political backdrop that the realist research agenda has emerged. One of the main purposes of this research is to distinguish the notions of protection from the police and protection from crime, and take them both seriously (Young and Kinsey 1985: 16). It also exposes Labour's shameful underestimation of crime as a social problem – a problem which has the greatest impact upon those groups that the Labour Party ostensibly claims to represent, namely, the unemployed, women, ethnic minorities, and the 'working class.' Labour's failure to take crime seriously has been electorally damaging (Cowell, Jones, and Young 1987; Lea and Young 1984). While Thatcherism exploits victimology to reinforce 'law and order,' realists pursue it to reinforce a range of broader claims about social justice. The pity is that this dimension of their project is obscured by their desire to present realism first and foremost as the vanguard of a 'paradigm shift' – apparently out of a nostalgia for the heady days of the mid 1970s when the New Criminology took the discipline by storm?

Some British realists have assumed that North American 'radicals' (too easily lumping together Canadians and Americans) are isolated from local political practice (Young, this volume) and hence assume that only the theoretical dimension of their project might be of interest outside the British context. My Canadian experience tells me otherwise. Progressive academics in Canada are involved politically, both within and against the state. The rest of this essay offers some thoughts on ways to continue this engagement in the 1990s.

New Politics, New Agenda: A Modest Manifesto

An agenda for the 1990s must obviously be predicated on certain decisions about what we want to achieve. We must ask what form of research and pedagogy is required to promote a society in which equality of outcome and social justice are secured by principles emanating from the new red/green feminist politics. Such principles/goals would include:
- equality of access to services, power, and wealth outside the realm of labour force participation;
- an ethic of cooperation and mutual aid in working and living relationships;
- environmental principles which ensure that production, work, and consumption are safe, socially useful, and personally satisfying;
- democratized and decentralized decision making in the economic political and social spheres;
- accountable public institutions;
- a small-business sector that is guided by the goal of self-reliance and environmental sustainability;
- ecological systems and biological diversity taking precedence over profit;
- indigenous people enjoying the right to self-determination and cultural continuity;
- governmental systems reformed to ensure public participation, protection of civil liberties, natural justice, and the protection of the rights of unions, women, ethnic minorities, the aged, and the young;
- non-nuclear, self-reliant, non-aligned defence; and
- non-violent resolution of conflict at all levels.

This sort of model has been called the 'conservatory' model of capitalist democracy (Smith 1990: 200). The challenge will be to uncouple social justice from economic growth. Neither the British Labour Party nor the Canadian NDP, CLC, and Liberal party appear as ready as the population at large to forsake material gains in order to forestall an impending ecological crisis. Indeed, some British realists, who are Labour activists no less, regard the 'doom and gloom' talk of environmental devastation as without empirical foundation and highly speculative (oral communication with J. Young and S. Walklate, 1 June 1990).

In Canada the main impetus for such a politics comes from the green movement, women's organizations, the Conference of Catholic Bishops, the Canadian Centre for Policy Alternatives, progressive trades unions such as CUPE, and indigenous people (Havemann 1987). But the task is daunting.

The distribution of income, wealth, and power in Canada from 1945 until the early 1970s was based upon an accord between labour and capital. This accord is no longer sustainable. A new business agenda now drives the political agenda. Big capital has declared that continentalism and free trade are to be the guiding principles (Warnock 1988; Carroll 1989) of the new order. In the process, the Canadian state has become decidedly anti-democratic and oligarchic. Conservative governments in the province of British Columbia, the Prairies, Quebec, and the Atlantic region have all moved towards a sort of authoritarian state minimalism. The Constitution Act of 1982 has brought about a 'legalization of politics' (Mandel 1989) that has further centralized power, and even the defunct Meech Lake Accord would have balkanized the country rather than making local governments more decentralized and accountable.

Meech Lake reflected the parochialism of settler capitalism while totally ignoring the idea that the First Nations are also 'distinct' (Hall 1989). The notion of an elected senate was a mere talking point, and there was not even discussion of the desirability of proportional representation to break the traditional two party stranglehold. Meech Lake (Beaudoin 1989: 387) promised that the federal executive would make selections for the Supreme Court bench based on lists of candidates supplied by the provinces, but without any provision for a public or even parliamentary hearing process of the sort that so effectively eliminated Judge Bork, Reagan's candidate, from the US Supreme Court bench.

Continentalism, the partial Americanization of the Canadian juridical-political system, and the free-market aspirations of big capital represent an ideology inimical to social justice. Academics have played a crucial role in constructing and reproducing this hegemony. Progressive academics, isolated and beleaguered though they may have been, have a critical role to play in providing the empirical and conceptual vocabulary for a counter-hegemonic ideology.

Against 'Hyphenated' Criminology: For Justice Studies

Canadian progressive academics should continue on a course that abandons the label 'criminology,' even the hyphenated critical-radical-Marxist-liberatory versions of it, and employ 'justice' as their organizing concept. In doing so, they are not in any sense abandoning recognition of the seriousness of crime or the coerciveness of the criminal justice system. We recognize that criminology may be an institutional 'flag of convenience,' but it should no longer serve as a signifier for a progressive political project (see Hirst 1975; Schwendinger and Schewendinger 1975; Spitzer 1980; Bankowski and Mungham 1977; Couse et al. 1982; Sumner 1983; O'Malley 1988). Important landmarks in this sense are the establishment of the School of Human Justice in Regina, the appearance of the *Journal of Human Justice*, and the change in name of *Crime and Social Justice* to *Social Justice*. This holistic and interdisciplinary focus on pedagogy, research, and community service has parallels in such fields as women's studies and peace studies, with which justice studies has very explicit affinities. These developments have occurred contemporaneously with British realism, although they are not derivative of it – at least not in the United States and Canada, although, like British realists, North American progressives have been involved in the fight against law-and-order policies and the dismantling of the welfare state (or its US equivalent) (see Platt and Takagi 1977, 1981; Michalowski 1983; Gross 1982; Cohen 1985, McMullan 1986).

At the School of Human Justice in Saskatchewan the realization that a 'small-r' realist agenda was necessary found expression in a paper entitled 'The False Promises of Criminology: The Promise of Justice.' This was collectively written in 1982/3 by the faculty and staff (owing its final rendering and erudition to Dr J. Harding). Its table of contents reveals the scope of the critique, which owes much to the 'New Criminology' of Taylor, Walton, and Young (1973, 1975):

1.1 Technical Fix: A History of the Canadian State's Search for the Cure for Crime
1.2 From Social Pathologist to Government Paid Obscurantist
1.3 The Paradigm of Criminology
1.4 From Legalism to Medicalization: Illogical and False Analogies in Criminology
1.5 Law versus Justice in Criminology: Lifting the Veil
1.6 The State and Law in Old and New Criminologies
1.7 The Patriarchal Make-up of Old and New Criminologies
1.8 How Critical is Critical Criminology?
1.9 Radical Criminology in Canada?

Had British realism been anticipated I dare say that 1.10 might have read 'Realism, Pragmatism or Idealism.'

Some Attributes of Justice Studies

The justice studies approach generally rejects criminologies which pathologize or romanticize the criminal or blame the victim. It is based on a recognition that:

- it is necessary to intervene in the policy process so as to reformulate the problematics offered by government and to challenge these through public-policy advocacy;
- since the victimized and marginalized are virtually voiceless, a participatory research approach must be adopted (local crime surveys ought not to be conflated with participatory research no matter how 'politically correct' the instrument or empathetic the interviewer);
- government agencies at local and national levels are not monoliths and that their internal contradictions allow for the forging of certain kinds of alliances; further, that state employees are little different from ourselves and have multiple identities as neighbours, students, and public employees;
- conventional pedagogy overemphasizes the cognitive; critical courses seldom go beyond a description of the gap between real and ideal, so that students are often left without any sense of concrete political practice;
- progressives are often faced with an invidious choice between attacking the arbitrary and intrusive aspects of state welfarism (Taylor 1980) or defending these as remaining bastions of a decommodified service sector (Offe 1984); for women, the implications have been the requirement to choose between dependencies on either public or private patriarchy (Barrett and McIntosh 1982);
- there is a material basis to fear of crime and demands for more 'law and order';
- there is a need for a minimalist and non-coercive criminal justice system;
- no single academic disciplinary or disciplinary amalgam can address 'holistically' the nature and causes of marginalization, victimization, and crime;
- there can be no peace without social justice, and no local justice without global justice;
- demarcations among the caring, controlling, and containing apparatuses of the state are artificial; notions of penality, transcarceration, displacement, net-widening, and informal processes reveal a 'seamless web' that 'criminology' alone cannot unravel;
- 'justice' offers an organizing framework for the development of a political economy of criminal justice institutions and reform practices in welfare-state capitalism. Justice studies can offer community-based education and a participatory research agenda that recognizes the personhood of research subjects and the degree to which respect for individual and collective worth are integral to any sort of 'critical,' 'insurgent,' 'liberating,' or 'empowering' political mission – a mission which one presumes the labels 'critical,' 'left,' or 'realist' criminology also imply. But hyphenated criminology's dependency upon a criminocentric and reactive response to what are essentially state-constructed problems renders it oxymoronic.

Reinventing the Future: Some Tasks for Progressive Intellectuals

The Academy as a Site of Struggle against Incorporation. The agenda for the 1990s must include the site in which much of our work is done: namely, the academy. We must continue to document, expose, and resist the ongoing incorporation of the academy into the New Right's project to commodify knowledge and harness it exclusively to the imperatives of the market-place (Newsome and Buchbinder 1987; Havemann 1987). Justice studies will have to compete with administrative criminology in the research and teaching arenas, and continue to challenge the state's construction of criminology as the research and development bench for the scientistic legitimation of social-control and containment technologies (Hackler 1979; Couse et al. 1983; Arnold 1984; Ratner 1985; Brickey 1989).

Pedagogy. Critical and liberatory pedagogy requires a context in which recognition and enhancement of the interpersonal and affective aspects of the teaching process are possible. We must be vigilant in the protection of teaching as a worthwhile activity, as our colleagues have argued for some years. We must campaign for smaller classes and an open-textured justice studies curriculum. Such pedagogy also requires continued production of accessible, challenging materials.

Freedom of Inquiry. Freedom of inquiry from overt and covert intellectual suppression, from above and from one's peers, must be acknowledged and addressed through public and collective action. The learned societies, faculty associations, and professional bodies to which we belong must be urged to support 'whistle-blowers' and victims of suppression. To do this will require our active involvement in these bodies, since they are unlikely to enter these arenas without some stimulus.

Feminist Process. Our collegial practice must be informed by a feminism which challenges gender hierarchy. Too often hierarchy manifests itself in the deliberate or unselfconscious abuse of social power. We are what we do. Strength rather than weakness or naïvety, plus concern for listening, for consensus seeking, for healing and tolerance are necessary.

The imperatives of individual survival must not lead us to adopt the privatized, alienated, or exploitative postures which seem almost inevitable in the incorporated academy. The post-Fordist era in which we live demands collective, public, and principled stand-taking.

The erosion of the liberal vision of the university is both rapid and gradual. It involves minute and major transactions which progressives cannot now leave to the 'others.' Progressives must play an active part in constructing curriculum, admitting students, setting research priorities, reviewing peers, editing journals, and so on. We must all do the 'housework.'

The academy – like the welfare system, the industrial-military complex, transnational capital, and the criminal justice apparatus – must become the object of critical scrutiny. Justice studies must include research into the academy's personnel practices, student policies, budget allocations, and links to business, the military, and the state.

Cross-Disciplinary Linkages. The interdisciplinary linkages successfully forged with feminist and critical legal scholars must continue. We must seek to include bio-ethecists, natural scientists, urban planners, ecologists, and the like, and strengthen links with those in 'radical social work' and 'critical social policy.'

Research and Practice – Taking Sides. The tendencies to succumb, to what Cohen (1988) describes as 'distancing' oneself from the old debunking paradigm of radical demystification, now takes many forms, such as 'radical' impossibl-ism, post-modern apocalyptic nihilism (Hebdidge 1989), and co-opted quanti-tative obscurantism, within the administrative sciences. They obviously deflect us from helping even to bring about incremental positive change. Progressive academics can and must harness their conceptual sophistication, methodological and communication skills, and access to information to serve marginalized social groups. Our relatively privileged status, the ideology of academic free-dom, and national and international networks all oblige us to engage in low- and high-risk research and consulting tasks in the public arena.

Alternatives to the Research Industry. These tasks include doing, documenting, and disseminating research which counters the hegemony of administrative criminology, whether it be produced at the behest or on behalf of the state. The state-sponsored evaluative research industry must be examined and exposed to reveal its contract-tendering processes and ideological editing procedures, both overt and covert.

Official Discourse and Official Statistics. The implicit and explicit ideologies which can be disgorged from official discourse and official statistics must assume a higher profile on our agenda – especially where we are excluded from the data or the process of data collection and interpretation.

Participatory Research. Research should be for – or preferably with – marginalized people rather than for the state. Such research can be used to counter disinformation that legitimates punitive practices and cut-backs; challenge the classificatory, excluding, pathologizing processes implicit in much research; and investigate territorial injustices, official abuse, neglect, maladministration, and oppression.

This research inevitably requires new techniques and attitudes on our part. It is low budget, both qualitative and quantitative, ethnographic – and polemical at times. Our co-researchers should include unions, prisoners, environmental groups, women's organizations, the poor, and Aboriginal people.

As part of the 'peer review' process in the academy and learned journals, we must give such research parity of esteem with more positivist and conventional forms. Alternative media such as *The Critical Criminologist* and *The Journal of Human Justice* must be enhanced to overcome the censoring process of the academic, government-controlled or corporate-owned media we have traditionally used as vehicles for disseminating our research.

Reformism in Practice. Research, training, consultation, and public-policy advocacy offer media through which progressives can work. The spheres where justice studies can take place include:

a urban and rural planning;
b community-based correctional programs, e.g., diversion;
c public consultative or representative advisory committees for social and recreational programs;
d campaigns against prison building; selecting sites for institutions, factories, waste dumps, and nuclear facilities without meaningful public consultation; logging; denials of Aboriginal rights; infractions of workplace safety regulations;
e campaigns against school closures, welfare cuts, prison overcrowding, homelessness, rent-hikes;
f the auditing and countering of official social and environmental impact statements;
g crime surveys; and
h police commissions and community boards for non-governmental organizations.

Often a justice studies perspective will lead the progressive academic to reformulate problems and suggest alternative modes of analysis, intervention, and bases of comparison. The 'list' above is not exhaustive, but merely indicative of the knowledge base and processes which should be integrated into the research, pedagogy, and practice of justice studies. One hopes that it goes without saying that the political economy of crimes against the poor, of the powerful, in the corporate sector, by the state, against the environment, and against women will continue to be part of the agenda. We must, however, liberate our work from the apparent necessity of using crime as a Trojan horse to enter other realms of inquiry.

Conclusions: Social Rights and Democracy

As social, political, and economic 'rights' are such key concepts in the liberal discourse which still forms the main terrain on which our transformative project takes place, we must take rights seriously. The 'rule of law' is a qualified social good. Social-rights strategists must be self-conscious about the implications of the 'legalization of politics' and the counter-insurgent backlash that an empty rights rhetoric can produce.

Part of the research and political agenda must be to continue to promote and evaluate rights strategies and discourses at local and international levels. We must take care to ensure that the politics of rights – as opposed to the myth of rights – informs our politics (Scheingold 1974). Also we must be aware of the limits of entrusting our project to predominately juridical institutions.

The social impact of the Canada–United States Free Trade Agreement, and the oligarchic nature of the process of 'making' the Charter and the Meech Lake Accord, and the militarization of relationships with Aboriginal people at Oka and elsewhere must become part of our agenda. The 'nuanced' democratization of our institutions holds the key to asserting a new political agenda. We must be critical of simplistic majoritarianism. For example, not only must the Canadian Senate be elected (currently, members of Senate are appointed), but it must be elected on the basis of proportional representation. We must point out that the Meech Lake Accord did not attempt to decentralize power; it provincialized it, placing it in the hands of local oligarchs whose sectoral interests are antagonistic to larger redistributive social reforms. Supreme Court of Canada appointments must be subject to public hearings, and not just reflect the whim of the local premier. And so on ...

The justice studies project aims to create the vocabulary for rewriting the terms of the relationship between the people and the state so as to secure an ecologically sound socialist and feminist future. This process of rewriting involves strengthening alliances and becoming involved in participatory research with organized labour, the liberatory church, local communities, political movements, Aboriginal people's movements, women's organizations, social justice coalitions, and so on.

The dictum that good process yields good outcomes must inform our practice. This at least is my 'realist' agenda for the 1990s.

References

Albo, G., and J. Jenson. 1989. 'A Contested Concept: The Relative Autonomy of the State,' in W. Clement and G. Williams, eds., *The New Canadian Political Economy*, 180-211. Montreal and Kingston: McGill-Queen's University Press

Arnold, B. 1984. 'Criminal Justice Education in British Columbia: A Political Perspective.' *Canadian Criminological Forum*, 7: 21-40

Bankowski, Z., and G. Mungham. 1977. 'Radical Criminology or Radical Criminologist?' *Contemporary Crisis*, 1: 37-52

Barrett, M., and M. McIntosh. 1982. *The Anti-Social Family*. London: Verso

Beaudoin, G. 1989. 'Constitutionalizing Québec's Protection at the Supreme Court and in the Senate,' in M.D. Behiels, ed., *The Meech Lake Primer: Conflicting Views about the 1987 Constitutional Accord*, 385-390. Ottawa: University of Ottawa Press

Brickey, S. 1989. 'Criminology as Social Control Science: State Influence on Criminological Research in Canada.' *Journal of Human Justice*, 1 (1): 43-63

Brown, P., and R. Sparks, eds. 1989. *Beyond Thatcherism: Social Policy, Politics and Society*. Milton Keynes: Open University Press

Carroll, W. 1989. *Corporate Power and Canadian Capital*. Vancouver: University of British Columbia Press

Cohen, S. 1985. *Visions of Social Control*. Cambridge: Polity Press

– 1988. 'Taking Decentralization Seriously: Values, Visions and Policies,' in S. Cohen, *Against Criminology*, 213-234. Oxford: Transaction Books

Couse, K., G. Geller, J. Harding, P. Havemann, R. Matonovich, and R. Schriml. 1983. *The False Promise of Criminology: The Promise of Justice*. Regina: Prairie Justice Research, University of Regina

Cowell, D., T. Jones, and J. Young. 1987. *Political Affiliation, Victimization and Attitudes to Penalty*. London: Middlesex Polytechnic, Centre for Criminology

Gross, B. 1982. 'Some Anti-Crime Strategies for a Progressive Agenda.' *Crime and Social Justice*, 19: 13-22

Hackler, J. 1979. 'The Commercialization of Criminological Research in Canada.' *Canadian Journal of Criminology and Corrections*, 21: 197-199

Hall, Tony. 1989. 'What Are We? Chopped Liver? Aboriginal Affairs in the Constitutional Politics of Canada in the 1980s,' in M.D. Behiels, ed., *The Meech Lake Primer: Conflicting Views about the 1987 Constitutional Accord*, 423-456. Ottawa: University of Ottawa Press

Havemann, P. 1987. 'Marketing the New Establishment Ideology in Canada.' *Crime and Social Justice*, 26: 11-37

Hebdidge, D. 1989. 'After the Masses.' *Marxism Today*, January: 48-53

Hirst, P. 1975. 'Marx and Engels on Law, Crime and Morality,' in I. Taylor, P. Walton, and J. Young, eds., *Critical Criminology*, 203-232. London: RKP

Kennedy, M. 1988. 'The New Global Network by Corporate Power and the Decline of National Self-Determination.' *Contemporary Crises*, 12: 245-276

Kinsey, R., J. Lea, and J. Young. 1986. *Losing the Fight against Crime*. Oxford: Basil Blackwell

Lea, J., and J. Young. 1984. *What Is to Be Done about Law and Order?* Harmondsworth: Penguin

McMullan, J. 1986. 'The Law and Order Problem and Socialist Criminology.' *Studies in Political Economy*, 6 (A): 7-34

Mandel, M. 1989. *The Charter of Rights and the Legalization of Politics in Canada*. Toronto: Wall and Thompson

Michalowski, R. 1983. 'Crime Control in the 1980s: A Progressive Agenda.' *Crime and Social Justice*, 15: 13-22

– 1991. '"Niggers, Welfare Scum and Homeless Assholes": The Problems of Idealism, Consciousness and Context in Left Realism,' in B.D. MacLean and D. Milovanovic, eds., *New Directions in Critical Criminology*, 31-38. Vancouver: Collective Press

Newsome, J., and H. Buchbinder. 1987. *The University Means Business*. Toronto: Garamond Press

Offe, C. 1984. *Contradictions of the Welfare State*. London: Hutchinson

O'Malley, P. 1988. 'The Purpose of Knowledge: Pragmatism and the Praxis of Marxist Criminology.' *Contemporary Crises*, 12: 65-79

Platt, T., and P. Takagi. 1977. 'Intellectuals for Law and Order.' *Crime and Social Justice*, 8: 1-16

– 1981. 'Law and Order in the 1980s.' *Crime and Social Justice*, 15: 1-7

Ratner, R. 1985. 'Inside the Liberal Boot: The Criminological Enterprise in Canada,' in T. Fleming, ed., *The New Criminologies in Canada*, 13-36. Toronto: Oxford University Press

Scheingold, S. 1974. *The Politics of Rights*. New Haven: Yale University Press

Schwendinger, J., and H. Schwendinger. 1975. 'Defenders of Order or Guardians of Human Rights?' in I. Taylor, P. Walton, and J. Young, eds., *Critical Criminology*, 113-146. London: RKP

Scraton, P., ed. 1987. *Law, Order and the Authoritarian State*. Milton Keynes: Open University Press

Smith, D. 1990. *Capitalist Democracy on Trial*. London: Routledge

Spitzer, S. 1980. 'Left "Wing" Criminology – An Infant Disorder?' in J.A. Inciardi, ed., *Radical Criminology: The Coming Crisis*, 169-190. Beverly Hills: Sage

Sumner, C. 1983. 'Rethinking Deviance: Toward a Sociology of Censure.' *Research in Law, Deviance and Social Control*, 5: 187-204

Taylor, I. 1980. *Law and Order: Arguments for Socialism*. London: Macmillan

– 1987. 'Theorizing the Crisis in Canada,' in R. Ratner and J. McMullan, eds., *State*

Control: Criminal Justice Politics in Canada, 192-224. Vancouver: University of British Columbia Press
– 1988. 'Left Realism, the Free Market Economy and the Problem of Social Order.' Paper presented at the American Society of Criminology, Chicago, November
Taylor, I., P. Walton, and J. Young. 1973. *The New Criminology*. London: RKP
– eds. 1975. *Critical Criminology*. London: RKP
Turpel, M.E. 1989. 'Aboriginal Peoples and the Canadian Charter: Interpretive Monopolies, Cultural Differences.' *Canadian Human Rights Handbook*, 6: 4-45
Warnock, John W. 1988. *Free Trade and the New Right Agenda*. Vancouver: New Star Books
Young, J. 1986. 'The Failure of Criminology: The Need for a Radical Realism,' in R. Matthews and J. Young, eds., *Confronting Crime*, 4-30. London: Sage
Young, J., and R. Kinsey. 1985. 'Crime Is a Class Issue.' *New Statesman*, 11 January: 16-77

6 Crime and Justice in Socialist Cuba: What Can Left Realists Learn?

Raymond J. Michalowski

During the 1980s that segment of English-language criminology known as critical or radical developed several divergent approaches to the study of crime and justice.[1] The most policy-oriented of these *new* 'new criminologies' has been variously labelled 'realist criminology' (Young 1987), 'radical realism' (Matthews 1987), and 'left realism' (Taylor 1988). In the following discussion I will use the term *left realism* in order to distinguish 'realism' among critical criminologists from the 'realism' characteristic of conservative and neoconservative approaches to the crime problem (e.g., Wilson 1975; Wilson and Kelling 1982; Van den Haag 1975).

The following inquiry compares left-realist *theory* about criminology and crime control with the *practice* of criminology and crime control in socialist Cuba. This comparison is motivated by the claim by some left realists that the search for solutions to the crime problem in contemporary capitalist societies must be guided by socialist principles, with the ultimate goal being the eventual establishment of socialism itself (Taylor 1980). Or as MacLean has stated: 'Socialism does not guarantee that crime will be resolved or that reification will be eliminated, but it represents *a necessary first step*' (1986: 372; my emphasis).

I am sure some will take issue with my suggestion that the 'socialism' imagined by left realists has anything in common with 'socialism' as practised in current or former socialist nations, particularly those, such as Cuba, that are guided by what Taylor characterizes as the kind of 'democratic centralist party so beloved of the revolutionary left' (1982: 6). With the demise of one-party socialist systems throughout Eastern Europe and the Balkans at the end of the 1980s, the claim that these countries, dominated as they were by Stalinist institutions, were never truly socialist became an ideological shield for many leftists in the face of claims that the bankruptcy of socialism has been proven once and for all, and that the 'end of history' has arrived in the form of what Fukuyama (1989) has characterized as an 'unabashed victory of economic and political liberalism.'

The reality of actually existing (or formerly existing) socialism, however, cannot be so easily sidestepped or dismissed by those who claim to be socialists. If the long-term goal of 'socialism' for left realists refers to something other than reproducing the existing social democracies of the developed world,[2] then the twentieth-century experiments with state-owned and state-managed economies cannot be dismissed as 'not socialism.' Despite the degree to which many on the left would care to disown them, and however significant their failures, these experiments represent the only concrete attempts in the modern epoch to develop social systems at a national level that are not organized around private-production economies. Those who are interested in finding the much discussed 'third way' should undertake close analyses of the 'second way' – real-world socialism – as much as they have of the 'first way' of capitalism.

My grounding assumption, then, is that not only do left realists need to take crime seriously, they also need to take actually existing socialism seriously – not necessarily approvingly, but seriously. Left realists must undertake a careful examination of real-world socialist societies in order to understand the successes and failures of others who have pursued the construction of what they perceived to be socialist crime-control policies.

The following comparison of left realism and Cuban crime control consists of two parts. First, I examine three specific elements of crime prevention and crime control in Cuba: (1) the relationships among class, socio-economic inequality, and rates of crime; (2) the public culture of self-worth; and (3) community-based measures for the prevention and control of crime. Second, I discuss the implications of these real-world socialist crime-control measures for left-realist strategies of (1) localism, (2) community prevention, and (3) improving social equality.

The Cuban data presented here are derived from six working trips to that country during the period from 1985 to 1990. During each of these trips I interviewed ordinary citizens, government officials, justice system personnel, and university law school professors; collected contemporary and historical documents related to crime and criminal justice policies in Cuba; and visited various criminal justice agencies and facilities. In spring 1989 my work in Cuba included a four-month period of participant observation in a law collective (*bufete colectivo*).

Class, Inequality, and the Crime Problem in Cuba

The central tenets of Cuban criminology are: (1) the problems of lawbreaking develop within specific historical contexts, (2) the form of the crime problem in any society is a reflection of the inequalities generated by its means of production, and (3) the central strategy in reducing problems of crime is the reduction of these inequalities (Viera 1986: 38). According to this model, the first step in addressing the problem of crime – but far from the only one – must be the elimination or reduction of the structurally induced inequalities of the given historically situated social formation. For instance, according to this model, the problems of crime in capitalist societies can be addressed only by first eliminating the kinds of inequalities that arise from the conflict between labour and capital under conditions of the private ownership of the means of production. Thus, the *first step* to be taken by any capitalist society that sincerely wishes to reduce its level of crime must be the replacement of a capitalist mode of production with a socialist one. For Cuba this has meant the elimination of the private ownership of the means of production (with the exception of land for small-scale farmers and personal tools for self-employed artisans), and state planning of nearly all production and most distribution.

In both theory and practice, socialism and a socialist mode of production, however, are not pure communism, and consequently structural sources of inequality exist in socialist societies. According to Cuban criminologists and legal theorists, however, the problems of crime under socialism do not arise from inequalities derived from the conflict between labour and capital, but from (1) inequalities that result from socialist distribution, including the wage-allocation principle of 'from each according to his or her ability to each according to his or her *work*'; (2) bourgeois ways of thinking and acting that continue to exist as cultural remnants from the pre-socialist era or reflect current ideological influences from the capitalist world; and (3) personal problems of psychological maladjustment, usually resulting from disorganization within the family. It is these things, they argue, that socialist criminologists must address in their search for further reductions in the crime problem, making their task somewhat different from that of criminologists in free-market societies. Socialist societies in the Third World, they add, face an additional source of crime resulting from the gap between legitimate popular desires for material consumption and the economic limits on the ability of less developed countries to fulfil these desires.[3]

Theoretically, it is interesting to note that Cuba's socialist criminology reorients the study of inequality from the relations of production when speaking of capitalist societies, to relations of distribution when the topic is the link between inequality and crime under socialism. Cuban Marxists adopt what paradoxically might be seen as variant of Weber's understanding of class (Giddens and Held 1982: 10) in so far as their focus tends to shift from the (already transformed) relations of production to the problems of socialist distribution. It could also be argued, however, that socialist distribution is not market distribution, and that those who study inequality under socialist distribution are confronting a form of social inequality distinctly different from that analysed by either Marx or Weber.

Every Cuban criminologist and jurist whom I interviewed, as well as most ordinary Cubans with whom I have talked, agree that the transition from a free-market capitalist economy to a centrally planned socialist system in Cuba was accompanied by a reduction in conventional forms of crime. Part of this claim, at least on the part of criminologists and legal professionals, is founded on the Marxist assumption that the 'exploitation of man by man [*sic*]' is *sui generis* criminal, and thus the socialist elimination of capitalist labour markets necessarily results in a reduction of crime. Beyond this tautology, however, we can also inquire into the level of ordinary crimes under conditions of socialist organization in Cuba.

The Official Picture of the Crime Problem

Table 6.1 reports the number and rate per 100,000 population for all crimes against persons and property; four specific categories of property crime (burglary, robbery, theft, white-collar crime); crimes against state security; and all other crimes for the years 1985, 1986, 1987, and 1988. Not included are offences reported to the police but subsequently determined to lack sufficient validity to warrant further investigation by a police investigator (*instructor de policia*).[4] These data represent crimes that could be prosecuted in *provincial* courts. The jurisdiction of these courts begins with offences that carry a possible penalty of more than one year of incarceration. Thus, the data presented here are for offences comparable in gravity to the kinds of felony offences listed as Part I crimes by the US Federal Bureau of Investigation in its annual crime reports.

The data reported in table 6.1 are not measures of the actual rates of *criminal behaviour* in Cuba. They are measures of what people report to government record-keepers, and what these record-keepers record.[5] Like all official criminal statistics, although they are not measures of crime per se, they can serve as a useful measure of a society's *crime problem*. As Sumner (1976) observes, 'crime' does not designate a fixed, transparent behavioural reality, but rather is a term of 'ideological censure'; that is, 'crimes' reflect those events deemed to be of sufficient gravity by the public *and* the formal institutions of state control to warrant the attention of the criminal justice system.

TABLE 6.1

Number and rate (per 100,000 population) for selected crimes in Cuba

Category	1985	1986	1987	1988
All personal crimes	13,927	17,840	19,657	19,608
		(175)	(190)	(186)
All property crimes	21,011	24,205	27,998	21,656
	(207)	(237)	(270)	(206)
Robbery	1,325	1,694	1,398	1,533
	(13)	(17)	(13)	(15)
Burglary	7,367	9,823	10,446	8,758
	(73)	(96)	(101)	(83)
Theft	7,084	8,944	10,499	6,531
	(70)	(88)	(101)	(62)
White collar	1,361	1,201	1,512	705
	(13)	(12)	(15)	(7)
State crimes	624	780	839	313
	(6)	(8)	(8)	(3)
Other offenses	3,250	3,619	3,304	4,109
	(32)	(35)	(32)	(39)
Total offenses	34,938	42,045	47,645	41,267
	(343)	(412)	(458)	(393)
Population	10,152,639	10,200,600	10,366,175	10,531,750

Source: Population – Annuario Estadistico de Cuba: 1986 (p. 57). Population data for 1987 and 1988 are projections based on reported growth anticipated between 1986 and 1990. Crime data provided by Fiscalia General de la Republica de Cuba, May 1989

It is difficult to make reliable comparisons between pre- and post-revolutionary crime statistics in Cuba (Salas 1979). Caution is required even when comparing crime statistics from one post-revolutionary period to those from another. Table 6.1, for example, indicates there was a noticeable decline between 1987 and 1988 in the number and rate of every category of crime except 'other offences.' However, this drop in 'crime' is less the result of behavioural changes than it is the consequence of the implementation of a new criminal code. This code, which went into effect on 30 April 1988, downgraded a number of offences from the jurisdiction of provincial (felony-equivalent) courts to municipal (misdemeanour-equivalent) courts; transformed a number of lesser property crimes into citation-only, non-criminal offences; and completely removed a number of acts that had formerly been defined as either white-collar crimes or crimes against state security from the legal jurisdiction of the state. The decline in recorded crime is significant in terms of Cuba's *crime problem*, however, in

TABLE 6.2

Number and rate (per 100,000 population) for selected crimes in Cuba and the United States, 1986

Category	Cuba	United States
Violent crime	17,840	1,448,140
	(175)	(617)
All property crimes	24,205	11,722,700
	(237)	(4,863)
Robbery	1,694	542,780
	(17)	(225)
Burglary	9,823	3,241,400
	(96)	(1,345)
Theft	8,944	7,257,200
	(88)	(3,010)
Total offences	42,045	13,171,440
	(412)	(5,480)

Source: United States – US Department of Justice, Federal Bureau of Investigation, Crime in the United States (1986: 41). Cuba – Fiscalia General de la Republica de Cuba

that it represents a *redefinition* of what behaviours are understood as posing sufficient social threats to warrant the attention of the criminal justice system.

Contrasting the perceived crime problem in Cuba with the perceived crime problem in the United States helps to put Cuba's crime problem into perspective. Table 6.2 compares the rate of recorded offences per 100,000 population in Cuba during 1986 with that of the United States. As this table shows, the recorded rates of common street crime in Cuba are substantially lower than reported rates for comparable crimes in the United States.

Cross-national comparisons of this sort pose a number of problems, particularly with regard to the comparability of crime definitions. The enormity of these differences, however, cannot be explained away as reflections of definitional differences or record-keeping practices. The simple fact, as those who have spent time in Cuba know, is that crime is less common there, and, when it does occur, it is less violent than crime in the United States and most of Latin America.

The Unofficial Picture of the Crime Problem

In Havana, Cubans do not fear crime in any degree comparable to that for residents of most major urban centres in the United States. In the Cuban countryside the fear is even less.

One of the best measures of the perceived level of safety in a society is the degree to which women are or are not fearful of crime. Women face not only most of the same threats of street crime as do men, but also the additional and significant threat of sexual assaults and gender-specific brutality and harassment (DeKeseredy, this volume). Consequently, I would argue the level of fear of crime among women is a good litmus test of the general perception of crime risks. A society or a city in which men feel relatively safe to move about may still be a hazardous place for women. By contrast, it is unlikely that, if women feel relatively safe from crime, men do not share a similar sense of security.

In Havana it is common at night to see women of all ages walking alone on the streets or taking buses unaccompanied. All but one *Habanera* (female resident of Havana) with whom I have spoken, and it is a question that I have asked more than forty Cuban women over a period of five years, said that they were not afraid to go out alone at night. The one exception was a woman in her middle fifties who told me that she 'felt nervous' walking down an empty street to a bus stop at 4:00 a.m. in order to be able to get to her job as a cook by 5:30. Even though she had never been threatened with a crime in her years of doing so, the empty predawn street still seemed ominous to her. Several women in their early fifties claimed that the situation for women in Havana had improved since the prerevolutionary era when the extraordinary level of prostitution designed to serve White, male North American visitors meant than almost any woman on the street was treated as though she was of easy virtue.

Not all victimization of women occurs on the streets. As local victim surveys have shown, women face the additional threat of violence in the home (Painter 1990). There are no victim surveys in Cuba comparable to either the official crime surveys in the United States and Britain or the local crime surveys conducted by left realists. Consequently, it is impossible to construct a statistical description of woman abuse in the Cuban home. The ethnographic information I have been able to obtain, however, suggest that while violence against women in the home occurs, there has been a decline in wife/lover beating in comparison to prerevolutionary levels. Various informants have attributed this to the fact that the guarantees of work and access to subsidized food, clothing, and housing means that women are less likely to feel they are the economic prisoners of their husbands than was the case in the pre-socialist era. While economic imprisonment is not the only factor influencing a violent home, it is an important one. As one young female attorney in Cuba said to me: 'The men know that if they want us to stay they cannot hit us like they used to.'

In addition to feeling relatively safe on the streets, unlike many residents of large cities in the United States, most Cubans do not feel a need to secure themselves behind bolted doors when they are at home. In Havana people usually lock their doors if they leave home for any length of time or when they are asleep. Frequently, however, they leave apartments or homes unlocked when visiting neighbours or stepping out for a short time. During the frequent warm weather, Cubans usually leave doors, windows, and shutter walls wide open if they are at home during the day. With the exceptions of one shanty-town of recent in-migrants into Havana along the Almendra River, and one particular street near the railway station, I was never told to avoid any areas of Havana because of the threat of crime. Nor did I ever feel threatened by crime at any time while I was in Cuba, even though in five years of travelling there I have explored both Havana and Cuba's western and central provinces widely. I cannot claim a similar lack of fear when I am in many of the US cities to which I travel.

These observations do not mean that Cubans live, or feel they live, in a crime-free society. Burglaries, thefts, robberies, sexual assaults, and other forms of interpersonal violence (usually arising from personal disputes) occur, as table 6.1 indicates. Yet, the comparatively lower level of crime means that Cubans do not live with a sense that they are besieged by crime, as do many people in the United States. Cubans with whom I have spoken, even those living in central-city Havana, the highest crime area of Cuba, claim they feel free to conduct their lives without devoting any significant portion of their attention to the threat of crime.

Explaining Cuba's Crime Rate

What are we to make of the low official rates of crime in Cuba and the fact that Cubans, in general, experience less fear of crime than do people in the United States and Britain? A number of Cubans with whom I have spoken – ordinary citizens as well as professionals in criminology and law – claim that Cuba's comparatively low rates of crime are *prima facia* evidence that the society's efforts to achieve a universal provision of basic necessities such as food, housing, health care, work, and education have substantially ameliorated many of the major social forces that generate crime.

There are several other possible explanations. First, some might suggest that Cuba's low rate of crime is the product of the deterrent effectiveness of a repressive criminal justice system. Contrary to US government claims (US Department of State 1987: 444), however, the sanctions provided by Cuba's criminal code are no more punitive than those in the United States, and in some cases they are less so (Michalowski 1989). Furthermore, the conditions in Cuba's prisons have been found to be comparable to those in other Western nations (Evanson 1989; United Nations 1989). Moreover, in recent years criminal justice policy makers in Cuba have actively promoted both depenalization and the expansion of non-prison alternatives for convicted offenders (Escasena Guillarón 1988) in notable contrast to the increasing use of imprisonment in the United States.

Another possibility is that the level of 'routine activities' in Cuba are such that the supply of available victims and attractive targets is low (Cohen and Felson 1979). With 42.4 per cent of its total population in the labour force, however, Cuba has a rate of labour force participation comparable to that of the United States and higher than that of any other nation in Latin America. The difference between Cuba and most other Latin American nations is even greater with respect to the labour force participation of women. In other words, on two social dimensions that presumably increase the number of potential crime targets – the proportions of homes vacant during the day and the number of people in transit – Cuba ranks substantially higher than most other Latin American countries and is comparable to the United States (International Labor Organization 1987). The number of homes that are vacant during working hours and the high proportion of people in transit is further increased in Cuba by the fact that nearly all children under age sixteen are in school and away from home during most of the day. Despite Cuba's high levels of the kind of routine activities that presumably elevate the risk of criminal victimization, the rate of crime there remains relatively low.

Another possibility is that the number of attractive targets for property crime is limited in Cuba because of the relatively narrowed range of options for personal consumption. In other words, where the amount of personal property and the level of individual differentiation in the ownership of such property is limited, there is relatively less reason to steal. The personal ownership of commodities in Cuba is not uniform. Some people have scarce items such as colour TVs, motorbikes, air-conditioners, and tape recorders, while others do not. The range of possibilities and the degree of differentiation, however, are narrower in Cuba than in most contemporary capitalist societies. Thus, the level of desirable items that one does not have and that can be obtained by theft is lower in Cuba than in both developed and less-developed market societies that have larger visible gaps between affluent classes and less advantaged segments of the society. It should be noted that Cuban criminologists would take the 'few things worth stealing' argument as evidence that the socialist economic strategy of reducing material inequalities is effective in reducing crime.

Available evidence suggests that Cuba's rate of crime cannot be explained adequately either by harsh penal practices or by low levels of victim-producing routine activities. Rather, the lower rates of property crime in Cuba, according to Cuban criminologists, results from certain fundamental characteristics of Cuba's socialist social formation. Specifically these are: (1) lower levels of obvious material inequality in comparison to capitalist societies, (2) a public culture within which social worth is measured less in terms of material possessions than in terms of a person's social participation, and (3) a neighbourhood system of surveillance and a highly developed gossip chain (*radio bimba*), which, when combined with low levels of material inequality, minimizes the possibilities that unexplained material acquisitions will pass unnoticed or unremarked.

Material Inequalities

The Cuban constitution designates the state as responsible for insuring that everyone has not only the right to work, but also the opportunity to work (Republic of Cuba 1976/81: 23). While there is competition for better-paying, more prestigious jobs, particularly in terms of professional careers requiring university education, Cuban socialism has, for the most part, made *entry* into the labour force non-competitive. As a result open unemployment in Cuba is low (Mesa-Lago 1989: 205).[6]

The salary scale in Cuba ranges from 100 to 450 *pesos* a month, with some specially skilled workers earning as much as 600 *pesos* per month. With housing costs generally held to 10 per cent of salary, and with extensive state subsidies for transportation, recreation, and rationed food and clothing items, Cubans who work are able to earn the Cuban equivalent of a basic standard of living. In addition, free medical care, free education, and universal old-age pensions relieve Cubans from many of the financial fears that people in market societies characteristically experience.

The class hierarchy – in the Weberian sense of being able to purchase life chances in the market – characteristic of capitalist societies is substantially compressed in Cuba. There are different levels of material consumption in Cuba, but there is neither great visible wealth nor the kind of deep poverty found in much of Latin America.

The feeling that one has not received a share of what the society has to offer is less likely to develop when the gap between oneself and those whom one perceives as 'average' is narrow. Many of the Cubans with whom I have spoken, regardless of the level of their lifestyle, claim that, while they do not have everything they desire, they 'have enough,' a phrase I heard repeatedly, during the 1980s, when I asked people about the material conditions of their lives.[7]

There is one important exception to this. Those living in Cuba who judge their lives primarily by the material possessions of Cubans in the United States or by the general media-transmitted image of lifestyles in the developed West are far more likely to express material dissatisfaction and economic frustrations. In some cases the resulting sense of deprivation relative to the developed West tempts these Cubans to try to leave Cuba without completing the formal procedures for immigration, procedures which are currently cumbersome and tedious, as much because of delays in granting visas on the US side as because of red tape (*papeleo*) on the Cuban side (Smith 1987). I spoke with several defendants who had been charged with attempting to immigrate illegally (*salida ilegal*). One said he wanted 'to have a car,' another said that his dream was 'to be free to buy more things,' and a third told me that 'you are just not free to make enough money in Cuba.' By US standards, individuals such as these would normally be treated as economic rather than political refugees. For its own political purposes, however, the US government tends to portray anyone who leaves Cuba as being motivated by desires to escape political or religious repression.

Particular efforts are made to minimize a sense of relative deprivation among young people in Cuba. For example, all Cuban school students wear uniforms. Consequently, status differentiation and status competition among young people at school, at least in terms of clothing styles, is minimized. By comparison, clothing serves as an important source of competition among students in US schools. In recent years in the United States the desire for certain high-prestige clothing items, particularly expensive basketball shoes and team jackets, has reached a point where students have been robbed and even murdered by their schoolmates *for their clothes* (Telander 1990).

Differentiation in clothes or other desired items is not entirely absent among young people in Cuba. Some children receive gifts from visiting relatives who live in the United States. Also, some parents whose professions involve travel overseas may have access to limited amounts of foreign currency that can be spent in the diplomatic stores (*diplotiendas*) on scarce imported items for themselves or their children.[8] The most popular items of youth consumption are up-to-the date imported clothing and personal electronics such as jamboxes, Sony Walkmans, or equivalents. There is some theft among young people of these items, and I have been told that these things will sometimes 'disappear' at school. In general, however, school and youth culture in Cuba are organized in ways that minimize rather than promote the competitive display of material markers of status. In so far as much street crime is youth crime, the reduced emphasis on and opportunity for status competition in terms of material display among Cuban youth may be an important factor contributing to the relatively lower overall rate of street crime in Cuba.

Public Culture and Material Life

When I have asked Cubans what life is like in Cuba their responses invariably included statements such as 'Here everyone has food,' 'Here everyone has work,' or 'In Cuba health care is free.' These same people often went on to talk about problems with transportation, particularly the buses, with the erratic telephone system, and with housing – these being the most common areas of popular material dissatisfaction in Cuba. Yet, the dominant theme often remained the nation's efforts to meet the basic needs of all Cubans, and most Cubans I have spoken with refer to these efforts with some pride and satisfaction. It is important to note that even the most dissident Cubans with whom I spoke supported a continuation of constitutional guarantees for food, work, housing, health care, and education. Their complaints were often focused on the failure to provide these things at what they viewed as a satisfactory level, not with the *idea* that these substantive provisions should remain as part of the fundamental *rights* of citizens to be guaranteed by the government.

I am not suggesting that Cubans do not have material frustrations. There are many scarce, imported items such as cars, colour TVs, VCRs, the latest in clothing styles, and air conditioners that Cubans would like to own, and many would like a better or larger place to live. Additionally, the limited supplies of certain food items, such as garlic, coffee, meat, and seafood (particularly shellfish, much of which is directed to the export market), is an ongoing source of popular frustration. These lacks, however, do not appear to translate into a sense of personal failing or inadequacy, and are attributable, in part, to the discontinuity between a Cuban's salary and what a Cuban can purchase.

The ability to buy many of the most desirable items, particularly imported commodities, depends not on one's earning power, but on either having been given the opportunity to buy a scarce item as a specific recognition of exemplary work or having access to foreign currency. Both cases are understood to represent *exceptional* opportunities, and being excluded from these opportunities does not indicate that one is a 'failure.'

Part of Cuba's socialist ideology is that all work is social, and therefore all accomplishments are collective in nature. Certain scarce goods may be given to those whose contributions are recognized as above average, but doing 'average' work as part of the general whole is not a sign of 'mediocrity.'

The *bufete* where I worked, for example, received three new Soviet-built Lada sedans in spring 1989. The *bufete* then had to determine who among its forty-six attorneys would be given the opportunities to buy the cars. A committee was elected by the workers in the *bufete* to examine the work records of the employees. The committee recommended that two of the most senior attorneys in the *bufete* each be given the opportunity to buy a Lada at the comparatively low, subsidized price of 4,000 *pesos* in recognition of their long careers of high-quality service to clients.[9] The third car, it was suggested, should be kept by the *bufete* for the general business use of the attorneys. This recommendation was unanimously adopted by the workers in the *bufete*. Because there were so few cars to distribute, and because those who received them were among the most experienced attorneys in the *bufete*, the other attorneys with whom I discussed the cars did not seem to feel that *not* having received a car was a comment on their own inadequacy. All of the attorneys with whom I spoke about the distribution of the cars said that it was appropriate and fair. The only negative comment was that it was too bad there were so few cars to distribute because there were so many really fine attorneys in the *bufete*.

Under conditions of obvious scarcity, such as the distribution of cars in the *bufete*, the inability to obtain desired items appears as the consequence of structural constraints rather than personal shortcomings. Under conditions of market distribution and presumed abundance, as in the United States, a similar inability takes the phenomenal form of personal failure and, I would suggest, is more potentially damaging to self-esteem. This weakened self-esteem, in turn, can lead to compensatory measures that, in some instances, may take the form of criminal behaviours.

The combination of a narrowed salary scale and a relative scarcity of many of the most desired items means the public culture of social worth and personal prestige have been substantially decommodified in Cuba. In Cuba the esteem one enjoys in the eyes of others is often based less on the ability for public (and often anonymous) display of high-status commodities than is the case in the United States. Prestige is much more closely tied to the personal evaluations made by one's co-workers or neighbours. Under these conditions motivations towards both ordinary crimes of theft and white-collar crimes are reduced, in part, because it is more difficult (although not impossible) to steal or cheat one's way to social prestige in Cuba. *How* one obtained the objects of material desire, not the mere possession of them, remains an important part of Cuba's more decommodified system of social evaluation.

Another important character of public culture in Cuba is the sense that many Cubans seem to have that they are personally involved in the country's attempts to meet substantive social and economic needs. A characteristic of statements regarding Cuba's social accomplishments is that Cubans, including young people, will more often use the term 'we' (*nosotros*) rather than such expressions as 'the government' (*el gobierno*) or 'the state' (*el estado*) to denote the subject of the accomplishments. Cubans have frequently said to me: '*We* are working to have one doctor on every block' or 'Since the Revolution *we* have eliminated malnutrition' or '*We* have achieved a sixth grade level of education for everyone here and in a few years *we* will reach the ninth grade level' (my emphasis). This way of speaking suggests that at an ideological level many Cubans identify their country's accomplishments as the consequence of collective, participatory efforts on the part of the Cuban people, of which they are a part. This popular culture of involvement may be a less fertile ground for breeding self-absorbed motivations and a lack of empathy for others, both of which are important accompaniments of street crime.

I want to emphasize here that I am talking about proportions, not absolutes. There are commodity-based desires and dissatisfactions in Cuba. There are people whose motivations are far more self-absorbed than they are social. And there are the kinds of street crimes that these things can breed. The seriousness and frequency of these crimes, however, appear to be substantially less in Cuba than in the United States. One of the reasons for this, I would argue, is that the public culture of social worth in Cuba is such that, in comparison to a competitive market society such as that of the United States, proportionally more Cubans feel themselves to be integrated into, and evaluated positively by, the wider society, than feel alienated from it.

Community Crime Control

Community, as understood by Cuban policy planners, is not a social phenomenon that results from simple residential proximity. Rather, community is seen as a dynamic, revolutionary *process*. 'Community' is dynamic in that it must be created and continually renewed, and is not a social formation that will naturally and automatically arise because people live together in a neighbourhood. 'Community' is revolutionary in that the expressed purpose of communities in Cuba is to be transformative. The goal of the Cuban government is to create communities that will serve as the mechanism for the revolutionary construction and reproduction of a socialist society. Community, in the eyes of Cuba's leadership, is the site for the creation and maintenance of 'revolutionary conscience' (*consciencia*). Community, in this context, is not something that *is*, but rather something that *does*.

The primary mechanism for creating community in revolutionary Cuba is what are termed 'mass and social organizations' (*las organizaciones sociales y de masas*). These consist of a variety of social and political institutions designed to communicate revolutionary ideology to the public and to provide citizens with organizational structures that enable them to: (1) address specific problems within their immediate level and legal sphere of jurisdiction, and (2) access lines of communication to institutions of state, government, and party. These mass organizations include bodies such as the Cuban Federation of Women (FMC – *Federación de Mujeres Cubanas*), the Congress of Cuban Trade Unionists (CTC – *Congreso de Trabajadores Cubanos*), and the Committees for the Defense of the Revolution (CDR – *Comités de Defensa de la Revolución*).

Of the various mass organizations, the Committees for the Defense of the Revolution are most closely connected with 'community' as a residential grouping. CDRs consist of block-level units of citizens organized into a hierarchical structure that follows Cuba's ubiquitous democratic-centralist principles of organization. The CDRs are multi-purpose social, political, and cultural organizations that, in the words of one Cuban, 'do everything from inoculating dogs, to taking the census, to policing the neighborhood, to throwing parties.'[10]

CDRs are the basic and broadest level of revolutionary organization in Cuba. Whether employed or non-working, young or old, male or female, single or married, everyone can participate in the local CDR. Because CDRs are organized on the most basic level, participation in CDR activities also serves as the minimum indicator of whether or not an individual is 'integrated' into the Revolution.

The CDRs also serve as the most basic instrument of crime prevention and crime control in Cuba. Through the institution of *la guardia*, the night-time patrol, CDRs are responsible for ensuring the general safety of their *barrio*. Each night, two members of the CDR are supposed to patrol the neighbourhood, keeping a watch out for criminal, counterrevolutionary, or socially disruptive activity. It is difficult to know for sure how closely the real patrol activity of the *cederistas* follows the ideal, however, most of the Cubans with whom I have spoken indicate that patrols take place in their neighbourhood, and they feel their neighbourhoods are safer for them. In a case with which I am personally familiar, a close Cuban friend awoke one night in spring 1990 to the sound of would-be burglars rummaging about in his living-room. They had gained entrance by sending a small boy or a very thin person through the wrought-iron bars that typically cover shutter windows kept open at night. The intruder then unlocked the front door for the others. My friend ran out his back door and began shouting '*Ladrón Ladrón!*' (Thief! Thief!). The *guardia* who were on the corner of his block came running, and the burglars fled empty-handed. My friend estimates that less than two minutes passed between the time he raised his alarm and the time help arrived, demonstrating the superior response time afforded by community crime patrols in comparison to that of regular police.

The community patrols play an important role in responding to the problems of crime in Cuba in several ways. First, the CDRs increase the possibility of detection, thus strengthening the deterrent efficacy of the justice system.[11] Second, as several police investigators for the Ministry of the Interior with whom I spoke suggested, it is likely that the presence of the *guardia* is important, not only for its ability to deter serious crime, but also because it limits the possibilities for pre-criminal deviance among adolescents by mobilizing community intervention at an early age. Third, the CDRs increase citizen feelings of safety by providing someone who will (or should) come to your aid if you need it on the street at night. Fourth, the CDRs serve as a practical mechanism to strengthen the idea that crime control and public safety are a *public* rather than an exclusively state responsibility. In this sense the CDRs serve to multiply, many times over, the social-control functions that are almost exclusively the function of police in many other societies.

Implications of Cuban Crime Control for Left Realism

Cuba appears to have made inroads against the kinds of street crimes that left realists feel critical criminologists should take seriously. The strategies used by Cuba provide a useful standpoint from which to reflect on certain of the crime-reduction strategies proposed by left realists – specifically their arguments for (1) localism, (2) community crime control, and (3) reductions in inequality with an increased emphasis on production for social need.

Localism

As Hunt (1982: 2) notes, one of the underlying assumptions of left realism is that critical criminologists must address the problems people face with crime in terms of their daily lives. These problems, left realists argue, are more immediate, more meaningful, and more arresting than the distant, complex, and less visible problems associated with larger issues of political economic organization. The Cuban approach, on the contrary, is based on a more holistic understanding of social problems, and on a belief that ordinary citizens are *capable* of, and *interested in*, understanding the relationship between their day-to-day problems and the larger organization of society. Official presentations about crime in Cuba usually emphasize the relationship between levels of crime and the society's level of 'social development' in terms of its ability or inability to meet social needs.[12] Similarly, discussions of crime-control policies almost always incorporate concerns for the ability of the economic and social system to integrate or reintegrate offenders into the productive sphere.

The emphasis on localism within realist criminology is a natural outgrowth of the valid concern that day-to-day problems with crime be taken seriously by critical criminologists. However, it also runs the risk of narrowing the project of left realists to responding to working-class problems of crime on the lowest level of analysis, rather than using those concerns to develop both popular understanding and concrete research regarding the link between everyday crime problems and the wider social forces that engender them.

Community Crime Control

Most left realists view decentralized community crime-control strategies as one of the basic elements of a progressive agenda for the control of crime (Matthews 1987: 389). As Cohen (1979) and others (Taylor 1982; Matthews 1987) have noted, however, this emphasis on the crime-control potential of 'communities' is situated in a historical moment when the kinds of stable, community-based, social relations central to minimizing crime are well along a trajectory of decline in Britain, Canada, and the United States.

As discussed above, Cubans have developed relatively effective and universal community crime-control strategies through the CDRs and neighbourhood patrols. These activities, however, are based on a systemic integration of communities of residence into an overall plan for socialist social relations that raise two questions regarding the possibility of community crime prevention in Western societies dedicated to certain liberal traditions.

First, to the extent that community crime control in Cuba works, it does so because it presumes it is appropriate for people to keep track of the comings and goings in their neighbourhood and the behaviour of their neighbours. This means, among other things, that people live with an awareness that their activities are noticed – not so much in the sense of surveillance by the formal institutions of a repressive state, but rather in the sense of being under the watchful and oftentimes judgmental eye of their neighbours. The CDR and community patrol systems attempt to reproduce life in a small village where individual behavioural options are limited by public scrutiny. The wife of a defendant charged with illegal possession of foreign currency, for example, said to me that the police investigated them because some 'jealous neighbours' reported that the people living in her house had many things that are more easily purchased with foreign currency (i.e., a colour TV, a VCR, several fans, an air-conditioner, and new gold jewellery). And the neighbours were right. These things had been purchased with illegally obtained foreign currency.

The ideology and social values of liberal democracies privilege and presume freedom from interference in one's daily life, including surveillance for criminal activity, by anyone other than officially designated representatives of the state, and then only in accordance with specified rules of procedure. Community crime prevention such as occurs in Cuba poses a direct challenge to the value placed on individual liberty in Anglo-American culture. Left realists need to confront the question of individualism and privacy as it relates to surveillance as they attempt to develop strategies for community crime control because effective community crime control can very easily contradict contemporary liberal definitions of due process and privacy rights.

Second, the formation of communities as sets of binding social relations rather than simple residential groupings necessitates widespread commitment to some overarching set of principles or beliefs. Contrary to my earlier writing on the subject (Michalowski 1983: 19), I doubt that community crime patrols or other stable, community-based crime-prevention strategies can be organized around concerns for crime control *alone*. They must be based in a broader sense of community, on a sense of mutual concern for the well-being of others. Community crime control requires an altruistic surrendering of a portion of one's free time to the general well-being of the community, and a personal involvement with its members. Such strategies are unlikely to meet with broad acceptance in most communities in industrialized capitalist societies, particularly in heterogeneous, anonymous urban neighbourhoods. To the extent that individuals are motivated primarily by a private and personal desire to be free from crime, buying better locks, guard dogs, and guns, and similar individualistic strategies will remain for most people more rational and desirable responses to the problem than surrendering a portion of one's discretionary time to the discipline of community-organized crime-prevention activities similar to the CDR *guardia* in Cuba. Even where communities come together for crime-prevention activities under conditions of extreme threats of crime, such organization is based on a response to *crisis* rather than arising from pre-existing social relations. In short, community crime-control strategies as an expression of stable community relations must be *preceded* by the construction or reconstruction of *communities*.

Inequality and Production for Need

Taylor argues that 'the need to organize production to fulfill continuing and unmet *social needs* for goods, services, and employment' is essential to the reduction of motivations towards crime (1982: 12). The most fundamental element of crime reduction in Cuba has been just that, the organization of production that privileges the fulfilment of basic social needs over the unequal satisfaction of personal commodity desires. Related to this are Cuba's efforts to decommodify personal worth and social status, in order to undercut many of the significant motivations towards property crime.

The Cuban route to production for general social needs and the relative decommodification of social worth has been achieved through abrogating the right of markets to determine the production, importation, and distribution of basic goods, most services, and desirable items of consumption beyond the basic level. As a system of production and distribution capitalism has historically always limited the access of some individuals, groups, or classes to labour and commodity markets. Cuba's efforts to surmount these limitations and the social disruptions they produce took the form of socializing the means of production and the institutions of distribution, and reorganizing these functions through a state-planned and centrally administered economy. As the events in Eastern Europe during the late 1980s and early 1990s demonstrated, centrally planned economies such as Cuba's are not sufficient by themselves to guarantee either social harmony or social equality. Centrally planned socialist economies, like other political-economic social systems, combine with the sedimented history and the culture of a society to produce concrete social formations that can create their own versions of inequality, exclusion, and privilege.

In general, left realists, I suspect, would reject policies leading to significant restructuring of contemporary capitalist systems, along the lines of a Cuban-style state-planned economy. A subtext of left realism, at least according to my reading of it, is that discussions about radical transformation of the political-economic system of Western capitalist societies would be considered as 'ideal-istic,' or perhaps, unrealistic at this time. Critical criminologists, they tell us, should focus instead on developing crime-control strategies that are immediate, practicable alternatives to the crime-control policies of the right. This rejection of 'idealistic' solutions, when combined with the claimed socialist orientation of left realists, however, results in an apparent ambivalence regarding the role of the state as the site for the production of social change. Taylor argued that the state should serve as 'both an arena of job creation and a source of investment for production' (1982: 12) What is absent from such proposals about reducing social inequality through state mechanism, however, is an explanation of how this is to be done *effectively* without some radical restructuring of those markets in a society whose social order is predicated on the relatively free operation of labour and commodity markets.

If left realists discuss the problem of reducing inequality at all, it is often in terms of state mechanisms that can minimize some of the worst consequences of market-based distribution such as 'marginalization' of select populations (Lea and Young 1984: 208). Other left realists suggest that such problems be addressed, not through a reorganization of class relations, but through a better understanding of marginalized groups as subcultures (Taylor 1988: 21).

Developing welfare-state strategies to reduce inequality, or an increasing sensitivity to the subcultural characteristics of marginalized populations, does not, however, constitute a particularly socialist response to problems of crime. Instead, it is reminiscent of the liberal and social-democratic anti-poverty campaigns of the 1950s and 1960s.

Conclusion

In order for language to be useful, words must possess relatively stable mean-ings. Historically being a 'socialist' or being 'on the left' has signified a fundamental concern with issues of social class and class conflict (in a Marxian sense). Practical crime-control policies that do not address the problems of class, class conflict, and ownership and control over the means of production are not 'left' policies simply because they are formulated by Marxists or others who endorse the *idea* of socialism.

I am not arguing that, because many of the policy suggestions of left realists are not specifically aimed at transforming class relations in capitalist society, they are not worth pursuing. This kind of left purism is self-indulgent. There are many good reasons for critical criminologists to explore the development of practical policy alternatives to the crime-control strategies of current conservative governments. Many men and women in Britain, Canada, and the United States, as well as elsewhere in the modern capitalist world, live with an ever-present fear of street crime. Women live with the additional, life-organizing fear of sexual assault and harassment. Simultaneously, prisons are bursting with ever-larger, more crowded populations. In simple humanitarian terms these things must be addressed, and left-realist attempts to address them are to be applauded.

At the same time, I am concerned that left realists, by mislabelling liberal and social-democratic policies as 'left' policies, will derail the search for a critical, class-based sociological and historically grounded understanding of the relationship between crime and society. I think this problem is potentially greater in parliamentary democracies where left realists can hope to become the crime control think-tank for labour parties. Where political opportunities exist to improve the conditions and lives of both the victims and the doers of crime, they should be taken by critical criminologists. But I think there is a need to be cautious that in the current political climate we do not automatically identify anything that is 'not conservative' as 'left.'

In short, left realists may be leftists, but comparing most of their crime-control policies to those in Cuba, I would have to conclude that most left-realist policies are liberal in character in that they are designed to ameliorate some of the worst consequences of crime in capitalist societies, rather than to transform structural composition of market relations in those societies. On this point, I suggest that left realists consider the words of Boris Kagarlitsky: 'The market can serve as a guarantor and defender of individual interests, but it can never automatically serve common interests. For just this reason it cannot and must not occupy a central place in the system of values of a society striving to be democratic and humane. Each individual, irrespective of their talents, earnings and luck, must have the right to a dignified life. A society which turns this principle into its everyday practice will be a socialist society. People who have made this principle central to their lives must inevitably become socialist' (1989: 35).

Those of us who are interested in developing crime control policies from a socialist perspective should not mislead ourselves into thinking that simply because certain policies are in accord with common-sense popular wisdom about crime, can be adapted to the existing structure of labour and commodity markets, and can be implemented in the short term, that they will necessarily work, or that they represent an accurate analysis of the problem. Pragmatism may make for good politics in the short term. It does not necessarily make for either sound social inquiry or effective strategies for long-term social change.

Notes

1 Schwartz (1989) has suggested that, in addition to realist criminology, it is possible to identify emerging criminological paradigms associated, respectively, with deconstruction, the various models of feminism, and linguistics/semiotics.

2 By 'social democracy' I mean social formations wherein private ownership of the means of production is combined with a more or less extensive welfare state designed to ameliorate the worst socio-economic consequences of the private-sector economy.

3 Personal interview with Juan Escalona Riguera, Cuban minister of justice, 1985

4 According to Miguel Angel Garcia of the Office of the Attorney General, the only cases excluded are crime reports deemed false by the police or other investigating units. All other reported crimes are included, regardless of subsequent investigative or prosecutorial outcomes.

5 The data presented here have not been 'cooked' for foreign consumption. These are the same data used by the Cuban Ministry of Justice, the Office of the Attorney General, and the Ministry of the Interior for policy planning and personnel projections. They are consistent with seven-year aggregate figures on crime provided to the National Assembly, and with the distribution of offence types within my own compilation of case data from the archives of the *bufete*. The errors of reporting, recording, and transmission contained in these data are more or less consistent with those frequently discussed by criminologists, rather than deriving from some exceptional political motivation.

6 There are also some people, usually young men between the ages of eighteen and twenty-five, who choose not to work, even though they could. Various informants have estimated that these *desocupados* may account for as much as 8 per cent of the eighteen-to-twenty-five age group, although there is little way of verifying these estimates.

7 Since this research was conducted, the Cuban economy has had to absorb a number of shocks as a result of the deroutinization of its trade relations with the Soviet Union and other Eastern European nations. The government has conceded that economic growth is unlikely in the short term, and that Cubans must prepare for the sacrifices

of a wartime economy without war (Benjamin 1990; Zimbalist 1990). By the summer of 1992, Cubans found themselves struggling to maintain their former levels of consumption, given Cuba's weakened trade position. It remains to be seen if Cuban's will continue to support non-market forms of production and distribution, in the face of deepening economic problems.

8 Current regulations permit Cubans working outside the country to spend either the foreign currency paid to them or the unused portion of their per-diem allocation, at the *diplotiendas* (foreign currency stores) within ten days of their return to the country.

9 While in Cuba during spring 1989 I roomed with a Soviet ecologist for several weeks. He complained to me bitterly that the Cubans could buy Ladas for 4,000 pesos while the average Soviet citizen had to spend 8,000 of what he claimed were more valuable Soviet rubles to buy the equivalent car.

10 In preparation for the Fourth Congress of the Cuban Communist Party, scheduled for December 1989, considerable discussion occurred concerning a redefinition of the roles of the CDRs and the local-level FMC committees in order to eliminate areas where their functions currently overlap.

11 Personal interview with Denio Commacho, Chair of Legislative Review Committee of the Cuban National Assembly, 1990

12 Personal interviews with Renen Quiros, professor of law, University of Havana, 1989 and Julio Arranz, assistant professor, Faculty of Law, University of Havana, 1989

References

Anuario Estadistico de Cuba. 1986. Havana: Comite Estatal de Estadisticas

Benjamin, Medea. 1990. 'Things Fall Apart.' *NACLA: Report on the Americas*, 24 (2): 13-23

Cohen, Lawrence, and Marcus Felson. 1979. 'Social Change and Crime Rates: A Routine Activity Approach.' *American Sociological Review*, 46: 505-524

Cohen, Stanley. 1979. 'Community Crime Control.' *New Society*, 15 March

Escasena Guillarón, Jóse. 1988. 'Apuntes Sobre Algunas Modificaciones al Libro 1 del Codigo Penal.' *Revista Cubana de Derecho*, 34: 123-144

Evanson, Debra. 1989. *The Changing Role of Law in Revolutionary Cuba*. Madison, WI: The Institute for Legal Studies

Fukuyama, Francis. 1989. 'Entering Post-History.' *New Perspectives Quarterly*, 6 (Fall): 49-52

Giddens, Anthony, and David Held. 1982. *Classes, Power, and Conflict*. Los Angeles: University of California Press

Hunt, Alan. 1982. 'Law, Order, and Socialism: A Response to Ian Taylor.' *Crime and Social Justice*, 16 (Winter): 16-21

International Labor Organization. 1987. *Yearly Labor Statistics, 1983-1987*. The Hague: United Nations

Kagarlitsky, Boris. 1989. 'The Importance of Being Marxist.' *New Left Review*, 178 (Nov./Dec.): 29-36

Lea, J., and J. Young. 1984. *What Is to Be Done about Law and Order?* Harmondsworth: Penguin

MacLean, Brian. 1986. 'Alienation, Reification, and Beyond: A Political Economy of Crime,' in B.D. MacLean, ed., *The Political Economy of Crime*, 365-375. Scarborough, ON: Prentice-Hall

Matthews, Roger. 1987. 'Taking Realist Criminology Seriously.' *Contemporary Crises*, 11: 371-401

Mesa-Lago, Carmelo. 1989. 'The Cuban Economy in the 1980s: The Return of Ideology,' in I.L. Horowitz, ed., *Cuban Communism*, 187-226. New Brunswick, NJ: Transaction

Michalowski, Raymond. 1983. 'A Progressive Agenda for Crime Control.' *Crime and Social Justice*, 19 (Summer): 13-23

– 1989. 'Human Rights in Cuba.' Paper presented at the American Society of Criminology annual meeting, Reno, November

Painter, Kate. 1990. 'Women, Crime, and Social Space.' Paper presented at Realist Criminology: Crime Control and Policing in the 1990s, University of British Columbia and Simon Fraser University, Vancouver, May

Republic of Cuba. 1976/81. *Constitution of the Republic of Cuba*. Havana: Editoria Politica

Salas, Luis. 1979. *Social Control and Deviance in Cuba*. New York: Praeger

Schwartz, Martin. 1989. 'The Undercutting Edge of Criminology.' *Critical Criminologist*, 1 (2): 1-2, 5

Smith, Wayne S. 1987. *The Closest of Enemies*. New York: W.W. Norton

Sumner, Colin. 1976. 'Marxism and Deviance Theory,' in P. Wiles, ed., *The Sociology of Crime and Delinquency in Britain*, vol. 2: 159-174. London: Martin Robertson

Taylor, Ian. 1980. *Law and Order: Arguments for Socialism*. London: Macmillan

– 1982. 'Against Crime and for Socialism.' *Crime and Social Justice*, 18: 4-15

– 1988. 'Left Realism, the Free Market Economy, and the Problem of Social Order.' Paper presented at the American Society of Criminology meeting, Chicago

Telander, Paul. 1990. 'Your Sneakers or Your Life.' *Sports Illustrated*, 14 May: 37-43

United Nations. 1989. *Final Report of the Human Rights Commission*. Geneva

US Department of State. 1987. *Reports on Human Rights Practices in Cuba*. Washington, DC: USGPO

Van den Haag, Ernst. 1975. *Punishing Criminals*. New York: Basic Books

Viera, Margarita. 1986. *Criminologio*. Havana: Ministerio de Educacin Superior

Wilson, James Q. 1975. *Thinking about Crime*. New York: Vintage

Wilson, James Q., and George Kelling. 1982. 'Broken Windows.' *The Atlantic Monthly*, March: 29-38

Young, J. 1987. 'The Tasks Facing a Realist Criminology.' *Contemporary Crises*, 11: 337-356

Zimbalist, Andrew. 1990. 'Does the Economy Work?' *NACLA: Report on the Americas*, 24 (2): 16-19

7 Beyond Realist Criminology

Robert Menzies

However politically expedient and morally sensitive this [realist] solution might seem, it is prone to theoretical amnesia. What is gained by giving up the romantic and visionary excesses of the 1960s is lost by forgetting the truisms of the new criminology of that decade: that rules are created in ongoing collective struggles; that 'crime' is only one of many possible responses to conflict, rule breaking, and trouble; that the criminal law model (police, courts, prisons) has hopelessly failed as a guarantee of protection and social justice for the weak; that crime control bureaucracies become self-serving and self-fulfilling. These are truths that have not been refuted. (Cohen 1988: 271)

Times are hard for progressive criminologists. Nearly two decades have slipped away since Taylor, Walton, and Young's *The New Criminology* (1973) first turned heads. Megawatts of computer time have been burned up, movements mobilized, associations formed and fractured, the lines drawn and redrawn with seismographic regularity. But with what effect? From without, there is the unrelenting barrage of news about counterrevolution in Eastern Europe, Asia, and Latin America; the contradictions of Tiananmen Square; ten years and more of neoconservative politics in the flagship nation-states of the northwest. Inside the discipline, the engines of law and order churn remorselessly onward. The Good Ship Criminology has veered scarcely a fraction to port. In the centre of dissent, the mainstream has simply turned down the volume and gone on working.

Criminology still means criminal justice. And for those who had cut their teeth on New Left ideas and ideals, the revolutionary romance with crime has lost much of its lustre. The 1980s were a decade for recanting and reformulation. In the swirl of revision, crime and justice were two of the principal casualties. *En masse*, critical criminologists have turned to alternative fields of struggle, in legal studies, feminism, politics, labour, history, and the Third World. Those radicals who held onto the old disciplinary identities have been left to contend with their uneasy institutional alliances, to reflect on the roots of their disempowerment, and to bear witness to the right's increasing domination of the crime-control agenda. Critical criminology has limped painfully into its crisis of middle age.

The news gets even worse. From within the critical academy itself has come the left-bank onslaught of post-structuralism and post-modernism. The old radical categories are being ripped asunder. From Barthes to Baudrillard, Lacan to Lyotard, a deconstructionist, almost terrorist, impulse has invaded the human sciences and inspired an ontological implosion. For a time immune, or at least oblivious, radical, socialist, and feminist criminologists are increasingly both the authors and the subjects of this new-wave assault on totalization. At risk are not only the signs and politics of the oppressors, but the discursive and doctrinal glue that has held the criminological discipline together: 'the abolition of the criminal justice system is part of deconstructive strategy, as is also the abolition of criminology as a coercive signification system' (Hirvonen 1989: 70).

Nor are subversive categories themselves exempt from subversion. The very corner-stones of critical theorizing in criminology – the constitution of power in modes of production and patriarchy; the dialectical materialist understanding of history; the centrality of social class, gender, race and ethnicity in capitalist social relations; the concept of praxis as politically energized human agency; the juxtaposition of capitalist and socialist politico-economic formations – are subjected to the forces of ontological abolitionism (Davis and Schleifer 1985; Derrida 1976; Dews 1987; Foucault 1972, 1977a; Nicholson 1990; Ryan 1982; Said 1983). All rationalist modes of thinking, enlightenment philosophies of left and right, promises and refusals, utopias and dystopias alike have been decoded as so many interchangeable fictions. Like Burroughs's virus from outer space (see Lydenberg 1987), the parallel projects of post-structuralism and post-modernism have spread rapidly and seem to play no political favourites.

For many this is a troubling trend. As Palmer writes, the realm of discourse is not necessarily a land of life. 'Left to its own devices, poststructuralist theory will always stop short of interpretive clarity and a relationship ... premised on political integrity and a contextualized situating of [human] agents within structures of determination. Whatever insight can be gleaned from discourse theory and its privileging of language needs to be balanced with other appreciations drawn from more resolutely historical and materialist traditions. Without this balance, interpretation descends into discourse' (1990: 14). In its critique of the rational, its concentration on the Text, its kaleidoscopic conception of power-knowledge, its radical idealism, its silencing of the human subject, post-structuralism gainsays the very possibility of a dialectically constituted revolutionary politic. It offers a powerful critique of the referential, repressive, and normalizing structures that pass off experience as truth (Foucault 1977b, 1980), but its neo-Nietzchean method disallows either revelation or programmatic practice on behalf of the oppressed. In an epistemological anti-system where progress makes no sense (literally), it allows no vision of a 'progressive' political practice or an alternative social order.

Socialists and socialist feminists, in contrast, dwell in a world of political moralities, centralized power systems, human classes, ideological conversions, and structured possibilities for social change. In criminology, as elsewhere, a radical resistance to the deconstructionist campaign is grounded in these largely incommensurable epistemologies, and in the mutually alien practices they invoke. For post-structuralism and post-modernism, socialism represents one more rationalist residual of the enlightenment. For the latter, this new wave is a dangerous diversion, which threatens to dissolve not just the edifices and languages of oppression, but along with them much that is politically transformative about the modernist sensibility (Dews 1987; Kroker and Cook 1987; Palmer 1990).

The Realist Revival

Now in the very midst of this maelstrom – between New Right politics and deconstructionist discourse – has come the realist revival in criminology. This 'most recent contender from the radical stable' (Young 1988: 178) has been spawned in turbulent waters. It has emerged as a threefold strategic and tactical response: against the fusion of modernism and conservatism in the 1970s and 1980s ('right realism'); against the deconstructive dazzle of the post-modernist alternative ('the descent into discourse'); and finally, in the context of these rival transgressions, against what is perceived to be the New Left's own lethargic lurch towards isolationism, culturalism, theoreticism, and political suicide ('left idealism').

Whether explicit or unspoken, self-conscious or otherwise, the left-realist message is very much about reconstituting the progressive agenda. It is about restoring order, working backward and inward towards a progressive core, delivering a manifesto for action and accountability, sketching the correspondences between modernist philosophies and political struggles. And for criminology, it is about nothing less than disciplinary survival – a reaction to the 'decriminalization of criminology' (Shearing 1989) and to the attendant monopolization of the law-and-order question by positivists and managerialists alike (Cohen 1988; Young 1979, 1988).

All of this has much appeal. Whatever its epistemological contradictions – in particular, its uncharted relationship to *philosophical* realism (see Giddens 1976; Keat and Urry 1982; O'Neill 1972) – a criminological realism of the left promises to preserve its radical constructs and to clarify praxis.

Realism draws in the critical lens, shedding peripheral utopian diversions, and localizing its fields within familiar contours of time and space. It works in a world of questions and answers, actions and outcomes, problems and solutions, cause and effect. As a rationalist system, realism exudes a conviction in the stability and practicality of empirical knowledge. It holds: 'that there are general standards of scientificity, of what counts as an adequate explanation, of what it is that we must try to achieve by scientific theories, of the manner in which empirical evidence should be used to assess their truth or falsity' (Keat and Urry 1982: 44). Its promotion of reason is realism's antidote for the problematization of knowledge and existence. Against the guerrilla methods of deconstruction movements (Baudrillard 1975, 1987; Newman 1985), realism represents the victory of logic over revelation, structure over dissolution, science over faith, essential over phenomenal, local over global, the past and present over the future. And when aligned with a progressive politic, realism may present an enticing prospect, especially to disillusioned New Left veterans in search of winnable skirmishes.

Such has been the case with realist criminology. Realism about crime, law, and justice has been embraced largely on the strength of its philosophy of reassurance and its politics of immediacy. For critical criminologists in Britain (Kinsey, Lea, and Young 1986; Lea 1987; Lea and Young 1984; Matthews 1987a; Matthews and Young 1986; Taylor 1981) and their radical and liberal counterparts in North America (Currie 1985; Morris and Hawkins 1970; Pepinsky 1980), it also opens up a seeming wealth of programmatic possibilities. Realists are refreshingly aware of their own limitations. Constraints of structure and imagination are to be acknowledged as immanent features of the progressive environment. What is impossible should be suspended or abandoned altogether. Pragmatism must prevail. Criminal justice, law, order, and punishment can all be resurrected and converted into instruments of empowerment. The old categories are once again to be 'taken seriously' in critical practices: crime rates, legal codes, violence, victimization, social defence, policing, local government, the community. The state and its institutions, rather than being an ineluctable organ of oppression, are a latent ally. 'Realism rejects a utopian strategy of waiting for the state to wither away, knowing that we would only have to reinvent it if it did' (Lea 1987: 369).

Over the course of the past decade and more, realist criminology has been energized by the experience of exclusion, by the quest for relevancy, by a generalized sense of impotence among progressive criminologists, and by the frustrations that cascade out of criminology's multiple failings and domestications. Critical approaches to crime and justice have not punched many holes in the enterprise or its conventional problematics. It turns out that Inciardi (1980) was right – and that the crises in radical criminology did arrive precisely on schedule. And on the leeward side of the discipline, for administrative criminologists and positivists, it has largely been more and more (and more) of the same. Thirty minutes of shmoozing around an ASC conference lobby are worth a thousand petulant paragraphs on the history of ideas.

The point for realists is not to deconstruct or reconstruct the world of law and order, but to take care of business in the here and now. And if the business of criminology is crime, for progressives it needs to be the experience, prevention, and control of crime on behalf of those who, on the basis of their class, gender, race, ethnicity, sexuality, ideology, and so on, are casualties of the capitalist patriarchal order. Such a strategy is viewed as a major reinvestment in the criminological discipline as an accountable player in the law-and-order derby. It demands new scripts for a radical criminology that throughout the New Right era has been painfully far-sighted. According to Lea and Young's six-point manifesto (1986: 359-363), it is high time to regrind the lens:

1. Crime really is a problem.
2. We must look at the reality behind appearances.
3. We must take crime control seriously.
4. We must look realistically at the circumstances of both the offender and the victim.
5. We must be realistic about policing.
6. We must be realistic about the problem of crime in the present period.

All of these items are embedded in a populist, participatory, and particularistic discourse. Realists aspire to bring human beings back into the crime-control equation, as a stark contrast to the abstractions of left idealism; to the poststructuralist dismemberment of subjectivity; and, in particular, to the faceless gloom of administrative criminology (Young 1988). They spurn intellectualism and Leninism. Their criminological *perestroika* is geared to programs of alliance, reconciliation, and democratization. They are willing to serve and protect. If they stop short of representing an 'amazing new left law and order campaign' (Steinert 1985), realist criminologists are at least candid about their position on the problem of urban crime. And they are willing to make moral bargains, to dirty their hands, to inflict punishment as a tool of social justice. Like Wolff, Moore, and Marcuse (1970), they recognize that an anodine tolerance can often be the purest form of repression. Much better to join the fight against crime, and to work with what works. Their beverage of choice is beer not Beaujolais.

Against Realist Criminology

So, what is wrong with this left-realist agenda? Whatever the nuances and overtones, the realist quest for engagement is plainly both necessary and vitalizing. The attractions of realism have been the subject of much dynamic and persuasive writing (Lea and Young 1984; Young 1975, 1979, 1987, 1988; Taylor 1982), although this is not the place to review that literature. As a revivalist program there is no question that realism contains at least the seeds of a people's criminology. This observation has been made recurrently by Young (1975, 1987). And even a diffident critic like Cohen concedes that realism 'moves closer to the commonsense, public knowledge of what constitutes the crime problem' (1988: 19) and that its concerns are 'clear and convincing' (1987: 368).

Still, in what follows I argue that, for all its attractions, the realist impulse harbours some dangerous precedents for critical work on crime and justice. All is not well on the front lines. If indeed 'the tide *is* turning for radical criminology' (Matthews and Young 1986: 1), the outcome is still very much in doubt. Philosophically, politically, and pragmatically, realism is far more ambiguous, more contradictory, than either sponsors or opponents would concede. In taking realism itself seriously, in trying to contextualize this 'general air of hard-nosed realism' (Sumner 1983: 187), it is not especially helpful either to proclaim the movement to be a disciplinary panacea or to renounce it paranoically as an opportunistic coalition with the centre and right. Neither in itself is an accurate depiction.

For one thing, there are many realisms. After fifteen years and more of realist criminologies from right, left, and centre, it is apparent that this body of work is a political, discursive, and programmatic amoeba. It defies condensation. Like its predecessors in art, literature, cinema, architecture, philosophy, and law (Cotterrell 1984; Crisp 1988; Frank 1949; Hunt 1978; Lee 1989; Marcus 1986; Rhode 1976; Smith, 1986), the criminological variant of realism is highly diffuse, historically conditioned, author specific, and (ironically) resistant to glib categorization. Further, it embodies intriguing projective properties that are as revealing about the wider discipline as about realism itself. For all of the reasons outlined above, and throughout this book, the project in its various forms is an apt catalyst for debate about critical options in the 1990s. It mirrors, even if in highly refracted images, the multiple dimensions of radical thought and action in criminology.

The writings of realists and their critics recurrently circulate around critical criminology's Great Identity Crisis. It is precisely here – in its prescriptive content, its offering of resolutions, its self-promotion as a radical liberator – that realism stakes its central claim, and where it ultimately implodes. Realism recommends internal medicine for what ails criminologists on the left. Its epitaph might well read 'For Criminology.' The preservationism that characterizes realist approaches to state, law, and crime is also onanistically applied. In a chorus of voices, not always in harmony, its proponents unite in pushing disciplinary reconstruction – back from radical humanism in its many forms, and from interdisciplinary dependencies, and towards the reaffirmation of criminology as a progressive force with which to be reckoned (it is significant, for example, that much of the momentum has come from British institutes, schools, and centres of criminology more so than from cognate fields). If it is true that 'one must belong to a tradition to *hate* it properly' (Adorno, cited in Cohen 1988: v), the same might be also said for *love*. And realism's monogamous relationship with criminology translates into a one-sided and uncritical acceptance of the core discipline, its domain assumptions, and its principal constructs.

Space precludes a comprehensive critique of the central underlying concepts in realist criminology. But a brief glance at three of these – the 'state,' the 'community,' and the 'victim' – should help to cement my point. Realist analysis's cavalier treatment of these fundamental issues lays bare its arid qualities and its questionable politics. The hazards of realist practices begin to emerge. Holes open everywhere, and contradictions abound.

First, criminological realism has yet to yield a coherent theory of the state. Its drift away from socialism and towards social democracy has come at the cost of a theoretically energized praxis. In realist writings, the immediate problems of crime are excised from wider questions of capitalist and patriarchal formations, class and gender struggles, and the political economy of nation-states. This separation of issues has been principally the product of its members' introduction to, or reconciliation with, labour-party politics in the desperate hours of the neoconservative revolution (Addario and Gavigan 1983; Taylor 1981, 1983). Against the Thatcherite juggernaut, social-democratic policies and strategies took on a renewed relevance. Pockets opened up at the local-council level, particularly in inner-city London and the north, which offered zones of relative immunity from the New Right onslaught. It was within these municipal arenas that social-democratic practices survived, and realist policies on crime, welfare, policing, law, order, and justice were forged. Criminologists invested heavily in local governments of the left, working with community policing initiatives (Kinsey, Lea, and Young 1986), serving as researchers and consultants on drugs, prostitution, young offenders, and urban violence (Dorn and South 1985; Kinsey, Lea, and Young 1986; Matthews 1986; Matthews and Young 1986), and turning out a steady stream of survey research in rebuttal to Home Office depictions of crime patterns (Hanmer and Saunders 1984; Jones, MacLean, and Young 1986; Jones, Lea, and Young 1987; Kinsey 1984).

In the process, however, the centralized state, and its institutions of surveillance and coercion, have been relegated to the political backstage. Revolutionary strategies have been replaced by democratic tactics. Aspirations have been scaled down, the time frame telescoped, and the state itself dichotomized into fragmented venues of activism at the local level, and centralized monoliths of reaction globally. For realists, the latter have largely been reserved as the site for some future electoral contest. This is a costly deferral. As Michalowski (this volume) writes: 'I am concerned that left realists, by mislabelling liberal and social democratic policies as "left" policies, will derail the search for a class-based understanding of the relationship between crime and society. I think this problem is potentially greater in parliamentary democracies where left realists can hope to become the crime-control think-tank for labour parties ... I think there is a need to be careful that in the current hegemonic conservative political climate we do not automatically identify anything that is "not Right" as "Left."'
Further, in realist writing there is little theorization about how the proximate and central states, or the private and the public, are to be articulated within a comprehensive social-democratic program. On the subject of crime control, realist formulations are alarmingly undeveloped. Lea simply asserts that 'realism is an attempt to work out a new form of relationship between centralized criminal justice and community alternatives' (1987: 365) and that popular practices and organizations can float 'alongside criminal justice.' But there is no attempt to chart the form or content of these relations, or to explore their implications. Seemingly oblivious to the warnings of political theorists and revisionist writers on social control (see Abel 1982; Cain 1985; Henry 1983; Lowman, Menzies, and Palys 1987), realists resort to rather hollow reassurances about the mutually regulating features of pluralistic systems. The proposition that decentralization equates with democratization – that 'healthy conflict' will prevail between various levels of the state, and between state and civil society – appears oddly utopian, particularly when couched in the sharp resonance of realist discourse.

Nor do realists come to terms with the structural contradictions of their own populist ideology. What is it that separates the localized and nationalized populisms of the realist left and right, particularly when it comes to law and order? How can the social-democratic local state sustain and expand its counter-hegemonic basis of support without simply emulating the law-and-order policies of national neoconservatives? How are realists to street-proof themselves – to guard against the authoritarian drift that so often accompanies the long-term exposure of policy makers to the 'realities' of crime control? On these and related questions, realist writing is strangely silent.

Second, there is realism's sanguine reliance on programs of 'community' policing and 'community' justice. Sedimented through realist writing is the tendency to confound populism with democracy, to presume that smaller is better, and to ignore the ideological contradictions of 'people's power' and 'people's justice.' The uncritical reliance on localized and particularized politics-from-below, without a recursive and historically specific relational analysis, is perilous. The state, the political economy, the law, ideological and cultural formations, cannot be so conveniently bracketed off. The struggles cannot be insulated within state-proof pockets of local activism, without in the long term risking the co-optation or annihilation of progressive practices.

Whereas it is necessary to take community seriously as an empowering source and site of popular politics, the exclusive reliance on community power – public or private – can amount to playing with dynamite, unless organized horizontally and vertically along multiple fronts, and unless situated dialectically in an enabling structural and ideological environment. Otherwise, community justice can rapidly disconnect from the rule of law, and community policing can devolve into vigilantism as recent experience in Brazil and Columbia have chillingly shown. As Hunt writes, 'the appeal to popular justice is an open invitation to make use of exemplary punishments in response to social or moral panic' (1982: 17). Such 'romanticizing of the community' is a leitmotif in realist criminology, as even its own advocates have at times conceded (Lea and Young 1984).

Experience with people's justice in revolutionary Cuba and Nicaragua, along with other progressive Third World nations (see Michalowski, this volume), is especially germane. Community politics, justice, and policing in Cuba, as constituted in the CDRs (Committees for the Defense of the Revolution), are highly integrated and operate as mediators between citizens and the state. The role of the CDRs extends far beyond the securing of social order, based on the recognition that local law-and-order activities need to transcend issues of public safety alone. This is the lesson to be taken from popular justice practices in socialist states: namely, that the defence of the community must be projected far beyond the narrow boundaries of crime and criminology, and towards alliances with women's support groups, shelter/homelessness issues, health care, day care, recreation, education, and so forth. Such multiple community fronts present a great progressive advance over single-issue campaigns that concentrate on social protection alone (and that can unwittingly reinforce the hegemonic command of the authoritarian right). As Michalowski writes (this volume), a genuinely democratic community movement 'necessitates widespread commitment to some overarching set of principles or beliefs.'

Third, there is the realist promise to contribute a radical victimology. Here as well, realists reveal their preservationist inclinations – their confidence in the capacity to radicalize the traditional pursuits, methods, and preoccupations of criminology *as* criminology – to occupy mainstream epistemologies and projects and give them a politically correct ideological twist.

This is a seductive reconstruction project, but with troubling implications. There is danger in deproblematizing the victim. Despite periodic gesturing by some realists towards notions of 'social symmetry' (Lea and Young 1984; Young 1988), for the most part their radical victimology devolves into public protectionism, raising palpable rigid lines of demarcation between criminal victims and offenders. In the process, they risk bypassing the victim concept altogether as a catalyst for social change. The counterhegemonic power of feminist work on *inter*-gender violence (Edwards 1989; Gregory 1987; Hanmer and Maynard 1987; MacKinnon 1987) does not transpose easily when applied to the *intra*-class and *intra*-ethnic transgressions studied by realists. In zooming in on the victim, progressive criminologists need to avoid divesting the construct of critical content. Victim research on the left must open up the concept, acknowledging that victimology is about more than crime, law, order, and violence. It should be concentrating on the correspondences between crime and related victimizations.

In taking the victim seriously – and in rightfully retiring for good the false-consciousness premise that frames the hostility of so many critical criminologists to victimology and fear-of-crime research – realists need also to restrain their own tendencies towards reification. They have to maintain a tension between experience and interest, avoiding the uncritical acceptance of victims' perceptions as primal. That too is an epistemological split and political straitjacket.

Finally, criminal victimization is not an insular phenomenon. It *does* continue to intersect with victimization by sexism, racism, political corruption, corporate mayhem, illiteracy, sexual harassment, overpolicing, undersupport, and so forth. These old 'idealist' insights still apply. And it is through these convergences that a criminological victimology might conceivably function as an instrument of empowerment, in highlighting people's strengths, not weaknesses (Cohen 1988: 264-265), and in resisting the tendency to harness the revelations of crime victims into a rationale for intensified control programs in alleged defence of the weak.

Towards a Reflexive Alternative

Just where exactly are the windmills against which realist criminologists have been tilting since the mid to late 1970s? What is this idealist illusion that Cohen (1988) sardonically characterizes as a 'thought crime'? In the realist literature idealism seems to assume many faces, many facets, many forms: constructionism, abolitionism, Fanonism, phenomenalism, instrumentalism, functionalism, culturalism, post-structuralism, post-modernism, this-ism, that-ism ...

Now, some of these have presented easy and disturbingly convenient targets. It is hard not to choke on concepts like the 'problematic situation' (Hulsman 1986) and 'radical non-intervention' (Schur 1973). The 'deviance, yeah, right on' impulse that Pearson (1975) wrote about so beautifully did indeed carry the critical project farther and farther outward, away from the hard cruel world of evil and pain; through increasingly digestible safety zones of inquiry, politics, and practice; and towards romantic fields where deviance could be appreciated, celebrated, and often joined. Out there in the New Left soap opera (Mairowitz 1976), it was not so surprising that the subjects were so damned attractive and alluring. They were often ourselves. And of course the middle fingers in those heady times were at best pointed only vaguely in the direction of the Establishment, and the decontrol talk centred on retracting the talons, leaving people alone wherever possible, refusing to deviantize (and certainly to criminalize) social diversity (Taylor, Walton, and Young 1973), and so on and so on.

But that is all a jaded tale, better told elsewhere (Wiles 1976; Cohen 1981, 1988; Young 1988). It is also far more mythic than the realist literature would allow. While it may be true that the revolutionary drift precipitated a sometimes hoary humanism drained of realpolitik, this was hardly a one-sided affair. After all, contrary to some accounts, the Old Left did not self-immolate in 1968. And its materially grounded agenda was very much a part of the struggles taken up by the 'new' criminologists from Sheffield to Berkeley. In their caricatured retrospective on the adolescence of progressive criminologies, realists have paradoxically done *themselves* a disservice most of all. For embedded in their assault on idealism is a rather strained, self-referential, and autocritical *cri de coeur*. And at least to some degree this amounts to a rewriting of criminological history.

Many of the projects and projections of the NDC, and even of North American radical criminology, *were* on the right track; they *did* confront the 'realities' of crime (even if these were pluralized, deconstructed, opened up, shouldered away from the discipline's gravitational core); and they *still* merit the 'cautious reaffirmation' advised by Cohen (1987: 368). Looking back, for most people, for the most part, the infantile disorder (Spitzer 1980) decried by realism either proved to be quickly fatal or it soon built up immunities and ran its course. This is not to say that idealism in the wrong hands did no damage (Young [1979; 1987] accurately – if one-sidedly – documents the worst of those times). But the last song in that particular opera was sung a long time ago, and in any event we have faced the Enemy, and more often than not it, too, was ourselves, looking through the past darkly.

And when it comes to the question of constructing a dialectical and politically animated alternative, I think that it is simply wrong to suggest that a genuinely socialist-feminist-humanist criminology is remotely in danger of relinquishing the crime problem to the centre and right. But in working these muddy frontiers between critique and action, it is imperative that progressive criminologies contend with and transcend the various barriers that have paradoxically been thrown up through the realist reflex. Among the most seductive of these sidetracks have been the *insulation* of crime and criminalization from political economy, patriarchy, ideology, organization, culture, and the workplace; the *essentializing* of crime through superhistorical and inevitiblist discourse and practice (the undercurrent of realism's misleading campaign against 'impossibilism': see Matthews 1987b); and the *hypostatization* of crime as a primal and reified 'social problem.'

In combating these realist tendencies, and others, an historically informed and recursive praxis remains the key. When it comes to criminological programs, analysis and action must remain open. Different crimes and oppressions involve different sets of relations, different methods, and different politics. Crime is not a unitary phenomenon, nor is it ontologically accessible on its own, or anterior to its official legal construction. Superficial gesturing to these pivotal notions (as in Lea and Young 1984) is not enough.

Along with this, non-criminal pains, deprivations, and victimizations are imminently intertwined with crime in the experiences of women; the working class; the underclass; lesbians, bisexuals, and gay men; ethnic, racial, and ideological minorities; imperialized and colonialized peoples; and various other oppressed groups. A radical victimology is about more than fists, syringes, wallets, guns, and broken windows (contrast Matthews and Currie, this volume). The crime concept as social currency must be allowed to float.

At the level of theory, idealism versus realism is a disorienting dualism. It is a Manichean Jeckyl/Hyde split, where each side becomes a single spectral half of the radical personality. This strange separation amounts to yet another depressing example of the more suicidal inclinations among the criminological left. Reaction and counterreaction are too often internalized, directed against competitive dissenters, cleaving ultimately into a blinding disarray of oppositions: material versus ideal, essence versus appearance, form versus content, pessimism versus optimism, local versus global, individual versus state, victim versus offender, short versus long term, criminology versus politics, reformist versus structural change, and so on and so on.

Neither realism nor idealism can singly ignite a progressive politic or practice in criminology. A fusion, a genuinely reflexive criminology (to borrow the concept from Gouldner [1970] and O'Neill [1972]), can be neither ideal nor real, abstentionist nor preservationist, voluntarist nor determinist, romantic nor condemnatory, future- nor present-sited, state- nor community-centred. On this point I would dispute Cohen's contention that 'the old choice still remains: between visionary politics and realpolitik' (1988: 233). I think the very notion that one needs to *make* a choice, that a progressive fight against crime is somehow incompatible with alternative visions about the order of things, has been the legacy of defensive formalism in an era dominated by the push of Thatcherism, Reaganism, monetarism, and realism on the right, and the pull of post-structuralist and post-modernist carnage on the left.

But a radical reconstruction of criminology simply cannot be premised on a foreclosure of the critical imagination. Heads cannot entirely replace hearts. The dense discourse of rationality and expediency that characterizes so much of realism has to be tempered with a cautious reaffirmation, not a bracketing, of humanism – that 'squeak of hope' preferred by Maureen Cain (1985). And this requires a criminology with a future tense (a theory of the state, ideology, patriarchal relations, and socialist practice), as much as the past and present tenses in which realism is encased (through its quest to resolve, respectively, the aetiological crisis of criminology and the political problem of crime).

Can all of this be confined solely within the boundaries of a discipline called criminology? My answer is obviously no. I think we have drifted far beyond the point where purely criminological prescriptions for either order or disorder will help us much. The shifts in the orthodoxy charted so well by Jock Young have solidified the centre and right. These latter have bulked up, generating currents of resistance and management that can easily destabilize and deconstruct progressive projects that are thrown up from the inside. With Michalowski, Carlen (this volume), and others, I harbour deep misgivings about the social-democratic, *tercerista*, neo-Fabian inclinations that define the most dominant strain of realism in Britain and North America (with its mixed-economy relation to justice and its formalism, incrementalism, and preservationism). I wonder about the capacity of realist criminology *as* criminology to maintain a progressive edge, within a largely hostile academic, correctional, and political environment, in its advocacy of such apparently restrained criminal justice measures as demarginalization, minimalism, and pre-emptive deterrence (cf. Lea and Young 1984).

When Nils Christie spoke at the opening of the Sheffield Centre for Criminology, he remarked that the criminologist's role should be to close not open such centres (see Cohen 1988: 10). One need not be an abstentionist, nor even (entirely) an abolitionist, to take his point. Although this too may devolve into a Hobson's choice (between criminology and nothing), the question remains whether British, European, US, and Canadian criminology as currently constituted (politically, discursively, institutionally) is capable, in this particular configuration of time and space, of steaming entirely under its own disciplinary momentum towards a socialist, feminist, anti-racist, anti-imperialist politic and practice.

I, for one, think it needs help. And on this point – its lack of vision, and its failure to evoke a genuinely transformative politic outside of the criminological realm – the realist program must be rejected. As Cohen writes (1988: 228): 'the further we move from the discourse of *criminal* justice, the more likely we are to find the conditions for realizing [progressive] values' and 'to be realistic about law and order must mean to be unrealistic (that is, imaginative) about the possibilities of order without law.' Or, in a convergence too bizarre for words, Klockars said something similar: 'imagination is one thing, criminology another' (1980: 93).

My point is simply this. In that lonely last Althusserian instance, when the dialectic dance has come full circle, realism may come to play its most important role, but not as a radical odyssey back to the core of criminology nor as a progressive antidote to the crime problem. Instead, it may fashion its place in criminological history as a kind of antithesis, the oppositional force that might very well, and at long last, push critical criminology beyond its theoretical, political, and discursive boundaries towards a genuine fusion – a socialist, feminist, humanist enterprise that embraces both the transcendental visions of idealism and the hard politics of a realist agenda. And after all these years, Paul Hirst (1975) might yet have the last word. Such a synthesis could once and for all transport us far beyond the fringes of criminology altogether.

I would like to thank Dorothy Chunn, John Lowman, and Ted Palys for their comments, as well as students in my 1990 graduate seminar in criminological theory.

References

Abel, Richard, ed. 1982. *The Politics of Informal Justice*, vol. 1: *The American Experience*, vol. 2: *Comparative Studies*. New York: Academic
Addario, S.M., and S.A.M. Gavigan. 1983. 'An Interview with Jock Young.' *Canadian Criminology Forum*, 6 (1): 107-116
Baudrillard, J. 1975. *The Mirror of Production*. St Louis: Telos
– 1987. *Forget Foucault*. New York: Foreign Agents/Semiotext(e)

Cain, M. 1985. 'Beyond Informal Justice.' *Contemporary Crises*, 9: 335-373

Cohen, S. 1981. 'Footprints on the Sand: A Further Report on Criminology and the Sociology of Deviance in Britain,' in M. Fitzgerald, G. McLennan, and J. Pawson, eds., *Crime and Society: Readings in History and Theory*, 220-247. London: Routledge and Kegan Paul

– 1987. 'Taking Decentralization Seriously: Values, Visions and Policies,' in J. Lowman, R.J. Menzies, and T.S. Palys, eds., *Transcarceration: Essays in the Sociology of Social Control*, 358-379. Aldershot: Gower

– 1988. *Against Criminology*. New Brunswick, NJ: Transaction

Cotterrell, R. 1984. *The Sociology of Law: An Introduction*. London: Butterworths

Crisp, C.G. 1988. *Eric Rohmer: Realist and Moralist*. Bloomington: Indiana University Press

Currie, E. 1985. *Confronting Crime: An American Challenge*. New York: Pantheon

Davis, R.C., and R. Schleifer, eds. 1985. *Rhetoric and Form: Deconstruction at Yale*. Norman: University of Oklahoma Press

Derrida, J. 1976. *On Grammatology*. Baltimore, MD: Johns Hopkins University Press

Dews, P. 1987. *Logics of Disintegration: Post-structuralist Thought and the Claims of Critical Theory*. London: Verso

Dorn, N., and N. South. 1985. *Helping Drug Users*. Aldershot: Gower

Edwards, S.M. 1989. *Policing 'Domestic' Violence: Women, the Law and the State*. London: Sage

Foucault, M. 1972. *The Archaeology of Knowledge and the Discourse on Language*. New York: Pantheon

– 1977a. *Language, Counter-Memory, Practice: Selected Essays and Interviews*. Ithaca, NY: Cornell University Press

– 1977b. *Discipline and Punish: The Birth of the Prison*. New York: Pantheon

– 1980. *The History of Sexuality*. vol. 1: *An Introduction*. New York: Vintage

Frank, J.N. 1949. *Courts on Trial: Myth and Reality in American Justice*. Princeton, NJ: Princeton University Press

Giddens, A. 1976. *New Rules of Sociological Method: A Positive Critique of Interpretative Sociologies*. London: Hutchinson

Gouldner, A.W. 1970. *The Coming Crisis of Western Sociology*. New York: Avon

Gregory, J. 1987. *Sex, Race and the Law*. London: Sage

Hanmer, J., and M. Maynard, eds. 1987. *Women, Violence and Social Control*. Atlantic Highlands, NJ: Humanities Press International

Hanmer, J., and S. Saunders. 1984. *Well-Founded Fear: A Community Study of Violence to Women*. London: Hutchinson

Henry, S. 1983. *Private Justice: Towards Integrating Theorizing in the Sociology of Law*. London: Routledge and Kegan Paul

Hirst, P.Q. 1975. 'Marx and Engels on Law, Crime and Morality,' in I. Taylor, P. Walton, and J. Young, eds., *Critical Criminology*, 203-232. London: Routledge and Kegan Paul

Hirvonen, A. 1989. 'Forget Criminology: The Radical Strategies of Abolition and Deconstruction,' in B. Rolston and M. Tomlinson, eds., *Justice and Ideology: Strategies for the 1990s*, Working Paper no. 9, 60-72. London: The European Group for the Study of Deviance and Social Control

Hulsman, L.H.C. 1986. 'Critical Criminology and the Concept of Crime.' *Contemporary Crises*, 10 (1): 63-80

Hunt, A. 1978. *The Sociological Movement in Law*. London: Macmillan

– 1982. 'Law, Order and Socialism: A Response to Ian Taylor.' *Crime and Social Justice*, 18: 16-22

Inciardi, J. A. 1980. *Radical Criminology: The Coming Crises*. Beverly Hills: Sage

Jones, T., J. Lea, and J. Young. 1987. *Saving the Inner City: The First Report of the Broadwater Farm Survey*. London: Middlesex Polytechnic, Centre for Criminology

Jones, T., B.D. MacLean, and J. Young. 1986. *The Islington Crime Survey*. Aldershot: Gower

Keat, R., and J. Urry. 1982. *Social Theory as Science*. 2d ed. London: Routledge and Kegan Paul

Kinsey, R. 1984. *First Report on the Merseyside Crime Survey*. Liverpool: Merseyside City Council

Kinsey, R., J. Lea, and J. Young. 1986. *Losing the Fight against Crime*. Oxford: Basil Blackwell

Klockars, C.B. 1980. 'The Contemporary Crises of Marxist Criminology,' in J.A. Inciardi, ed., *Radical Criminology: The Coming Crises*, 92-123. Beverly Hills: Sage

Kroker, A., and D. Cook. 1987. *The Postmodern Scene: Excremental Culture and Hyper-Aesthetics*. Montreal: New World Perspectives

Lea, J. 1987. 'Left Realism: A Defence.' *Contemporary Crises*, 11: 357-370

Lea, J., and J. Young. 1984. *What Is to Be Done about Law and Order?* Harmondsworth: Penguin

Lee, A. 1989. *Realism and Power: Postmodern British Fiction*. London: Routledge

Lowman, J., R.J. Menzies, and T.S. Palys, eds. 1987. *Transcarceration: Essays in the Sociology of Social Control*. Aldershot: Gower

Lydenberg, R. 1987. *Word Cultures: Radical Theory and Practice in William S. Burroughs' Fiction*. Urbana: University of Illinois Press

MacKinnon, C.A. 1987. *Feminism Unmodified: Discourses on Life and Law*. Cambridge, MA: Harvard University Press

Mairowitz, D.Z. 1976. *The Radical Soap Opera: Roots of Failure in the American Left*. Harmondsworth: Penguin

Marcus, M.J. 1986. *Italian Film in the Light of Neorealism*. Princeton, NJ: Princeton University Press

Matthews, R. 1986. *Policing Prostitution: A Multi-Agency Approach*. London: Middlesex Polytechnic, Centre for Criminology

– 1987a. 'Taking Realist Criminology Seriously.' *Contemporary Crises*, 11: 371-401

– 1987b. 'Decarceration and Social Control: Fantasies and Realities,' in J. Lowman, R.J. Menzies, and T.S. Palys, eds., *Transcarceration: Essays in the Sociology of Social Control*, 338-357. Aldershot: Gower

Matthews, R., and J. Young, eds. 1986. *Confronting Crime*. London: Sage

Morris, N., and G. Hawkins. 1970. *The Honest Politician's Guide to Crime Control*. Chicago: University of Chicago Press

Newman, C. 1985. *The Post-Modern Aura*. Evanston, IL: Northwestern University Press

Nicholson, L. J., ed. 1990. *Feminism/Postmodernism*. New York: Routledge, Chapman and Hall

O'Neill, J. 1972. *Sociology as a Skin Trade: Essays towards a Reflexive Sociology*. New York: Harper and Row

Palmer, B.D. 1990. *Descent into Discourse: The Reification of Language and the Writing of Social History*. Philadelphia: Temple University Press

Pearson, G. 1975. *The Deviant Imagination*. London: Macmillan

Pepinsky, H.E. 1980. *Crime Control Strategies*. New York: Oxford University Press

Rhode, E. 1976. *A History of the Cinema from Its Origins to 1970*. New York: Plenum

Ryan, M. 1982. *Marxism and Deconstruction: A Critical Articulation*. Baltimore, MD: Johns Hopkins University Press

Said, E. 1983. *The World, the Text, and the Critic*. Cambridge: Cambridge University Press

Schur, E.M. 1973. *Radical Non-Intervention: Rethinking the Delinquency Problem*. Englewood Cliffs, NJ: Prentice-Hall

Shearing, C.D. 1989. 'Decriminalizing Criminology: Reflections on the Literal and Tropological Meanings of the Term.' *Canadian Journal of Criminology*, 31 (2): 169-178

Smith, M.J. 1986. *Realist Thought from Weber to Kissinger*. Baton Rouge: Louisiana State University Press

Spitzer, S. 1980. '"Left-wing" Criminology – An Infantile Disorder?' in J.A. Inciardi, ed., *Radical Criminology: The Coming Crises*, 169-190. Beverly Hills: Sage

Steinert, H. 1985. 'The Amazing New Left Law and Order Campaign.' *Contemporary Crises*, 9 (4): 21-38

Sumner, C. 1983. 'Rethinking Deviance: Toward a Sociology of Censures,' in R.J. Simon and S. Spitzer, eds., *Research in Law, Deviance and Social Control*, vol. 5: 187-204. San Francisco: JAI Press

Taylor, I. 1981. *Law and Order: Arguments for Socialism*. London: Macmillan

– 1982. 'Against Crime and For Socialism.' *Crime and Social Justice*, 18: 4-15

– 1983. *Crime, Capitalism and Community: Three Essays in Socialist Criminology*. Toronto: Butterworths

Taylor, I., P. Walton, and J. Young. 1973. *The New Criminology: For a Social Theory of Deviance*. London: Routledge and Kegan Paul

Wiles, P. 1976. *The Sociology of Crime and Delinquency in Britain*, vol. 2. Oxford: Martin Robertson

Wolff, R., P.B. Moore Jr., and H. Marcuse. 1970. *Critique of Pure Tolerance*. Boston: Beacon Press

Young, J. 1975. 'Working Class Criminology,' in I. Taylor, P. Walton, and J. Young, eds., *Critical Criminology*, 63-94. London: Routledge and Kegan Paul

– 1979. 'Left Idealism, Reformism and Beyond: From New Criminology to Marxism,' in B. Fine, R. Kinsey, J. Lea, S. Picciotto, and J. Young, eds., *Capitalism and the Rule of Law*, 11-28. London: Hutchinson

– 1987. 'The Tasks Facing a Realist Criminology.' *Contemporary Crises*, 11: 337-356

– 1988. 'Radical Criminology in Britain: The Emergence of a Competing Paradigm.' *British Journal of Criminology*, 28 (2): 159-183

8 The 'Left Regulation' of Prostitution: Reconciling Individual Rights and Collective Interests

John Lowman

In Canada over the past ten years there has been a concerted effort to suppress street prostitution. The conventional wisdom has been that the street trade grew uncontrollably after a series of court decisions in the late 1970s are said to have rendered unenforceable the law that made it illegal to 'solicit any person in a public place for the purpose of prostitution.'[1]

Whether jurisprudence really was responsible for the sorts of problems that police and residents' groups across Canada attributed to it is debatable. Against this view, the Special Committee on Pornography and Prostitution (Fraser Committee 1985) argued that the problem was not so much the demise of the soliciting law, but the contradictory and self-defeating nature of the various Criminal Code sections[2] relating to prostitution (see also Lowman 1986a, 1989: 178-194). The combined effect of these sections is the determination that, while prostitution is technically legal, it is virtually impossible to operate as a prostitute without committing a criminal offence. The committee reasoned that street prostitution would be unlikely to abate until the legislature confronted the issue of where prostitutes should work. To this end it suggested that one or two prostitutes working from a single location should be exempt from bawdy-house legislation and that the provinces should be empowered to license small-scale prostitution establishments.[3] But the Conservative government at that time rejected this proposal, apparently in the belief that to liberalize bawdy-house laws would be tantamount to condoning prostitution. This sort of reasoning has much in common with arguments that condemn needle-exchange programs for encouraging intravenous drug use, or refuse to give prisoners condoms on the grounds that to do so would encourage homosexual liaisons. The cost of such reasoning has quite literally been a death sentence for many of those who do not toe the line.

Instead of confronting head on the question about where prostitution should be located (should it be in brothels, red-light districts, private residences, etc.?), the Conservatives tried to turn back the clock to the good-old days when the soliciting law supposedly held street prostitution in check. The soliciting section was replaced by a law making it an offence to 'communicate' in public for the purpose of buying or selling sexual services. But in many Canadian cities very little seems to have changed (cf. Canada, Department of Justice Canada 1989; Lowman 1989), thus throwing further into doubt the idea that the expansion of the street trade was caused by jurisprudence.

It is against this backdrop that recent commentary on prostitution in Britain would seem to be particularly relevant to the Canadian debate. English and Canadian prostitution laws are similar, although in England – and this is a key difference – a single prostitute can work out of a residence; in Canada, bawdy-house law prohibits such activity. This facet of British law is of particular interest to anyone involved in the process of overhauling prostitution policy in Canada because, to this point, the legislature has baulked at the proposal to 'liberalize' the Criminal Code even this much. It is in this respect that two articles by Roger Matthews on prostitution control in Britain are of particular interest. In one (1986a), he celebrates the putative success of a 'multi-agency' initiative in ridding Finsbury Park of street prostitution. In the other (1986b), he offers a critique of proposals to decriminalize prostitution, opting instead for what he calls 'left regulationism.'

The Finsbury Park study is noteworthy mainly for its conclusion that street prostitution is more opportunistic than is often supposed. Already this argument has been appropriated by Brannigan and Fleischman (1989: 90), two Canadian researchers, to bolster their opportunity model of prostitution, and the neoconservative argument flowing from it that 'the appropriate legal posture towards prostitution is the same as that towards the other petty offences which young, impulsive persons engage in: deterrence and re-education' (for commentary, see Lowman 1991).

Brannigan and Fleischman's use of the Finsbury Park study aside, I have argued elsewhere (Lowman 1992a) that the evidence Matthews presents, especially when it comes to displacement, does not permit the conclusion that he draws.[4] As a counterpoint to Matthews's analysis, I provided a description of twenty years of prostitution control in Vancouver, a story of a series of displacements of street prostitution in response to various control initiatives. One point of this juxtaposition was to suggest that the multi-agency approach may have been successful in Finsbury Park because street prostitutes did have somewhere else to work – private residences – whereas Vancouver prostitutes did not. The best way to have thrown light on this possibility would have been to interview prostitutes about their response to the multi-agency initiative. Unfortunately, they were excluded from both the initiative and the analysis (the only information about prostitutes is drawn from secondary sources).

In response to this criticism, Matthews (1992) has acknowledged that different types of people have different levels of 'commitment' to prostitution, and implies that intravenous drug users, of whom apparently there were not very many in Finsbury Park, are likely to have a much greater commitment. Methodological issues aside, one cannot help but think that in his discussion of 'motivational questions' (ibid.: 20), the choice to prostitute has floated free of the social relations of production and reproduction in which it should be analytically grounded. Where are patriarchal social relations, age and gender employment structures, and the feminization of poverty in this account, which seems much too individualistic?

When it comes to the policy implications of the analysis of street prostitution displacement in Vancouver, Matthews misrepresents the argument when he says that 'Lowman suggests that one way of squaring the circle of accepting street prostitution while trying to minimize its negative effects upon afflicted neighborhoods is to adopt a zoning policy; he argues that certain streets should be designated for the use of prostitutes and their clients and that by implication, prostitution should be decriminalized' (1992: 21).

In fact, I came to no such conclusion (Lowman 1992b). And when it comes to 'decriminalization,' I did not have in mind the model that Matthews describes (1986b: 195). The purpose of this essay is thus to talk about where prostitution might be located, and to comment about the logic of decriminalization. To do this, I use Matthews's left-regulationist approach as a foil.

Left Regulationism

Although he is opposed to criminalizing prostitution as such, Matthews rejects both legalization (state-run brothels and/or some form of licensing system) and decriminalization (removal of all reference to prostitution from the criminal law)[5] on the grounds that neither tries to suppress prostitution. And, although advocates of decriminalization oppose legalization because it would legitimize the objectification and commodification of women, Matthews argues that decriminalization would end up doing much the same thing. He also rejects 'impossibilism' – the view that prostitution is inevitable (1986b: 196) – which he sees as being central to arguments for both legalization and decriminalization.

While not all advocates of decriminalization assume that 'prostitution' is 'inevitable' (I don't), and although it is difficult to see why the apparent inevitability of an activity would lead anyone to argue that it should be legal (imagine applying this argument to murder, theft, or assault!), there can be no doubt that there is a widespread belief that, try as we might, there are no quick fixes to the problems associated with prostitution. In Canada, it is becoming more and more clear that the most realistic way to deal with the exploitative and nuisance aspects of prostitution is to institute some sort of system of formal toleration, be it in the form of state-run brothels (or some other system of licensing) and/or red-light districts, or in allowing prostitutes to work out of private residences.

To the extent that Matthews supports extending the exemption from bawdy-house law to two prostitutes working out of a residence, he obviously *does* support the formal toleration of prostitution in certain circumstances. The irony of his taking this position is that the Fraser Committee's (1985: 546-553) proposals to do the same in Canada have been opposed for the same sorts of reasons that Matthews cites in opposing legalization and decriminalization; i.e., it would be tantamount to the state condoning prostitution. It is thus only with the aid of smoke and mirrors that Matthews is able to sidestep the charge that left regulationism also condones prostitution. In fact, although he does not seem to want to admit it, Matthews ends up where I believe we ought to end up: talking about controlling the circumstances in which prostitution takes place.

The question is, does left regulationism lay out a coherent strategy for realizing what appear to be fundamentally contradictory goals: i.e., the recognition of the right of the individual to prostitute, and the desire to suppress prostitution? A review of Matthews's portrayal of the putative pros and cons of legalization and decriminalization sets the stage for some comments about the tensions that characterize left regulationism.

Against Legalization

In Matthews's account, legalization is a system which purports to recognize the positive aspects of prostitution and allows the state to benefit from it. The appeal of legalization has consisted in its putative potential for:

a controlling venereal diseases;
b minimizing the nuisances associated with street prostitution;
c creating an outlet for male sexual desire that might otherwise be channelled elsewhere;
d offering prostitutes protection from the police, pimps, and 'bad tricks';
e creating a more congenial work environment for prostitutes; and
f allowing the state to accrue revenue through taxes and reduce expenses by cutting back criminal justice expenditures on prostitution control.

Against these claims, Matthews argues that there is little empirical evidence that prostitution does act as a sexual outlet protecting other women from male lust, or that it really is a major source of venereal-disease contagion. He suggests that legalized prostitution does not solve the problem of public nuisance because not all prostitutes are prepared to work under a government-controlled regime. Most importantly of all, he suggests that, *by legitimating the objectification of women, legalization reinforces the notion that women are sexual objects to be bought and abused.* In this vein he suggests that establishments such as the 'eros centers' of West Germany represent not so much a movement towards the greater freedom of prostitutes, but a 'reversion to neo-slavery and traditional modes of female dependence' (1986b: 195).

With these remarks Matthews reiterates the view expressed by supporters of decriminalization (prostitutes' rights organizations and many feminists) that state-controlled prostitution simply substitutes one system of repression and exploitation (criminal-law stigmatization and private pimping) for another (stigmatization through licensing and state pimping).

Against Decriminalization

Matthews suggests that one of the main justifications for decriminalization – a call for the removal of all references to prostitution from the criminal law – is the proposition that prostitution should not be defined as a crime since it is an activity which involves neither a victim nor an offender (e.g., Reiman 1979). When prostitution involves consenting adults, who can be said to be the victim? And if it is agreed that the prostitute is socially and economically disadvantaged and in some senses 'driven' into prostitution, how can it be argued that she is fully 'culpable?'

According to Matthews, in the British context the strategy of decriminalization derives its appeal from its promised resolution of three tensions in the prevailing regulationist approach to prostitution: first, it offers to remove an outdated moralism from criminal law; second, it promises to overcome the inconsistent, discriminatory, and often counterproductive nature of prostitution law and law enforcement; and, third, it promises to end the convergence between prostitution and other illicit economies by freeing the prostitute from the domination of clients, pimps, and official agencies.

Matthews concedes that its advocates have successfully exposed the inequitable nature of prostitution law and its enforcement, but he rejects decriminalization on the grounds that it would:

a create a 'sexual free-for-all for men,' reinforcing the ideology which casts women as sexual objects to used by men (1986b: 199);

b minimize 'the important role of protective legislation which, however paternalistic, recognizes the real vulnerability of certain groups of women' to pimps, exploiters, and other predators (ibid.);

c probably increase the overall exploitation of prostitutes by giving a free hand to organize prostitution as a legitimate business – Matthews suggests that 'the choice between existing [British] regulationism and decriminalization in real terms may strategically be a choice between relatively small scale local exploitation by pimps and various parasites, and the large scale exploitation by well organized faceless business interests' (ibid.);

d do nothing about the nuisances caused by prostitutes and their customers in areas affected by street prostitution (ibid.: 200-201).

He argues that underlying decriminalization is a 'pluralistic vision of society composed of free-willed atomistic individuals freely pursuing their own best interests apart from the unnecessary intervention by the state' (ibid.: 201). From this point of view, criminal legislation is evaluated in terms of its effects on individual prostitutes rather than on social relations in general. Thus it is because of what happens at the level of social relations – and, specifically, gender relations – that Matthews advocates criminal-law intervention. If the prevailing ideology which treats women as sex objects is to be confronted and transcended, law should be directed to the control and reduction of prostitution, Matthews argues, not its legitimation and expansion: 'Even with its serious limitations ... [law] has still managed to provide important defensive and protective elements, while acting as a general deterrent' (ibid.: 202). For Matthews, the issue is how to use law more effectively and constructively rather than abandon it altogether. To do this, he argues, we have to transcend the libertarian discourse which has so far informed so much ostensibly radical intervention. 'Left regulationism' becomes the vehicle for this transcendence.

The Goals of Left Regulationism

Left regulationism seeks to realize four main objectives through criminal law (Matthews 1986b: 205-209):

a general deterrence of both prostitutes and customers and condemnation of prostitution as an unacceptable form of commodification and exploitation of female and youth sexuality;

b protection of third parties from the disturbance, nuisance, and harassment associated with street prostitution;

c protection of prostitutes from pimps; and

d prevention of the development of large-scale, highly commercialized styles of prostitution.

The question is, can these different objectives be reconciled with each other in practice, an acid test of any 'realist' policy? The Canadian experience suggests that they cannot.

General Deterrence

One of the main strategies of left regulationism is to retain criminal-law sanctioning of prostitution to send out the message that prostitution really ought to be something that we try to dissuade. To this end, Matthews would want to write the criminal law in such a way that it would serve to censure prostitution. To maximize the deterrent capacity of the law it would be written in gender-neutral terms and include clients as well as prostitutes, in order to 'question and potentially undermine the widely-held male expectation that women and/or young men ought to be purchasable to service their sexual desires and fantasies' (1986b: 205).

As already noted, however, the law would be written to allow two prostitutes to work from a residence in order to provide them with some degree of protection and autonomy. And when it comes to the customers of prostitutes, Matthews rejects the idea that purchasing sexual services should itself be criminalized. He suggests that the criminalization of the customer would be unfeasible because of the consensual nature of prostitution and because of the types of entrapment techniques and dubious surveillance methods that would have to be employed to enforce such a law successfully.

This is a curious argument on two counts. First, practical issues aside, if one of the purposes of left regulationism is to undermine certain widely held attitudes, would it not make sense to criminalize the trick rather than the prostitute? Surely a different sort of argument is relevant here: assuming that we are not going to criminalize the act of selling sexual services, by what logic could we justify criminalizing the purchase of a commodity or service that is perfectly legal to sell? Criminalizing the purchase of sexual services would certainly censure a certain construction of male sexuality, but at what price? If the buyer were to be criminalized, it would be difficult to control the location and circumstances in which prostitution occurs, in which case prostitutes would continue to confront the same sorts of problems that they now face.

Second, in a left-regulationist regime, the criminal law controlling customers would relate *only to their public activity*. Something rather peculiar has happened here. Given the recognition of the prostitute's right to work (and right, perhaps, even to communicate with a potential client in a public place, as long as no nuisance occurs), the question becomes, what is it about left regulationism that would act as a deterrent to buying and selling sexual services? Certainly, commercialized prostitution organized by third parties would be prohibited. And the activities of street prostitutes and their customers would be subject to criminal penalty. But buying and selling sexual services would remain quite legal.

Left regulation, then, appears to be more about *controlling the circumstances* under which the sale and purchase of sexual services occurs than about suppressing prostitution itself. Since it does not actually criminalize prostitution, it is difficult to see how it would act as a 'general deterrent.'

Is the Prostitute Inevitably a 'Sexual Slave'?

Arguments favouring the abolition of prostitution appear to assume that the sale of sexual services is necessarily and inevitably a form of 'sexual slavery,' no matter what its social-structural context (e.g., Pateman 1983). Others have objected that, although prostitution in its current form may be morally undesirable in the sense that it is one of the worst forms of male exploitation of women, commercial sexual relations do not necessarily have to take their present form (Shaver 1988; Shrage 1989); nor should all contemporary commercial sexual relations be characterized this way. Prostitution is not all of a piece.

Some commentators have argued that commodifying sex takes it out of the realm of reciprocal desire, thereby debasing it (Pateman 1983). Perhaps it does. But on what grounds would it be legitimate to translate this set of values into criminal prohibitions? Why should sex be legislatively limited to a situation of reciprocal desire? What should be the legal response to men who pay to be sexually and otherwise humiliated by a domina? And what about women who pay men for sex?

It might be argued that prostitution would disappear in a more egalitarian society, but as long as the products of a complex division of labour are distributed through a market-place, it is likely – though not inevitable – that some individuals will decide to commodify their sexuality.

Decriminalization, the Inevitability of Prostitution, and Control of the Body

Matthews suggests that the logic of decriminalization is based, among other things, on the belief that prostitution is inevitable. It may well be that some advocates of decriminalization believe this to be the case, or at least they believe that prostitution is not likely to disappear quickly in market societies. But such a belief is not necessary to the logic of decriminalization.

As Matthews recognizes, one of the main rationales for decriminalization is that, historically, prostitution law has created a double jeopardy for women. Not only is the act of prostitution supposedly one of female subjugation, but, when it is criminalized, it is the already subjugated woman who is usually prone to punishment. But there are other reasons for decriminalizing the act of selling sexual services. On what grounds should the state be empowered to criminalize a person for taking money for something that would otherwise be perfectly legal? To argue that he or she should be allowed to make this choice, even though it is circumscribed by various social structures (what choice isn't?), is not quite the same as the liberal-rights position described by Reiman (1979), nor does it require buying into the 'abstract contractarianism' advanced by Ericsson (1980). Decriminalization does not have to be based on a 'pluralistic vision of society composed of free-willed atomistic individuals pursuing their own best interests apart from the unnecessary interference by the state' in the way that Matthews suggests (1986b: 201). More important, it is an argument about the limits of state power. While Matthews does acknowledge this, he minimizes the importance of this part of the argument. Also, he does not seem to acknowledge that, when it comes to individual rights, there is considerable overlap of liberalism and certain kinds of socialism (cf. Hunt 1985). Questions about rights are relevant to socialism too. Indeed, different strains of socialism can be distinguished according to how they conceive individual rights in relation to state power. It is difficult to see how one can talk about placing limits on state power without resorting to some notion of individual rights, Carol Smart's (1989) reservations about the discourse on rights notwithstanding.

Consider some of the other implications of criminalizing a person for selling sexual services. Even in the United States, in most states where prostitution is criminalized, neither premarital or extramarital sex is illegal, nor is 'sexual promiscuity.' So why criminalize prostitution, which is distinguished from some of these other legal sexual experiences only by virtue of the payment involved? By criminalizing females for selling sexual services the state is effectively saying that, if women are going to engage in multiple sexual relationships, they must do so without compensation! Or, to put it more bluntly, women should give themselves away for free!

It is one thing to want to criminalize third parties for exploiting a woman's sexuality, but quite another to say that she should not be allowed to exploit it on her own behalf. Why would the state preclude this sort of remuneration when women are already disadvantaged? In an economic sense, to do so would be to disadvantage them further.

A word of clarification: none of this is to disagree with Matthews when he insists that the act of prostitution cannot be analysed apart from its social, economic, and political context (see also Shrage 1989). It has no single transhistorical and transcultural form. And although he argues that prostitution is an undesirable human relationship, he does *not* argue that the selling and buying of sexual services should themselves be criminalized. If we agree with this position, then again it would seem that the best we can hope to achieve is manipulation of the circumstances in which prostitution occurs – in which case, some form of regulatory system would seem to be desirable. But what should it look like?

Does Decriminalization Mean No Regulation?

Matthews suggests that many advocates of decriminalization leave the impression that there should be no control of prostitution whatsoever. He chides prostitutes' rights advocates for not even mentioning the problems residents in areas of street prostitution might experience, let alone discuss what might be done about such problems. It is probably for this reason that, in Canada, groups opposed to street prostitution have mistakenly interpreted arguments for decriminalization as favouring the rights of prostitutes to work the street, when most prostitutes' rights groups not only oppose red-light districts and brothels, but some of them have said that they are not in favour of street prostitution either[6] (primarily because it is so dangerous for prostitutes). What these activists take issue with is the use of criminal-law sanctions to control street prostitution when the legislature refuses to tackle head-on the issue of where prostitutes should work; given that they refuse to provide any information about where prostitutes and customers should meet, how can legislators justify punishing street prostitutes and their customers for working the street? And why should prostitutes and customers be subject to criminal sanctions when other forms of street commerce are controlled by civil law?

Matthews is on firm ground when he points out that, if decriminalization is taken to mean the removal of all references to prostitution from the Criminal Code, it is difficult to see how it would be possible to avoid the development of large-scale brothels and prevent the crass commercialization and exploitation of prostitutes without putting some other form of regulatory system in place. That is precisely why Canadian advocates of decriminalization favour a regulationist strategy (e.g., Shaver 1985), but one that is based on civil law, with generic criminal laws controlling extortion and nuisance. In his description of decriminalization, Matthews does not really do justice to the logic that opposes regulation by criminal sanctioning.

Very few other activities are criminalized only because a payment is involved (examples being bribery and kickbacks, and in these cases the payment is proscribed because of the unfair advantage that it bestows on the parties involved). In contrast, in various systems of regulation, the circumstances of payment are controlled in all sorts of ways. Perhaps civil regulations might be a much better vehicle than criminal law for controlling prostitution.

The Protective Role of Criminal Law

Matthews suggests that advocates of decriminalization show little recognition of the idea that the criminal law is a 'protective instrument of social defence.' He also argues that 'there can be little serious doubt that legal intervention over the past century, with all its anomalies and inconsistencies, has acted to reduce the level of prostitution and provide some protection for women and girls against exploitation' (1986b: 199). Well, I for one doubt that criminal law has had much of a deterrent effect when it comes to prostitution. Probably much more important as a deterrent is the general stigmatization of prostitution in Western societies that is rooted in Christian beliefs about original sin, sex, and the family. The law certainly has helped to consolidate this censure, but at what cost? The law consolidates the 'outlaw' identity of the prostitute, and in the process makes female prostitutes, in particular, more vulnerable to exploitation and violence. Because she or he is an 'outlaw,' the prostitute is hardly going to turn for protection to the police, who represent a threat of another kind. The criminal sanction thus helps to create the social niche that the pimp steps into, that of protector, even if most of the protection provided is from himself and other pimps.

Matthews laments that supporters of decriminalization display little concern for residents bothered by street prostitution. In Vancouver, however, where a variety of different neighbourhood organizations have formed with the sole purpose of ridding their neighbourhoods of prostitution, they have voiced virtually no concern about the problems facing prostitutes (note that the multi-agency approach in Finsbury Park apparently did not include dialogue with prostitutes, thus consolidating the us/them mentality that goes along with the disapproval of prostitution and reinforcing the notion that prostitutes are disposable women). The response of the Canadian legislature has been similar. It ignored the Fraser Committee's recommendations and enacted the communicating law without changing any of the other sections relating to prostitution. In other words, the government resolutely tried to protect residents from nuisance, but did nothing to deal with the problems facing prostitutes; nor did it clarify the legal status of prostitution. In Vancouver since 1986 some twenty-five prostitutes have been murdered, and an unknown number are robbed, assaulted, and/or raped on any given night. The current law relating to prostitution must be held at least partly responsible for this awful situation. Only recently has there been any public outcry that something must be done about it. Otherwise, public propriety and property values have overwhelmed all other issues.

Note, this is not to argue in favour of prostitutes' rights over residents' rights. Rather, it is to argue that we have to reconcile the two.

Nuisance Control

When it comes to controlling street prostitution, Matthews would limit criminal-law intervention 'to those forms of soliciting or importuning which involve annoyance, harassment or public disturbance' (1986b: 205). In wanting to respect the civil rights of prostitutes and clients, Matthews suggests that 'convictions against either party should require *some proof of annoyance* based upon objective evidence and should not be reliant on police evidence alone' (1986b: 206; emphasis added). But one wonders exactly how this kind of nuisance law would be worded. Recent Canadian experience suggests that the writing of such legislation is anything but easy. Given the experience with the soliciting law, the prevailing opinion in Canada would seem to be that, if a law designed to control street prostitution requires police to do much more than simply establish that a person offered to provide a sexual service for a fee or offered to purchase such services, convictions are difficult to secure. It was precisely this kind of proof that the courts required once it had been established that 'soliciting' consisted of 'pressing and persistent' behaviour – it was the *pressure and persistence* that constituted the *proof of annoyance*. When interpreted this way, it became very difficult to obtain convictions since prostitutes were rarely pressing and persistent in approaching would-be customers. Of course, one might argue it was this particular way of defining nuisance that was the problem, but it is probably safe to assume that most prostitutes would be quick to adapt their behaviour to just short of about any definition of nuisance that one might employ.

It was for this kind of reason that the federal government did not adopt the street-prostitution law proposed by the Fraser Committee (1985: 538-543). The Fraser Committee proposed that everyone who 'stands, stops, wanders about in or drives through a public place for the purpose of offering to engage in prostitution or employ the services of a prostitute, and *on more than one occasion*, (i) beckons to, stops or attempts to stop pedestrians or attempts to engage them in conversation, (ii) stops or attempts to stop motor vehicles, or (iii) impedes the free flow of pedestrian or vehicular traffic, or of ingress or egress from premises adjacent to a public place … is guilty of an offence punishable on summary conviction' (1985: 539; emphasis added).

The communicating law enacted in December 1985 was based on this wording, but the phrase 'on more than one occasion' was deleted. And a new clause was added so that now it is an offence in a public place or any place open to public view to 'in any way communicate or attempt to communicate with any person for the purpose of engaging in prostitution or of obtaining the services of a prostitute' – a law that Matthews apparently would oppose. One indication of the difficulty police experience in using anything other than the last clause of the new law is that of the 2,180 charges laid in Vancouver in 1986 and 1987, all but one related to a person's 'communication' with a police decoy (Lowman 1989). The law thus effectively criminalizes the act of communication; the communication itself is treated as the nuisance.

Groups in Vancouver lobbying the federal government for tougher laws against street prostitutes and their customers have explicitly rejected the kind of street-prostitution nuisance law that Matthews proposes, reasoning that it would not be enforceable. Instead, they argue that it is the visibility of the prostitute on the street that is the nuisance (see Lowman 1989: A149-A189). They also argue that many of the nuisances caused by street prostitution (such as traffic congestion, increased general noise levels, and the lowering of property values) cannot be reduced in a legal sense to a particular individual and thus could not be brought under control by a nuisance or disturbance law. The only way to deal with these general problems is to get prostitution off the street – in which case we are back to the question of where it should be located and how it should be organized.

Aside from these issues, there is another problem that a street-prostitution nuisance law raises; i.e., if prostitution is legal, it is not clear why a criminal nuisance law should be written with reference to prostitution only, rather than applying to nuisances generically. There are already several Canadian Criminal Code sections (as there are in English law), such as 'causing a disturbance,' which deal with public nuisances. Why not apply these generic laws to the nuisances that can be attributed to specific prostitutes and customers?

In Canada several religious organizations promote their ideas on street corners by distributing various publications, such as *Awake*, which include treatises against such things as homosexuality, abortion, and evolutionary theory. None of these treatises constitutes a nuisance in the sense being discussed here, but when their distributors stand in shop doorways they sometimes interfere with pedestrian traffic. They are much more of a nuisance when they knock at the doors of private houses in order to peddle their ideas, but there is no criminal law to prevent them from doing so. Some people similarly find market researchers in shopping precincts a nuisance when they ask inane questions about such things as the preferred coating on chocolate raisins, or how much cheaper than bottled beer would canned beer have to be before people would buy it. At least this is annoyance with a human face. More irksome is the computer that random dials private residences to ask the same kinds of questions. Academic researchers can, no doubt, be similarly bothersome. What separates these kinds of annoyances from the nuisances caused by prostitutes, other than their different moral connotation? Certainly prostitution is concentrated in relatively small areas, and is ongoing. But why should a prostitute be subject to criminal penalty when the business activities of other people in public places are not? If the answer is that other types of person are not creating the kinds of problems associated with prostitution, my retort in the case of the Canadian situation would be that, since the structure of prostitution law does not provide any viable alternatives in which a prostitute might operate legally, it is the law that is creating the problem, not the prostitute. If the law enabled a single prostitute to work from a fixed location, as in Britain, then the same sorts of laws which prevent other businesses from setting up shop in the street could be used to regulate prostitution. From this perspective, street commerce generally would be the object of control. Regulated this way, it would be possible to confront directly the issue at stake here – the *location* of prostitution – rather than to have to deal with it tangentially (i.e., by intervening only in terms of nuisances that are created in the process of conducting the business).

The general principles underlying the way we write criminal laws are also important when we consider how to control prostitution, not the least because any criminal law is subject to judicial interpretation and can be struck down if it breaches such principles. In this regard, consider the consequences of defining nuisance according to the *status* of the actor (prostitute or customer) rather than the act itself. In Canada until 1972, street prostitution was controlled by a vagrancy provision. This law, which made it an offence for a 'common prostitute or nightwalker' to be found in a public place without being able to 'give a good account of herself,' was repealed because it was a *status offence*. For one thing, a prostitute was, by definition, female. Neither male prostitutes nor customers (nearly all of whom were men) were susceptible to prosecution. Rather than criminalize a specific act, it criminalized a person's status – being a known prostitute in a public place – even though the act of prostitution was not, technically, illegal. Any law that criminalizes nuisances according to the status of the actor (i.e., prospective prostitute or customer) is little different. The problems created by such offences are brought into sharp relief when we realize that, under the provisions of the communicating law, one can stand on the street corner all day long, arrange to engage in all manner of sexual activities with all manner of people, and do so perfectly legally as long one does not require remuneration for said activities.

Certainly the type of nuisance law that left regulationism would employ is an improvement over the Canadian communicating law. But, like that law, and like the provision recommended by the Fraser Committee, the nuisance law described by Matthews would lead to a status offence; the status of the actor (someone wanting to buy or sell sexual services), rather than the act itself, would be criminalized.

If one were to retort that these kinds of arguments are unrealistic, that non-prostitute women do not stand on street corners propositioning passers-by, or that other businesses do not cause the kinds of nuisances that prostitutes and their customers do, it should nevertheless be recognized that the law is, and ought to be, constructed according to certain principles – the means are as important as the ends.

Preventing Exploitation

Controlling the Pimp. Some feminists (e.g., McLeod 1982) have argued that laws relating to pimping should be repealed because they are paternalistic (see also Fraser Committee 1985: 543). But this paternalism does not bother Matthews who, although wishing to rewrite protective criminal legislation in such a way as to allow the differentiation of the exploitive 'parasite' from the prostitute's friends, nevertheless believes that protective legislation specifically relating to prostitution should be kept in place. One problem with this proposal is that Matthews gives no indication as to exactly how the law that he has in mind might be worded, in this case to show how it would be possible to distinguish a 'friend' from an 'exploiter.' Just what would the legal definition of a 'parasite' look like? It is the difficulty in drawing this line that led the Fraser Committee (1985: 543) to recommend that only when a person is, by force or threat of force, coerced into engaging in prostitution should the criminal law be invoked to protect her or him. Advocates of decriminalization (e.g., Shaver 1985: 499) have suggested that generic laws relating to assault and threats be used to protect prostitutes. In other words, one can use the criminal law to protect prostitutes without having to relate its wording specifically to prostitution.

The Role of Other Third Parties. In terms of reducing the objectification and commodification of female sexuality, Matthews (1986b: 209) suggests that more police efforts should be devoted to closing down escort services and massage parlours. As we have already seen, one of the main differences between decriminalization and left regulation is that the latter retains criminal laws to prevent the development of commercialized prostitution establishments. Without some such regulatory mechanism in place, decriminalization would be tantamount to legalization. But, in reflecting on Matthews's desire to prevent third-party profit from prostitution, two questions arise: (a) Is it possible for off-street prostitution to occur without some third parties playing a role in bringing prostitutes and customers together? and (b) Are all forms of third-party involvement necessarily 'exploitative'?

If prostitution were, for the most part, to be removed from the street, the very act of making the trade less visible creates a niche for third parties to become

involved in bringing the prostitute and customer together. If off-street prostitution were to be decentralized in the way that Matthews suggests, with prostitutes
working in pairs out of private residences – the Fraser Committee dubbed this the
'cottage industry' model of prostitution – how would customers find them? One
mechanism would be some kind of advertising publication, but in Canada the
publishers would risk prosecution for living on the avails of prostitution and for
procuring. Another mechanism would be for prostitutes to meet patrons in bars
or clubs – although we should guard against forcing alcohol and prostitution
together – in which case the organizers would again risk prosecution for living
on the avails of prostitution.

Matthews recognizes that the 'relative isolation and the maintenance of
prostitutes as a pariah and outcast group has served to occlude the real levels of
violence and exploitation to which they are often subject' (1986b: 207). In
Canada, escort services generally do help to protect prostitutes, even if some of
them are run by superpimps who make vast profits in the process. Because a third
party monitors the activities of escorts and their customers (by virtue of wanting
to know the identity of the customer and the location at which services will be
rendered – in Vancouver, several escort agencies require an escort to ring in to
the office when she meets the trick and again when she is leaving), escorts appear
to be far less prone to violence than are street prostitutes. Thus, while escort
agencies should be condemned for their exploitation of prostitutes, they do
provide a minimal level of protection. What if these agencies were to be worker-
owned and -operated? What if escort services or other venues were to be run by
non-profit societies, with some of the revenues being used to provide services for
prostitutes?

Under the current law, it is easy to imagine what effect a crackdown on escort
services would have on street prostitution, and just as easy, therefore, to
understand the current police and crown policy of not enforcing living-on-the-
avails and procuring laws against such enterprises (even though several convictions have been obtained). Through the system of 'quasi legalization' that
currently prevails in Canada, and because of the emphasis on nuisance control
at the expense of all other issues (particularly youth prostitution and violence
against prostitutes) large-scale commercialized escort prostitution is already
flourishing. All because legislators refuse to come to grips with the question the
Fraser Committee challenged them to answer.

Despite the enactment of the communicating law in 1985, in most Canadian
cities street prostitution continues unabated. It may well be that relaxing the
bawdy-house laws would reduce street prostitution significantly. In other words,
no matter how one looks at it, to diminish the kind of large-scale commercialized
prostitution that already exists in Canada will probably require open and

deliberate acknowledgement of the right of the individual to sell sexual services in order that a different style of decentralized off-street prostitution, not exploited by third parties, can emerge.

'Benign' Displacement – From Whose Point of View?

Rather than confronting head-on the issue of where prostitutes should work by trying to bring about 'positive displacement' (i.e., displacement into some predetermined location, be it on the street or off), Matthews (1992) prefers 'negative displacement'[7] (i.e., displacement of prostitution away from certain areas). Following Barr and Pease (1990), he argues that displacement can be both 'malign' and 'benign.' The comments by Barr and Pease are well taken: displacement is a relative concept, and we should reject the notion that it operates on a 'one-for-one basis'[8] (Barr and Pease 1992: 215). But when Matthews argues in favour of 'negative' displacement, 'to remove street prostitution and kerb-crawling away from those areas where they cause the most nuisance and have the most detrimental effects' (1992: 21), the main reason that he can call it 'negative' is because it is mostly the interests of residents that he has in mind.

In Vancouver over the past fifteen years, one of the main strategies of the authorities has been to try to achieve negative displacement. In some cases, prostitution has simply moved to other residential districts – hardly a 'positive' result. And when it has been 'negative,' it has not always been 'benign.' That is because what is benign from the point of view of persons bothered by prostitutes is often malign when viewed from the point of view of prostitutes. For example, some police initiatives in Vancouver have involved relocating street prostitution in poorly lit industrial warehouse districts where prostitutes are much more prone to violence.

By way of analogy, we might say that, under Canadian law, the practice of negative displacement is something like steering a car around an obstacle course without the benefit of a steering-wheel. The occupants have to throw their weight from side to side to get the car to negotiate corners. But as the car careens down the road, it injures and kills various onlookers. In the left-regulationist version of negative displacement, the car has a steering-wheel, but the occupants of the car find their hands tied behind their back so that they cannot use it.

Conclusion

The kind of system that Matthews outlines, especially the liberalization of bawdy-house laws to allow one or two prostitutes to work out of a premise, has been opposed in Canada on the grounds that it would be tantamount to the state's condoning prostitution. The irony is that, although Matthews is reluctant to admit it, he most certainly does identify a location – the private residence – for prostitution to take place. In the process of not wanting to be accused of condoning prostitution, he refuses to contemplate positive measures that might guide it into the location that he recommends.

When it comes to left regulationism, the question remains, if one (a) recognizes the individual right of a person to sell or purchase sexual services; (b) requires that public liaisons for either of these purposes create tangible 'annoyances' in order to warrant criminal conviction; and (c) allows prostitutes to work out of their own homes, what aspect of the criminal law would actually serve to deter prostitution? When it comes to undermining the belief that women's bodies should be available for men to rent, the system that Matthews proposes would not seem to make things much more difficult for customers than either decriminalization or legalization. Rather, left regulationism is about controlling the circumstances in which prostitution can occur. But, in his belief that prostitution is undesirable, Matthews refuses to admit this.

In the short term, if prostitution is not going to be criminalized, we must decide where to locate it so that prostitutes are protected from violence and exploitation, and bystanders are protected from nuisance. In the longer term, the overall goal of social policy ought to be geared to creating the circumstances in which prostitution would be more of a choice. I have suggested that the criminal law can play only a minor role in achieving this long-term objective, and that we should turn to civil law, supplemented by generic criminal laws, to achieve the short-term goals.

Notes

1 For details of these cases, see Fraser Committee (1985: 419-426).
2 As the Canadian Criminal Code currently stands, a variety of activities related to prostitution are prohibited. There are five clusters of statutes relating to prostitution: (1) 'Bawdy house' laws prohibit the keeping of 'places' as prostitution establishments or the frequenting of such places; (2) a series of statutes prohibit living on the avails of prostitution; (3) it is an offence to procure a prostitute for another person (the bawdy house, procuring, and living on the avails laws have remained virtually unchanged since 1920); (4) a new statute enacted on 1 January 1988 criminalizes the purchase of (or offer to purchase) sexual services from anyone under eighteen years of age; and (5) the 'communicating' law prohibits the public purchase or sale of sexual services or the offer to purchase or sell such services.
3 For commentary on these proposals see Kanter (1985) and Lowman (1986b).
4 In response, Matthews reasons, 'all the evidence available ... both formal and informal, indicated that although a few of the women working as prostitutes in

Finsbury Park area moved to other parts of London, most of the women for whom there were records (approximately one sixth of the total) were not working as prostitutes three years after the intervention was implemented' (1992: 19). But, the fact remains that the only attempt by Matthews to measure displacement was a check of records of women arrested in Amhurst Park, the nearest street-prostitution area, for a six-month period. This method of measurement simply cannot sustain the conclusion Matthews draws from it. Also, the fact that some of the women were no longer prostituting three years later begs a variety of questions: What are these women doing now? What evidence is there that it was the Finsbury Park multi-agency initiative that caused them to give up the game? And how reliable is this apparently impressionistic evidence anyway?

5 For more detailed descriptions of these different models, see Fraser Committee (1985) and Shaver (1985).

6 See, for example, the interview with representatives of Prostitutes and Other Women for Equal Rights (POWER) in Lowman (1989: 196-210).

7 In the process, Matthews says that 'positive zoning has been tried extensively in America with little long term success' (1992:21). It has? Where? In all but one state, selling sexual services is a criminal offence – and even in Nevada, street prostitution is illegal. It would have been helpful if some references had been supplied here and some indication of what period Matthews is referring to.

8 Interviews with Vancouver prostitutes (Lowman 1989: A344) reveals that some of them probably were deterred by the new communicating law, but all the evidence suggests that this was only a small minority of the people involved. Of forty-five prostitutes interviewed, thirty said that they did not know anyone who had quit because of the introduction of the new law; twelve said they knew 'a few' people who had quit; and only three said they knew 'many.'

References

Barr, R., and K. Pease. 1990. 'Crime Displacement and Placement,' in M. Tonry and N. Morris, eds., *Crime and Justice: A Review of Research*, vol. 12: 277-318. Chicago: University of Chicago Press

– 1992. 'A Place for Crime and Every Crime in Its Place: An Alternative Perspective on Crime Displacement,' in D.J. Evans, N.R. Fyfe, and D.T. Herbert, eds., *Crime, Policing and Place: Essays in Environmental Criminology*, 196-216. London: Routledge

Brannigan, A., and J. Fleischman. 1989. 'Juvenile Prostitution and Mental Health: Policing Delinquency or Treating Pathology.' *Canadian Journal of Law and Society*, 4: 77-98

Canada, Department of Justice. 1989. *Street Prostitution, Assessing the Impact of the Law: Synthesis Report*. Ottawa: Ministry of Supply and Services

Ericsson, L. 1980. 'Charges against Prostitution: An Attempt at a Philosophical Assessment.' *Ethics*, 90: 335-366

Fraser Committee (Special Committee on Pornography and Prostitution). 1985. *Pornography and Prostitution In Canada*. Ottawa: Ministry of Supply and Services

Hunt, A. 1985. 'What Price Democracy?' *Marxism Today*, May: 25-30

Kanter, M. 1985. 'Prohibit or Regulate? The Fraser Report and New Approaches to Prostitution and Pornography.' *Osgoode Hall Law Journal*, 23: 171-194

Lowman, J. 1986a. 'Street Prostitution in Vancouver: Notes on the Genesis of a Social Problem.' *Canadian Journal of Criminology*, 28 (1): 1-16

- 1986b. 'You Can Do It, But Don't Do It Here: Some Comments on Proposals for the Reform of Canadian Prostitution Law,' in J. Lowman, M.A. Jackson, T.S. Palys, and S. Gavigan, eds., *Regulating Sex: An Anthology of Commentaries on the Badgley and Fraser Reports*, 193-213. Burnaby, BC: School of Criminology, Simon Fraser University

- 1989. *Street Prostitution, Assessing the Impact of the Law: Vancouver*. Ottawa: Department of Justice Canada

- 1991. 'Street Prostitutes in Canada: An Evaluation of the Brannigan-Fleischman Opportunity Model.' *Canadian Journal of Law and Society*, 6: 137-164

- 1992a. 'Street Prostitution Control: Some Canadian Reflections on the Finsbury Park Experience.' *British Journal of Criminology*, 32 (Spring): 1-17

- 1992b (forthcoming). 'Street Prostitution Control: Against Red Light Districts.' *British Journal of Criminology*

Matthews, R. 1986a. 'Policing Prostitution: A Multi-Agency Approach,' Paper 1. London: Middlesex Polytechnic, Centre for Criminology

- 1986b. 'Beyond Wolfenden? Prostitution, Politics and the Law,' in R. Matthews and J. Young, eds., *Confronting Crime*, 188-210. London: Sage

- 1992. 'Regulating Street Prostitution and Kerb-Crawling: A Reply to Lowman.' *British Journal of Criminology*, 32 (Spring): 18-22

McLeod, E. 1982. *Women Working: Prostitution Now*. London: Croom Helm

Pateman, C. 1983. 'Defending Prostitution: Charges against Ericsson.' *Ethics*, 93: 561-565

Reiman, J. 1979. 'Prostitution, Addiction and the Ideology of Liberalism.' *Contemporary Crises*, 3: 53-68

Shaver, F. 1985. 'Prostitution: A Critical Analysis of Three Policy Approaches.' *Canadian Public Policy*, 11 (3): 493-503

- 1988. 'A Critique of the Feminist Charges against Prostitution.' *Atlantis*, 14 (1): 82-89

Shrage, L. 1989. 'Should Feminists Oppose Prostitution?' *Ethics*, 99 (1): 347-361

Smart, C. 1989. *Feminism and the Power of Law*. London: Routledge

9 Why Company Law Is Important to Left Realists

Rob McQueen

Company law is a meeting-point for various class interests. Contrary to the impression given by much literature on 'corporate' crime, company law is not the province of a particular class or faction of capital. Rather, it is the product of a series of compromises arising out of the conflict among and within various interests. It is also the case that company 'law' is not solely contained in the legislative enactments of the state. A plurality of rules, practices, 'laws,' and sanctions operate on and 'legitimize' or 'delegitimize' corporate actors. Various class forces engage on the battleground of corporate law(s), characterized by the dynamic interplay of those rules, practices, and 'laws' which recognize, regulate, and punish the corporation. As a consequence, company law should not be seen, as some past researchers have tended to do, as a relatively static edifice, largely immutable, except to change that is in the interest of 'capital.' While not the primary concern of this essay, the whole question of the fashion in which the insights of legal pluralism may illuminate the travails of corporate regulation (conceived of in terms of state laws relating to corporations) and the potential of properly conceived self-regulatory regimes (in contradistinction to much of the left literature which rejects self-regulation out of hand) is a matter of some considerable importance.[1]

One of the significant connections between the issue of appropriate strategies for regulating corporate crime – the question of what is meant when we refer to corporate 'law' – is that of what can be regarded as the 'normal' corporation and what effects different normative conceptions of the corporation might have on the alleviation of certain unacceptable behaviours and practices among corporate citizens. Related to the issue of the interconnections between different normative conceptions of the corporation and the 'policing' of corporations is also the issue of whether – and, if so, how – transformations in the normative content of the corporation might be brought about.

These twin issues – the normative content of the corporate form and strategies for its transformation, the subject of this essay – have been largely neglected by criminologists specializing in white-collar crime. Many of them have simply been content to argue for a stronger and/or more effective regulatory system rather than for the transformation of the corporate form itself.

The precarious state of the 'normal' company is rarely recognized in the criminological literature. The aperture for normative arguments *vis-à-vis* the corporate form crystallized conflicts between different factions of capital (e.g., finance and industrial capital) over the manner in which corporate entities are composed and the terms upon which incorporation is granted are rarely mentioned in analyses of 'white-collar' crime. Nor have the possibilities for opening a debate on the nature of the corporation created by the frequent discord between small and large capital over the conditions upon which incorporation is granted and the regulatory requirements that attend incorporation legislation been seized upon by criminological researchers. It is also the case that the issue of the appropriate balance of broader 'community' interests and those of private capital is crucial in the broader terrain of company 'law,' yet the preconditions for effective interventions of community groups is an area which has been little researched. Quite often left researchers have employed theoretical assumptions, such as the power of corporate capital to explain the lack of impact of 'community' organizations on corporate behaviour and regulation. These explanations have been often made at the expense of more constructive programs which might analyse the parameters and preconditions for community interventions which challenge prevailing notions of the 'normal' corporation.[2]

It is important to recognize that, as the result of such an uneasy and dynamic balance of class forces, company law is vulnerable to challenge. In particular, it must be understood that an array of class interests, not traditionally associated with company law, may be reflected in legislation relating to the formation and regulation of corporations. State law relating to corporations – in particular, companies – and securities legislation are *not* the exclusive province of any one class.

Corporate law must cease to be considered in discussions of 'white-collar' criminality as an essentialist reflex of capitalist forces of production, and the corporate form as some sort of immutable construct that forms the backdrop for various forms of regulatory intervention. It is asserted in this essay that 'white-collar' criminologists should turn their attentions away from attempts to establish which forms of regulatory intervention are most effective against the 'corporation' and begin instead to explore the manner in which different normative conceptions of the corporate form itself may impact on 'corporate' behaviour. Approaching these deficiencies from a somewhat different perspective Kelvin Jones remarks that the problems of the legal regulation of corporations are more complex than has been generally recognized as being the case by 'white-collar' criminologists: 'they cannot be reduced to the capitulation of law enforcement agencies and the genuflection of state in the face of almighty corporate power. One thing 'white collar' criminology does not seem to consider in any great detail is the possibility that corporate activity cannot be regulated by classifying it as real crime and utilizing the machinery of law, that criminalization may not be a viable means of controlling corporate crime' (1982: 16).

The following discussion attempts to place such an analysis of the potential effects of different normative conceptions of the corporate form in a left-realist setting. The potential strategic possibilities of a radical questioning of the normative content of the corporate form is examined against the backdrop of the call for greater accountability of social agencies which lies at the heart of some significant recent left-realist analyses of law and order and policing (e.g., Lea and Young 1984). In examining the issue of accountability in the context of corporations, a number of the characteristic normative features of the modern 'corporation' – limitation of liability, the requirement that social considerations be subordinated to the interests of shareholders in the management of the corporation, and the idea that corporate regulation should not be so strict as to interfere with 'legitimate' business activities – have been chosen to demonstrate the manner in which variations in the normative content of company law may have significant effects on commercial behaviour and provide a range of benefits to the broader community by lessening (or extinguishing) the incidence of certain unacceptable behaviours of corporate actors.

Claims for greater accountability of corporations may cohere around one or a number of these characteristic normative features. For instance, it might be claimed by certain sectional representatives of an affected 'community' that corporate interests should, at least in certain instances, be routinely subordinated to social needs. For instance, polluting the living environment of community members is unacceptable, and no matter what other benefits in terms of employment and infrastructure the relevant corporation may bring into the community, the interests of the polluting corporation on this issue are to be regarded as subordinate to the community interest in a clean and safe living environment. The usual response of the state to such claims has, at least in the recent past, been to subject the polluting corporation to regulatory action (a fine, a warning, and so on). A genuine challenge to the legitimacy of the corporation's right to ignore social interests would, however, be constituted by providing the affected community, or a representative organ(s) of the various sectional interests in the community, a voice within the corporation itself if it failed to respond to more conventional regulatory interventions. Thus, one means by which the current barrier between the rights of a corporate actor as a 'private' domain and 'public' interest might be modified, if not obliterated, would be to make the right of corporate 'privacy' contingent upon the corporation's respecting 'public' rights to clean air, clean water, a safe environment, and so on.

The manner in which such challenges to the normative content of the corporate form might realistically be tied to a campaign to make corporations more democratically accountable to those groups which are affected by their actions (workers, local communities which are affected by hazards created by business residents, creditors who are affected by defalcations of the businesses to whom they have money, and so on) is further examined in succeeding parts of this essay.

Versatility Unlimited: The Uses and Abuses of Limited Liability

In the first version of modern English company legislation – that embodied in the Joint Stock Companies Act of 1844 – limited liability was not conferred on companies registering under that 'general' legislation. While incorporation was granted as a *right* upon the conditions of the 'general' legislation being satisfied, limitation of shareholders' liability was still regarded as a *privilege*, and could be obtained only by securing a charter or by a private act of Parliament conferring such a status on shareholders.

In a number of systems of corporate law, only particular types of shareholders are provided with the shelter of limited liability. In other varieties of corporate legislation, not all types of corporate entities are considered to require the protection of limited liability – for instance, only those enterprises with a demonstrable need for such a device in order to attract capital are given the right to limit liability as a matter of course. In particular, it is the case in a number of European systems of corporate law that the active members of small corporate enterprises remain liable for an unlimited amount in the case of certain contingencies, such as the failure of the undertaking to pay its creditors or the enterprise being held liable for damages arising from a negligent action.

It has been suggested by some observers that it was only through a series of legal 'accidents' that small enterprises (private companies) obtained the protection of limited liability in the English model of company legislation (Kahn-Freund 1944). The debates that ranged around the phenomenon of the 'private' company throughout the nineteenth century in England clearly indicate that the availability of incorporation and the concession of limited liability were not always considered inseparable. The evidence of many witnesses before the Royal Commission on the Depression in Trade (1886) is a reflection of this continuing ambivalence concerning the concession of limited liability to all varieties of corporate entity.

Despite the many arguments raised during the nineteenth century against the desirability of making the combination of corporate personality and limited liability available to all enterprises, whether large or small, the decision in the famous case of *Salomon* v. *Salomon* (1897) AC 22, and the subsequent amendments to English company legislation in 1907, which formally recognized the 'private' company, constituted a defeat for those who wished to keep the question of limitation of liability separate from that of incorporation. The ideology established as a consequence of the resolution of these debates has only rarely been challenged since. As Perrott (1982: 83) has noted: 'we are still living under a dominant ideology regarding limited liability that ... was at its height around ... 1910. [This] ideology has assumed that freely obtainable corporate personality ... and limited liability go naturally and indivisibly together, and that each is crucially important to the other in promoting the degree of investment that made our current level of commercial and economic activity possible.'

What is important to recognize in regard to the period of historical ascendancy of the principle of limitation of liability in England is that, for much of that period, the majority of English business was still being conducted by partnerships. That is, during the nineteenth century, within most sectors of business, the incentive of limited liability was not necessary to attract capital. The potential risk of loss attending such organizational arrangements was arguably productive of a more attentive membership and a greater level of financial responsibility. As one of the commercial witnesses to the Davey Committee in 1895 stated: 'The social and personal consequences of bankruptcy, which result from unlimited liability, impose prudence on private traders; but being non-existent in the case of limited companies, business involving large risks is more easily undertaken by such companies. This fact considerably handicaps ordinary traders with unlimited liability in their competition with companies with limited liability, and has a tendency either to drive them out entirely, or to induce them to abandon their cautious rules of conduct in trading' (Board of Trade on Company Law 1895: 65).

It might, however, be suggested that, whereas in the past corporate identity and limitation of liability were separable, such is no longer the case. Today, removing the right of limited liability would be impossible because of the expectations that have accumulated on the basis of the connection between the two.

A number of recent developments within both English and European law indicate, however, that one can separate limited liability and incorporation without doing irreparable damage to the fabric of capitalism. Indeed, a process has begun whereby the pendulum is swinging back towards regarding limitation of liability as a *privilege* extended by the state which can be withheld in certain circumstances rather than as a *right* of every undertaking wishing to incorporate.

For instance, one of the current 'penalties' in the case of a company trading beyond its capacity to pay is to make directors personally liable up to an unlimited amount for all those debts contracted beyond the time in which the company could be reasonably expected to be able to repay. This is a legislative recognition that the concession of limitation of liability is contingent rather than absolute in nature. It is lost if certain conditions are not met. Perhaps, even more dramatic than the provisions in respect to the liability of directors has been growing preparedness of legislatures to fracture the connection of corporate identity and limitation of liability in the case of enterprises which do not trade, in particular those companies which are set up for the principal purpose of reducing tax liabilities. To sever the ties between corporate personality and limited liability is easier in such cases, as quite clearly none of the reasons originally advanced for making limited liability available to enterprises (e.g., attracting risk capital) apply. Instead of providing an incentive for constructive investment in new industrial projects, limitation of liability in this context merely offers unscrupulous persons the opportunity to rob the public purse.

Even more so than in systems of company law based on the English model, European legislatures have recently begun to turn away from the ideology of the inseparability of corporate status and limitation of liability. For instance, the French *Loi sur les sociétés commerciales*, 66-537, of 24 July 1966 provided in articles 114 and 248 that, if the managers of a company have acted contrary to the company's constitution or the rules of company law, or are otherwise at fault in running the company, they can be made personally liable to restore losses thereby occasioned (Le Gall 1974: 249-250). Similar developments have also occurred in German company law (Cohn 1968:69 ff; Meinhardt, 1978).[3]

The relevance of this discussion to left realists is that many of the apparently insuperable problems of corporate regulation raised in the 'corporate crime' literature might be more constructively dealt with by re-examining the relationship between corporate identity and limitation of liability. In the case of some of the more intractable arenas of regulatory failure, the severance of that link is possible. So too is the reorientation of community opinion from the prevailing ideology that incorporation with limited liability should be available as a right. Instead these artifices should be a regarded as a privilege, extended only to certain types of undertaking. Such campaigns are winnable, precisely because they cut across class lines. As one critic of the unfettered availability of limited liability incorporation noted:

[A desire among management] for the protection of limited liability as a shelter from the consequences of inefficiency does not obtain. In fact the concept of limited liability for corporate involvement is not particularly well understood among businessmen, as distinct from their lawyers, and often what is understood is not liked. A manager is just as likely, perhaps more likely, to identify with the unpaid creditor of an insolvent business, as with the original investors in that business. A bad debt owing to his company is often an irritation to him personally, and when he sees the owners of his debtor avoiding liability although they are well able to pay, and the bankers of his debtor are debenture holders, being paid in priority to his company, he is likely to be very irritated at both groups, and to doubt the commercial wisdom of limited liability and of floating charges. And even the management of banks themselves will try, in the interests of their company, to avoid the effects of limited liability by insisting on personal guarantees from the management of their private company debtors in appropriate cases. Moreover, those private guarantees are perhaps most willingly given by precisely the entrepreneurial, risk accepting managements, considered economically desirable, whom limited liability is supposed to encourage. (Perrott 1982: 115-116)

Legitimacy and Illegitimacy in Commercial Behaviour

For over a century company law has been the domain in which the distinction between the 'legitimate' and 'illegitimate' in business has been worked out. Since the nineteenth century, it has been the role of the legislature and the courts to split hairs in distinguishing the careless from the criminal. The key issue raised for the legislature in each of the recurrent panics around the 'abuse of the corporate form' has been how to punish and/or restrict 'illegitimate' practices without also affecting 'legitimate' business activities. This problem is significant because the line between what is and what is not 'legitimate' in business is considerably blurred. For instance, most citizens probably believe that trading while a company is illiquid is illegitimate. When a corporate entity so indulges itself, it puts both business creditors and employees at risk of financial loss. Continuing to trade beyond the point where one has any realistic expectation of repaying suppliers, lenders, and employees is indeed one of the most common characteristics of business failure. However, it is also true that almost *all* businesses, whether small or large, have at some stage in their existence traded while they were illiquid. Trading in such circumstances is regarded by most people in the commercial world as a normal, if undesirable, business practice. The risks that attend trading in such circumstances are regarded as being among the 'normal' risks of business. Consequently, so the argument goes, if you absolutely prohibit companies trading while illiquid, and stringently enforce such a provision, you will not only catch the dishonest and the reckless in business, but also stifle initiative among 'legitimate' risk takers.

The quandary for the commercial community is, therefore, that despite their native antipathy to regulation, they also desire government intervention to deal with the more parasitic and dishonest elements in their midst. Company law is a meeting-point of various intra- and interclass conflicts within capitalism because it performs the crucial role of setting the parameters for all regulatory interventions into business affairs. However, the difficulty in drawing any precise line between the legitimate and the illegitimate has resulted in the immobilization of company law; the confining of legislative reforms within a strait-jacket dictated by the overall protection of arbitrarily defined 'legitimate' business activities. Caution has prevailed lest commercial initiative be stifled, a situation that has almost certainly been contrary to the immediate interests of the broader community and at times has even acted against the long-term interests of capitalism itself. The historian of ICI, William J. Reader, commented in this regard that he was convinced that 'early dedication of the limited liability company to the interests of investors has been a source of weakness ever since' (1982: 200). Another commentator on modern company law stated some two decades ago: 'The history of Companies Acts could be written in terms of a century of sporadic and ill-planned endeavor to mitigate the more intolerable consequences of a basic premise that business, even when conducted under the special conditions of limited liability, is an affair between consenting ... adults. We need to build carefully but anew, from a different premise – that limited liability is an artifice sanctioned by the community, deriving as a privilege from them, and subject accordingly, to the paramount rule of their welfare' (Finer 1966: 588).[4]

The dividing line currently set by company law between legitimate and illegitimate activity, because of its conservative cast, encourages unsavoury conduct. It also, of course, allows many 'respectable' businesses to remain respectable, even when at their most errant. This has been one of the predominant reasons for the present boundaries remaining static for so long. Nevertheless, the preparedness of both business and governments to redraw the boundaries between the legitimate and the illegitimate, the fraudulent and the careless, has changed in recent decades, partly as a result of growing public intolerance towards corporate malfeasance and a heightened perception of community interest. The shift in attitude in regard to what is and is not legitimate in business has also in part stemmed from a changed perception among the business community itself as to how parasitic and dishonest elements in their own ranks should be dealt with. This altered view has manifested itself in a greater preparedness on the part of commercial victims of corporate malfeasance to prosecute offenders in the courts, rather than to have such matters dealt with informally.

Those areas where redefinition of the boundary between the legitimate and the illegitimate has been most dramatic are those concerned with the stark conflict between commercial motive and community interest. Issues such as pollution control, environmental degradation, and occupational injury and disease have become important to the recasting of the parameters of what is considered 'legitimate' in business. A recitation of traditional arguments about commercial necessity are no longer sufficient where long-term costs to the community are involved.

There are mounting signs that a similar recasting of the boundaries of acceptable conduct in business are taking place in response to the economic effects of the actions of particular capitalists. Community interests (read: 'capital in general') must be protected at the expense of individual interest (read: 'particular capitalists'). In response to the recent travails of Australian corporate regulation one commentator remarked: 'Continued inaction to settle the chaos, criminal behaviour and collapses pervading the corporate sector will make the task of rejoining the fraternity of accepted and respected dealers in world capital very difficult' (Westfield 1990: 23).

A change in emphasis in the manner of dealing with commercial practices which walked the fine line between the legitimate and illegitimate was suggested as an essential part of a strategy for rescuing Australian capital from its current crisis. Community interests have been compromised as a result of 'the lack of prosecutions for egregious corporate behaviour and the high number of so-called "commercial solutions" imposed on wrongdoers' (ibid.).[5]

This current redefinition of boundaries of behaviour can have little effect, it is submitted, unless the redistribution of the balance between community and private interests is enshrined in corporate legislation. This is more than a polemical device, such as the labelling of all corporate behaviour as 'criminal.' Rather, it constitutes a major structural shift in the underpinning of most current regulatory schemes aimed at corporate behaviour. The reasons are explored below.

Whose Interests Should the Corporation Serve?
Recasting the Balance between Shareholders and the Community

The limited liability company was developed for the benefit of owners of capital and with their interests almost solely in mind. Other parties concerned with such an enterprise's business – employees; customers; suppliers; competitors; and, more remotely, the general community – were not considered by the architects of modern company law to have any legitimate voice in the conduct of the undertaking. Limited liability companies were totally dedicated to serving the interests of their investors (Reader 1982: 200-202).

During the 1960s and 1970s, a number of challenges were made to the exclusive subservience of the 'company' to the interests of shareholders. Most such challenges were concerned with establishing the legitimate interest of workers in corporate decision making. However, instead of attempting to do so by significantly broadening the underlying interests, a company's management was required to take account of worker concerns in their decision making. These attempts predominantly relied upon the clumsy device of the 'worker director.'[6] In response to the introduction of amendments to Norwegian company law which provided for worker representation on company boards, Aubert (1976) comments: 'These new provisions in the Company Act include the employees in the circle of "brothers" ... But as long as the Company Act in other respects remains unchanged, and the traditional interpretations of its basic principles continue to be current, board members can hardly as a matter of principle work for a change of the goal of industrial life ... The structure of the Company Act gives the capital owners a legitimation to give priority to profit. The Company Act has no similar legal legitimation to give priority to conditions of work, increase of pay, environmental considerations, and societal usefulness of production, etc.' (cited in Mathieson 1980: 61).

The question of the consideration of broader community interests in corporate decision making remained untouched in the spate of reforms to company legislation inspired by considerations of 'industrial democracy' during the 1970s. Indeed it might be suggested that these reforms further legitimated the existing subordination of corporate decision making to purely private economic concerns by co-opting 'worker directors' to a structure which set the parameters within which decisions could be made. The acquiescence of worker representatives to a structure that made 'shareholder interests' pre-eminent in decision making could be seen as an admission of the marginal status of the claims of other interests to be considered in the corporate decision-making process.

One of the reasons why a recognition of the plurality of interests involved in the corporate decision-making process is so vital to left realists is the effect it would have on recasting community attitudes to what is and what is not legitimate behaviour on the part of corporations. For instance, it would clearly be impermissible for a company to continue trading while it is illiquid without adverting to the effects this might have on creditors, employees, and customers. If there were no evidence that these interests were not considered, then this could constitute *prima facie* evidence of an offence being committed. If these matters were considered, the record of those deliberations would constitute evidence of the reasonableness of the corporation's decision to continue to trade.

Perhaps most important, a recognition of the legitimacy of a range of interests besides those of shareholders in corporate decision making would open up a range of possibilities with regard to sanctions that would normally be opposed by corporate interests. These include: legal audits, equity fines, probation orders, and the application of community-service orders to corporations. Current sanctions applied to corporations or to corporate officers judiciously avoid touching the interior life of the corporation. Regulatory schemes presently in force are not aimed at rehabilitating 'bad' corporations or 'bad' executives. The imposition of a fine or a short term of imprisonment leave intact the structures which were implicated in the corporate transgression; the readjustment of internal factors implicated in offending are left to the corporation itself.

If, however, the community was seen to have a legitimate interest in the manner in which corporate decisions were reached, then the community could be considered to have a legitimate interest in intervening in the internal governance of corporations which offended against community norms (and, particularly so, in the case of persistent offenders). For instance, if a corporation involved in timber production failed to take account of community interests in conducting its logging operations (e.g., by logging in an area subject to an environmental protection order) or a demolition company knocked down a historical building in defiance of community interests in the preservation of that building (e.g., evidenced by a Heritage listing), then those companies might be required to issue shares to a community representative – in the former case, say, to an environmental group, and in the latter, to the National Trust. In other words, offenders would expose themselves to a range of unpalatable interventions by outside organizations into their internal affairs, rather than being simply exposed to a monetary penalty which left their corporate structure untouched.

Disciplining and Punishing Corporate Offenders

In the conclusion to his excellent study, *Regulating Fraud* (1987), Michael Levi suggests that, if certain varieties of corporate malfeasance are to be dealt with at all, then social control must be dispersed and, at least in part, privatized (he cites the eradication of insider trading and the enforcement of prohibitions on unauthorized dealing in securities as examples of these principles). Surveillance by external bodies is clearly an ineffective and inappropriate mechanism for dealing with such matters.

Much of the recent literature on self-regulation has taken on a very different guise from that which emerged from the New Right's assertion of the merits of deregulation in the 1980s. Unlike their predecessors, recent analyses have been concerned with making corporations more accountable to the broader community through the operation of certain 'self-regulatory' strategies. Such strategies – the establishment of ethics committees and audit committees; the rule that directors of public corporations are responsible for losses that result from business judgments which do not conform to community standards; the imposition of unlimited liability on corporate officers for losses suffered by creditors, investors, and so on, when they continued to operate their corporation beyond the time it could be reasonably expected to trade out of difficulties – are all concerned, in one way or another, with making corporations and those who run them more accountable.

Of course, many of the above strategies have failed in practice or are difficult to implement. This, however, does not detract from the point that there is currently in train a series of 'self-regulatory' strategies which collectively challenge prevailing normative conceptions of the corporation.

Before turning to a more detailed examination of possible mechanisms by which the normative content of the corporate form might be transformed, it is worth dwelling on the limitations of any strategy which relies, as the one adumbrated here does, on a greater degree of 'accountability' on the part of corporations to the community or communities who are affected by their actions and on a greater role for these communities in corporate decision making. The issue of what 'accountability' might look like, if it were to have a true transformative role, has been explored by John Lea and Jock Young with respect to policing. They conclude that, for 'accountability' to have any real effect, it would have to assign a significant role to local communities in relation to the deployment and the strategies of policing adopted in the relevant geographical area. They also identify a problem that also applies to 'community' involvement in the policing of corporations – this is the issue of how one might properly identify the 'community' for the purposes of such programs. The difficulty experienced in identifying the relevant 'community' is identified by John Lea and Jock Young in the following passage: 'The most important issue that has to be faced is precisely what do we mean by the *local community* under whose control we are proposing that many aspects of policing be placed? It is one thing to argue that the national political process excludes significant social interests; it is quite another to argue that the locality can somehow be constituted as a political entity with sufficient political coherence to control its own policing policy' (1984: 237).

The problem identified in this passage applies equally to community interventions into corporations. The affected 'community' to which corporate behaviour must be made more 'accountable' lacks political coherence, and is as subject to 'capture' by particular interest groups as is the community to which police must become more accountable. But as Lea and Young argue, this is not a reason to abandon the project of making social institutions more accountable. Indeed, they suggest that leftist conceptions of the 'withering away' of such institutions are idealistic pipe dreams. Consequently, we must look at ways in which such institutions (police, corporations, etc.) can be made more genuinely accountable and responsive to the community which they, at least nominally, serve. Three other propositions advanced by Lea and Young offer some insight into the conditions for a successful implementation of such a strategy of community accountability. First, Lea and Young suggest the community affected by policing is best placed to define its 'policing' needs. It could similarly be argued in respect to corporations that the community (or communities) affected by their actions are the best-placed groups to identify regulatory needs.

Second, Lea and Young suggest that debate around such issues will lead to a greater degree of cohesion in the local community (i.e., participation in genuine decision making is likely to play a significant role in reconstituting the now fractured 'community'). In the case of corporate behaviour, the process of fragmentation of the 'communities' affected by it and their 'capture' by particular interests (e.g., trade unions being seen as the voice of the community of workers) might be halted as a consequence of providing the members with a real voice in corporate regulation.

Third, Lea and Young advance the view that the effectiveness of institutions will be achieved only when they are properly integrated with community needs. For instance, in the case of the police, clear-up rates are currently so low because of community mistrust of the police. If the police were genuinely accountable to the community, Lea and Young assert, they would be more effective. Again it could be asserted that, if corporations were seen as 'public' institutions with certain 'private' elements accountable to the 'communities' affected by their actions, then an overall improvement in corporate behaviour might result with benefits to both corporate citizens and communities. Effective monitoring of corporate financial activities would lead to a lower morbidity rate among corporations and to flow-on effects to the economy. More directly ineffective and dangerous work practices would be eliminated, creating greater company productivity. Greater scrutiny of tax compliance would lead to larger public revenues and the possibility of expanded welfare budgets, public work projects, and infrastructural development. As with policing, the relationship between community and corporations need not be seen as an antagonistic one. Properly implemented, accountability would be a policy with mutual benefits to the community and the corporate sector.

Any attempt to make corporations more 'accountable' will have a long-term normative effect on the institution in question. Donzelot's work on the family is a possible point of departure for a better understanding of how a variety of sanctions and self-regulatory mechanisms might be used in reconstituting the 'private' sphere of the corporation. In *The Policing of Families* (1979),[7] Jacques Donzelot explains how the modern family is not exclusively a private domain, as is sometimes assumed, but rather is a hybrid of public and private domains. While the family is apparently quarantined off from public life, politics, and the economy, it is also susceptible to interventions by state institutions concerned with the care and control of children. Donzelot asserts that, as a consequence of this hybrid status, the intimate space of the family cannot be understood other than as an environment which is reconstructed through the action of social policy. Different family members are entrusted with the enforcement of particular biopolitical objectives; in other words, certain members of the 'private' sphere of the family 'police' the family to ensure that it meets certain objectives which originate in the 'public' domain. The family doctor and public-health visitor both act as inspectors to ensure these objectives are being met and to define the competences of various family members in respect to particular 'policing' functions.

Much of the literature on the history of nineteenth-century companies regards the family estate as the real exemplar of the modern corporate entity, rather than the 'republican' model implied by the formal 'democratic' structure recited in company law statutes (see Reader 1982; cf. Fraser 1983). As conceived in the 'private' sphere, the company was considered to be an unsuitable candidate for public interventions. The architect of modern English company law, Robert Lowe, reiterated time and again the undesirability of the government's directly intervening in the affairs of corporate enterprises, even when the actions of those enterprises may have had 'public' consequences. The corporation was never constructed as a private panoptic space in the way in which the family was. The members of the 'family estate' of the corporation entrusted with enforcing certain types of conduct were not so successfully enmeshed in their 'policing' functions. The 'general body of shareholders' responsible for ensuring that managers discharged their duties honestly were denied the information upon which they could adequately perform that task. Auditors quite often were dissuaded from 'whistle-blowing' on the grounds that they would tarnish the public reputation of the corporation and create economic havoc.

In the case of corporations, it was not solely the reluctance of 'insiders' to perform a policing role that led to a quite different intersection of the public and private, but also the lack of effective public demand to inspect and socially evaluate the internal functioning of the corporation. For most of the past century, company registrars regarded their functions as merely ministerial. Even when the company legislation prescribed penalties for specific instances where the corporations internal functioning broke down, the registrar of companies was rarely given explicit power to intervene. Nor was any other public official.

Also, while the competence of and forms of relationship between different individuals and groups within the corporation were at first precisely defined, the extant company legislation gave members few rights of access to financial and other information upon which they could intelligently intervene in the affairs of the corporation. When more information was required of management by the legislation, the legal position in regard to the distribution of power in the enterprise changed in favour of management so that the members could no longer intervene and run the affairs of the corporation when management had been financially irresponsible or had otherwise erred (Gower 1979: 144).[8]

An understanding of the means by which to constrain the worst excesses of corporate activity cannot be obtained without a consideration of the intersection of the public and private in the 'policing' of corporations. A reconstruction of the private sphere of the corporation will be necessary to rein in the more antisocial aspects of corporate behaviour. As suggested above, one technique which should be employed is the introduction of 'community interests' into the decision-making processes of the corporation. Another technique of facilitating the intersection of the public and private in the 'regulation' of corporations is to embed in 'public' sanctions for malfeasance a whole array of devices to allow outsiders to penetrate the 'private' sphere of the corporation.

Sanctions presently employed against errant corporations have been largely ineffective in decreasing levels of malfeasance. A variety of reasons have been advanced to explain the failure of current strategies. These explanations range from those that place the blame on the ineffectiveness of regulatory agencies to those which suggest the real problem lies in not setting fines at a level that is truly deterrent.[9] Most of the criticisms of current practices regarding the application of sanctions thus fall into the trap of proposing that the current difficulties would be overcome if 'more' was done: sanctions would be effective if more resources were devoted to the regulatory agencies charged with their enforcement; fines would have real deterrent effects if their dollar amounts were more substantial; sanctions against company officers would be more effective if more individuals in management positions were prosecuted; and so on.

The 'more is better' syndrome in respect to corporate sanctions needs to be broken. Regulation of corporations by mechanisms which leave untouched the private domain of the corporation will *never* be effective because the corporation is not exclusively an economic or legal unit. Like the family, it is also a 'political' unit. This dimension is important to recognize for most current systems of sanctions dealing with corporate malfeasance assume that corporate decision making can be explained by reference to factors external to the corporation. As one recent commentary on the inefficacy of sanctions observed:

Both neo-classical and Marxian economics accept the subordination of enterprise decisions to external conditions. Neo-classical economics reduces the functioning of enterprises to a series of rational responses designed to maximize profits subject to abstract constraints placed upon decisions by 'the market'. Marxism conceives individual enterprises as mere fragments of the totality of capital in motion ... The inadequacy of these explanations of enterprise decisions is evident from their failure to specify the mechanisms whereby the profit maximization objective, the market or capitalist relations of production act as determining principles in corporate decision making ... There are aspects of enterprise organization and behaviour which bear little direct relation to macro-economic considerations. (Lowe 1987: 37)

Consequently, even if one could set fines at an optimum level of effectiveness by means of some form of calculus, they would still be unable to curb malfeasance because they would leave untouched a variety of 'political' factors which may have significantly contributed to the corporate decision in question. If corporations are not always economic rationalists in their decision making, then financial disincentives in respect to decisions which run counter to community interests may be at best only partially effectual. As Fisse and Braithwaite (1984) have pointed out, 'fines against corporations pose a monetary threat which is not well-tuned to the non financial decision-making factors which pulse through organisations.' They continue: 'Corporate personnel conceive their own ends in terms which may diverge substantially from the goals of their corporation or its organizational sub-units. For instance, lower management may falsify pollution compliance reports to avoid closure of an obsolete plant, not so much to maximise profits for the firm as to save their own jobs or reputation in the local community' (p. 132). In order for a regime of more effective corporate 'regulation' to be instituted, the irony is that some 'deregulation' will need to take place. 'More of the same' will simply not solve the current crisis in corporate regulation as its faith that structures external to corporations motivate their behaviour is misplaced. Regulatory strategies based on such assumptions fail to comprehend the necessity of an intertwining of private and public domains of corporate activity in any effective 'regulatory' strategy. A number of proposals for alternative forms of sanctions put forward by analysts of business regulation provide examples of how the public and private may combine to produce a potent regulatory strategy.

The first such alternative sanction which we will examine is the 'equity fine' which was first elaborated by John Coffee. The proposal advanced by Coffee is, in its simplest form, explained in the following manner: 'when very severe fines need to be imposed on the corporation, they should be imposed not in cash, but in the equity securities of the corporation. The convicted corporation should be required to authorise and issue such number of shares to the state's victim compensation fund as would have an expected market value equal to the cash fine necessary to deter illegal activity. The fund should then be able to liquidate the securities in whatever manner maximises its return' (1981: 413). As suggested earlier, a variant on this would to be to require the offending corporation to issue shares to some appropriate representative community organization – for instance, in the case of an offence against pollution laws, the corporation could be required to issue shares to a consortium of environmental groups who would manage them on behalf of the community (McQueen 1989).

The use of equity fines would create an aperture into the private 'political' realm of the corporation. They would provide a point of intersection for the private and the public domains. First, they would do so by creating a 'political' motivation for managers and corporate officers to desist from making decisions that may lead to a 'watering' of capital. The spectre of a shareholder backlash to managerial initiatives which compromised their stake in the corporation would lead to greater circumspection on the part of managements in considering whether to engage in antisocial practices, particularly where there was a relatively high probability of being discovered. Second, if a corporation did transgress, the introduction of a block of shareholders (with the right to appoint one or more directors) into the private domain of the corporation would constitute a mechanism whereby there could be a constant internal monitoring of the corporation's behaviour. Just as specific family members may be charged with monitoring certain familial behaviours (e.g., the mother ensuring that the father does not sexually or physically abuse the children), the 'community' shareholder/director, appointed to the corporation as a consequence of past transgressions, would be charged with ensuring that further malfeasance did not occur. The effective functioning of this self-regulatory mechanism would be further ensured by regular 'inspections' by public bodies charged with regulating aspects of corporate behaviour (pollution control bodies, equal opportunity agencies, companies and securities commissions, and so on).

The use of equity fines alone, however, would not be sufficient to bring about the transformation of corporate regulation. They are only suitable for dealing with certain forms of malfeasance. Also, they provide only a limited ingress into the private domain of the corporation. Despite the 'political' dimensions to their operation, they still rely primarily on financial incentives to deter corporate malfeasance. Fisse and Braithwaite have noted in this regard: 'As regards congruence with non-financial values in organizational decision-making, equity fines ... fall short. Dilution of equity could have some adverse effects upon corporate and managerial prestige and power, yet the impact of the sanction would remain predominantly financial ... Coffee has urged that equity fines would play on managerial fear of hostile take-over bids ... however ... the bloc of shares created by an equity fine would have to be very large indeed to create any serious risk of take-over bid for a large company' (1984: 135).

A further form of sanction which might be deployed as part of an overall strategy for the 'regulation' of corporate behaviour is to require offending corporations (or offending divisions of a larger corporate structure) to subject themselves to annual (or even bi-annual) legal audits. The idea is that a qualified outsider is appointed by the courts or an administrative agency to monitor the compliance of the corporation in question to the range of regulatory provisions to which they are subject. The 'legal auditor' would have full access to all corporate documents and decision-making processes. To return to our analogy with the family, it would be like having a live-in social worker placed in a problem family.

Such an arrangement in the corporate context has often been tied to another mechanism imported from the criminal law. This is the idea of probation orders. Instead of fining a corporation, it would be placed on probation, with the requirement that it demonstrate to the court or regulatory agency within a specified period of time that it has conducted a review of its internal managerial processes to determine the factors responsible for the breach, and that it has adjusted its internal functioning so that a repetition will not occur. The 'legal auditor' mentioned above would act as an independent consultant in the conducting of the review. Some years ago a South Australian government committee (Mitchell Committee 1977) suggested that such a system should be adopted. The benefits, both in cost and in efficiency, were seen to be particularly attractive: 'Essentially, internal discipline orders would require a corporation to investigate an offence committed on its behalf, undertake appropriate disciplinary proceeding, and return a detailed and satisfactory compliance report to the court issuing the particular order ... the object of internal discipline orders thus would not be to produce guilty individuals to the prosecuting authorities, but to cast part of the burden of enforcement squarely upon the enterprise on whose behalf an offence has been committed' (Mitchell Committee 1977: 361-362). Again, this is a form of sanctioning which depends upon an intersection of the private and public, rather than reinforcing the divide which separates the two spheres in present regulatory practice. As has been suggested throughout this essay, the only real hope for effective regulation of business practices is to abandon regulation from outside, relying upon macroeconomic 'pleasures and pains' to ensure good citizenship on the part of corporations. Instead regulatory strategies should be aiming at operating from inside the corporate structure. The corporation should no longer be conceived of as an inviolate private domain but as a meeting-point of private and public concerns. Just like the modern family, it could take on certain panoptic characteristics. Members of the corporation, just as is the case with members of the modern family, could be 'required' to police the corporation.

Conclusions

Most leftist responses to the regulation of corporate offending have been inadequate. A number of members of the broad left eschew any interest in the question of company law at all. They regard such legislation as irredeemably capitalist in nature. There can, according to such arguments, be no inscription of socialist or progressive values into company law because the form and content of regulation is prescribed in advance by the forces of production.

Other leftists have been more adventurous and have proposed a number of desirable reforms to company law. These have included the proposal that worker representatives be included on company boards, suggestions that a variety of alternative sanctions applied to corporations and the agencies responsible for the regulation of corporate malfeasance be restructured. However, most of these sorts of 'leftist' positions are difficult to distinguish from 'small-l' liberalism Many of these positions also are located on a continuum with current legislative and regulatory provisions and practices. They often involve proposals for an augmentation to the bureaucratic machinery currently charged with corporate regulation. Proposals which entail self-regulation are avoided because both leftists and small-l liberals doubt that capitalist enterprises can regulate their own activities without 'cheating.'

In a tentative and preliminary manner, this essay has attempted to suggest how a distinct 'left' program of corporate law restructuring might be developed around a demand for greater accountability on the part of corporations, and those who run them, towards the members of the communities in which they are situated. I have also proposed ways in which the demand for greater accountability on the part of corporations might be utilized to challenge the long-held belief that at least certain of their activities are inviolate as a result their essentially 'private' nature. It has been suggested that the division between 'private' and 'public' in this context is false.

It has also been suggested that, on the one hand, the proposed approach avoids the trap of assuming that current regulatory strategies have failed simply because company law is in its 'form' capitalist in nature and thus irredeemable; on the other hand, the proposed approach avoids making the assumption that the failure is attributable to insufficient resources being dedicated to company regulation. The suggestion here is that leftists examine strategies to make certain self-regulatory strategies work in favour of those affected by corporate behaviour. The problems of regulating the corporation have been compared with the problems involved in regulating that very 'private' space – the family. The manner in which those latter problems were addressed in the late nineteenth century with the incorporation of the family into the new domain of the 'social' provides an example of the manner in which intersection of the private and public might occur in the realm of corporate 'regulation' (cf. Sargent 1989).

Corporate entities have generally been regulated on the basis that their internal functioning is part of an inviolate 'private' domain. Intervention in the 'political' processes internal to the corporation has been considered to be particularly sapping to commercial initiative. As public interventions to the internal domain have been ruled out because they might stifle business initiatives, the corporation has been extended considerable rights by the state. Rights such as limitation of liability have been extended to corporate entities with little or no benefits flowing to the community as a consequence. The supposed benefit to the community in terms of greater amounts of risk capital being extended to business is doubtful, and certainly has no application in the case of enterprises which do not trade or have no 'public' investors.

Accountability of corporations to the 'communities' in which they are situated should become a key demand for progressives interested in company law. Also, community interest in the internal affairs of enterprises should be asserted as a right. Decision making in corporations should be, at least in part, subservient to community concerns. The assertion of this right on the part of the 'public' is a necessary prerequisite for a reconstruction of regulatory practices.

Above, an analogy was made between the corporation and the family. Donzelot describes the family as neither a truly public nor a private domain; in terms of regulation, it is a hybrid of the two. The same intersection of public and private 'regulation' might also occur in respect to the corporation. Certain corporate members could be made responsible for ensuring the corporation does not, for instance, discharge dangerous chemical residues into public waterways. If such a transgression took place, *they* would be responsible for the offence, along with the corporation. Just as a mother might be disqualified from assuming her maternal role (e.g., when her children are taken from her and made wards of the state), a director of a corporation held responsible for pollution offences might be prohibited from acting as a director for a specified period of time if an infraction of pollution regulations occurs.

This 'mode' of 'policing' drawn from Donzelot's account of how the normative content of the modern family is arrived at and how the antisocial family is kept in check, when applied to the corporation, suggests ways in which a number of the regulatory 'problems' arising from the claimed inviolability of the 'privacy' of even the most antisocial of corporations may be overcome. It also suggests how certain problems relating to attributing blame to corporate officials might be overcome by making a corporate official 'accountable' to those in the 'community' when it comes to ensuring compliance.

In addition, it demonstrates the possible means for deploying effective non-financial sanctions against corporate transgressors. Just as persistent antisocial behaviour within a family leads to greater and greater interventions into the private domain of the family by state officials, and to greater and greater pressure on members of the family who have 'failed' to be 'good' parents to retrieve their social standing and self-esteem as such, so too in the corporate domain a persistent record of offending should allow for greater and greater intervention on the part of 'public' officials or publicly appointed representatives of the community into the private domain of the corporation.

Unlike many of the current mechanisms of corporate regulation, the type of strategy outlined is flexible. It can deal with the different characteristics of different types of company – the 'public' company, the 'private' company, the family trust company, and so on. It can also deal with the specificity of particular transgressions – different intersections of the private and public might be appropriate to deal with financial malfeasance than is the case with transgressions in respect to environmental discharges.

By adopting a program along the lines suggested in this essay, the left will not only arm itself with a workable alternative to current corporate regulatory strategies, but also avoid becoming immersed in many of the hoary chestnuts which inhabit the debates in this area, such as the relative merits of regulation versus deregulation and the long-term effects of the separation of ownership and control. Much, however, still needs to be done. One area that needs to be explored in the process of constructing a 'carceral archipelago' of the type suggested in this essay is the question of how to avoid a differential application of the panoptic principle to particular varieties of corporate actor. In the area of the policing of families, the full application of the techniques outlined in Donzelot's exegesis has occurred only in the case of the marginal family; the destitute urban family being the site where such 'policing' is in full operation. In the case of companies it might also prove to be the case that the form of private/public intersection I have advocated can only be fully effective in the case of those corporations at the margins. For the large respectable corporate enterprise, the intervention of the public world into the private domain of the enterprise may be unacceptable. However, the mechanisms I have outlined may enmesh such enterprises, at least for a time, in their own 'self-regulatory' rhetoric.

Notes

1 For an excellent critical discussion of the literature on legal pluralism see Griffiths (1986).

2 Frank Pearce (this volume) has made an important contribution in this area by showing,

via a re-evaluation of data collected by the second Islington Crime Survey, the considerable concern expressed by members of a local community in respect to white-collar crime.

3   See Articles 300 *et seq* of the *Aktiengestez (AktG)*, 1965, as amended.

4   The same emphasis on the fact that the rights attached to incorporation and the privileges enjoyed by officers of corporations are conferred at too low a cost is present in a number of the comments made at a recent Australian Institute of Criminology seminar on the policing of corporate crime. Dr Sutton, of the Bureau of Crime Statistics and Research, made the following comment in the course of questions to the panel: 'I would suggest from the little reading I have done of the *Companies Act* that enormous protections have been developed for people who operate companies [yet those protections are obtained at little personal cost to those individuals] ... Directors are not required to pass tests, they are not required to submit themselves to periodical examinations, and they are not required to participate in disclosure other than that which is specified in the *Annual Reports* and the like which is really not enough to determine whether or not what they have done has been carried out in any sort of ethical manner' (Institute of Criminology 1987: 81).

5   See also the letter from Gough Whitlam, the former prime minister of Australia, to the *Sydney Morning Herald* (1990).

6   However, provisions in respect to both were introduced into English company legislation during the 1970s. In addition to providing for 'worker' directors, English company legislation was amended to require mangers to take account of employee interests in the course of their decision making. This is now enshrined in s. 309 (1) of the Companies Act, 1985 (UK) which reads: 'The matters to which the directors of a company are to have regard in the performance of their functions include the interests of the company's employees in general, as well as the interests of its members.' In a 1989 Australian report on directors' duties this provision was said to be 'largely unenforceable' (p. 87). The report then went on to cite Sealy (1987) approvingly to the effect that s. 309 of the English Companies Act 1985 was 'either one of the most incompetent or one of the most cynical pieces of drafting on record.' See also the discussion of employee interests in Hull and Docksey (1981: 207).

7   For an extensive discussion of Donzelot's arguments and the criticisms which have been directed at them, see Minson (1985).

8   Gower states in this regard: 'Until at least the end of the nineteenth century it seems to have been generally assumed that the principle remained intact that the general meeting was the company whereas the directors were merely the *agents* of the company subject to the control of the company in general meeting ... In 1906, however, the Court of Appeal, in *Automatic Self-Cleansing Filter Syndicate Co.* v. *Cunninghame* [1906] 2 Ch 34 ruled that the division of powers between the board and the company in general meeting depended ... entirely on the construction of the articles of association' (1979: 144).

9 An excellent summary of the various critical accounts of 'business regulation' can be found in the introductory chapter to Jones (1982).

References

Board of Trade on Company Law. 1985. *Report*. London: HMSO

Coffee, J.C. 1981. 'No Soul to Damn, No Body to Kick: An Unscandalized Inquiry into the Problem of Corporate Punishment.' *Michigan Law Review*, 79: 386-459

Cohn, E.J. 1968. *Manual of German Law,* vol. 2. London: Dobbs Terry

Cooney Committee, Company Directors' Duties. 1989. Report of the Social and Fiduciary Obligations of Company Directors. Canberra: Standing Committee on Legal and Constitutional Affairs, AGPS

Donzelot, J. 1979. *The Policing of Families*. London: Pantheon

Finer, M. 1966. 'Company Fraud.' *The Accountant*, 5 November: 583-588

Fisse, B., and J. Braithwaite. 1984. 'Sanctions against Corporations: Dissolving the Monopoly of Fines,' in R. Tomasic, ed., *Business Regulation in Australia*, 129-146. Sydney: CCH

Fraser, A. 1983. 'The Corporation as a Body Politic.' *Telos*, 57: 5-40

Gower, L.C.B. 1979. *Principles of Modern Company Law*, 4th ed. London: Stevens and Son

Griffiths, J. 1986. 'What Is Legal Pluralism?' *Journal of Legal Pluralism and Unofficial Law*, 24: 1-56

Hull, J.K., and C.A. Docksey. 1981. 'Implications for Employees of the New Companies Act.' *Company Lawyer*, 2: 203-214

Institute of Criminology. 1987. *Policing Corporate Crime*. Sydney

Jones, K. 1982. *Law and Economy*. London: Academic Press

Kahn-Freund, O. 1944. 'Some Reflections on Company Law Reform.' *Modern Law Review*, April: 54-66

Le Gall, J. 1974. *French Company Law*. London: Oyez Publishing

Lea, J., and J. Young. 1984. *What Is to Be Done about Law and Order?* Harmondsworth: Penguin

Levi, M. 1987. *Regulating Fraud: White Collar Crime and the Criminal Process*. London: Tavistock

Lowe, G. 1987. 'Corporations as Objects of Regulation.' *Law in Context*, 5: 30-46

McQueen, R. 1989. 'The New Companies and Securities Legislation: A Fundamental Departure?' *Australian Quarterly*, 61: 481-497

Mathieson, T. 1980. *Law, Society and Political Action*. London: Academic Press

Meinhardt, P. 1978. *Company Law in Europe*. Aldershot: Gower

Minson, J. 1985. *Genealogies of Morals*. London: Macmillan

Mitchell Committee. 1977. *Report*. Adelaide: South Australian Government Publishing Office

Perrot, David. 1982. 'Changes in Attitude to Limited Liability – The European Experience,' in T. Orhnial, ed., *Limited Liability and the Corporation*, 81-121. London: Croom Helm

Reader, W.J. 1982. 'Versatility Unlimited: Reflections on the History and Nature of the Limited Liability Company,' in T. Orhnial, ed., *Limited Liability and the Corporation*, 191-204. London: Croom Helm

Royal Commission on the Depression in Trade. 1986. *Report.* London: HMSO

Sargent, N. 1989. 'Law, Ideology and Corporate Crime: A Critique of Instrumentalism.' *Canadian Journal of Law and Society*, 4: 39-77

Sealy, L.F. 1987. 'Directors' "Wider" Responsibilities – Problems, Conceptual, Practical, and Procedural.' *Monash Law Review*, 13: 164

Snider, L. 1991. 'The Regulatory Dance: Understanding Reform Processes in Corporate Crime.' *International Journal of Sociology of Law*, 19: 209-236

Sydney Morning Herald. 1990. 'Letter from Gough Whitlam on the *Corporations Act Case*,' 15 February: 12

Westfield, M. 1990. 'A Blinkered View from the Bench,' *Sydney Morning Herald*, 9 February: 23

PART THREE
Left Realism and Feminism

10 Women, Crime, Feminism, and Realism

Pat Carlen

This essay focuses on women's lawbreaking and the academic, social, and political responses to it. It does not discuss female victims of crime, or women working in the criminal justice or penal agencies. The primary purpose of this essay is to assess the potential of realist criminology to inform: (1) analyses of women's lawbreaking and criminalization; and (2) campaigns and policies aimed at redressing the discriminatory wrongs that women presently suffer in the courts and prisons.

Before assessing the contribution that realism has to make to current debates and concerns about women, crime, and criminology, however, it is necessary to consider whether there is a need for a special theory of women's lawbreaking, and to touch on questions concerning the potential for, and/or desirability of, a feminist criminology and/or jurisprudence.

The essay is therefore divided into five parts: the first two parts examine the contributions and limits of feminism in relation to women, crime, and criminology; the third and fourth explicate the limits and potential of realist criminology in relation to women, crime, and social policy; finally, part five outlines an agenda for the realization of some attainable ideals both in the deconstruction and theorization of 'women and crime' questions and in the development of policies designed to ensure that the penal regulation of females does not further increase their oppression as unconventional women, as Black people, and as poverty-stricken defendants.

1. Women, Crime, and Criminology: The Contributions of Feminism and Feminists

Since the publication of Carol Smart's *Women, Crime and Criminology: A Feminist Critique* in 1976, there has been a much more sustained focus upon lawbreaking women, a topic almost ignored by criminologists prior to the mid 1970s (see Adler 1975; Simon 1975; Smart and Smart 1978; Heidensohn 1985; Carlen et al. 1985; Messerschmidt 1986; Naffine 1987; Adelberg and Currie 1987; Allen 1987; Carlen and Worrall 1987; Carlen 1988; J. Allen 1988; Cain 1989; Worrall 1990). Not all the authors writing on women in the criminal justice and penal systems have explicitly claimed that their works have been informed by 'feminist' theories or concepts. Nor have all explicitly styled themselves 'feminist.' Yet because they have collectively contributed to a demolition of certain sexist myths concerning women's lawbreaking and have called into question the more discriminatory and oppressive forms of the social control and regulation of women, I shall in this section use 'feminist' very loosely to refer to all those who, in writing of women lawbreakers, have been concerned to remedy the wrongs done to women criminals by criminologists, police, courts, and prisons. Their achievements have been diverse.

One of the first concerns of the new wave of writers on women and crime was to put 'women' on the criminological agenda, to demonstrate that most previous explanations of crime had in fact been explanations of *male* crime, and to argue that when women break the law they do so in circumstances that are often very different from those in which men become lawbreakers (see, for example, McRobbie and Garber 1976). A constant theme in these analyses has been that women's crimes are preeminently the crimes of the powerless (see Box 1983; Messerschmidt 1986; and Carlen 1988).

A second concern has been to demonstrate how essentialized and sexualized typifications of womanhood, gender, and femininity have fashioned not only criminological explanations of women's lawbreaking, but also the treatment of deviant women by the welfare, criminal justice, and penal systems (see Carlen 1983; Edwards 1984; Eaton 1986; Worrall 1990).

Third, some writers have joined with campaigning organizations and/or women ex-prisoners to campaign for a better deal for women in trouble, before the courts, or in prison (see Carlen et al., 1985; Seear and Player 1986; Padell and Stevenson 1988; Casale 1989). And some of these latter have not disdained an explicit policy orientation (see Seear and Player, 1986; Carlen, 1988, 1990; Casale, 1989).

Finally, some writers (usually, but not always, explicitly eschewing empirical and policy-oriented work altogether) have been concerned to debate (variously): (1) whether the development of a feminist criminology is a possible theoretical project (Cousins 1980; Carlen et al. 1985); (2) whether the focus on women lawbreakers is a 'proper' concern of 'feminism' (Allen 1988; Smart 1990); and (3) the desirability (or not) of a feminist jurisprudence (see Boyle et al. 1985, for Canada; MacKinnon 1987, for the United States; Smart 1989, for England; and Stang-Dahl 1987, for Norway). As the first two questions will be touched on below, in Part 2, I end this section by assessing the extent to which a feminist jurisprudence might benefit women in conflict with the criminal law.

As Carol Smart has recently observed: 'The search for a feminist jurisprudence signals the shift away from a concentration on law reform and "adding women" into legal considerations to a concern with fundamental issues like legal logic, legal values, justice, neutrality and objectivity' (1989: 66). Yet although Smart argues that we do indeed need to theorize women's oppression, she expresses reservations about the quest for a feminist jurisprudence. Such reservations stem from: (1) fears that a feminist jurisprudence would merely replace one closed and global system of 'Truth' with another; and (2) her own analyses, which well illustrate that when women go to the law in civil cases they frequently find that even when their claims are rooted in the apparent logic of legislative reforms that could be expected to right women's wrongs, 'once enacted, legislation is in the hands of individuals and agencies far removed from the values and policies of the women's movement' (ibid.: 164). For these (and several other) reasons Smart sounds a 'warning to feminism to avoid the siren call of law' (ibid.: 160). Avoidance of law, however, is not an option open to those women who stand before it not voluntarily seeking remedy but rather involuntarily awaiting punishment.

I take Carol Smart's point that a 'feminist jurisprudence' might merely replace one closed and global system of truth with another and that, consequently, application of some principles of a feminist jurisprudence (e.g., 'equality,' 'the appeal to rights') might merely result in advancing certain feminist claims to the detriment of others. But, at the same time, I would argue that use of the indefinite article can put *any* jurisprudence in its place. For although I can conceive of the possibility of several feminist jurisprudences – i.e., perspectives on the interpretation and administration of laws that are informed by the knowledge that women's life experiences are different from men's – I can think, too, of several other jurisprudential and political considerations that might also rightly inform decision making and assessments in criminal cases involving women. For instance, officials and campaigners might sometimes correctly calculate that, if they argue for equality of provision for their women clients, their claims will be answered by withdrawal of the existing facilities in question from their male clients. Likewise, a competent probation officer might know both that her client will gain advantage if it can be demonstrated that she is a good housewife and mother, *and* that by privileging that woman's housewifely and mothering performances she will also be colluding in, and promoting, the stereotype of the *criminal* woman who is not a wife and mother and thereby possibly disadvantaging single, divorced, childless, and lesbian female offenders.

The existence of dilemmas like those outlined above should not be surprising. The varied constellations of political, ideological, and economic conditions in which penal philosophies are realized mean that we can seldom expect to read off a penal policy from a jurisprudence – whatever it is called. This is Smart's point, too, and it is because she recognizes both the limits to theory and the effectivity of law that she recommends that feminists adopt a deconstructionist approach to law and constantly call into question its claims to 'Truth.' None the less, because of the 'involuntary' relationship between women lawbreakers and the criminal law, and because of the dominance of the metaphor of the 'rational man' in the criminal courts, I shall argue in the final part of this essay that in relation to this (criminal) branch of law, feminists might both engage in the deconstructionist struggle *and* suggest principled ways in which the criminal justice and penal systems might become more *women-wise*.

2. Women, Crime, and Criminology: The Limits to Feminism/Feminist Theory

The Limits to Feminism in Providing an Explanatory Theory of Women's Lawbreaking and Criminalization

One of the major problems of writing specifically about women as lawbreakers is that such gender specification can imply that reasons women-as-a-biological-grouping have for committing crime are *essentially* different from men's. Indeed, once biological explanations of crime have been abandoned, why is a special theory required to explain women's lawbreaking? For as Cousins (1980) pointed out ten years ago, *any* global explanations of a taken-for-granted *'female criminality'* must be as reductionist and essentializing as the much-maligned biological ones. Rather, in order to theorize the relationships between the agency of criminal law and the organization of sexual difference, theorists should abandon stable referents for the categories 'male' and 'female' and 'masculine' and 'feminine' on the grounds that these categories are 'produced as definite forms of difference by the particular discourses and practices in which they appear' (ibid.: 117). However, once the historically and socially specific discourses and practices within which lawbreaking and criminalization occur in Britain, the United States, Canada, and Australia *are* investigated, a concern with gender constructions rapidly merges with questions concerning class, racism, and imperialism. Certainly, feminist assumptions about the relative powerlessness of women and the ways in which gender typifications structure the administration of criminal law have resulted in building up a body of knowledge demonstrating that women's law violations are in the main committed and criminalized under different ideological and political conditions than are men's; prevailing typifications of femininity do result in lawbreaking women being seen as doubly deviant – as citizens and as women – and prevailing typifications of gender differentiation do result in women being judged less on the seriousness of their offences and more on the extent to which their lifestyles violate conventional notions of women's proper place. Yet, although it could be argued that the studies producing this knowledge were provoked by a set of feminist propositions concerning the position of women in society, it could not be argued that present knowledge about women and crime has been developed via explanatory concepts that could be called distinctly feminist, unless one counts as 'explanatory' the (usually descriptive) use of the word 'patriarchal' – but see Cousins (1978) for a critique of such usage. Nor can I conceive of any theory (feminist or otherwise) focusing solely on 'women as a group' that could adequately explain three major features of women's lawbreaking and imprisonment: that women's crimes are, in the main, the crimes of the powerless; that women in prison are disproportionately from ethnic minority groups; and that a majority of women in prison have been in poverty for the greater part of their lives.

Women (as a group) in the penal system are a striking example of what Laffargue and Godefroy (1989) have referred to as the '"hard core" of repression,' whose criminalization has been overdetermined by the threefold effects of sexism, racism, and the class injustices of an increasingly repressive state. Because explanations of racism, class structure, and gender structure are not reducible one to the other (cf. Cain, 1986, on gender and class structures), it is likely that people wishing to engage in criminological work that may have some theoretical, policy, or campaigning pay-off in relation to women's crimes and women's imprisonment, will not wish to rely solely on the insights of feminism into gender structure when mounting their investigations. However, some feminists, including several who also would advocate a deconstructionist stance, argue that the topic 'women and crime' is not a proper subject for feminist engagement at all!

The Topic 'Women and Crime' Is Not a Proper Concern of 'Feminists'

Two major arguments are advanced by writers claiming that feminists should not study 'women and crime.' One I will call 'deconstructionist agnostic,' the other 'deconstructionist libertarian.'

The 'deconstructionist agnostic' position on women and crime argues against the discipline of 'criminology' per se. It implies that specification of empirical referents at the outset of an inquiry must inevitably entail investigations forever trapped in essentialist categories that obstruct the production of new knowledge (see Cousins 1978; Brown 1986; Allen 1988; and Cain 1989). This is not such a new insight as deconstructionists have claimed. It was an awareness that the empirical referents of social-scientific discourses are already endowed with more taken-for-granted and ideological meanings with discursive effects than are discourses in the physical sciences that led earlier sociologists to develop the notorious 'sociological jargon' (or 'sociologese') so particularly sneered at by their traditionalist opponents. Yet deconstructionists have access to modes of thought that should diminish the radical theorist's perennial fear of the ideological power of the empirical referent. In particular, they can adopt the methodological protocol of Bachelard (1940), that systems of thought must say 'no' to their own conventions and conditions of existence. Additionally, they can take comfort from Saussurian linguistics (Saussure 1974), which demonstrate that individual words themselves have no essential meaning but rather acquire meaning only within syntagms that, through differentiation, assign the value of a specific sign. If by taking the assumptions of Bachelard and Saussure as prescriptive and working on the contradiction that the already known has to be both recognized and denied, deconstructionists use a 'bricolage' of concepts from other disciplines (Derrida 1976), then there is no reason why they should not *both* take seriously (i.e., recognize) and deny the empirical referents' material and ideological effects (see Burton and Carlen 1979.) Thereafter, whether such investigations are pursued under the political sign of 'feminism' or the academic sign of 'criminology' is important only in so far as such signifiers provide the author with a support group or a salary! From a deconstructionist perspective, labels such as 'feminist' or 'criminological' (or 'left realist') are irrelevant; none can guarantee the Truth of the arguments. (Although I have hoped that my work might contribute to – or at least not obstruct – some feminist projects, this is one reason I have never called myself a feminist 'criminologist.')

The 'deconstructionist/libertarian' stance on 'women and crime' is one sometimes implicit in the work of Carol Smart (1990: 524) – though not always held to (1989: 165). It implies a denial that a reduction in women's crime is a proper concern of criminologists and that therefore criminologists should not seek to justify policy proposals on the grounds that they might help criminal women keep out of trouble in future. (According to J. Allen [1988], who on this takes a line similar to Smart's, however, it is okay to seek to reduce *men's* lawbreaking!) This is a position very close to that which Jock Young (1986) has called 'left idealist,' and together with the 'deconstructionist agnostic' reluctance to engage with the empirical reality of women's lawbreaking and criminalization, it could result in policy on 'women and crime' being abandoned either to what Carol Smart (1990) has referred to as the 'macho left' (realists?) or to the realists of the right. To my mind, neither alternative would be acceptable.

Feminism Is a Politics, Not a Guarantor of Theoretical Truth

As far as the topic 'women and crime' is concerned, it should by now have become apparent that: (1) I do not believe there is a distinctly feminist theoretical conceptual system that might adequately explain (or call into question) the empirical phenomenon; and (2) I am in any case in agreement with those feminists who would argue against global, essentialist theories seeking to guarantee certain 'Truths' – including feminist 'Truths.' (The absurdity of the notion that there is a distinctly feminist *method* in criminology or sociology is discussed below.)

I do, none the less, disagree with feminists who argue for a non-interventionist stance on women's lawbreaking and criminalization. For, as a matter of political calculation (and not as a guaranteed theoretical recipe for a desired outcome), knowledge gained from theoretical work can be used in part to inform policy interventions. The *way* it is used and its effects will be dependent upon the balance of competing ideological, material, and political conditions of the time, and there is, of course, no reason any social scientist working on 'women and crime' and calling herself a feminist should feel obliged to make such interventions. There is a need for all types of work – quantitative, qualitative, rational deductive, ethnographic, purely theoretical, and so on. Yet, just as one cannot read off an interventionist politics from a theory, neither can one read off from any theory a politics of *non-intervention*. My personal view is that if *no* academics were prepared to compromise their claims to theoretical rectitude (or consistency) by committing themselves *as academics* and *as feminists* to campaigns to redress the specific wrongs suffered by women lawbreakers in the criminal justice and penal systems, it would be to the further disadvantage of those very women who are already among the worst casualties of the gender and poverty traps.

3. Women, Crime, and Social Policy: The Potential of Left-Realist Criminology

One of the best things about left-realist criminology is that its main proponents take crime (and its effects) seriously. In thus confronting the challenge of right-wing realist and administrative criminology (Wilson 1975) and in an attempt to repossess some of the ground predominantly occupied by the right on questions of crime control, Jock Young and his associates (see Lea and Young 1984; Kinsey, Lea, and Young 1986; Young 1987; Lea 1987; Matthews 1987) have developed the following major tenets:

THEORETICAL:
1 'The basic triangle of relations which is the proper subject-matter of criminology [is] ... the offender, the state, and the victim' (Young 1986).
2 Theoretical explanations must be symmetrical – there must be the same explanation for social action and social reaction.
3 'Man [*sic*] is a creator of human nature' (Young 1987) and therefore explanations of crime should not be deterministic and people should be seen as responsible for their actions.

POLITICAL:
1 Crime is a real problem and especially to working-class people who suffer disproportionately from personal crime, i.e., robbery, assault, burglary, rape.
2 The 'left' should attempt to develop a credible [populist?] approach to crime control to prevent the 'right' from having a monopoly on the 'crime problem.'
3 The purpose of theorizing should be to make practical interventions into law-and-order issues.
4 To reduce crime, there is a need to achieve a higher level of cooperation between police and public and this will be best achieved by a democratization of local control of the police.

A vast body of critique of left-realist criminology has been developed during the last 10 years (see Middlesex Polytechnic 1989). In the remainder of this section, however, I shall discuss only its potential for informing theoretical and political work on women's lawbreaking and criminalization. Concomitantly, I shall be pointing out the extent to which I think some elements of left-realist criminology can supplement, are in accord with, or are in opposition to either the deconstructionist theoretical perspective and/or the feminist politics that I favoured above, in Part 2.

Taking Crime Seriously – Left Realism as a Politics

As I said above, one of the most important aspects of left realism in criminology is that it explicitly identifies the criminal justice arena as a site of political struggle. Because of the deconstructionist theoretical program that I have advocated, I see no reason why feminists should be wary of engaging in theoretical debate about the possible meanings of the peculiar mix of ideological, political, and economic conditions in which 'women as a status group' break the law, are criminalized, and, in a minority of cases, are imprisoned.

Realism's Advocacy of Empirical Investigation Is an Essential Prerequisite of Theoretical Relevance and Political Interventions

In talking of theoretical relevance I am not intending to imply that theoretical concepts have essential relationships with empirical referents. Rather, I am assuming that because the effects of racism, class exploitation, and gender discrimination require different explanations, and also because the discourses and practices of women's lawbreaking and criminalization vary across time and between places, it can never be assumed that discourses and practices of gender differentiation *necessarily* play primary parts in the conditioning of that lawbreaking and criminalization. Close observation and investigation of the empirical phenomenon have a part to play in the shaping of the questions to be asked and the concepts to be used – though the theoretical system constructed to answer them should also lead to their displacement and the requirement of further theoretical and/or empirical work. Such strategies of investigation and theorizing might or might not involve the use of concepts having claims to be labelled 'feminist.' Almost certainly, however, they will often draw on political theories and jurisprudential concepts where the rights and wrongs of *women* are not the primary concern and where political intervention on issues regarding women and crime centres chiefly on racism or class injustice.

'The Starting Point for Realism Is the Strategy of Democratization' (Lea 1987: 368)

It is in left realism's emphasis on a democratization of the criminal justice system that I see a major (formal, if not substantive) convergence with feminist concerns. For realists take seriously not only lawbreaking, but also people's experiences of it as *victims*. Indeed, the realists' work on women as victims of crime has been one of their major contributions to both feminist struggle and criminology (see Jones, MacLean, and Young 1986). What they have not taken so seriously are people's experiences of crime as suspects, lawbreakers, defendants, and prisoners. (See below for criticisms of those parts of the 'taking crime seriously' program that have frequently substituted populism for analysis, and moralism for theory.) Yet an understanding of crime and criminal justice from the offender's standpoint is a prerequisite to the reduction of crime (Box 1987: 29) and to a diminution of the increased oppression that women incur because of their lawbreaking (Carlen 1988, 1990). This is the main justification for pursuing qualitative investigations that take seriously women's (and men's) own perceptions and experiences of their offences and the state's response to them. It is not because of any distinctly 'feminist method' that 'allows women to speak for themselves' (see Jupp 1989). Such a procedure would be rampant (populist) empiricism rather than theoretical investigation. Rather, it is in the symbolic interactionist (realist) tradition, which assumes that if people perceive things as real they will be real in their effects (Thomas 1951). Taking seriously women's views of their lawbreaking might lead to: political demands for a diminution of the oppressive conditions in which much of women's lawbreaking is committed; the democratic construction of feasible interventionary programs in relation to the drug taking, thieving, and other crimes that often cause misery to women other than the offender, as well as aggravating the existing problems of the woman lawbreaker herself; and the democratic management of housing and other schemes for women in trouble.

4. The Limits to Left Realism and the Need for Feminist and Socialist Ideals

Although left realists have specified some theoretical tenets concerning the left-realist approach to thinking about crime, it is often difficult to work out exactly why they have termed their program 'realist.' One difficulty stems from their conflation of a political program with a set of theoretical assumptions that do not emanate from either the philosophical realism of, say, Karl Popper or the sociological realism of, for instance, Emile Durkheim. Another difficulty results from their juxtaposition of their own left 'realist' theories to those that they call left 'idealist' and where 'idealist' is not being used in its usual sense to refer to theories that *explain* the present by reference to some not yet realized ideal, but merely to condemn theories that would not, according to the realists, lead to any realizable programs of crime control. Perhaps because they do not clearly define and distinguish 'realism as theory' and 'realism as politics,' left realists produce both theoretical propositions that appear positivistic and essentialist, and a penal politics that can appear to be marred by opportunism, populism, and moralism.

Realism, Idealism, and Common Sense

Whereas the realism of Durkheim (1964) and Popper (1972) was aimed at subverting common sense, left realists appear to call for a theory of crime that will fit the facts of crime as popularly conceived of in common sense (cf. Jones,

MacLean, and Young 1986: 3-4). Hence the often uncritical use of the victim survey.

The Essentialism of Crime as a Unifier (see Hogg 1988: 32)

One of the strongest attacks on left realism has been that it is essentialist, that it attributes to the common-sense phenomenon 'crime' – a phenomenon that consists of many different types of lawbreaking and many different modes of criminalization – a unitary existence known to all people of goodwill and common sense. In other words, there is an easily recognizable reality 'out there' known as crime that can be understood through empirical investigation and in its own terms.

In answer to the foregoing criticisms, Young (1987) has claimed that, far from being essentialist, left realists aim to 'deconstruct' the crime phenomenon. However, it turns out that by 'deconstruct' he means that the common-sense 'crime' is broken down into small substantive dimensions for analysis – but not an analysis that might subvert the common-sense meaning. Indeed, once the common-sense meaning is denied, it is unlikely that the new explanation will have popular appeal!

The Essentialism of Criminology as a Unifier

Because they portray crime as a unitary concept, it follows that left realists idealize 'criminology' as a unitary discipline rather than as an organizational site for the investigation of lawbreaking and criminalization. Linked with this thrust towards the unification of theory and politics is the left-realist criticism that other theories are 'partial' – that explanations fail in so far as they are not symmetrical, that is, in so far as they do not provide the same explanations for social action and reaction. Yet one of the greatest contributions of 1960s' interactionism was the insistence that lawbreaking and criminalization are two separate processes, each requiring entirely different explanations (Kitsuse and Cicourel 1963). Furthermore, and as I have argued elsewhere (Carlen 1980) a deconstructionist position assumes that:

the theoretical relationships between the criminal law, juridical relations, criminalization processes, and lawbreaking are embedded in asymmetrical practices and discourses. These discourses are 'neither mirror images of each other nor reducible one to the other.' 'Today,' as Foucault points out, 'criminal justice functions and justifies itself ... only by perpetual reference to something other than itself, by its unceasing reinscription in non-judicial systems ...' (Foucault, 1977: 22). [The preconditions and effects of] criminal law, juridical relationships, and criminalization processes are asymmetrical to each other. Once they are inscribed within and around notions like morality, freedom, guilt, and retribution ... they fragment into ironic icons of juridical relations ... [the] effect [of which] is dispersed not in criminological but in economic, religious, or political discourse. (p. 16)

Deconstructionist approaches to questions of women and crime can no more be confined within the parameters of a populist criminology than they can be solely and indissolubly tied to the concerns of feminism or the concepts of a 'feminist' theory. For deconstructionism – whether in 'criminology' or in 'feminism' – has constantly to say 'no' to the conditions of its own existence.

Left Realists' Idealistic and Moralistic Notions of Responsibility

Considering all previous explanations of crime to be deterministic, left realists insist that individuals must take responsibility for their crimes, and thus operate within the simplistic 'free will' versus 'determinism' dichotomy. In reply to the crude 'social conditions cause crime' claim, they answer that individuals choose to commit crime. They appear to think that deterministic (sociological?) explanations of lawbreaking alienate from a leftist politics those working-class people who, though living in less-than-ideal conditions, do not commit crime. Yet can such a simplistic dichotomy be justified on either theoretical or political grounds? Of course, 'people choose to act, sometimes criminally, [but] they do not do so under conditions of their own choosing. Their choice makes them responsible, but the conditions make the choice comprehensible. These conditions, social and economic, contribute to crime because they constrain, limit, or narrow the choices available' (Box 1987: 29, emphasis in original).

Furthermore, is it either logical or justifiable for left realists to use an anti-socialist rhetoric of individualism in the furtherance of socialist political ends? I think not. And this crude invocation of free will seems to me to be the worst example of the theoretical bad faith that results from attempting to fashion a theory in the service of a politics. By attempting to appeal to an electorate via populist and individualist conceptions of criminality, left realists lose an opportunity to show how individualized problems of criminal justice are also problems of social justice in general. To follow their example when posing questions of women and crime would be to make it impossible to assume that the experiences of 'women as a status group' have any ideological, economic, and political preconditions that are distinctly different to the experiences of 'men as a status group.'

The Need for a Principled Idealism to Counter the Impossibleness
of Left Idealism and the Opportunistic Tendency of Left Realism

A major concern of left realism (and one that I totally support) has been to counter the 'impossibleness' of left-idealist theories that claim that nothing can be done about crime until there is a fundamental change in the present exploitative class relations constitutive of capitalism. Yet a refusal to abandon the space of politics should not also entail an abandonment of a principled theoretical commitment to calling into question all already known explanations of crime, including those developed under the auspices of socialism, feminism, and/or left realism. The task of theory is to produce new knowledge; a task of politics is to calculate how, when, and if new knowledge can be used to change balances of power and induce desired social change. Principled commitment to an open-ended deconstruction-ist theoretical program, plus political commitment to sets of collectivist (feminist and/or socialist) ideals or aspirations is required to help ensure that theoretical production and political practice are neither opportunistically conflated nor opportunistically reduced, the one to serve the other. This is why I am reluctant to endorse the more conflationary and/or reductionist theoretical and political claims of both feminism and left realism when they invoke either a politics to justify their theories or, conversely, a theoretical position to guarantee the rectitude of their politics and/or policy interventions.

5. An Agenda

In this final part of my essay, I offer a potential agenda for realizing some attainable ideals in the deconstruction and theorization of 'women and crime' questions and in the development of policies aimed at righting some wrongs encountered by women lawbreakers in the criminal justice and penal systems.

Academic Agenda

1 Detailed empirical investigation of both the context (i.e., economic, ideological, and political conditions) in which women break the law and of their subsequent careers through the welfare, criminal justice, and penal systems (cf. Carlen 1988).
2 Detailed empirical investigation of the ideological discourses within which women's lawbreaking is known (cf. Carlen 1983; Allen 1987; Worrall 1990).
3 Deconstruction of what is 'already known' about women lawbreakers via a 'bricolage' of concepts appropriated from a variety of theoretical discourses

to inform answers to questions about the four main features of women's lawbreaking and imprisonment in Britain, the United States, and Canada, i.e.:

- that the women's crimes are predominantly the crimes of the powerless;
- that disproportionate numbers of women from ethnic minority groups are imprisoned;
- that typifications of conventional femininity play a major role in the decision whether to imprison women; and
- that the majority of women appears to be law-abiding and when in trouble are much more likely to receive medical, psychiatric, or welfare regulation than to be caught up in the machinery of criminal justice.

4 The construction of a feminist jurisprudence, which in assuming and empirically documenting the ways in which: (a) women's experiences are different from men's and (b) the criminal law affects and protects women differently than men, might be advocated as one jurisprudential paradigm (among others), which could inform campaigning strategies and policy recommendations.

5 The establishment of women's law as a special area of study not just as an optional subject but as a component of all compulsory subjects. (See Stang-Dahl 1987, for an account of the lead in this direction given by the Institute of Women's Law at the University of Oslo where women's law has already been fully integrated into the degree scheme of the Faculty of Law.)

6 The dissolution of 'women and criminal justice' questions within an interrogation of women and social justice in general.

7 The development of more sophisticated models of the relationships between culpability, responsibility, and accountability in societies where class relationships, racism, and gender discrimination call into question the very general concept of social justice that must underpin the more specific concept of criminal justice.

Campaigning and Policy Agenda

Any campaigning and policy agenda might (ideally) comprise: (1) fundamental aims; (2) general strategies; (3) short-term achievable goals for the relief of women presently bearing the brunt of both gender discrimination and racist gender discrimination in the criminal justice and penal systems; and (4) long-term programs that, although not achievable under present political conditions, can be argued for based on a deconstructionist analysis of present penal discourses and practices.

1 FUNDAMENTAL AIMS
- To ensure that the penal regulation of female lawbreakers does not increase their oppression as unconventional women, as Black people, and as poverty-stricken defendants still further.
- To ensure that the penal regulation of lawbreaking men is not such that it brutalizes them and makes them behave even more violently or oppressively towards women in the future.

2 GENERAL STRATEGIES
- Remedial action to redress the present wrongs of women in the criminal justice and penal systems.
- Resistance to penal or other regulatory measures based on essentialized stereotypes of gender.
- Democratic exploration of the many different possible modes of living and learning in a variety of all-female (and, for women who want them, mixed) half-way houses, accommodation schemes, and self-help groups (see Carlen 1990).

3 SHORT-TERM ACHIEVABLE GOALS
- The monitoring (and remedying) of sexist and racist-sexist practices within the welfare, criminal justice, and penal systems.
- Development of feasible non-custodial programs for women that recognize that women's social responsibilities and resources are usually different from men's.
- Proper medical provision (especially Well-Women Clinics) for physically and mentally ill women in trouble or in custody.
- The setting of minimum standards for all prison establishments and the closure of all institutions not conforming to those standards.
- Rejection of any justification for the discriminatory treatment of women in the penal system that invokes the relatively few numbers of women prisoners as just cause of their less favourable treatment.

4 LONG-TERM PROGRAMS. Although idealistic, these need to be adhered to and worked on, to counter the conservative compromises based on pragmatism and opportunism, which usually have to be made to achieve short-term goals.

Whatever compromises are made in the name of realist politics, campaigners should not abandon the pursuit of long-term goals – even if, under present political arrangements they are idealistic (for example, the virtual abolition of women's imprisonment [Carlen 1990]). Nor should theorists abdicate (in the name of democracy) their responsibility perpetually to question existent forms of knowledge (including 'feminism' and 'realism'). Of course, campaigners must be prepared to live with, and work on, the contradictions between the actions required for attainment of short-term goals and the principles to be held to in the construction of new forms of justice. Likewise, theorists must work on the contradiction that ideological knowledge (i.e., the already known) is a necessary constituent of new knowledge. But these tensions are essential elements of any politics or theory that is against closure and committed to being open-ended. The concomitant implication for theorists is that they should forever be intent on seeking that loss of authorship which, in the production and recognition of new knowledge, renders the politically important signifiers 'feminist' and 'realist' irrelevant.

This article also appeared in a special issue of Social Justice, *'Ideology and Penal Reform in the 1990s' (Vol. 17, no. 4, 1990), which is available at P.O. Box 40601, San Francisco, CA 94140.*

References

Adelberg, E., and C. Currie. 1987. *Too Few to Count: Canadian Women in Conflict with the Law*. Vancouver: Press Gang Publishers

Adler, F. 1975. *Sisters in Crime*. New York: McGraw-Hill

Allen, H. 1987. *Justice Unbalanced*. Milton Keynes: Open University Press

Allen, J. 1988. 'The "Masculinity" of Criminality and Criminology: Interrogating Some Impasses,' in M. Findlay and R. Hogg, eds., *Understanding Crime and Criminal Justice*, 1-23. Sydney: The Law Book Company

Bachelard, G. 1940. *The Philosophy of No*, trans. by G.C. Waterson. London: Orion Press

Box, S. 1983. *Power, Crime and Mystification*. London: Tavistock

– 1987. *Recession, Crime and Punishment*. London: Tavistock

Boyle, C., M.A. Bertrand, C. Lacerte-Lamontagne, and R. Shamai. 1985. *A Feminist Review of Criminal Law*. Ottawa: Minister of Supply and Services

Brown, B. 1986. 'Women and Crime: The Dark Figures of Criminology.' *Economy and Society* 15 (3): 355-402

Burton, F., and P. Carlen. 1979. *Official Discourse*. London: Routledge and Kegan Paul

Cain, M. 1986. 'Realism, Feminism, Methodology and Law.' *International Journal of the Sociology of Law*, 14: 255-267

– 1989. *Growing Up Good*. London: Sage

Carlen, P. 1980. 'Radical Criminology, Penal Politics and the Rule of Law,' in P. Carlen and M. Collison, eds., *Radical Issues in Criminology*, 7-24. Oxford: Martin Robertson

– 1983. *Women's Imprisonment: A Study in Social Control*. London: Routledge and Kegan Paul

– 1988. *Women, Crime and Poverty*. Milton Keynes: Open University Press

– 1990. *Alternatives to Women's Imprisonment*. Buckingham: Open University Press

Carlen, P., D. Christina, J. Hicks, J. O'Dwyer, and C. Tchaikowsky. 1985. *Criminal Women*. Cambridge: Polity Press

Carlen, P., and A. Worrall. 1987. *Gender, Crime and Justice*. Milton Keynes: Open University Press

Casale, S. 1989. *Women Inside*. London: Civil Liberties Trust

Cousins, M. 1978. 'Material Arguments and Feminism.' *m/f*, 2: 63-70

– 1980. 'Men's Rea: A Note on Sexual Difference, Criminology and the Law,' in P. Carlen and M. Collison, eds., *Radical Issues in Criminology*, 109-122. Oxford: Martin Robertson

Derrida, J. 1976. *Of Grammatology*, trans. by Gayatri Chakrovorty Spivak. Baltimore, MD: Johns Hopkins University Press

Durkheim, E. 1964. *Rules of Sociological Method*. New York: Free Press

Eaton, M. 1986. *Justice for Women?* Milton Keynes: Open University Press

Edwards, S. 1984. *Women on Trial*. Manchester: Manchester University Press

Foucault, M. 1977. *Discipline and Punish*. London: Allen Lane

Heidensohn, F. 1985. *Women and Crime*. London: Macmillan

Hogg, R. 1988. 'Taking Crime Seriously: Left Realism and Australian Criminology,' in M. Findlay and R. Hogg, eds., *Understanding Crime and Criminal Justice*, 24-51. Sydney: The Law Book Company

Jones, T., B. MacLean, and J. Young. 1986. *The Islington Crime Survey*. Aldershot: Gower

Jupp, V. 1989. *Methods of Criminological Research*. London: Unwin Hyman

Kinsey, R., J. Lea, and J. Young. 1986. *Losing the Fight against Crime*. Oxford: Basil Blackwell

Kitsuse, J., and A. Cicourel. 1963. 'A Note on the Use of Official Statistics.' *Social Problems*, 11 (Autumn): 131-139

Laffargue, B., and T. Godefroy. 1989. 'Economic Cycles and Punishment: Unemployment and Imprisonment. A Time Series Study. France, 1920-1985.' *Contemporary Crises*, 13 (4): 371-404

Lea, J. 1987. 'Left Realism: A Defence.' *Contemporary Crises*, 11 (4): 357-370

Lea, J., and J. Young. 1984. *What Is to Be Done about Law and Order?* Harmondsworth: Penguin

MacKinnon, C. 1987. 'Feminism, Marxism, Method and the State: Toward Feminist Jurisprudence,' in S. Harding, ed., *Feminism and Methodology*, 125-156. Milton Keynes: Open University Press

McRobbie, A., and J. Garber. 1976. 'Girls and Subcultures,' in S. Hall and T. Jefferson, eds., *Resistance through Rituals*, 202-222. London: Hutchinson

Matthews, R. 1987. 'Taking Realist Criminology Seriously.' *Contemporary Crises*, 11: 371-401

Messerschmidt, J. 1986. *Capitalism, Patriarchy and Crime: Towards a Socialist Feminist Criminology*. Totowa, NJ: Rowan and Littlefield

Middlesex Polytechnic. 1989. *Realism: A Select Bibliography*. London: Middlesex Polytechnic, Centre for Criminology

Naffine, N. 1987. *Female Crime*. Sydney: Allen and Unwin

Padell, U., and P. Stevenson. 1988. *Insiders*. London: Virago

Popper, K. 1972. *Objective Knowledge*. Oxford: Oxford University Press

Saussure, F. 1974. *Course in General Linguistics*. London: Fontana

Seear, N., and E. Player. 1986. *Women in the Penal System*. London: Howard League for Penal Reform

Simon, R. 1975. *Women and Crime*. Lexington, MA: Lexington Books

Smart, B., and C. Smart. 1978. *Women, Sexuality and Social Control*. London: Routledge and Kegan Paul

Smart, C. 1976. *Women, Crime and Criminology*. London: Routledge and Kegan Paul

– 1989. *Feminism and the Power of Law*. London: Routledge

– 1990. Review of 'Women, Crime and Poverty, by Pat Carlen.' *Journal of Law and Society*, 16 (4): 521-524

Stang-Dahl, T. 1987. *Women's Law: An Introduction to Feminist Jurisprudence*. Oslo: Norwegian University Press

Thomas, W.I. 1951. *Social Behavior and Personality*. New York: Social Science Research Council

Wilson, J. 1975. *Thinking about Crime*. New York: Basic Books

Worrall, A. 1990. *Offending Women*. London: Routledge

Young, J. 1986. 'The Failure of Criminology: The Need for a Radical Realism,' in R. Matthews and J. Young, eds., *Confronting Crime*, 4-30. London: Sage

– 1987. 'The Tasks Facing a Realist Criminology.' *Contemporary Crises*, 11 (4): 337-356

11 Feminism and Realism in the Canadian Context

Dawn H. Currie

As the interest in socialist realism grows, writers are beginning to question the potential for realist criminology to address the concerns of women. The answer to this question is not an easy one, judging by the mixed reception with which realism is received by feminist scholars. Responses to socialist realism range from critical but qualified support (see DeKeseredy and MacLean 1990; DeKeseredy, this volume), on the one hand, to outright rejection, on the other (Smart 1990; see also Gelsthorpe and Morris 1988). Supporters credit realist victimology for being the first non-feminist criminology to recognize the importance of feminist scholarship (Thomas and O'Maolchatha 1989). In contrast, critics claim that realist criminology gives only token attention to gender and women (Gelsthorpe and Morris 1990: 8) or that it lacks a systematic theorization of patriarchy (Dobash and Dobash 1988; Yllo and Bograd 1988), reflecting its use of distanced, objective measures (Kelly and Radford 1987) which are ahistorical and remove violence against women from the complexity of its social context. At the same time, realist criminology is characterized as downplaying corporate crimes against women (DeKeseredy and Schwartz 1991).

However important these criticisms may appear, in my mind they do not present a serious challenge to the realist endeavour. Such is the case because they either misconstrue the realist project and in so doing set an agenda that probably exceeds original intentions – for example, the failure of realism to develop and test theories, especially of patriarchy – or, alternatively, suggest that problems can be resolved within the realist frame of reference, for example, by measuring corporate crime and intragroup variation (see Crawford et al. 1990; Ellis and DeKeseredy 1989; Smith 1990). What interests me, therefore, is a more serious claim, namely, that by clinging to an outdated empiricism and now discredited positivist commitment to cause-and-effect thinking, realism has missed the boat altogether. Smart (1990), as the major proponent of this line of criticism, argues that the question of an alliance between feminism and realism is a non-starter: while atavistic criminologists struggle on in search of the Holy Grail which will provide an undistorted, truthful picture of the social world, post-modern feminism has abandoned this kind of question altogether. From this perspective, feminism is characterized as transcending the expectation of 'discovering' the truth of crime, concerning itself instead with post-modern methods which help us to discover how truth itself is created. It is this criticism which I shall address here in assessing the relevance of realist criminology to Canadian feminism. In order to do so, I shall follow two lines of inquiry. The first concerns the historically specific question of the relationship between feminism and criminology, particularly in the Canadian and broader North American context. The second concerns analytical and more global questions about whether post-modernism does, indeed, represent the twilight of 'scientific' research in criminology. As we shall see, these questions are related: both are framed by the current political context within which knowledge about women's lives is constructed.

Feminism, Crime, and Criminology: Struggling against Male Violence against Women

To begin, it is important to recognize that the current interest shown by Canadian criminologists in violence against women is relatively recent, and has been gaining momentum throughout the 1980s. The women's liberation movement (WLM), where impetus came from community activists working within women's self-help groups rather than from university-oriented academics, first put the issue on the public agenda. Within the women's movement, feminists challenged both academic and common-sense notions about the normalized violence of heterosexual relations and definitions of crime. Against the official discourses of both the state and 'state-of-the-arts' criminology, feminists highlighted the reality of women's everyday resistance against the violence of husbands, lovers, relatives, friends, and acquaintances. Through activities such as consciousness raising and the formation of support groups, the women's movement created a space within which women's experiences of abuse could be articulated, defining woman abuse as an issue which 'begins with women's experiences and asserts that it is men who beat women, that they do so because they are allowed to, because the family/marriage is considered by society to be a private institution in which one must rarely, if ever, intervene, and because violence is accepted, with few exceptions, as an appropriate means of control to uphold men's authority over women. It also asserts that misogyny and women's economic dependence on men are mutually reinforcing' (Barnsley 1985: 73).

Included in the challenge to privatized patriarchal authority was the demand to end the invisibility and inaction which surround male violence against women. Thus, violence against women was included in the feminist mandate to 'politicize the personal' by transforming woman abuse from 'a private trouble to a public issue' (see Comack 1987). As a literal rather than rhetorical accomplishment, this transformation engaged feminists with advocacy groups, law reform commissions, and state agencies such as the Canadian Advisory Council on the Status of Women (CACSW). The history of these campaigns is too complex to discuss here, as are the controversies and criticisms about the orientation of various campaigns (that is, their liberal perspective) and their results (that is, emphasis given to criminalization of woman abuse through measures such as mandatory arrest).[1] The point here is that by the time the Canadian Advisory Council on the Status of Women produced its second report on wife battery in Canada, the Canadian state – for a number of reasons – had publicly endorsed feminist goals. Highlighting complaints in the earlier report (MacLeod 1980) that (1) police discriminate against women in enforcing Criminal Code provisions for assault; (2) women lack access to existing institutions which are mandated to protect women from violence; and (3) there is widespread public misperception and ignorance about, especially, wife assault, the Canadian state endorsed the recommendations of the Advisory Council Report. These recommendations included: ongoing training of all police officers (rather than only new recruits) to encourage consistency in the application of policies relating to wife battering; education for judges and Crown attorneys that would make them more sensitive and supportive of women and which would thereby 'prevent the problem of women refusing to testify, and so deflect the unnecessary and harsh use of contempt charges against women who are feeling frightened, vulnerable, and confused'; and better record-keeping systems by police agencies.

By endorsing the recommendations of the CACSW, the Conservative party increasingly linked itself to the progressive image which the Advisory Council provides through its platform of 'women's issues.' In reviewing the second CACSW report (MacLeod 1987), the minister responsible for the Status of Women declared that 'the issue of wife assault is one of the issues Prime Minister Brian Mulroney cares about the most.'[2] In response to its recommendations, the minister further announced that an integrated intervention strategy was being supported by the solicitor general. This strategy was to link police, social, and health agency needs and, according to the minister, would lead to program proposals for pilot projects dealing with family violence (see Currie 1990).

Within this context, funding priorities of both private and state-sponsored research granting agencies increasingly priorized the issue of family violence. At this point, criminology has begun to show more than a passing interest in violence against women, as evidenced by the virtual explosion of published academic work on violence against women. Indeed, woman abuse *has* been transformed from a private to public matter. But this transformation has created problems: as woman abuse was transformed through academic research from a private to public issue, it also was transformed from a women's issue, which emphasizes the continuum of violence in women's lives and its relationship to women's socially subordinate status, into a gender-neutral discourse, one that talks about 'family violence' and 'domestic assault,' for example.[3] The problem is, as Errington had already warned, within criminology: 'When we read about marital violence, we can't tell who is doing what. The language is completely neutral. It is completely de-sexed. So when we read things such as "violence between family members," something called "intra-family murder," "aggravated assault between husband and wife," and so on ... we are somehow beginning to see or begin to think or are looking at it as if, in fact, violence was being dispersed equally among adults in the family' (1977: 3). The narrow, gender-neutral perspective adopted by social agencies and employed by much of the value-free, academic research thus 'obscures the actual history of the feminist "discovery" of violence against women and discourages analysis of the problem from a context of societal male supremacy' (Breines and Gordon 1983: 508). Instead, Canadians are encouraged to see 'the family' as violent and therefore in need of remedial intervention, even though the vast majority of known situations of abuse concern women being beaten by their mates (DeKeseredy and Hinch 1991).

Far from arguing that women's issues are being ignored and neglected in Canada, women in the WLM are beginning to complain that women's issues have become 'institutionalized.'[4] Violence against women is one example of how the needs of women became incorporated into existing discourses about justice so that the logical solution to violence became the expansion rather than transformation of patriarchal institutions which, ironically, can be seen as giving rise to the problem in the first place. By meeting the needs of women for protection from male violence – a real, documented need – the problem of male violence appears to be addressed. The more radical impulse of the WLM has been diffused, while the state and its agencies are given the authority to define women's needs and the solutions to their problems. Within this context, the perspectives of academics and professionals – those deemed 'experts' by the state – have taken precedence over those of battered women. Thus, in the second CACSW report on wife battery, MacLeod (1987) notes that the expansion of services for women during the 1980s has not been an unequivocal success for the

WLM,[5] because it reflects the shift of authority over the problem from the women's community to accredited professionals who speak from a position of power, and therefore seldom against institutionalized privilege and power. MacLeod concludes that, in the final analysis, campaigns against wife battery have failed the test of reality – the reality of battered women's lives. Like other community-based researchers of the later 1980s, she notes that battered women do not necessarily find policies promoted by the criminal justice system, such as mandatory arrest, satisfactory solutions to their problems; in fact, they can make the situation worse (see Smith 1984; McGillivray 1987).

The Criminological Appropriation of Feminist Discourse

The WLM is experiencing a period of serious introspection about the way in which solutions to women's problems have been framed from a white, middle-class perspective (see Currie and Kline 1991). At the same time, critical thinkers within criminology are beginning to identify its role in the depoliticization of woman abuse in Canada. DeKeseredy and MacLean (1990), for example, point out that the Conflict Tactics Scale, one of the most popular instruments employed by criminologists to measure the frequency and distribution of domestic violence, seriously downplays the extent of battery against women, while overestimating assault against male partners. In a historical overview of theoretical approaches, Ahluwalia (1987, 1988) shows how woman abuse has been transformed within social-scientific discourses[6] into 'self-abuse.' She links this to the tendency to simply add women into existing explanatory frameworks. Starting from the female victim as the more readily identifiable population, researchers compared women in order to identify differences between battered and non-battered women, as well as between women who stay in abusive situations and those who leave violent husbands. In terms of the 'type' of women who are battered, they suggested that the cause of battering can be located in women's low self-esteem (Swanson 1985), the wife's psychiatric instability (Rounsaville and Weissman 1977/8), their belittling and tormenting behaviour (Rae-Grant 1983), or their failure to adapt to their wifely role (Goodstein and Page 1981). Clarehart, Elder, and Janes (1982) suggest that battered women are deficient in problem-solving skills, while Ferraro (1983) identifies ways in which battered women rationalize their behaviour as contributing to the violence. Snell, Rosenwald, and Robey (1964) proclaim that 'a husband's behaviour may serve to fill a wife's need even though she protests it ... such wives [are] ... aggressive, efficient, masculine and sexually frigid ... masochism ... is typical. The periods of violent behaviour by the husband served to release him momentarily from his ineffectiveness as a man, while, at the same time, giving his wife apparent masochistic gratification and helping probably to deal with the guilt arising from the intense hostility expressed in her controlling, castrating behaviour' (cited in Ahluwalia 1987: 78). In terms of why women would stay in abusive situations, it seemed logical to speculate that motivation and self-perception must play an important role. Along these lines, Walker (1977/8) suggested that women cannot leave because the are manifesting 'learned helplessness': after repeated abuse that women are unable to control, they give up hope that their actions can effectively change things. Other researchers have suggested that the prevalence of depression in battered women is further evidence of this phenomenon (Straus 1977; Swanson 1986).

Turning to the question of intervention, academics have drawn upon exchange theory to study the underlying dynamics of power relations within families. Viewing family dynamics as an exchange of personal resources, Goode (1971) argued that violence will be invoked only when individuals lack other ways of exercising power. He reasoned that most people do not willingly choose overt force when they command other means because the costs of force are high, especially in the family, where it may destroy the possibility of achieving goals other than mere conformity, such as affection and respect. Consequently, Goode suggested a general rule that the greater the other resources an individual can command, the more force he or she can muster, the less he or she will actually deploy it in an overt manner. Thus the husband in the middle- or upper-class family is characterized as not having to use force or its threat.

From the proposition that the relationship between power and marital violence depends upon the alternatives to violence that are available, Allen and Straus (1980) developed an 'ultimate resource theory of violence.' Quite simply, the theory stipulates that husbands who lack certain personal traits and material possessions substitute physical violence in order to maintain their superiority within the marriage. Allen and Straus then empirically evaluated several hypotheses emanating from this 'theory,' many of which predicted an inverse relationship between the social class of husbands and their use of force or threats of force. While many of these hypotheses have not borne out empirically, the tenets of exchange theory were used to give scientific credentials to the common-sense notion that mandatory arrest would act to deter violent husbands. Humphreys and Humphreys (1985: 267), for example, argue that wife battery exists because the 'costs' of abuse are not great enough to counteract the 'rewards.' They claim that the imposition of mandatory arrest will act as deterrent to wife battering by correcting this calculation. In the now controversial Minneapolis experiment, American researchers Sherman and Berk (1984) provided empirical evidence – currently being challenged – that mandatory arrest works. The point to be emphasized here is that social-scientific research, in the final analysis, while beginning from the problem of male violence, has helped to avoid framing the issue in terms of a serious critique of patriarchy.

Recognizing this problem, Dobash and Dobash (1983: 262) conclude that traditional approaches are simply inadequate in that they are too narrow to capture the dynamics and complexity of domestic violence. They attribute this narrowness to the practice of abstraction which arises from the strict separation of ideas (theories) and observation (method) by positivist social sciences. When studying domestic violence, researchers develop abstract concepts and propositions separated from their social context and meaning, from which generalized scientific hypotheses are deduced through reasoning or logic. Researchers ignore anything beyond established categories which are then verified through the system of rules about what counts, rules which gave rise to the categories in the first place. Rejecting the tenets of positivism as such, Dobash and Dobash advocate what they call 'a critical, holistic, and contextual approach that includes historical, institutional, and interactional analysis' (1983: 262). This approach requires unstructured personal interviews in order to begin with the experiences of victims, characterized by 'a consideration of the wider history of relationships between men and women, along with the social, cultural, and economic background of the institution of marriage.' Although beginning from a specific context and an 'event,' they propose that the researcher's goal is to 'develop explanations of social phenomena through a substantively informed theoretical discourse in which concepts, propositions, and assertions are rooted in specific, delimited and empirical contexts' (ibid.). From this 'contextualized' explanation of the social world, meaningful strategies for social action can be developed.

While Dobash and Dobash thus remain within the causal framework of standard sociological investigation, Smart (1990) takes the critique of positivism somewhat farther. She argues: 'The problem of positivism ... lies in the basic presumption that we can establish a verifiable knowledge or truth about events: in particular, that we can establish a causal explanation which will in turn provide us with objective methods for intervening in the events defined as problematic. Given this formulation, positivism may be, at the level of political orientation, either socialist or reactionary. The problem of positivism is, therefore, not redeemed by the espousal of left politics. Positivism poses an epistemological problem; it is not a simple problem of party membership' (1990: 72). Smart (ibid.) specifically rejects socialist realism which she characterizes as driven by the positivist search for the 'cause and solutions' to social problems.[7] She questions 'whether "scientific" work can ever provide a basis for intervention as positivism would presuppose. This is not to argue that intervention is inevitably undesirable or impossible, but rather to challenge the modernist assumption that, once we have the theory ... which will explain all forms of social behaviour, we will also know what to do and that the rightness of this "doing" will be verifiable and transparent' (ibid.). On this basis, she also rejects two dominant trends in feminist social science, identified by Harding (1986) as feminist empiricism and feminist-standpoint epistemology. While the former continues to privilege the male as norm, the latter has not, to date, been sympathetic to the study of masculinity.[8] Because Smart equates 'standpoint' epistemology with realism, she dismisses the possibility of an alliance between feminism and left realism. She implies that through the post-modern deconstruction of knowledge and shift away from causal systems of explanation, feminism will (somehow) transcend current analytical and political problems characteristic of both criminology and legal theory.

Beyond Sociological Positivism (?)

Following especially Foucault,[9] Smart dismisses both the construction of grand theories of women's oppression and theoretically inspired empirical investigation. She maintains that as post-modern social scientists[10] it is not the 'Truth' (of crime) that we are after, but rather an understanding of processes through which truth (especially in law) is constructed and operates to exclude alternative knowing. Employing the literary method of deconstruction, Smart (1989) proposes to create space for feminism as a form of knowledge which until now has been continuously disqualified. Smart notes that, in the study of systems of knowledge, Foucault directs us to systems of rules whereby true and false are separated and the effects of power attached to that designated as 'True.' As an example of how post-modernism can take us beyond the limitations of current attempts to eliminate violence against women, Smart describes how recent reforms by feminists of the Criminal Code have failed. Specifically, she is concerned with the replacement of the gender-specific offence of rape with the gender-neutral offence of sexual assault. The purpose of this reform was to better reflect women's experiences of rape as an act of violence rather than of sex. The legal issues are important because law is a signifier of masculine power and because judicial decisions set and reset the discursive parameters within which rape is dealt with in practice more generally throughout society (Smart 1989: 26). Smart further maintains that the rape trial distils all the problems which feminists have identified in relation to law, and on that basis she provides a detailed examination of what happens in the courtroom. In doing so, she explores the way in which consent is discursively linked to (masculine) notions of pleasure. Here she notes that male and female sexualities are distinctly different: construction of this difference renders the female body a signifier of sex, in a way which the male body is not. Within the Western tradition, 'woman' has been equated with the body, 'man' with mind or reason (see Currie and Raoul 1991). Beginning from this sexualized difference, she deconstructs the broader system of binary logic which requires us to think in these kinds of oppositional terms. Within this logic, opposites are not equal: 'Truth' is established through exclusion of the devalued. When binary opposites, such as truth/untruth, guilty/innocence, consent/non-consent, are applied to the ambiguities of rape, women's experiences of rape are discounted as untrue (1989: 33).

In the final analysis, these types of deconstructive readings make a powerful contribution to our understanding of legal process and our struggles against domination through law. Specifically, they debunk 'naturalized' categories[11] – these in law, others in theory – revealing them as culturally specific and historical constructs. In so rejecting universal categories, post-modernism abandons the notion of a political reality unified by an appeal to overarching, theoretical concepts – such as that of 'woman.' Central to post-modernism is the notion that one's experiential identity is a political point of departure, and a motivation for action (see Alcoff 1989). The politics of post-modernism is of 'diversity' and 'resistance,' so that bell hooks (1989), for example, maintains that for many exploited and oppressed people the struggle to create an identity, to name one's reality is an act of resistance.

While this appeal to localized resistance based on the diversity of women's concrete experiences may appear to empower women because it avoids over-generalized theoretical prescriptions, a number of writers point to the pitfalls inherent in post-modern politics. Carby (1990: 85) points out that theories of difference and diversity in practice leave us fragmented and divided but unequal in our ability to conceive of radical social change. This fragmentation is reflected in the increasing tendency to talk about 'oppression' rather than 'systems of exploitation,' and to substitute the term 'resistance' for 'revolution.' The problem is that while the latter terms denote collective struggle, their replacement by terms which correctly emphasize the contextual and partial nature of all knowledge leads to a pluralism that is thoroughly compatible with the individualism of liberal-democratic societies. For this reason Carby (1990: 84) maintains that the politics of difference within contemporary post-modern feminist thinking and practice is an example of the way in which the politics of race is actually being avoided, displaced, or abandoned, even though it appears that racism is being dealt with directly. Similarly, Hartsock (1987: 201) claims that while the retreat from historical agency, foundational grounding, and anything except local, contingent theory in order to insist upon a fragmented, decentred self may be useful for those with power, these post-modern tenets pose dangers for those on the margins of society.

While these types of debates are likely to be unresolved for some time yet, I am among those reluctant to abandon the potential of a humanist emancipatory project for marginalized peoples. There is a lot of hard work ahead in the struggle for a just and free society. As Currie and Kline (1991) have argued elsewhere, the deconstruction of power must occur in the real as well as conceptual realm: this means that 'patriarchy' – as well as other socially constructed institutions which are oppressive – must be deconstructed in the real as well as the discursive realm. My worry is that the academic agenda of post-modernism, with its focus on language and tendency to discount reality outside the text, will fail to engage intellectuals in this work. It surprises me that a discourse grounded in recognition of the politically constructed nature and effects of truth pays so little attention to the relations and conditions of its own production.

A primary concern of a 'critical' social science is how to generate knowledge in ways that transform thought into emancipatory action (see Lather 1988). Along these lines, I think that the analytical work of academics has the potential to help transform 'identity politics' into *political identity*. However, as I shall argue, this requires generalizing theoretical categories, such as those of race, class, and gender. This is because I disagree with Flax's (1990: 49) suggestion that 'perhaps "reality" can have "a" structure only from the falsely universalizing perspective of the master.' My everyday observations of the university, for example, suggest that privilege can blind us to the dynamics of structured authority. In contrast, I believe that persons marginalized and oppressed by privilege have tacit, operating knowledge of the centralization of power as a condition of their exclusion. For this reason, perhaps the powerless, more than the powerful, need a comprehensive 'theory' about the relations and conditions of their exclusion and oppression. This is where I find post-modernism lacking and, in fact, dangerous for women engaged in political struggles to end the real material experience of women's oppression. Before being able to address the question of realism, it is necessary to explore this theme at greater length.

From Identity Politics to Political Identity: Standpoint Epistemology Revisited

The ability to name our experiences in order to validate the claim that we are oppressed has been central to feminism from the 1960s onward. The primary vehicle for this naming is 'consciousness raising' (CR), a strategy borrowed from Marx's analysis of working-class oppression. Within feminism, CR has been defined as a subjective process of becoming conscious of something not formerly perceived, raising something from the unconscious to the conscious mind, or to heightening the consciousness of oneself or a state of affairs (Cassell 1977). In this way, CR has been likened to becoming aware of the patriarchal nature of social relations by drawing upon women's unarticulated experiences of oppression. It also underlies the notion of claiming oppression through the constructed identities of gender, ethnicity, heterosexual orientation, and so on. Although adopted as feminist practice by many who are theoretically opposed to Marxism, CR is directly linked to Marx's concept of change through the political action of a group united by their recognition of shared oppression. When Marx analysed working-class oppression, he argued that liberation requires class identity that would come through recognition by workers, not only of their 'subjective' sense of having a common identity and interests, but also of their 'objective' interests which arise from their relationship to the means of production. It is the conjuncture of the objective and the subjective which creates class consciousness: unless the proletariat is a 'class for itself,' as well as a 'class in itself,' it will not take action on its own behalf (Jaggar 1983: 333). For Marx, then, the role of the philosopher/intellectual is to no longer simply speculate about the need for change, but to actively participate in the political project of shaping of working-class consciousness.

I do not reject CR as feminist practice. However, recognition of one's *political* membership in an oppressed group goes beyond simply identifying with that group through the post-modern affirmation of subjective self. If our goal is to acknowledge but overcome the marginalization associated with all kinds of identities, we must transform 'identity politics' into political identity. While the former implies that identification with an oppressed group is itself political action, the latter requires recognition of the nexus of social relations through which both the identity, as well as the oppression, of groups is constituted. This recognition is complex because, as Marx noted, social relations are not always immediately apprehensible: there is no necessarily obvious connection between how experiences are 'subjectively' interpreted and how they are 'objectively' constituted. To Marx, mystification of this connection is characteristic of a capitalist society constituted through the 'liberation' of the peasantry from feudal obligations and their transformation into 'free' economic agents. He noted that while power relations of feudal societies are immediately visible, in capitalist society they are obscured by the appearance of individuals as free, self-determining agents and the emergence of the 'individual' who constructs meaning through participation in the market. As free economic agents, contemporary cultural critics have noted how the search for meaning has shifted from production to consumption. Within post-modern culture, individuals 'create' a 'personal' identity through a 'popular' culture which reflects the commodification of gender and sexual identity through fashion, cosmetic, fitness, and other 'industries.' While the quest for individual meaning is expressed in the cultural realm, however, it is the conditions and relations of the production of that culture which help us, as social scientists, to understand cultural meanings.[12]

Describing the tendency for humans to acquire meaning through commodities

– and vice versa – as commodity fetishism, Marx connected the subjective experience of the market to the objective relations through which commodities are produced. In this way, he understood experiential categories, those through which the subject is created, as expressions of social relations. As Hartsock (1985) notes, Marx was able to gain this understanding by taking the perspective of the underclass, rather than accepting as given dominant meanings constructed by bourgeois economic theory. In doing so, Marx posited two epistemological systems: one at the level of appearance, given by exchange activities of the market through which profit is realized; the other at the level of real relations, rooted in the activities of the working class through which value is produced and appropriated by the capitalist. By thus articulating a theory of exploitation, Marx illustrated that while the experienced need of the proletariat for waged employment fosters the appearance that economic processes are in the interests of both the capitalist and the working classes, objectively the interests of these classes are mutually antagonist. It is this recognition of objective interests which transforms the proletariat from a *class in itself* into a *class for itself*. By bringing to awareness the social relations of class oppression, Marx's theory of exploitation provides the epistemological standpoint from which to direct a proletarian economic revolution.

In a similar way, by viewing women as an oppressed group, Smith (1987) differentiates two epistemological systems: the official one in which masculine rationality and modes of action dominate and through which male interests are furthered through positivist science; the other embedded in women's everyday activities and experiences, historically excluded from public and political discourse. In an examination of how women's knowledges are excluded from official texts, Smith begins with these texts in order to examine the process of their production. She thus uses a standpoint epistemology to develop a distinctly feminist mode of sociological inquiry. Despite the diversity of women's identities and experiences, Smith notes that women share a common standpoint because of their shared exclusion from social relations which control the production culture and knowledge, including knowledge about what it means to be a woman. As I shall outline below, this method can help us to identify the objective social relations which give rise both to women's exclusion and to the meanings affixed to this exclusion.[13]

Smith (1987) begins by noting that power relations in advanced industrialized societies have been mystified by the growth of bureaucratic knowledges and procedures which exclude women but which, although authored from a male perspective, are caste in gender-neutral, universal terms. Associated with the authority of the 'expert' who remains obscured behind the text, official knowledge appears to be without a gendered (or other) identity and as coming from no identifiable location within the nexus of social relations. Smith (ibid.: 78-88) observes that the expert, as knower, claims to construct this neutral, totalizing perspective by combining and distilling partial views, and detaching them from their origin in particular groups, classes, or localities in the social structure. Consistent with this neutrality and objectivity, texts are written in the abstract mode: institutionalized knowledge is characterized by the passive voice and an externalized perspective which cannot be linked to any particular place or person. Smith calls this practice one of the 'head' speaking and writing, which denies the body, the material work involved, and the social context in which this work is produced.

Smith notes that, in order for the production of texts to occur in this way, the writer must suppress sensations produced by the act of writing – such as the feeling of the pen in hand or the chair upon which one sits, as well as bodily sensations of hunger, fatigue, and so on – in order to operate in the abstract mode. No attention is paid to the manual labour of the working classes which produces the pen, the chair, and so on; nor to the domestic labour of women which feeds the body and restores it to working order; nor the clerical work, again of predominantly women, which enables the academic – usually male – to operate in this mode. Thus Smith brings to view what the positivist model suppresses because of what it presupposes: divisions of all kinds – between 'mental' and 'manual' labour, between men and women, and (potentially)[14] between individuals on the basis of race. While expressed in the conceptual realm as an abstract mode of presentation, academic claims to knowledge reflect relations of ruling in the material world of patriarchal capitalism.[15] Privilege of all kinds occurs not simply in our minds or in the discourses of the academic, but is what makes the production of texts possible. Thus, opening new subject positions within the text requires the transformation of relations of ruling, not simply the development of new modes of expression; patriarchal knowledge can be displaced only when the processes – and not simply the discourses – include women, an accomplishment which requires material as well as conceptual change. The ability to help us understand how this might be achieved is missing from post-modern texts. By arguing that universalizing categories such as race, class, and gender, are fictions, constructed within the text, post-modernism robs us of the conceptual tools to understand how the meanings which it deconstructs are produced through relations of ruling which are racial, gendered, and based on class.[16] What I find conspicuously absent from post-modern inquiry, as a method grounded upon critique of privilege, are analyses of the privilege which allows the post-modern intellectual to declare that the emancipatory potential of humanism is dead.

In the final analysis, both Smart and Smith are interested in a method which can demystify discursive practices which operate to exclude women and marginalize their knowledge. The difference is, however, that through standpoint epistemology, Smith analytically reveals the material process of exclusion. She brings into awareness a number of changes implied by the transformation of women from objects of patriarchal discourse to subjects of feminist inquiry: specifically, she connects women's exclusion from the production of culture and official knowledge to their material oppression, experiential to theoretical knowledge, subjective to objective knowing, feminist epistemology to feminist politics. In this way, Smith helps us understand the ways in which feminism, as an alternative mode of inquiry,[17] has the potential to challenge both patriarchal ways of knowing and official knowledge. Returning to the question of discourses on violence against women, we can see that there is nothing inherently oppressive about theory or method. Although the problems of theory may appear to be academic ones – *viz.* the separation of theory and research or the tendency towards reified formulations – they reflect the conditions and relations of its production: the separation in the real world of mental and manual labour, along the lines of class, gender, and race. It is for this reason that I believe that feminism must necessarily be 'socialist' as well as 'realist.' Whether or not this means that 'realist criminology' is a viable feminist project is the next question.

The Potential of Realist Criminology in Canada

Realism – like feminism – is about reclaiming the discourse on crime and women's safety (see Jones, MacLean, and Young 1986; MacLean 1991). In order to accomplish this, realist criminology devotes considerable attention to estimating the frequency, distribution, and impact of violence and crime against women, which is why realist discourses emphasize empirical rather than purely theoretical concerns. To read this as simply empiricist or as a new search for the 'Truth' of crime seriously misconstrues the political nature of the project. Realism theoretically, methodologically, and politically challenges those processes through which the 'Truth of Crime' is officially created. Although concerned with the measurement of crime, realist criminology emphasizes that crime is a political process, historically located within a patriarchal society. The features of socialist realism which I find most promising include: its rejection of academic idealism; its advocacy of politics informed by a thoroughgoing inclusion of consideration of race, class, and gender; and its insistence on beginning from the standpoint of respondents rather than those of the police, criminal justice administrators, or criminologists. When one acknowledges that women's experiences and concerns about crime have been historically excluded and trivialized, one can hardly accuse realism of pandering to 'common sense' notions of crime.[18] At the same time, it is important to remind ourselves of Young's (1991) view of the role of the criminologist: it is to debate with the public and policy makers over crime priorities, not to bestow priorities. Given that these tenets are not simply theoretical considerations, we are going to have to roll up our sleeves and engage in the dirty work of research.

Young (1991) dispels many of the horrors raised by contemplating such a task. In the final analysis, realism frightens me less than much of what is currently dubbed 'critical' criminology in Canada because it attempts to be accountable: to those about whom it speaks through its research methods, and to those engaged in the political struggle for a more equitable society. It thus has the potential to be linked to movements for accountable policing[19] (see Currie, DeKeseredy, and MacLean 1990). The extent to which this potential can be realized, however, is a political question: Canadian criminologists do not figure prominently in political struggles,[20] particularly those around policing. This absence of critical public discourse by the criminological community in Canada draws attention to significant differences between the orientation of social scientists in North America and Britain. Whether or not these differences suggest that realism is culturally specific, and will not spread beyond Britain, is a political, not an academic question: in my opinion, criminology can be socialist and realist only by political engagement. It is not simply a question of theoretical or methodological orientation.

As we have seen above, although violence against women is currently receiving considerable criminological attention, this issue was first put onto the agenda by community activists, rather than university-oriented academics,[21] who challenged both academic and common-sense notions about heterosexual relations and definitions of crime. As we have seen, this challenge required extensive research, conducted by feminists, from women's perspectives. While the successful reform of legislation and policing practices surrounding violence against women reflects a complex process, it was made possible, in part, through the establishment of an alternative discourse on 'justice' by the women's liberation movement through direct political action and through the continuing struggle to provide alternative, feminist accounts of the social world through women's studies. Unlike criminology, women's studies as an academic discipline is an 'arm of the women's movement' (Tobias 1978). Thus, unlike criminology, women's studies emphasizes and struggles to maintain a meaningful relationship to its community-based constituency. This struggle to remain accountable to the WLM is a difficult and ongoing one which has created serious divisions between feminists and is the subject of serious introspection (see Ramazanoglu 1989; Currie and Kline 1991). However, this type of introspection is glaringly absent from critical criminological discourse. It is here where criminologists – especially left realists – can learn from the recent experiences of socialist feminists.

Feminism began from recognition of women's oppression as constituted through patriarchal processes which historically have excluded women from the construction of official discourses and knowledge. Here the literary method of post-modernism is a useful one for feminists, because it makes us aware of this exclusion and reveals the potential for subversive 'knowing.' However, this exclusion eventually leads us to further questions about who has been included in the production of 'official' feminism, and who can speak on the behalf of those remaining outside the production of the official discourses of the women's movement. Above I have tried to highlight the reasons why discursive acknowledgment of exclusion and diversity is not enough. Democratic, inclusionary practices require material transformation through the redistribution of resources – a healthy, albeit painful lesson, for contemporary feminism. Clearly, the lesson here is that we need to bring to the fore the conditions and relations of feminism themselves as an 'object' of transformation. This requires analytical and introspective work of all kinds, some of it theoretical. In the meantime, acknowledgment of the exclusionary nature of academic practice increases the relevance of theoretical constructs (such as race, class, and gender) as well as the necessity for valid, empirical research. As long as the production of official discourses remains the domain of academics, feminist research, with its emphasis on participatory, action-oriented research, has the potential to be an inclusionary practice.[22] However, this focus on action in no way should be read as a retreat from theory.

No matter how complex and contradictory the struggle for change through deliberated intervention, I am not sure that we should reject the notion of 'cause and effect' in order to claim that we have transcended the search for 'Truth.' I agree with Smart (1990) that we may want to abandon 'cause and effect' formulations of a positivist criminology which argues, for example, that 'poverty causes crime' or 'patriarchy causes violence against women.' However, unlike Smart, I do not think that we should abandon systematic, empirical investigation in order to develop theory. What I reject are the types of formulations which reflect reified thinking about the social world. While the above types of statements which causally link, for example, crime to the social conditions of its existence, are useful in the heuristic sense, for the large part they reflect the academic naturalization of social relations and, as such, are theoretical expressions of the relations of their production. This is where the method of literary deconstruction is both useful and limited. On the one hand, it brings to awareness the politically constructed nature of theoretical knowledge and the ways in which other kinds of knowing are excluded. On the other hand, deconstructing categories is like 'sawing off the branch on which one is sitting.' While philosophers may define this act as a clear-sighted recognition that there is no ground to fall on, for women I agree that it is still reckless sawing (see Hekmen 1990: 4). As women we are only just beginning to name the world as we experience it. The problem is not simply that feminism is an alternative or another partial, competing knowledge: feminism continues to be a marginalized discourse.[23] 'Grand' categories still have relevance because they help us to identify processes of our exclusion, to name relations of ruling and power, and to highlight both the diversity of women's relationships to this process and the divisions which this diversity brings. The problem with many analyses provided by what is claimed as 'post-modernism' is that they mistake *the way* in which domination and oppression are perpetuated – i.e., through texts and discourses – for the *cause* of this oppression by discounting a reality beyond the text.

In a position which I read as compatible to socialist realism, Cain (1990: 129) uses the term 'intransitive' to describe the reality created through and by social relations. To say that these realities exist whether we think about them or not, however, is not to say that we can ever be sure that our knowledges correspond to any or all of them. However, once people think about them, the realities may become transitive, changed by the ways in which people think about and relate to them. While this raises questions about what methodologies are appropriate to their 'discovery' that are beyond the scope of the present discussion, I think that we want as our goal to produce valid and reliable knowledge, i.e., knowledge that is open to 'democratic' investigation and critique. However, to claim that knowledge about intransitive phenomena is valid and reliable – whether of the natural world or the social – is not to claim that these empirically verifiable facts are universal 'Truths': the shift from the former to the latter is one which takes us from contextual to absolutist thinking. As many feminists have argued, we might like to start replacing the notion of scientific knowledge legitimated by claims to its truth-value by demonstrations of the desirability of its effects. While this obviously raises moral/ethical/political questions, we are only fooling ourselves if we believe that they are not already on the scientific agenda. As realists have continually noted, decisions about a 'just' society are political and not academic.

This does not mean, however, that as academics we can overlook the struggle against oppression at the local level. As academics we need to become more cognizant of the privilege that enables us to speak about minority struggles, on the behalf of those excluded from official discourse. What is becoming clear is that the 'failure' of much academic work to meaningfully address political questions – whether feminist or 'malestream' – is not a failure of research or theory: rather, it reflects in many ways the conditions of production of an 'official' knowledge. The articulation of demands became the specialty of 'experts,' those who 'speak the language of power' (see Barnsley 1985). Reflecting the involvement of accredited experts, the voice of the oppressed is that of primarily white, middle-class, educated men and women who discuss oppression within dominant discursive categories. While feminists critical of this process draw attention to the ideological realignment implied by shifts in discourse – like the ones from 'wife battering' to 'domestic violence' and from 'social equality' to 'criminal justice' – also important (but usually neglected) is the need to discuss the ways in which those who produce this discourse, regardless of intentions, are working within, and to maintain, relations of ruling.[24]

At the purely discursive level, the acceptance of criminal justice discourse is not simply a result of the internalization of ideological modes of thinking, however, so that problems can be corrected through purely intellectual effort. As feminists like Findlay (1988) who are engaged in and committed to the WLM have indicated, this acceptance occurs within the immediacy of a context requiring strategies that are practical, acceptable, and expedient. In a similar way, social-scientific discourses are produced within a context of academic requirements which directly reflect the actual, 'material' separation of intellectual and political decision making. While these observations raise more questions than can be answered here, they imply that our analytical task is to reconnect the production of discourses and their effects to their non-discursive context. As I hope that I have shown above, the result is a contextualized study that reflects the way in which post-modern critiques, while not displacing empirically grounded investigation, have transformed the ways in which we think about 'social scientific' study.

While the debates raised by post-modern critiques are unlikely to be resolved for some time yet, the lessons for feminism concern the plurality of knowledge which is hidden by both discursive and non-discursive processes of exclusion; recognition that while there may not be 'truths' there are real, experienced effects of knowledge; and the need to include ourselves as academics in introspective accounting of how both repressive and 'liberatory' discourses are constructed. In the final analysis, while there is both the necessity and potential for alliances between feminists and criminologists in the struggle against violence against women, realization of this potential will depend for a large part on the extent to which criminology in Canada is willing and able to learn from feminism. In particular, criminology requires greater consideration of the social relations of its discipline and the role which criminology plays in the construction of knowledge about crime, criminalization, and victimization. Realist criminology has come a long way towards this recognition by emphasizing the way in which criminal statistics are a product of the complex interrelationships between the offender, victim, police, and the community. Because the quality of these relationships determine the kind and frequency of official crime, realist surveys attempt to include measures of relationships which produce the social construction called 'crime.' Although realist approaches have broadened the analysis of the construction of crime by emphasizing the four-way interaction between offender, victim, police, and the community (see MacLean 1991), however, I hope that I have drawn attention to the glaring absence of the criminologist as researcher in this configuration. In the final analysis, what will bring realism and feminism closer together is recognition that criminological discourses are the result of *the complex interraction between offender, victim, police, community, and researchers.* This means that the incorporation of a feminist perspective within criminology – realist or otherwise – is more than a discursive practice: it mandates real transformation of patriarchal relationships within criminology, as well as transformation of the relationship between university-based criminology and the community in Canada.

I would like to thank John Lowman and Brian MacLean, as well as Meda Chesney-Lind, University of Hawaii at Manoa, and Frank Pearce, Queen's University, for their comments on this essay.

Notes

1 For an overview see Currie (1990).
2 In British Columbia, Carol Gran, the Social Credit party minister responsible for Women, similarly appropriated the issue of wife battery to endorse a televised campaign to inform the public that wife battery is a crime. I say 'appropriated' because the Socred government offers funding which is inadequate to ensure the survival of community-based women's self-help groups.
3 In particular, use of the term 'family violence' reflects the fact that child abuse is not an exclusively male domain. However, while the term 'family violence' may be often usefully employed, the increasing tendency to use this term when it is more correct both analytically and politically to view violence as a matter of gender *is* problematic.
4 It is not that we do not want women's issues to be incorporated into official agendas: the problem is that this has very often resulted in the accommodation and expansion of current patriarchal institutions instead of their transformation. Institutionalization most often is accomplished by incorporating women into bureaucratic hierarchies, who then become active agents of patriarchal institutions. This paradox has resulted in serious rifts over the issue of 'working within/against the institution.' Obviously, there are serious differences of opinion here.

5 MacLeod notes that the government support which this growth reflects – a growth since halted and even reversed by funding cutbacks – has been 'both a facilitator and a product of changes in philosophy among many shelter workers' (1987: 54). There is a growing tendency to hire staff with formal educational credentials and professional qualifications. While many workers welcome this because it strengthens the credibility of shelter staff in the community and helps to link transition houses with other professional services, it has transformed the relationship between battered women and transition-house workers (see also Morgan 1981), and has created a division between community-based and professional feminists. While boards of directors had previously consisted of staff and community members who shared the philosophical orientation and goals of the staff, they are now likely to be lawyers, accountants, teachers, or social workers (MacLeod 1987: 57).

6 These discourses are not exclusively located within the domain of criminology; nor are they necessarily the product of male scholarship.

7 In this way, by treating any appeal to the notion of 'causality' as 'positivistic,' Smart conflates positivism and philosophical realism. While realism is scientific, it is not positivistic and does not resemble the portrait Smart offers here (see, especially, Keat and Urry 1975).

8 I will merely draw attention here to the emerging interest by realist criminologists in the relationships between masculinity and masculine culture in the perpetuation of male violence. See especially DeKeseredy (1988).

9 While no one has ever accused Foucault of being a feminist, it is also important to recognize that he did not consider himself as a 'post-modernist' either. See Lather (1988).

10 This is not Smart's term. As with the notion of a post-modern criminologist, it strikes me as an oxymoron.

11 Because of this, Tong (1989: 219) argues that deconstruction is necessarily anti-essentialist. Ironically, however, if used to revalorize the feminine it can ironically affirm gender dichotomies. This is apparent in the imagery used by some post-modern writers to 'write the female body' (see Currie and Raoul 1991).

12 Here I am hinting at the (necessary) connection between analytical emphasis on culture and a political movement which, ironically, rests on affirmation of cultural identity.

13 That is, that this exclusion testifies to the 'fact' that women cannot have valid, reliable knowledge.

14 'Potentially' is not developed in Smith (1987) where this method is laid out.

15 Obviously, this applies to academic feminist knowledge. The difference between traditional knowledge and feminist knowledge – especially that from a standpoint epistemology – is that the latter acknowledges the way in which the production of official knowledge presupposes, yet renders invisible, the labour of subordinated

groups. Whether all feminism follows through on this is, of course, another matter (see Currie and Kline 1991).

16 Once again, this testifies to the post-modern notion that 'privilege' refers to the conceptual, rather than material, realm.

17 *If* an alternative mode of inquiry (not all 'feminist' approaches are)

18 By redefining crime to acknowledge actual but officially unrecorded rates of violence against women and to include other harmful behaviours which are not recognized as such, the Islington Crime Survey can hardly be accused of pandering to 'common sense' definitions of crime (see Scraton 1985, 1987, 1990). This criticism is obviously sexist and élitist.

19 A good example of where critical criminologists could become engaged (but have not) is the struggle by First Nations for indigenous policing of reserves.

20 I think that this differs substantially from the situation of academic lawyers who, quite visibly, can claim a public, political practice.

21 Some of these were members of universities as well.

22 As feminism is now being included in the production of knowledge and official policy, the question of exclusion is still relevant, particularly for minority women who continue to be marginalized within women's studies and other official bureaucracies. Thus Currie and Kline (1991) point out that Smith's standpoint epistemology is useful if extended to involve questions about who is included in the production of official feminism. This should also make it apparent why I disagree with Smart's understanding of feminist-standpoint epistemology which she implies is speaking about women as a unitary group. A 'standpoint' is the result of social relations. A feminist epistemology based on the notion of standpoint is important in asking questions about social relations between women.

23 While there has been some inclusion and accommodation of feminism within official agendas, feminism remains marginal to mainstream institutions, especially universities and government bureaucracies.

24 The way in which 'critical' criminologists are often engaged in this process is best illustrated by the example of one of my male critical-criminologist colleagues attending a national public forum who discounted the political work of a long-time feminist prison activist on the grounds that the abolitionist movement is inadequately informed by the theoretical 'fact' that prisons serve a function for the Canadian state.

References

Ahluwalia, S. 1987. 'A History of Domestic Violence: Implications for Medical Intervention in Saskatchewan.' MA thesis, University of Saskatchewan
– 1988. 'Diminished Conceptions of Women in Domestic Violence Research,' in D.H.

Currie, ed., *From the Margins to the Centre: Selected Essays in Women's Studies Research*, 69-94. Saskatoon: Social Research Unit

Alcoff, L. 1989. 'Cultural Feminism versus Post-Structuralism: The Identity Crisis in Feminist Theory,' in M.R. Malson, J.F. O'Barr, S. Westphal-Wihl, and M. Wyer, eds., *Feminist Theory in Practice and Process*, 295-326. Chicago: University of Chicago Press

Allen, J.M., and M.A. Straus. 1980. 'Resources, Power and Husband-Wife Violence,' in M.A. Strauss and C.T. Hotaling, eds., *The Social Causes of Husband-Wife Violence*, 188-208. Minneapolis: University of Minnesota Press

Barnsley, J. 1985. *Feminist Action, Institutional Reaction: Responses to Wife Assault.* Vancouver: Women's Research Centre

Breines, W., and L. Gordon. 1983. 'The New Scholarship on Family Violence.' *Signs: Journal of Women in Culture and Society*, 8: 491-553

Cain, M. 1990. 'Realist Philosophy and Standpoint Epistemologies or Feminist Criminology as a Successor Science,' in L. Gelsthorpe and A. Morris, eds., *Feminist Perspectives on Criminology*, 124-140. Milton Keynes: Open University Press

Carby, H.V. 1990. 'The Politics of Difference.' *Ms.*, September/October: 84-85

Cassell, J. 1977. *A Group Called Women: Sisterhood and Symbolism in the Feminist Movement.* New York: David McKay

Clarehart, S., J. Elder, and C. Janes. 1982. 'Problem-Solving Skills of Rural Battered Women.' *American Journal of Community Psychology*, 10 (5): 605-613

Comack, E. 1987. 'Women Defendants and the "Battered Wife Syndrome": A Plea for the Sociological Imagination.' *Crown Counsel's Review*, 5 (5): 6-10

Crawford, A., T. Jones, T. Woodhouse, and J. Young. 1990. *Second Islington Crime Survey.* London: Middlesex Polytechnic, Centre for Criminology

Currie, D.H. 1990. 'Battered Women and the State: From the Failure of Theory to a Theory of Failure.' *Journal of Human Justice*, 1 (2): 77-96

Currie, D.H., W. DeKeseredy, and B.D. MacLean. 1990 'Reconstituting Social Order and Social Control: Police Accountability in Canada.' *Journal of Human Justice*, 2 (1): 29-54

Currie, D.H., and M. Kline. 1991. 'Challenging Privilege: Women, Knowledge, and Feminist Struggles.' *Journal of Human Justice*, 2 (2): 1-37

Currie, D.H., and V. Raoul. 1991. 'The Anatomy of Gender: Dissecting Difference in the Body of Knowledge,' in D. Currie and V. Raoul, eds., *The Anatomy of Gender: Women's Struggle for the Body*, 1-39. Ottawa: Carleton University Press

DeKeseredy, W. 1988. *Woman Abuse in Dating Relationships: The Role of Male Peer Support.* Toronto: Canadian Scholars Press

DeKeseredy, W., and R. Hinch. 1991. *Woman Abuse: Sociological Perspectives.* Toronto: Thompson Educational Publishing

DeKeseredy, W., and B.D. MacLean. 1990. 'Researching Women Abuse in Canada: A Realist Critique of the Conflict Tactics Scale.' *Canadian Review of Social Policy*, 25 (May): 19-27

DeKeseredy, W., and M. Schwartz. 1991. 'British Left Realism on the Abuse of Women: A Critical Appraisal,' in R. Quinney and H. Pepinsky, eds., *Criminology as Peacemaking*, 154-171. Bloomington: Indiana University Press

Dobash, R.E. and R. Dobash. 1983. 'The Context-Specific Approach,' in D. Finkelhor, R.J. Gelles, G.T. Hotaling, and M.A. Straus, eds., *The Dark Side of Families*, 261-276. Beverly Hills: Sage

– 1988. 'Research as Social Action: The Struggle for Battered Women,' in K. Yllo and M. Bograd, eds., *Feminist Perspectives on Wife Abuse*, 51-74. Beverly Hills: Sage

Ellis, D., and W. DeKeseredy. 1989. 'Marital Status and Woman Abuse: The DAD Model.' *International Journal of Sociology of the Family*, 19: 67-87

Errington, G.B. 1977. *Family Violence – Is It a Women's Problem?* An address to the Symposium on Family Violence held in Vancouver (March). Vancouver: Women's Research Centre

Ferraro, K.J. 1983. 'Rationalizing Violence: How Battered Women Stay.' *Victimology: An International Journal*, 8 (3/4): 203-212

Findlay, S. 1988. 'Feminist Struggles with the Canadian State: 1966-1988.' *Resources for Feminist Research*, 17(3): 5-9

Flax, J. 1990. 'Postmodernism and Gender Relations in Feminist Theory,' in L. Nicholson, ed., *Feminism/Postmodernism*, 39-62. New York: Routledge

Gelsthorpe, L., and A. Morris. 1988. 'Feminism and Criminology in Britain,' in P. Rock, ed., *A History of British Criminology*, 93-110. Oxford: Clarendon Press

Goode, W. 1971. 'Force and Violence in the Family.' *Journal of Marriage and the Family*, 33 (4): 624-636

Goodstein, R.K., and A.W. Page. 1981. 'Battered Wife Syndrome: An Overview of Dynamics and Treatment.' *American Journal of Psychiatry*, 138 (8): 1036-1044

Harding, S., ed. 1986. *The Science Question in Feminism*. Milton Keynes: Open University Press

Hartsock, N. 1985. *Money, Sex, and Power: Toward a Feminist Historical Materialism*. Boston: Northeastern University Press

– 1987. 'Re-thinking Modernism: Minority vs. Majority Theories.' *Cultural Critique*, 7: 187-206

Hekmen, S.J. 1990. *Gender and Knowledge: Elements of a Postmodern Feminism*. Cambridge: Polity Press

hooks, bell. 1989. *Talking Back: Thinking Feminism, Thinking Black*. Boston: South End Press

Humphreys, J.J., and W.O. Humphreys. 1985. 'Mandatory Arrest: A Means of Primary and Secondary Prevention of Abuse of Female Partners.' *Victimology: An International Journal*, 10 (1-4): 267-280

Jaggar, A.M. 1983. *Feminist Politics and Human Nature*. Sussex: The Harvester Press

Jones, T., B. MacLean, and J. Young. 1986. *The Islington Crime Survey: Crime, Victimization and Policing in Inner-City London*. Aldershot: Gower

Keat, R., and J. Urry. 1975. *Social Theory as Science*. London: Routledge and Kegan Paul

Kelly, L., and J. Radford. 1987. 'The Problem of Men: Feminist Perspectives on Sexual Violence,' in P. Scraton, ed., *Law, Order and the Authoritarian State: Readings in Critical Criminology*, 237-253. Milton Keynes: Open University Press

Lather, P. 1988. 'Postmodernism and the Human Sciences.' *Psychology and Postmodernity*, a special issue of *The Humanist Psychologist*, 18 (1): 64-84

McGillivray, A. 1987. 'Battered Women: Definition, Models and Prosecutorial Policy.' *Canadian Journal of Family Law*, 6: 15-45

MacLean, B.D. 1991. 'In Partial Defense of Socialist Realism: Some Theoretical and Methodological Concerns of the Local Crime Survey.' *Law, Crime, and Social Change*, 15: 213-254

MacLeod, L. 1980. *Wife Battering in Canada: The Vicious Circle*. Ottawa: Minister of Supply and Services

– 1987. *Battered But Not Beaten: Preventing Wife Battery in Canada*. Ottawa: CACSW

Morgan, P. 1981. 'From Battered Wife to Program Client: The State's Shaping of Social Problems.' *Kapitalistate*, 9: 17-41

Rae-Grant, Q. 1983. 'Family Violence – Myths, Measures, Mandates.' *Canadian Journal of Psychiatry*, 28 (7): 505-512

Ramazanoglu, C. 1989. *Feminism and the Contradictions of Oppression*. London: Routledge

Rounsaville, B., and M. Weissman. 1977/8. 'Battered Women: A Medical Problem Requiring Detection.' *International Journal of Psychiatry in Medicine*, 8 (2): 191-202

Scraton, P. 1990. 'Scientific Knowledge or Masculine Discourses? Challenging Patriarchy in Criminology,' in L. Gelsthorpe and A. Morris, eds., *Feminist Perspectives in Criminology*, 10-25. Milton Keynes: Open University Press

– 1985. *The State of the Police*. London: Pluto

– ed. 1987. *Law, Order and the Authoritarian State*. Milton Keynes: Open University Press

Sherman, L., and R. Berk. 1984. *The Minneapolis Domestic Violence Experiment*, Police Foundations Reports no. 1. Washington, DC: Police Foundation

Smart, C. 1989. *Feminism and the Power of Law*. London: Routledge

– 1990. 'Feminist Approaches to Criminology or Postmodern Woman Meets Atavistic Man,' in L. Gelsthorpe and A. Morris, eds., *Feminist Perspectives in Criminology*, 70-84. Milton Keynes: Open University Press

12 Counting What Counts: The Study of Women's Fear of Crime

Seema Ahluwalia

In the late 1960s, British feminists expressed disillusionment with the male left because of the marginalization of women's issues on the socialist agenda (Kelly 1988; Malos 1972). At this time, many women were drawing attention to violence against women by calling for criminal justice and social service reform. These efforts were dismissed by the male left as either a concession to the bourgeois state or a form of moral entrepeneurship (Young 1988a).

By the mid 1970s, feminist writers had exposed criminology as a sexist domain from which women were excluded or in which they were portrayed in stereotypical ways (Smart 1976; Klein 1973; Heidensohn 1968). Dissatisfaction with the pervasive sexism in criminology has resulted in a body of feminist work developed outside of traditional and 'radical' discourses (Gelsthorpe and Morris 1988).

Today, British feminists have generally dismissed both traditional and radical criminology as gender-blind (Kelly 1988; Gelsthorpe and Morris 1988; Smart 1976). At the same time, however, left realists have claimed to share many of the methodological concerns and political aims of feminists. This essay explores potential connections between 'radical feminism' and left realism by comparing their approaches to the study of women's fear of crime. This particular phenomenon has been chosen because it constitutes a common ground for radical feminists and left realists, both of whom challenge the idea that crime is a rare occurrence (Walklate 1990). Contrary to conventional wisdom, left realists and feminists involved in survey research have attempted to demonstrate that women's fear of crime is based on an accurate assessment of risk rather than the overactive imaginations or hysterical tendencies of females.

This essay begins by describing survey research conducted by British femi-

Smith, D. 1987. *The Everyday World as Problematic: A Feminist Sociology.* Toronto: University of Toronto Press

Smith, M. 1990. 'Patriarchal Ideology and Wife Beating: A Test of a Feminist Hypothesis.' *Violence and Victims,* 5: 257-273

Smith, P. 1984. *Breaking Silence: A Descriptive Report of a Followup Study of Abused Women Using a Shelter.* Ottawa: National Clearinghouse on Family Violence

Snell, J.E., R.J. Rosenwald, and A. Robey. 1964. 'The Wifebeater's Wife.' *Archives of General Psychiatry,* 11: 107-112

Strauss, M.A. 1977. 'Sociological Perspectives on the Prevention and Treatment of Wifebeating,' in M. Roy, ed., *Battered Women: A Psycho Social Study of Domestic Violence,* 194-238. New York: Van Nostrand Reinhold

Swanson, R.A. 1985. 'Recognizing Battered Wife Syndrome.' *Canadian Family Physician,* 3 (1): 823-825

– 1986. 'Signs and Symptoms of Abuse.' Paper presented at Saskatchewan Health Department Conference: The Spouse Abuse Victim as a Hospital Patient, Saskatoon

Thomas, J., and A. O'Maolchatha. 1989. 'Reassessing the Critical Metaphor: An Optimistic Revisionist View.' *Justice Quarterly,* 6: 143-72

Tobias, S. 1978. 'Women's Studies: Its Origins, Its Organization, and Its Prospects.' *Women's Studies International Quarterly,* 1 (1): 85-97

Tong, R. 1989. *Feminist Thought: A Comprehensive Introduction.* Boulder and San Francisco: Westview Press

Walker, L. 1977/8. 'Battered Women and Learned Helplessness.' *Victimology: An International Journal,* 2 (3/4): 525-534

Yllo, K., and M. Bograd. 1988. *Feminist Perspectives on Wife Abuse.* Beverly Hills: Sage

Young, J. 1991. 'Asking Questions of Left Realism,' in B.D. MacLean and D. Milovanovic, eds., *New Directions in Critical Criminology,* 15-18. Vancouver: Collective Press nists (Hall 1985; Hanmer and Saunders 1984; Hanmer, Radford, and Stanko 1989; Radford 1984; Kelly and Radford 1987; Stanko 1985) and left realists on women's victimization. I will demonstrate that these two lines of inquiry share certain features and differ from traditional approaches in criminology. Finally, I consider research on fear of crime, a topic that has become a matter of some preoccupation in criminology in recent years. Described by Hanmer and Stanko as an 'Achilles heel for the state and for criminology' (1985: 369), it has generated research which perpetuates certain essentialist notions of women, including the idea that we are irrationally fearful and passive in our response to crime victimization.

Left-Realist Methodology

A fundamental tenet of left realism is that 'street crime' really is a problem. This insistence is partly a reaction to those 'left idealists' who romanticize crime by seeing it as political action. Also it spurns the British Home Office research machine which has devoted much time, effort, and money to establish that most citizens overestimate their risk of being victimized.[1] It has been argued that the real dimensions of criminal victimization have been missed because much criminological research has ignored the processual nature of crime, focusing instead singularly on the offender, the victim, the police, or the community (Jones, MacLean, and Young 1986; Ahluwalia and MacLean 1986). Left realism attempts to integrate these various levels of analysis.

Since crime is geographically and socially clustered (Sparks 1981), the assessment of who is at risk of criminal victimization and what kind of effect victimization (or threat of it) has on people's lives has become central to the left-realist research agenda. Such an assessment would require an accurate victimology and, in order to achieve this, left realists have established their own tradition of victimization surveys[2] which are claimed to be theoretically informed and committed to an understanding of crime that reflects the views of the public (Walklate 1989; Jones, MacLean, and Young 1986; Young 1986). This implies a problematization of official constructions of crime and the creation of an alternative definition which is not based upon police practice.

Young (1986) has criticized large-scale, government-funded surveys such as the British Crime Survey for constructing notions of 'global risk rates' of 'average citizens,' including the strange insight that an 'average person' suffers criminal injury approximately once every hundred years (Hough and Mayhew 1983). Such abstractions serve to 'conceal the actual severity of crime amongst significant sections of the population whilst providing a fake statistical backdrop for the discussion of "irrational" fears' (Young 1986: 23).

Instead, left-realist research has shown that criminal victimization is not distributed evenly, either geographically or socially. Through the use of locally based surveys, left realists have been able to demonstrate that victimization is a product of risk rate and vulnerability (Jones, MacLean, and Young 1986; Young 1986). Crime is not randomly distributed, and left realists point to the role that factors such as age, sex, race, and class play in shaping patterns of victimization.

The impact of crime victimization has also been a key area of left-realist research. Surveys have shown that fear of crime and the financial, physical, and emotional consequences of criminal victimization often influence the way people structure their daily lives (Crawford et al. 1990; Jones, MacLean, and Young 1986).

Critical examinations of definitions of crime and victimization have been a starting-point for left realists who have pointed out that official crime statistics are more likely a reflection of law-enforcement policy on resource deployment than an assessment of the scope and frequency of crime in the community (Kinsey, Lea, and Young, 1986; Ahluwalia and MacLean 1986; MacLean 1986). Racial and sexual biases in police decision making shape official statistics and, as in so doing, can seriously distort the community's experience (Young 1986; Ahluwalia and MacLean 1986; Kinsey, Lea, and Young 1986). As a result, left realists advocate the development of an alternative set of statistics based on the police response to both victim and offender, the police response desired by the public, and the public's notion of its safety needs (Walklate 1989).

Left realists have placed victim-centred definitions of crime, policing, and public safety needs at the heart of their research agenda in order to move beyond the typical subject-matter and mandate of administrative criminology. This allows for further exploration of what Stanko (1985) refers to as 'invisible victims,' and is particularly relevant to crimes involving female victims, particularly domestic violence and sexual assault.

It is in this respect that local crime surveys in the left-realist tradition have been particularly sensitive to issues surrounding the criminal victimization of women. For example, one of the key objectives of the Islington Crime Survey (ICS) was to 'attempt to measure, where possible, the differential impact that crime and policing has for women compared to men, the effects this might have on their perceptions and behaviours in relation to safety, and to what extent the particular needs of women in terms of public safety are either being met or ignored by the criminal justice apparatus' (Jones, MacLean, and Young 1986: 157).

The preceding discussion indicates that left realists have not been silent on the issue of the criminal victimization of women. The expression of a commitment to explore the extent to which victimization is mediated by gender at least holds the promise of a feminist initiative.

Feminist Methodology

There is much debate over whether or not there is a distinct 'feminist methodology.' However, Gelsthorpe and Morris (1990) suggest that it is possible to identify 'core elements' of feminist work, including: an anti-positivist stance, criticism of stereotypical portrayals of women, the use of women's experience as a starting-point of analysis, and a commitment to generate and utilize methods of research which are sensitive to such concerns.

In Britain, a common starting-point for feminists has been the observation that women's lives are controlled by the threat and reality of men's violence (Hanmer, Radford, and Stanko 1989). This has led for a call to examine patriarchal power in relation to race, class, and sexuality. Feminists have variously examined violence against women, theories about that violence, the state's response to it, and women's resistance to the violence of men (Hanmer, Radford, and Stanko 1989; Kelly and Radford 1987).

Kelly and Radford (1987) argue that male violence against women is a defining feature of patriarchal societies, and that it is often condoned by the state to ensure male domination and female subordination. According to this perspective, violence against women is assumed to be widespread and its threat ever present. The key problem is not so much to establish methods of counting instances of such violence as it is to demonstrate the ways that criminology and victimology have obfuscated and distorted the criminal victimization of women.

The starting-point for many feminists, then, has been to deconstruct criminological definitions of violence. Hatty notes that such definitions reflect 'malestream' standards of 'visibility and quantifiability, thereby excluding the invisible and diffuse' (1989: 71). The focus has been upon physical injury rather than psychological or emotional trauma. One response by feminists to this problem has been to reject abstractions of female experience and produce definitions by talking to women themselves in order to reflect the totality of their experience. Since definitions can and do change over time, it is important to pay attention to the ways in which women define and describe various forms of sexual violence (Kelly and Radford 1987). Feminists have developed new terminology to reflect experiences which have hitherto been neglected by criminologists. For example, a recent study of sexual violence in England (Kelly 1988) includes the categories 'coercive sex' and 'pressurized sex' to indicate behaviour which might be considered less serious than rape, but has been reported by women to be traumatizing. Concurrently, a shift has occurred from viewing various forms of male violence, such as rape and domestic violence, as separate phenomena to a view that such acts are specific variations of the general phenomenon of sexual violence against women (Hanmer, Radford, and Stanko

1989; Gelsthorpe and Morris 1988; Kelly 1988; Radford 1985). Viewing male violence against women as a continuum allows for an exploration of the links between individual acts of men and socio-structural forces. This approach is evident in a variety of feminist works (Radford 1985; Gilbert and Webster 1982; Marolla and Scully 1979) but is most clearly utilized in the recent work of Kelly (1988) who describes a 'continuum of sexual violence' in which a wide array of violent acts are directed at women *because they are female*.

If an understanding of violence against women is to be grounded in female experience, then traditional research methods which separate the researcher from the 'object' of research must be rejected. Considering the sensitive nature of the subject-matter, feminists designing surveys have sought to develop methods that take into account the difficulty of the research subject in conveying her experiences. Attention is given to how questions are formulated, the structure of interviews, and, perhaps most importantly, the encouragement and ongoing support that are offered to women who agree to discuss such painful experiences. While such concerns may not be seen as uniquely feminist, feminist research has been unique in remaining faithful to all three. Support might include referral to relevant community services, setting up self-help groups and organizing community meetings (Kelly and Radford 1987; Radford 1985; Stanko 1985). Feminist research aims to move beyond merely documenting women's experience of violence to developing strategies to change their conditions. Such strategies might include the development of services such as refuges for battered women, self-defence and assertiveness training, or campaigns to facilitate law and policing reform.

Feminists carrying out surveys have rejected approaches which distinguish different forms of violence against women and treat them as instances. Rather, feminist surveys of violence seek to explore how different forms of violence are experienced over a lifetime. Such an exploration would also need to consider the impact of pornography on women generally and the impact of sexual harassment at work and to document childhood experiences of physical, sexual, and emotional abuse (Hanmer 1989). Considering the nature of such research and the feminist commitment to democratize the research process (Hanmer and Saunders 1984), small-scale research projects have been favoured over government-sponsored crime surveys, since the former involve less expense, and 'expert' knowledge is eschewed in favour of sensitivity to women's experience (Hanmer 1989). Nevertheless, there has been recognition of the need for statistics that challenge official definitions of women's experiences; various researchers have attempted to use survey methods to demonstrate that violence against women is a regular occurrence (see, for example, Russell 1982; Hanmer and Saunders 1984; Hall 1985; Radford 1984).

By contending that women's experiences are characterized by a lifetime of exposure to male violence, feminists raise the questions of how and why women are not protected from such exposure, and, therefore, policing has taken centre stage in many feminist research projects. Women's individual complaints about male violence allow feminists to construct a general understanding of the role of the police in maintaining existing relationships of gender, race, class, and sexuality (Hanmer, Radford, and Stanko 1989). In this pursuit, feminists have noted the reluctance of the police to take action against men who are violent to women, the insensitivity of their intervention techniques, and the police failure to refer women to other agencies that might provide support (Hanmer, Radford, and Stanko 1989; Hall 1985; Stanko 1985; Pahl 1985; Binney, Harkell, and Nixon 1981; Dobash and Dobash 1979).

Finally, feminists have noted that traditional victimology portrays female victims of violence as passive and helpless. The concern is that such a portrayal, especially when sustained by the media, has a negative effect on women in general and discourages women from resisting the dominance they experience. Feminists have thus begun to describe the ways that women resist violence (Hanmer, Radford, and Stanko 1989; Ahluwalia 1988; Kelly 1988; Radford 1985). In so doing, the traditional language of victimology has been problematized. As Kelly and Radford explain: 'While women are victimized on a regular and recurring basis, the term victim implies a passive response to the events themselves and their aftermath. Feminists prefer the term survivor, thereby drawing attention to the many ways that women resist violence and to the coping strategies they use in dealing with the effects of sexual violence on them over time. Feminists seek to validate and encourage women to build on the strength they have demonstrated in resisting and coping' (1987: 247).

Some Common Themes

In terms of their research interests, left realists and feminists seem to be united on several counts. Both are committed to deconstructing traditional notions of crime and victimization in order to replace them with definitions that emerge from information yielded by research subjects. Both express dissatisfaction with previous victimization studies because they abstract the experience of victimization by restricting analysis of the interrelationships among race, class, and gender. For both, policing is an important area of research. Finally, both conceive of research as one way of engaging in political struggle with state agencies.

An analysis of fear of crime will serve to demonstrate the common characteristics of feminism and left realism by showing how they differ from traditional conceptions of women's fear of crime.

Studying Fear of Crime

Police crime statistics and various victimization surveys have putatively shown that women are less at risk of victimization than are men (Hindelang, Gottfredson, and Garofalo 1978; Canada, Ministry of the Solicitor General 1985; Hough and Mayhew 1983). The fact that women express higher levels of fear has thus led many researchers to conclude that women are irrational. Despite the problematic nature of the evidence that women are a low-risk group,[3] the discordance between fear and risk seems to have been uncritically accepted in many quarters (Ahluwalia and MacLean 1986). For example, some researchers, claiming to present a more 'feminist' stance, have suggested that the social and physical vulnerability of women accounts for their fear of crime (Horton and Kennedy 1985; Skogan and Maxfield 1981; Riger, Gordon, and LeBailly 1978; Riger and Gordon 1981; Smith 1990); in other words, women's fear reflects the way they perceive the consequences of victimization rather than reflecting the actual consequences (Maxfield 1984). In this way, women's fear is cast as an irrational perception, not a reflection of actual risk. For example, a report from the British Home Office suggests that violence against women is not as serious a problem as women's irrational fear of crime (Hough and Mayhew 1983). These findings imply that feminist claims about the vast amount of unreported and unrecorded violent crimes against women are exaggerated.

National victimization surveys continue to focus on crimes in the public domain. This selectivity reinforces the notion that woman's main nemesis is the 'dark stranger' and that women are safest in their own homes. Such conclusions fly in the face of twenty years of feminist efforts to document the extent to which women are assaulted within the family or by persons well known to them.

Feminists and left realists have resisted the idea that women are irrational, putting the experiences and needs of the victim as she sees them at the centre of the research agenda (Hanmer and Saunders 1984; Radford 1984; Hall 1985; Jones, MacLean, and Young 1986; Kelly 1988). By doing so, they problematize two assumptions underlying traditional work on fear of crime: (a) that women are less at risk than men, and (b) that fear of crime can be understood by juxtaposing a 'subjective' expression of fear with an 'objective' measure of risk (Young 1988b).

Feminist Survey Research

Feminist studies of women's fear of crime have started from the assumption that such fear is widespread, ever present, and has as much to do with the violence that women experience at the hands of their family and friends as violence and harassment in public space. Unlike traditional victimization surveys, most feminist studies are not designed to reproduce official categories of crime in order to provide comparison; rather they are meant as a specific tool for demonstrating the ways in which women are victimized and harassed by males on a daily basis. For feminists, these forms of victimization are not discrete and unrelated events. Instead, they have tried to establish that there is a link between street hassling and rape. Viewed this way, male violence against women is not an 'aberrant' or 'pathological' behaviour, but in a real sense is 'normal.' Wife battering and rape emanate from broader patriarchal social relations.

Dissatisfied with 'malestream' interpretations of women's experiences, feminists have called for a new form of survey research to challenge traditional conceptions by creating an alternative set of statistics that can then be used to support and empower women (Radford 1984). Feminists eschew definitions that bracket away women's experiences, searching instead for definitions that can indicate the ever-present threat of male violence in women's lives. An example is Kelly's (1988) use of the term 'sexual violence' to refer to physical, visual, verbal, or sexual assault or threat of assault. Here, the term 'sexual' denotes acts of violence against women specifically because they are women. Kelly feels that such terminology helps to ground an understanding of women's fear of crime by helping to remind us that 'for many women, the accumulation of experiences of sexual violence results in a realization that no place is totally safe. The threat of violence becomes a backdrop for everyday life. Learning that friends have also been abused can reinforce women's sense of vulnerability ... the possibility that women's fear may be connected to a variety of actual, and possible future, experiences of sexual violence is not explored' (1988: 198-199).

Feminists reject the narrow definitions of violence used in national victimization surveys (Walklate 1989) and doubt that the concepts and methods of victimology can convey women's experience: 'The type of aggression, the main organizing principle for the criminal justice system's categorization of crimes against the person, is not the major principle used by the women interviewed. Because the basis for defining behaviours as violent differs, the women interviewed classed as threatening, violent or sexually harassing situations that fell outside the criminal law as well as within it' (Hanmer and Saunders, 1984: 32).

Critical of police statistics and victimization survey findings, feminists point to the inability of such data to capture meaningfully female victimization. Such a criticism is well placed in the case of the first sweep of the British Crime Survey, which uncovered only one incident of attempted rape among a total of 11,000 respondents (Hough and Mayhew 1983). The fact that violence against women in the home was not measured as a separate category of crime indicates the lack of serious consideration given to violence against women in such surveys.

A common criticism of police-generated crime statistics is the emphasis that they place on public dimensions of violent crime. Feminists have noted that such statistics fail to capture much violence against women that occurs in private space, especially in cases where the offender is known to the victim. Stanko (1988) notes that it is the home where women are most likely to be sexually or physically assaulted; yet it is these forms of assault that are the least likely to be reported to the police, and when they are, the police often do not intervene (for similar findings see Jones, MacLean, and Young 1986; Radford 1985; Hanmer and Saunders 1984).

This is not to suggest that women are any safer outside of the home. Feminists note that women's sense of security in public places is profoundly shaped by our inability to safely occupy that space (Hanmer and Saunders 1984). Twenty per cent of Ruth Hall's respondents reported being raped or sexually assaulted[4] while waiting for public transport (1985: 51).

Race and Gender

The combined impact of race and sex have largely been ignored in criminology and by feminists (Rice 1990; Mama 1990). But there are some notable exceptions. For example, Hall (1985) found that for some Black women, racial and sexual assault were inseparable: nearly one in eight women responded positively when asked if they were assaulted because of race or nationality and 20 per cent of women suffered racist verbal abuse of a sexual nature (1985: 51). For women of colour, the familiar taunt of 'Black bitch' defies dichotomization as *either* racist *or* sexist abuse.

As noted earlier, feminists have demanded that fear of crime should not be considered in isolation from various forms of harassment, criminal or otherwise, that women experience on a daily basis. Alongside the recorded violence – rape, sexual assault, domestic violence – feminists have studied the impact of being chased, shouted at, 'kerb-crawled,' exposed to, or being the recipient of obscene phone calls.

Feminists have found that fear is not just caused by the perpetration of an act of violence against a particular person. The threat of violence can have much the same effect. Women know that they are targets of violence and harassment. The fact that they do not know whether verbal harassment will simply end verbally exacerbates the anxiety they experience – and there is nothing irrational about this. Hanmer and Saunders (1984) argue that the potential of violence can have the same restrictive effects as violence itself. Stanko (1985) has found that women structure their lives so as to maximize personal safety, and many feel that they live in a 'state of siege.' Hall found that women expressed the greatest fear in situations where they felt most vulnerable (1985: 44) and Hanmer and Stanko (1985: 369) found that the more uncertain the outcome, the more terrifying the encounter: 'Harassed on the street by men in business suits or men in jeans, commonly sexually coerced or intimidated at work by men in positions which affect their jobs, or bombarded by sensationalist news stories which feature violence to women, women are surrounded by experiences and portrayals of women's vulnerability to men's physical and sexual aggression. Powerless to prevent intimidating and/or violent behaviour except through strategies of avoidance, women learn that they are unable to predict whether men's behaviour is deserving of trust. Women's uncertainty is related to their inability to predict outcomes.'

Some feminists are critical of the police for the way in which they intervene in cases of violence against women; it seems the protection is based on the perceived 'deservedness' of the victim (Walklate 1989). They note that if women decide that the police cannot or will not help, or that their help is inappropriate, their fear of public abuse will be accentuated. The result is effectively a curfew on women (Hanmer and Saunders 1984: 65). Radford (1984) found that many women did not report to the police incidents where they had been shouted at, flashed at, or followed because such incidents are so readily dismissed as trivial by the police. Hall (1985) found that only one in twelve women who had been raped reported the incident to the police. She also found that 10 of the 1,236 women in her sample claimed to have been raped or sexually assaulted by police officers.

Left-Realist Research

From the beginning, left realists have questioned the notion that women are less likely than men to be the victims of criminal victimization. Like feminists, left realists have argued that certain types of violence against women, such as sexual assault and domestic violence, are significantly underrepresented in police-generated crime statistics and victimization surveys (Jones, MacLean, and Young 1986). In order to combat this problem, the first sweep of the Islington Crime Survey (ibid.) used an instrument that was designed to be sensitive to women's victimization at the hands of intimates. The result was a much higher rate of disclosure than is the case with most victimization studies. For example, domestic violence, which is not reported as a separate category in official crime statistics and has not been a previous focus of concern in victimization surveys, was found to constitute almost 25 per cent of all violent assault in the community (ibid.: 97). Further, contrary to official definitions, the ICS revealed that sexual assault, a crime which is largely unreported to the police, was nearly as frequent in the community as bicycle theft (ibid.: 99-101). The ICS also found that women are also more likely to be the targets of personal theft (ibid.: 57).

Using comparable data, left realists have been able to demonstrate that women *really are* victimized more often than surveys such as the British Crime Survey indicate. Yet conventional research would have us believe that men are more at risk of violent assault. As left realists have noted, however, conventional victimology has not construed this as an indication of an 'irrational' *lack* of fear on the part of men (Crawford et al. 1990). Left realists have challenged the idea that women are irrational by measuring differential perceptions of risk. The ICS (Jones, MacLean, and Young 1986) established that 'men appear to be as likely as women to perceive risks for women' (p. 160). Left realists suggest that this finding reflects a community awareness of women's risk, one that is not captured by traditional research. If the fear expressed is not a reflection of actual risk, then it would seem that men are as 'irrational' as women.

In an attempt to contextualize their analysis, left realists have assessed the *impact* of criminal victimization on women. Jones, MacLean, and Young (1986) found that the impact of criminal victimization on women was severe, in terms of both physical and psychological injury – a finding which further demonstrates a rational basis for their fear (Ahluwalia and MacLean 1986). Reflecting on the finding that women's fear of crime is positively correlated with age, Jones, MacLean, and Young (1986) suggest that the older women's fear is shaped by life long exposure to sexual intimidation.[5]

Building on feminist research, left realists have also studied various forms of behaviour that are not officially defined as 'criminal' but are nevertheless a common feature in women's lives and serve to structure their activities in various ways. Variously referred to as 'non-criminal forms of street harassment' or 'incivilities,' these behaviours contribute to women's fear. The ICS (Jones, MacLean, and Young 1986) echoes the findings of Ruth Hall (1985) that there is a 'curfew' on women; many women experience this form of harassment, find it extremely intimidating, and try to avoid it.

Left realists have argued that women do not just fear crime in the streets; they are also fearful on public transport and in the home. In the second sweep of the ICS, Crawford et al. (1990) note that 57 per cent of women expressed feeling fearful on the street, while the first sweep (Jones, MacLean, and Young 1986) indicated that 20 per cent of women avoid public transport as a precaution against crime victimization.

Left-realist surveys provide evidence that the home cannot be assumed to be a safe place for all persons (Jones, MacLean, and Young 1986; Crawford et al. 1990). As noted earlier, domestic violence comprised nearly one-quarter of all assault discovered in the first sweep of the ICS. In the second sweep, nearly 50 per cent of female respondents said they felt unsafe in their homes, a finding which corroborates feminist claims that much sexual and physical assault occurs in the home (Stanko 1985; Russell 1982).

In contrast to the images produced by feminist and left-realist research, others have asserted that 'restricted personal mobility is largely unrelated to fear of crime' (Maxfield 1984: 35). Maxfield (1984) further argues that variables relating to 'type of person' (married, elderly, and so on) are more important determinants of mobility than is fear of crime. Yet, the second ICS (1990) found that 90 per cent of those women who do not go out alone after dark cited fear of crime as part of the reason, and 91 per cent of women who do go out after dark take precautions either often or fairly often to minimize the risk of victimization (1990: 49). Left realists have rejected Maxfield's claim because he fails to note the ways that gender can influence one's risk of criminal victimization as well as one's fear of crime. In both the first and second sweeps of the Islington Crime Survey, gender was found to be the most significant variable in the determination of fear of crime. These findings have convinced left realists that a gender-specific deconstruction of fear of crime is crucial in order to debunk the idea that women have an irrational fear of crime (Crawford et al. 1990).

Finally, left realists have paid attention to the idea that certain kinds of physical environment intensify women's fear of crime. In several community surveys conducted in London over the past few years, researchers have found that respondents were often more likely to suggest that environmental improvements, including better housing and street lighting, were a more effective deterrent to crime than intensified policing (Crawford et al. 1990; Painter 1988, 1989; Painter et al. 1989).

Through the issue of fear of crime, it has been possible to outline common ground between left-realist and feminist research agendas. Both have rejected the claim that women are irrational and both have sought to measure the frequency and prevalence of violence against women. Critical of traditional victimology for its inability to grasp the reality of women's experiences, feminists and left realists have made efforts to redress such deficiencies. These efforts include sensitive interviewing techniques, prioritizing the experience of the research subject, and providing an alternative understanding of criminal victimization.

Conclusion: Counting What Counts

Left realists have devoted much time and effort to refining the research instrument employed in victim research, a strategy which implies a continuing commitment to quantitative research techniques. Meanwhile, feminists have openly criticized surveys conducted by both left realists and the British Home Office and questioned whether such approaches are a meaningful way of understanding the nature of women's victimization (Walklate 1989). While both left realists and feminists are interested in measuring the scope and frequency of violence against women, debate occurs over what is counted and how it is counted.

A major criticism of feminist survey research is that its methods are problematic because clearly articulated operational definitions of the variables being measured are not provided; it is thus impossible to compare different studies. But dissatisfaction with positivist epistemology has left many feminists groping for new ways to measure old problems. For feminists doing survey research, such principles as comparability and generalizability of results have not guided research practice. The need to allow women to express their experiences in their own terms has meant that such definitional precision must be sacrificed. For this reason, a more inductive approach is taken.

Left realists, too, have challenged the methods and conclusions of traditional victimology, demonstrating how victimization surveys can pose challenges to official definitions of crime and victimization. Left-realist studies have constituted a watershed in terms of contributing to our understanding of the effects of policing both on crime rates and on the public's experience of victimization.

Left-realist victimology is committed to a methodology which still relies heavily on statistical analysis. While the reasons for adopting this approach include making their research comparable to other surveys, there is some speculation that an approach constrained in this way cannot, in the final analysis, be very radical because it does not move us very far beyond traditional research parameters (Walklate 1989). Feminists have been more keen to move beyond these parameters. Rather than measuring phenomena like 'rape' and 'domestic violence' as separate and isolated incidents, they suggest that what is needed is a radically different conception of what we are measuring. The desire to demonstrate linkages among different forms of violence against women has superseded issues of technological sophistication with regard to sampling and measurement procedures. Far from being a finished product, feminist research on violence against women is ongoing. Feminist studies have made an important contribution by calling into question both traditional and radical criminology, revealing their sexism and failure to challenge the *status quo*.

Both left realists and feminists have tried to show that crime, fear of crime, and victimization must be understood within a particular social context. They have also shown that one of the most salient features of crime victimization, particularly violence against women, is the identity of the victim and her relationship to the offender (Stanko 1988; Jones, MacLean, and Young 1986). And they both argue that unless researchers clearly establish the dimensions of gender stratification, violence against women will remain a hidden, but all too real part of women's lives.

Perhaps the greatest limitation of both perspectives is the somewhat romantic vision of 'community' they evoke. By suggesting that definitions need to emerge from the 'community' or from 'women,' we construct an image of a generic woman or community member who reflects the needs and desires of all other members. This construction runs counter to the premise that race, sex, and class mediate the experience of criminal victimization.

What is needed is a refined and multifaceted research initiative that does not produce a single-pronged vision of the future of the community. For example, the 'get serious on street crime' message of both left realists and many feminists in Britain will actually prove to be racist in its practice, well-meaning though it may be in principle.

While being different in many respects and containing distinct strengths and weaknesses, left-realist and feminist research on women's fear of crime reveals a number of shared goals and ideals. The way forward would surely be to cultivate cooperation rather than to proceed in isolation from each other. Left realism seems to hold out the promise of a more gendered analysis of crime and victimization – for example, Young (1988a) has acknowledged the theoretical debt of left realism to feminism. Meanwhile, left realists have been very successful in winning local government support for their research endeavours, a strategy that has proved to be an effective form of political engagement and one that would surely benefit feminist research. Feminists will now hold left realists accountable on their claims of feminist initiative, lest left realism becomes yet another male-dominated movement committed to 'social democratic reform.'

Notes

1 In 1983 the Home Office reported that fear of crime was greatly out of proportion to the risk of being victimized since, on average, a person can expect 'a robbery [only] once every five centuries, an assault resulting in injury (even if slight) once every century ... a burglary every forty years ... and a very low rate for rape and other sexual offences' (Hough and Mayhew 1983: 15).

2 This body of work dates back to 1984 and includes: the Merseyside Crime Survey (Kinsey 1984), the Islington Crime Survey (Jones, MacLean, and Young 1986), the Hilldrop Environmental Survey (Lea et al. 1987), the Edmonton Project (Painter 1988), the Tower Hamlets Study (Painter 1989), the Hammersmith and Fulham Crime Prevention Survey (Painter et al. 1989), and the Second Islington Crime Survey (Crawford et al. 1990).

3 The idea that women constitute a low-risk group in terms of criminal victimization has been contested by many researchers (for example, see Jones, MacLean, and Young 1986; Ahluwalia and MacLean 1986; Rhodes and McNeill 1985; Hall 1985; Stanko 1985; Hanmer and Saunders 1984).

4 In this survey, rape was defined as sexual intercourse without a woman's consent. Since sexual assault could not be defined without going into potentially distressing details, it was left to the woman responding to say if she had an experience that she would define as sexual assault (Hall 1985).

5 Jones, MacLean, and Young (1986) note that one of the shortcomings of the ICS was the use of bounding procedures. Bounding procedures, which are typically used as a safeguard against forward and backwards telescoping of events, can hamper the validity of the research, particularly when it comes to women's fear of crime. The fear of criminal victimization expressed by women is not a reflection of one year's previous experience, but of life-long exposure to threatening and violent behaviour. Bounding procedures thus decontextualize the experience of women.

References

Ahluwalia, S. 1988. 'Diminished Conceptions of Women in Domestic Violence Research,' in D.H. Currie, ed., *From the Margins to the Centre: Essays in Women's Studies Research*, 69-94. Saskatoon: Women's Studies Research Unit, College of Graduate Studies and Research, University of Saskatchewan

Ahluwalia, S., and B.D. MacLean. 1986. 'Racial Biases in Policing: The Case of the Female Victim,' in D.H. Currie and B.D. MacLean, eds., *The Administration of Justice*, 64-89. Saskatoon: Social Research Unit

Binney, V., G. Harkell, and J. Nixon. 1981. *Leaving Violent Men: A Study of Refuges and Housing for Battered Women*. Leeds: Women's Aid Federation

Canada, Ministry of the Solicitor General. 1985. *Canadian Urban Victimization Survey*, Bulletin 4: *Female Victims of Crime*. Ottawa: Ministry of Supply and Services

Crawford, A., T. Jones, T. Woodhouse, and J. Young. 1990. *Second Islington Crime Survey*. London: Middlesex Polytechnic, Centre for Criminology

Dobash, R., and R. Dobash, 1979. *Violence against Wives: A Case against the Patriarchy*. New York: Free Press

Gelsthorpe, L., and A. Morris. 1988. 'Feminism and Criminology in Britain,' in P. Rock, ed., *A History of British Criminology*, 93-110. Oxford: Clarendon Press

– 1990. *Feminist Perspectives in Criminology*. Buckingham: Open University Press

Gilbert, L., and P. Webster. 1982. *Bound by Love*. Boston: Beacon Press

Hall, R. 1985. *Ask Any Woman: A London Inquiry into Rape and Sexual Assault*. Bristol: Falling Wall Press

Hanmer, J. 1989. 'Women and Policing in Britain,' in J. Hanmer, J. Radford, and E. Stanko, eds., *Women, Policing, and Male Violence*, 90-124. London: Routledge

Hanmer, J., J. Radford, and E. Stanko. 1989. 'Policing Men's Violence: An Introduction,' in J. Hanmer, J. Radford, and E. Stanko, eds., *Women, Policing, and Male Violence*, 1-12. London: Routledge

Hanmer, J., and S. Saunders. 1984. *Well-Founded Fear*. London: Hutchinson

Hanmer, J., and E. Stanko. 1985. 'Stripping Away the Rhetoric of Protection: Violence to Women, Law and the State in Britain and the USA.' *International Journal of the Sociology of Law*, 13 (4): 357-374

Hatty, S.E. 1989. 'Policing and Male Violence in Australia,' in J. Hanmer, J. Radford, and E. Stanko, eds., *Women, Policing, and Male Violence*, 70-79. London: Routledge

Heidensohn, F. 1968. 'The Deviance of Women: A Critique and an Enquiry.' *British Journal of Sociology*, 19: 160-175

Hindelang, M., M. Gottfredson, and J. Garofalo. 1978. *Victims of Personal Crime: An Empirical Foundation for a Theory of Personal Victimization*. Cambridge, MA: Ballinger

Horton, J., and L. Kennedy. 1985. 'Coping with the Fear of Crime.' Paper presented at the Canadian Research Institute for the Advancement of Women Annual Conference, Saskatoon

Hough, J.M., and P. Mayhew. 1983. *The British Crime Survey: First Report*, Home Office Research Study no. 76. London: HMSO

Jones, T., B. MacLean, and J. Young. 1986. *The Islington Crime Survey*. Aldershot: Gower

Kelly, L. 1988. *Surviving Sexual Violence*. Cambridge: Polity Press

Kelly, L., and J. Radford. 1987. 'The Problem of Men: Feminist Perspectives on Male Violence,' in P. Scraton, ed., *Law, Order and the Authoritarian State*, 237-253. Milton Keynes: Open University Press

Kinsey, R. 1984. *The Merseyside Crime Survey: First Report*. Liverpool: Merseyside Metropolitan Council

Kinsey, R., J. Lea, and J. Young. 1986. *Losing the Fight against Crime*. Oxford: Basil Blackwell

Klein, D. 1973. 'The Etiology of Female Crime: A Review of the Literature.' *Issues in Criminology*, 8: 3-30

Lea, J., T. Jones, T. Woodhouse, and J. Young. 1987. *The Hilldrop Environmental Survey: First Report*. London: Middlesex Polytechnic, Centre for Criminology

MacLean, B.D., ed. 1986. *The Political Economy of Crime*. Scarborough, ON: Prentice-Hall

Malos, E. 1982. 'The Women's Liberation Movement in Britain.' *International Marxist Review*, 3: 44-52

Mama, A. 1990. *The Hidden Struggle*. London: London Race and Housing Research Unit

Marolla, J., and D. Scully. 1979. 'Rape and Psychiatric Vocabularies of Motive,' in E.S. Goldberg and N. Franks, eds., *Gender and Disordered Behavior*, 301-318. New York: Brunner/Mazel

Maxfield, M. 1984. *Fear of Crime in England and Wales*, Research Study no. 78. London: HMSO

Pahl, J. 1985. *Private Violence and Public Policy: The Needs of Battered Women and the Response of the Public Services*. London: Routledge and Kegan Paul

Painter, K. 1988. *Lighting and Crime Prevention: The Edmonton Project*. London: Middlesex Polytechnic, Centre for Criminology

– 1989. *Lighting and Crime Prevention for Community Safety. The Tower Hamlets Study First Report*. London: Middlesex Polytechnic, Centre for Criminology

Painter, K., J. Lea, T. Woodhouse, and J. Young. 1989. *Hammersmith and Fulham Crime and Policing Survey*. London: Middlesex Polytechnic, Centre for Criminology

Radford, J. 1984. *Violence against Women – Women Speak Out*. London: Wandsworth Policing Campaign

– 1985. 'Policing Male Violence – Policing Women.' Paper presented at the British Sociological Association Annual Conference, April

Rhodes, D., and S. McNeill, eds. *Women against Violence against Women*. London: Onlywomen Press

Rice, M. 1990. 'Challenging Orthodoxies in Feminist Theory: A Black Feminist Critique,' in L. Gelsthorpe and A. Morris, eds., *Feminist Perspectives in Criminology*, 57-69. Milton Keynes: Open University Press

Riger, S., and M.T. Gordon. 1981. 'The Fear of Rape: A Study in Social Control.' *Journal of Social Issues*, 37 (4): 71-92

Riger, S., M.T. Gordon, and R.K. LeBailly. 1978. 'Women's Fear of Crime: From Blaming to Restricting the Victim.' *Victimology: An International Journal*, 3 (3/4): 274-284

Russell, D. 1982. *Rape in Marriage*. New York: Macmillan

Skogan, W.G., and M.G. Maxfield. 1981. *Coping with Crime: Victimization, Fear, and Reactions to Crime in Three American Cities*. Beverly Hills: Sage

Smart, C. 1976. *Women, Crime and Criminology: A Feminist Critique*. London: Routledge and Kegan Paul

Smith, M. 1990. 'Patriarchal Ideology and Wife Beating: A Test of a Feminist Hypothesis.' *Violence and Victims*, 5: 257-273

Sparks, R. 1981. 'Surveys of Victimization – An Optimistic Assessment,' in M. Tonry and N. Morris, eds., *Crime and Justice: An Annual Review*, vol. 3: 1-60. Chicago: University of Chicago Press

Stanko, E. 1985. *Intimate Intrusions: Women's Experiences of Male Violence*. London: Routledge and Kegan Paul

– 1988. 'Hidden Violence against Women,' in M. Maguire and J. Pointing, eds., *Victims of Crime: A New Deal?* 40-46. Milton Keynes: Open University Press
– 1989. 'Missing the Mark? Policing Battering,' in J. Hanmer, J. Radford, and E. Stanko, eds., *Women, Policing, and Male Violence*, 46-69. London: Routledge

Walklate, S. 1989. *Victimology: The Victim and the Criminal Justice Process*. London: Unwin Hyman
– 1990. 'Researching Victims of Crime: Critical Victimology.' *Social Justice*, 17 (3): 25-42

Young, J. 1986. 'The Failure of Criminology: The Need for a Radical Realism,' in R. Matthews and J. Young, eds., *Confronting Crime*, 4-30. London: Sage
– 1988a. 'Radical Criminology in Britain: The Emergence of a Competing Paradigm,' in P. Rock, ed., *A History of British Criminology*, 159-183. Oxford: Clarendon Press
– 1988b. 'Risk of Crime and Fear of Crime: A Realist Critique of Survey-Based Assumptions,' in M. Maguire and J. Pointing, eds., *Victims of Crime: A New Deal?* 164-176. Milton Keynes: Open University Press

13 Confronting Woman Abuse in Canada: A Left-Realist Approach

Walter S. DeKeseredy

Many disadvantaged people are targets of predatory street crimes such as assault, burglary, and theft (Jones, MacLean, and Young 1986; Phipps 1986). While critical criminologists[1] claim to be working towards the development of a 'criminology both for and about the working-class' (Fleming 1985: 2), many of them have not taken the causes and consequences of 'crime from below' seriously (MacLean and DeKeseredy 1990).[2] Instead, they examine corporate deviance and other misdeeds of the powerful.[3] This 'abstentionist position' (Boehringer et al. 1983) on victimization among the disenfranchised has: (1) trivialized marginal groups' legitimate fears of predatory street crime (Currie 1985); (2) allowed right-wing politicians to manufacture ideological support for 'law and order' policies that ignore the wider social, political, and economic inequalities that perpetuate crimes of the powerless (Currie and MacLean 1992; Snider 1990; Caringella-MacDonald 1988); and (3) contributed to the right's hegemonic control over knowledge about crime and policing (MacLean 1989).

British left realism responds to both the left's 'selective inattention' (Dexter 1958) to street crime and the right's 'inhumane and repressive solutions against populations already victimized by structural forces' (Snider 1990: 143).[4] Occasionally referred to as 'critical' or 'radical realism', it is a 'radical' or 'new' victimology (Phipps 1986) that includes an explanation of street crime and offers transitional, socialist policies to reduce it. Moreover, in sharp contrast to the left's tendency to eschew the use of quantitative methods (Phipps 1986), critical realists use local surveys to obtain data on crime and policing (Jones, MacLean, and Young 1986).

The main purpose of this essay is to demonstrate how British left realism can contribute to the sociological understanding of woman abuse in Canada. The essay that follows: (1) briefly describes and critiques left-realist research on woman abuse; (2) provides a critique of Canadian surveys on female victimization; and (3) shows how left-realist survey technology can provide more suitable alternatives to the problematic methods used in Canadian woman-abuse studies.

Left Realism and Woman Abuse

Since the history and major tenets and criticisms[5] of left realism have been well documented elsewhere (Lea and Young 1984; Young 1986; Matthews and Young 1986; Kinsey, Lea, and Young 1986; MacLean 1989; DeKeseredy 1988a; DeKeseredy and Schwartz 1989; Taylor 1988), those subjects are not repeated here. My main concern is the left-realist position on woman abuse, a perspective that has been generally ignored in previous academic publications and conference presentations (DeKeseredy and Schwartz 1991).

Left-realist victimology is influenced by feminist research on male violence against women (Matthews and Young 1986; Jones, MacLean, and Young 1986; Young 1988a). In fact, left realists were among the first critical criminologists to recognize the importance of feminist scholarship (Thomas and O'Maolchatha 1989). For example, they have developed local crime surveys with an eye to moving beyond the British Crime Survey's (BCS) limited analysis of gender-specific issues such as woman abuse (Chambers and Tombs 1984; Hough and Mayhew 1983, 1985). According to Hough and Mayhew: 'For rape, the BCS can say little, except that in comparison to crimes such as burglary, the risks of rape – and particularly of rape committed by strangers – are very low' (1985: 35).

The Islington Crime Survey (ICS; Jones, MacLean, and Young 1986) was the first inner-city crime survey designed by left realists. Several other local surveys modelled after this study have been conducted in London (Gifford 1986; Harris and Associates 1987; Painter et al. 1989), including a second sweep of the ICS (Crawford et al. 1990).[6] These investigations are more geographically focused than national victimization research. They examine the four-way interaction of the victim, police, offender, and community that underlies the social construction of victimization. Left realists contend that local surveys are essential for the formulation of democratic assessments of police activities and community involvement in crime control and policy development (Jones, MacLean, and Young 1986).

Based on the data derived from their measures of (1) perceptions of risk; (2) fear of crime; (3) avoidance behaviours; (4) rates of criminal and non-criminal violence; and (5) the impact of domestic assault and rape, they assert that 'the ICS has shown that not only are women more fearful than men but they have very good reasons for this. An examination of the criminal forms of violence directed specifically against women showed that there was a high level of both physical and psychological injury sustained by women very frequently. This survey illustrates that women receive very little institutional support of a satisfactory nature and must take responsibility for their own protection as a consequence. This means that they must engage in more avoidance behaviours than men which restricts them in their activities more often, especially at night' (Jones, MacLean, and Young 1986: 182-183).

Realist data offer a better account of woman abuse than those derived from the BCS. For one thing, in sharp contrast to the BCS, the first sweep of the ICS shows that female victimization occurs frequently and thus should not be trivialized by the criminal justice system (Walklate 1989; Ahluwalia and MacLean 1986). Despite left realists' claims (e.g., Young 1988b) to be sensitive to feminist discourse, however, some major feminist issues have been overlooked by the ICS. Since they are discussed elsewhere (DeKeseredy and Schwartz 1991; Schwartz and DeKeseredy 1991), they will only be summarized here.

The Limitations of Left-Realist Research on Woman Abuse

First, although feminism includes various perspectives and research agendas (Simpson 1989; Daly and Chesney-Lind 1988), many feminist victimologists have examined the relationship between patriarchy and various types of woman abuse (e.g., Dobash and Dobash 1988; Yllo and Bograd 1988; Messerschmidt 1986). Jones, MacLean, and Young (1986: 3) recognize the importance of this issue; however, a rigorous analysis of how patriarchal power within working-class families perpetuates and legitimates female victimization is not apparent in the ICS and other left-realist writings (Taylor 1988; DeKeseredy and Schwartz 1991). Feminist scholars Gelsthorpe and Morris (1988: 103), maintain that this is a 'startling omission.' Moreover, Kelly and Radford state that left-realist research and policies on woman abuse provide 'only a tokenistic nod to the questions feminists have raised' (1987: 237).

Second, female victimization is not a class-specific problem. While violence against women is more likely to occur in lower-class intimate relationships (Smith 1985, 1990a; Straus, Gelles, and Steinmetz 1981; Kennedy and Dutton 1989), many women are abused in middle-class domestic settings. Left realism fails to address 'the independent importance of patriarchy and sexual inequality across the social formation as a whole' (Taylor 1988: 23).

Third, some feminists argue that 'distanced, objective research methods' (Kelly and Radford 1987: 242), such as those used in realist surveys and other empiricist inquiries (e.g., Straus and Gelles 1986; Straus, Gelles, and Steinmetz 1981), are flawed because they: are reductionist, tend to be ahistorical and remove woman abuse out of its larger historical and structural context (Breines and Gordon 1983; Dobash and Dobash 1979; DeKeseredy 1988b). Others contend that quantitative, empiricist methods provide biased, 'male-constructed' (Bograd 1988) accounts of violence against women which preclude a comprehensive understanding of abuse from the victim's own perspective (Kelly 1988; Walklate 1989; Bograd 1988).

Fourth, left-realist research has been accused of ignoring significant types of violence against women (DeKeseredy and Schwartz 1991). Although Lea and Young (1984) assert that working-class people are victimized by both the rich and the poor, the first ICS focused mainly on intraclass, predatory street crime and ignored corporate crimes against women. The authors of the second ICS (Crawford et al. 1990), however, responded to this criticism and included measures of 'commercial crimes' (Snider 1988), such as accidents and injuries in the workplace and consumer victimization.[7]

A fifth limitation of the left-realist approach is that it lacks an analysis of data on variations in woman abuse across marital-status categories. This is surprising since Young contends that 'a realist criminology must start from the actual subgroups in which people live their lives, rather than from broad categories which conceal wide variations within them' (1988b: 171). In order to clearly avoid the 'fallacy of homogeneity' (DeKeseredy and MacLean 1991), left realists must examine their findings on marital status since marital status relates significantly to risk of victimization. For example, US and Canadian studies show that, compared with married women, cohabiting, separated, and divorced women are more likely to be victimized by the men with whom they live or have lived intimately (Ellis and DeKeseredy 1989; Ellis 1989; Stets and Straus 1990; Yllo and Straus 1981; Lupri 1990; Smith 1990a; Kennedy and Dutton 1989; Schulman 1979).[8]

A sixth point is that, like most conventional researchers, left realists have not developed or tested theories of woman abuse.[9] Rather, their principal concern is to gather data that can be used to formulate 'humane policies which accurately reflect people's needs, which are guided by facts and which can be monitored effectively' (Jones, MacLean, and Young 1986: 6). This 'political commitment' (Walklate 1989) is important, but it does not adequately answer an important question: why do men victimize women in patriarchal, capitalist societies?

Despite these limitations, left-realist survey technology can help to overcome some of the major deficiencies of Canadian survey research on female victimization. These shortcomings are outlined in the discussion that follows.

Woman Abuse in Canada: A Critique of Survey Research

Many Canadian women are victimized by men in a variety of contexts, such as in marriage, while dating or cohabiting, and on the street. Most quantitative data on this problem are derived from the Canadian Urban Victimization Survey (CUVS) (Solicitor General of Canada 1985); independent national surveys (Lupri 1990); provincial surveys (Kennedy and Dutton 1989); surveys of university students (DeKeseredy 1989a), and city-wide studies (Brinkerhoff and Lupri 1988; Smith 1985, 1986, 1987, 1990a). In one way or another, most of these studies have employed the Conflict Tactics Scale (CTS) originally constructed by Straus (1979). While the estimates of woman abuse reported in these inquiries are superior to those presented in other widely cited Canadian studies (MacLeod 1980, 1987), they all can be said to misrepresent the social reality of female victimization. Furthermore, these estimates may be used to justify the denial of adequate state support for abused women and their children (DeKeseredy 1988b, DeKeseredy and MacLean 1991, 1990).

The Canadian Urban Victimization Survey

In response to criticisms of police generated crime statistics,[10] the Ministry of the Solicitor General of Canada, with the assistance of Statistics Canada, conducted the CUVS in 1982. A representative sample of more than 61,000 household residents, sixteen years of age or older, were interviewed by telephone in seven metropolitan areas: Greater Vancouver, Edmonton, Winnipeg, Toronto, Montreal, Halifax-Dartmouth, and St John's. Since Canadian victimology was in its early stages of development when the CUVS was conducted,[11] this research made a significant contribution by providing a more accurate estimate of the frequency of crime than that offered by the Uniform Crime Reports (Statistics Canada 1985); however, in terms of criminal and non-criminal violence against women, the CUVS offers little information on the 'multidimensional nature' (DeKeseredy and Hinch 1991) of woman abuse in Canada.[12] For example, the CUVS provides poor estimates of violence against wives because respondents were not asked directly if their husbands or ex-husbands had assaulted them (Smith 1987). The CUVS has also been criticized for its inability to elicit data on: (1) a wide range of psychological assaults, (2) sexual harassment in the workplace and on the street, (3) child abuse and incest, and (4) the incidence of female victimization among rural and homeless women (DeKeseredy and MacLean 1991).

Another major problem with the CUVS is that it incorrectly portrays all female respondents as members of a homogeneous group (DeKeseredy and MacLean 1991). Variations in the amount and type of abuse among different class and racial categories are not examined even though differences among female subgroups do exist (Jones, MacLean, and Young 1986; Straus, Gelles, and Steinmetz 1981; Smith 1990a). In Canada, for example, because of their low socio-economic status, isolation, and vulnerability to other social problems such as social dissolution and alcohol abuse (MacLeod 1987), Aboriginal women are more likely to be physically and sexually assaulted than their White, middle-class counterparts.

A final salient shortcoming of the CUVS is that it fails to contextualize its findings on violence against women. For example, no attempt is made to consider the wider patriarchal, social, and ideological forces that shape male-female dynamics and perpetuate and legitimate woman abuse (DeKeseredy and MacLean 1991).

In summary, the CUVS does not provide a comprehensive sociological understanding of female victimization, nor could it since this was not its intention. However, Canadian probability surveys that were designed to do so, and have employed the CTS, provide more accurate estimates of the frequency of woman abuse than does the CUVS (Smith 1987). Nevertheless, the CTS has numerous pitfalls which will be made explicit here.

The Conflict Tactics Scale

The most frequently used measure of non-sexual violence against women in both Canada and the United States is the CTS. It is a quantitative measure that comprises eighteen items, and measures three different ways of handling interpersonal conflicts in intimate relationships: reasoning, verbal aggression, and physical violence. The items are categorized on a continuum from least to most severe. For example, the first ten items describe non-violent tactics, and the last eight describe violent strategies.[13]

The CTS is generally described to the respondent in the following way: 'No matter how well a couple gets along, there are times when they disagree on major decisions, get annoyed about something the other person does, or just have spats or fights because they're in a bad mood or tired or for some other reasons. They also use different ways of trying to settle their differences. I'm going to read a list of some things that you and your (wife/partner) might have done when you had a dispute, and would first like you to tell me for each one how often you did it in the past year' (Straus, Gelles, and Steinmetz 1981: 256).

Canadian studies, cited above, which have employed the CTS have estimated that a range of 11 to 25 per cent of their respondents have engaged in at least one of the violent tactics in the past twelve months. DeKeseredy's (1989a) survey of woman abuse in university dating relationships found that 12 per cent of a convenience sample of Ontario male university students reported physically abusing women at least once in the twelve months prior to the study.

The CTS has been criticized for assuming that physical violence is worse than psychological abuse (Breines and Gordon 1983); missing major forms of physical and psychological abuse such as burning, suffocating, squeezing, sexual assaults, scratching, and sexual harassment (Smith 1987; DeKeseredy and MacLean 1990); as well as its inability to determine the context of and motivation for family violence (DeKeseredy 1989b; Breines and Gordon 1983; Saunders 1989). Also, researchers who employ this technique assume that acts coded as 'minor violence' such as slaps and shoves are less serious than the five or six items contained in the 'severe violence' scale – from 'kicked her' to 'used a knife or gun on her.' Another criticism of the CTS is that it situates abuse only within the context of settling quarrels or disputes in conflict situations; therefore, it can not capture violent incidents that occur beyond the realm of dating, cohabiting, and marital relationships (DeKeseredy and MacLean 1990).

Although survey technology based upon a left-realist perspective cannot overcome all of the limitations of the CUVS and the CTS, some of the methods included in both sweeps of the ICS can help Canadian victimologists capture a wider range of data pertaining to the extent, distribution, and multifaceted nature of female victimization. Moreover, the findings derived from these measures can be used to encourage state 'bureaucratic caretakers' (Gouldner 1968) to provide battered women and their children with social support services such as alternative housing that make them less available to be abused and services such as police intervention that deter men from abusing them (Ellis, in press; DeKeseredy and MacLean 1990).

Confronting Woman Abuse: New Directions in Empirical Research

Left-realist surveys have expanded their scope to include measures on three major issues largely ignored by most Canadian surveys of violence against women: (1) sexual harassment on the street; (2) subgroup differences; and (3) the physical, psychological, and financial impact of victimization. A summary of these measures and the analysis of the data they yield are presented here.

Sexual Harassment on the Street

One premise of the realist research has been that some male behaviours are threatening to women but are not officially designated as criminal. Because these behaviours are not, strictly speaking, 'criminal,' conventional surveys have not measured them, and it is for this reason in particular that different forms of sexual harassment on the street are given considerable attention in the realists' local crime surveys. For example, Jones, MacLean, and Young (1986) found that many women are victimized by leers, 'kerb crawlers,' lewd comments in the street, and unwanted sexual advances from both strangers and acquaintances. Despite the fact that these incidents are excluded from the purview of the law (DeKeseredy and Schwartz 1991; Quarm and Schwartz 1985), they are not insignificant because 'at the time women are followed/flashed at/harassed they do not know how the event will end. It is only in retrospect that such events can be defined as "minor"' (Kelly and Radford 1987: 242).

If Canadian victimologists were to adopt such measures and were to capture data on various types of 'non-criminal street violence' (Jones, MacLean, and Young 1986), they might find the data yielded to be useful in encouraging police departments to take women's 'well founded fear' (Hanmer and Saunders 1984) of sexual harassment seriously. There may be limits to such an approach, however. Some feminists have argued that 'law and order' solutions are problematic because they do not challenge the wider patriarchal, social and ideological forces that perpetuate and legitimate woman abuse (Snider 1990; Currie and MacLean 1992). In addition, police protection may be a 'trap' (King 1986) because it fosters female dependency on a patriarchal state. Such critique may be of little significance to women who are in the process of being battered, or who are frightened to walk on the streets (Schwartz and DeKeseredy 1991). For these people, police intervention is often perceived as the only practical response.

Subgroup Differences

By focusing on the amount and type of abuse among different racial categories, realist surveys avoid the 'fallacy of homogeneity' characteristic of most Canadian survey research on woman abuse (DeKeseredy and MacLean 1991). Except for Smith's (1985, 1990a) studies, none of the Canadian surveys on violence against women have examined ethnic variations in female victimization. Furthermore, some surveys (Solicitor General of Canada 1985; Smith 1985, 1987; Kennedy and Dutton 1989) used telephone interview methods that are weak and less sensitive measures of those who suffer from high rates of violence – homeless and low-income women (Smith 1985, 1990a; Kennedy and Dutton 1989; Lupri 1990; Harman 1989; DeKeseredy and MacLean 1991). Obviously, people who live on the streets cannot can be contacted by telephone. Moreover, many low-income women cannot afford telephones. Thus, according to Smith: 'The negative relationship between income and abuse compounds the low-income bias among households without telephones' (1989: 309).

Realists have avoided some of these problems in their research by using questions on ethnicity and face-to-face interviews, and by not employing telephone interviews. Rather, their approach has been to employ in-person interviews conducted by well-trained, sympathetic researchers. In this way people without telephones, such as the homeless, transients, or sojourners, can be incorporated into the sampling frame. Such a strategy seems particularly useful in that it is likely to encourage higher rates of disclosure of woman abuse than more 'distanced, objective' methods (Kelly and Radford 1987) such as telephone interviews because frankness, privacy, and rapport, central to disclosure, are much easier to establish in a face-to-face interview (Russell 1986). Furthermore, interviewers can provide their respondents with immediate social support, such as companionship or transportation to a crisis centre, if they become upset during an interview (Russell 1986).

Realists have also employed disproportionate sampling techniques which 'oversample' ethnic minorities. In this way, researchers are able to capture more meaningful and diverse data on the ethnic dimensions of woman abuse as well as to ensure that the Caucasian bias characteristic of more conventional research is somewhat reduced. In its 'ethnic minority booster sample' the ICS employed matched interviewers and for the Asian subsample a team of interviewers who spoke nine different languages was employed in order to ensure that respondents drawn from the sampling frame could be communicated with (MacLean, Jones, and Young 1986). The use of multilingual interviewers might prove useful in the Canadian context as well where there is a similar multi-ethnic composition of the population. Such a strategy might ensure that researchers are sensitive to the needs of ethnic women.

The Physical, Psychological, and Financial Impact of Victimization

None of the Canadian surveys designed specifically to examine woman abuse measures the impact of male abusive behaviours for the victim. Moreover, one of the principal concerns of the CUVS was to examine the impact of crime upon its victims, and in this regard, and at the time it was conducted, it was probably the best attempt to do so. Nevertheless, it is deficient in four ways. First, ethnic variations in the financial and physical impact of abuse are not reported. Second, direct measures of the emotional or psychological costs of victimization are not included.[14] Third, time lost from work as a result of their victimization is a form of economic impact not measured. Finally, measures of specific injuries such as black eyes, broken bones, and cuts are not made.

Left-realist surveys eliminate the above problems because they measure variations in the physical, psychological, and financial impact of abuse across racial categories. Specific personal injuries and time lost from work are also documented and analysed. Such measures are crucial to achieving the objective of accurately pinpointing social support needs of victims, such as transition houses, medical aid, and criminal justice intervention (DeKeseredy and MacLean 1990; Kennedy and Dutton 1989; Stets and Straus 1990).

Summary and Conclusions

The physical and sexual abuse of women is clearly a major social problem in Canada. While survey research carried out within a left-realist framework can provide a better sociological understanding of female victimization and its control than mainstream research, several key issues must be addressed in future work. These concerns are briefly discussed below.

One way in which Canadian realists can effectively respond to feminists' calls for more research on the relationship between patriarchy and woman abuse is by using Smith's (1990b) quantitative inquiry as a partial model for the development of new surveys (DeKeseredy and Schwartz 1991). The main objective of Smith's study was to 'test the feminist hypothesis that wife beating results from adherence by battering husbands to an ideology of familial patriarchy' (1990b: 258). Survey data gathered by telephone support this hypothesis. On the basis of interviews with female respondents, Smith concludes that men who adhere to an ideology of familial patriarchy are more likely to beat their spouses than are men who do not espouse patriarchal values and beliefs. Smith's findings also show that men with low incomes, low educational attainment, and low-status jobs are more likely than higher-status husbands to adhere to the sexist ideology.

Representative sample surveys have important strengths, and they should not be abandoned in favour of alternative techniques. However, a variety of methods can improve realist studies. For example, the context-specific approach of Dobash and Dobash (1979, 1983) could help realists bridge the gap between micro- and macro-level analyses of woman abuse because it combines quantitative strategies with historical, institutional and interactional research methods (DeKeseredy 1989c). Their example of methodological triangulation also demonstrates a sensitivity to feminist criticisms of empiricist studies discussed in above.

If methodological triangulation is desirable, then so is research in rural and Aboriginal contexts. So far, most of the Canadian woman abuse studies have been conducted only in urban areas. Thus, the abusive experiences of many farm and Aboriginal women are not recorded. This is a major omission because a substantial number of these people are battered, psychologically and economically mistreated, and sexually assaulted by male intimates (Lupri 1990; MacLeod 1987; Sharp 1990). In fact, woman abuse may be more prevalent in rural and Aboriginal communities than in cities or large towns (LaPrairie 1983). The key determinants of this variation are low socio-economic status, geographic isolation, and vulnerability to other problems, such as community erosion resulting from the 'fiscal crisis of the welfare state' (Griffiths and Verdun-Jones 1989) and high levels of alcohol consumption (MacLeod 1987; DeKeseredy and Hinch 1991).

Although, to date, realist surveys have been restricted to inner-city areas, this does not mean that they cannot be conducted in rural, isolated, and Aboriginal communities. In fact, realist criminologists are much more likely to conduct local surveys in these environments than are conventional researchers because they are strongly committed to the objective of developing policies which aid disenfranchised people throughout Canada. Realists do not regard the experiences of women, ethnic minorities, and working-class individuals who live in urban areas as more important than the encounters of other victims of oppressive political/economic conditions.

Another major issue, perhaps the most important, needs to be addressed in Canadian discussions of left realism. Currie, DeKeseredy, and MacLean (1990: 49-50) remind us that, while British research shows that realist survey technology can provide a defensible, alternative source of information which can be effectively used in political struggles against right-wing law and order campaigns, 'the question still remains *to what extent a similar strategy might be useful within a Canadian context.*' (emphasis in original). This is a practical question which must be answered practically. The only way left-realist research designs can be used in political attempts to end woman abuse is if Canadian critical criminologists develop similar strategies and advance them within practical local political forums (ibid.).

It is time for Canadian radical scholars to move beyond simply criticizing conventional research. Critique is necessary for advancing our understanding of female victimization; however, useful alternatives to conservative approaches should also be provided because 'critical discourse divorced from critical practice degenerates into mere literary criticism, the value of which is a *purely scholastic question*' (Currie, DeKeseredy, and MacLean 1990: 50; emphasis in original).

Financial support is necessary for the purpose of administering local crime surveys designed to inform progressive policies on abused women. Nevertheless, as Brickey (1989) points out, very few Canadian critical scholars ask state institutions to fund their research. Perhaps their rationale for not doing so is heavily informed by a school of thought which Edwards (1989) refers to as 'feminist idealism.' Proponents of this approach generally argue that 'the state and the law, the legal mechanism and the police are part of a patriarchal structure, under which attempts at legal reform are only tinkerings within the overall system' (Edwards 1989: 15). There is substantial evidence to support this position (see Snider 1990); however, 'feminist realist' Jane Ursel's (1990) state-sponsored research on wife abuse has helped many battered women receive better social support. Perhaps other criminologists can secure state monies to aid abused women, and there are signs that this goal can be achieved. In Ontario, for example, the provincial government is now run by the socialist New Democratic Party, which is apparently committed to ending woman abuse and other symptoms of patriarchal capitalism. Thus, critical criminologists should ask state agencies, such as the Ministry of the Solicitor General, to fund local surveys throughout urban and rural Ontario.

Progressive local community organizations, such as women's groups, aboriginal communities, and labour unions, might also provide funding. Even so, they tend to be overlooked by critical criminologists despite the fact that these groups recognize that radical research can help them in their political struggles (Brickey 1989).

In conclusion, Canadian realists must try to tap funding sources such as the above. If they do not, they will experience major obstacles in their attempts to formulate local crime surveys and progressive policies that stop men from abusing women at home, on the streets, and in the workplace.

I would like to thank Brian MacLean for his comments at the conceptual stages of this essay.

Notes

1 There are various definitions of critical criminology (see Lynch and Groves 1989; Hinch 1989; Thomas and O'Maolchatha 1989). However, for the purpose of this paper it is defined as 'that part of the discipline which sees the causes of crime as being at core the class and patriarchal relations endemic to our social order and which sees fundamental change as necessary to reduce criminality' (Young 1988a: 160).

2 Salient exceptions to this 'left idealist' (Young 1979) approach are critical studies on violence against women, children, and ethnic groups (Breines and Gordon 1983; Dobash and Dobash 1979; Schechter 1982; Russell, 1984, 1986).

3 See Box (1983), Goff and Reasons (1986), Ellis (1987), and Barak (1991) for detailed reviews of this literature.

4 US, Canadian, and Australian criminologists have also provided left-realist analyses of predatory street crime (Currie 1985, 1989; Michalowski 1983; Platt 1978, 1984; Schwartz and DeKeseredy 1991; DeKeseredy and Schwartz 1991; Alvi 1986; Ahluwalia and MacLean 1986; DeKeseredy and MacLean 1991, 1990; McMullan 1986, 1987; Hogg 1988; Hogg and Brown 1988; Boehringer et al. 1983).

5 See MacLean (1991), DeKeseredy (1990), and Young (1991) for responses to various attacks on left realism.

6 For more detailed information on the methods employed in the ICS, see MacLean, Jones, and Young (1986), Jones, MacLean, and Young (1986), and Crawford et al. (1990).
7 See Pearce (this volume) for more detailed information on this research.
8 Ellis and DeKeseredy (1989) contend that the DAD model may be helpful in explaining the relationship between marital status and woman abuse. According to this model, variations in abuse across martial-status categories are associated with variations in dependency, availability, and deterrence.
9 See Gelles (1980) and DeKeseredy (1988b) for more information on the dearth of theory construction and testing in family-violence research.
10 For comprehensive critiques of Canadian official statistics, see Evans and Himelfarb (1987), Hagan (1985), Lowman and Palys (1991), and MacLean (1986).
11 The CUVS is rooted in both the emergence of victimology as a major subdiscipline of criminology and practical Canadian criminal justice policy concerns (DeKeseredy and MacLean 1991).
12 For more information on the methods used in the CUVS, see the Research and Statistics Group's (1984) technical report.
13 DeKeseredy (1989a) and Smith (1987) modified the CTS by including an additional item – choking.
14 The 1985 replication of the CUVS included questions on the psychological impact of victimization (Solicitor General of Canada 1987).

References

Ahluwalia, S., and B.D. MacLean. 1986. 'Racial Biases in Policing: The Case of the Female Victim,' in D.H. Currie and B.D. MacLean, eds., *The Administration of Justice*, 64-89. Saskatoon: Social Research Unit, Dept of Sociology, University of Saskatchewan

Alvi, S. 1986. 'Realist Crime Prevention Strategies through Alternative Measures for Youth,' in D.H. Currie and B.D. MacLean, eds., *The Administration of Justice*, 112-127. Saskatoon: Social Research Unit, Dept of Sociology, University of Saskatchewan

Barak, G., ed. 1991. *Crimes by the Capitalist State: An Introduction to State Criminality*. Albany, NY: State University of New York Press

Boehringer, G., D. Brown, B. Edgeworth, R. Hogg, and I. Ramsey. 1983. 'Law and Order for Progressives?: An Australian Response.' *Crime and Social Justice*, 19: 2-12

Bograd, M. 1988. 'Feminist Perspectives on Wife Abuse: An Introduction,' in K. Yllo and M. Bograd, eds., *Feminist Perspectives on Wife Abuse*, 11-26. Beverly Hills: Sage

Box, S. 1983. *Power, Crime, and Mystification*. London: Tavistock

Breines, W., and L. Gordon. 1983. 'The New Scholarship on Family Violence.' *Signs: Journal of Women in Culture and Society*, 8: 491-553

Brickey, S. 1989. 'Criminology as Social Control Science: State Influence on Criminological Research in Canada.' *Journal of Human Justice*, 1 (1): 43-62

Brinkerhoff, M., and E. Lupri. 1988. Interspousal Violence.' *Canadian Journal of Sociology*, 13: 407-434

Caringella-MacDonald, S. 1988. 'Parallels and Pitfalls: The Aftermath of Legal Reform for Sexual Assault, Marital Rape, and Domestic Violence Victims.' *Journal of Interpersonal Violence*, 3: 175-189

Chambers, G., and J. Tombs. 1984. *The British Crime Survey: Scotland*. Edinburgh: HMSO

Crawford, A., T. Jones, T. Woodhouse, and J. Young. 1990. *Second Islington Crime Survey*. London: Middlesex Polytechnic, Centre for Criminology

Currie, D., W. DeKeseredy, and B.D. MacLean. 1990. 'Reconstituting Social Order and Social Control: Police Accountability in Canada.' *Journal of Human Justice*, 2 (1): 29-54

Currie, D.H., and B.D. MacLean. 1992. 'Women, Men, and Police: Losing the Fight against Wife Battery in Canada,' in D.H. Currie and B.D. MacLean, eds., *Rethinking the Administration of Justice*, 251-275. Halifax: Fernwood Publications

Currie, E. 1985. *Confronting Crime: An American Challenge*. New York: Pantheon

– 1989. 'Confronting Crime: Looking toward the Twenty-First Century.' *Justice Quarterly*, 6: 5-26

Daly, K., and M. Chesney-Lind. 1988. 'Feminism and Criminology.' *Justice Quarterly*, 4: 497-538

DeKeseredy, W. 1988a. 'The Left Realist Approach to Law and Order.' *Justice Quarterly*, 4: 635-640

– 1988b. 'Woman Abuse in Dating Relationships: A Critical Evaluation of Research and Theory.' *International Journal of Sociology of the Family*, 18: 79-96

– 1989a. 'Woman Abuse in Dating Relationships: An Exploratory Study.' *Atlantis: A Women's Studies Journal*, 14: 55-62

– 1989b. 'In Defense of Self-Defense: Demystifying Female Violence against Female Intimates.' Paper presented at the annual meeting of the American Society of Criminology, Reno, Nevada, November

– 1989c. 'Dating Violence: Toward New Directions in Empirical Research.' *Social Viewpoints*, 5: 62-74

– 1990. 'Confronting Woman Abuse: A Brief Review of the Realist Approach.' *The Critical Criminologist*, 2: 7, 8, 11

DeKeseredy, W., and R. Hinch. 1991. *Woman Abuse: Sociological Perspectives*. Toronto: Thompson Educational Publishing

DeKeseredy, W., and B. MacLean. 1990. 'Researching Woman Abuse in Canada: A Realist Critique of the Conflict Tactics Scale.' *Canadian Review of Social Policy*, 25:19-27

- 1991. 'Exploring the Gender, Race and Class Dimensions of Victimization: A Left Realist Critique of the Canadian Urban Victimization Survey.' *International Journal of Offender Therapy and Comparative Criminology*, 35: 143-161

DeKeseredy, W., and M. Schwartz. 1989. 'British and U.S. Left Realism: A Critical Comparison.' Paper presented at the annual meetings of the American Society of Criminology, Reno, November

- 1991. 'British Left Realism on the Abuse of Women: A Critical Appraisal,' in R. Quinney and H. Pepinsky, eds., *Criminology as Peacemaking*, 154-171. Bloomington: Indiana University Press

Dexter, L. 1958. 'A Note on Selective Inattention in Social Science.' *Social Problems*, 6: 176-182

Dobash, R. E., and R. Dobash. 1979. *Violence Against Wives*. New York: Free Press

- 1983. 'The Context-Specific Approach,' in D. Finkelhor, R.J. Gelles, G.T. Hotaling, and M.A. Straus, eds., *The Dark Side of Families*, 261-276. Beverly Hills: Sage

- 1988. 'Research as Social Action: The Struggle for Battered Women,' in K. Yllo and M. Bograd, eds., *Feminist Perspectives on Wife Abuse*, 51-74. Beverly Hills: Sage

Edwards, S. 1989. *Policing Domestic Violence*. Beverly Hills: Sage

Ellis, D. 1987. *The Wrong Stuff: An Introduction to the Sociological Study of Deviance*. Toronto: Collier Macmillan

- 1989. 'Male Abuse of a Married or Cohabiting Female Partner: The Application of Sociological Theory to Research Findings.' *Violence and Victims*, 4: 235-255

- in press. 'Post-Separation Woman Abuse: The Contribution of Social Support.' *Victimology: An International Journal*

Ellis, D., and W. DeKeseredy. 1989. 'Marital Status and Woman Abuse: The DAD Model.' *International Journal of Sociology of the Family*, 19: 67-87

Evans, J., and A. Himelfarb. 1987. 'Counting Crime,' in R. Linden, ed., *Criminology: A Canadian Perspective*, 43-73. Toronto: Holt, Rinehart and Winston

Fleming, T. 1985. 'Central Issues in the New Criminological Debate,' in T. Fleming, ed., *The New Criminologies in Canada: State, Crime, and Control*, 1-4. Toronto: Oxford University Press

Gelles, R. 1980. 'Violence in the Family: A Review of Research in the Seventies.' *Journal of Marriage and the Family*, 42: 873-885

Gelsthorpe, L., and A. Morris. 1988. 'Feminism and Criminology in Britain.' *British Journal of Criminology*, 28: 93-110

Gifford, L. 1986. *The Broadwater Farm Inquiry*. London: Borough of Haringey

Goff, C., and C. Reasons. 1986. 'Organizational Crimes against Employees, Consumers and the Public,' in B.D. MacLean, ed., *The Political Economy of Crime: Readings for a Critical Criminology*, 204-231. Scarborough, ON: Prentice-Hall

Gouldner, A. 1968. 'The Sociologist as Partisan: Sociology of the Welfare State.' *American Sociologist*, 7: 103-116

Griffiths, C., and S. Verdun-Jones. 1989. *Canadian Criminal Justice*. Toronto: Butterworths

Hagan, J. 1985. *Modern Criminology: Crime, Criminal Behavior, and Its Control*. Toronto: McGraw-Hill

Hanmer, J., and S. Saunders. 1984. *Well Founded Fear: A Community Study of Violence to Women*. London: Hutchinson

Harman, L. 1989. *When a Hostel Becomes a Home: Experiences of Women*. Toronto: Garamond Press

Harris and Associates. 1987. *Crime in Newham: The Survey*. London: Borough of Newham

Hinch, R. 1989. 'Teaching Critical Criminology and Critical Justice Studies in Canada.' *Journal of Human Justice*, 1 (1): 63-76

Hogg, R. 1988. 'Taking Crime Seriously: Left Realism and Australian Criminology,' in M. Findlay and R. Hogg, eds., *Understanding Crime and Criminal Justice*, 24-51. Sydney: The Law Book Company

Hogg, R., and D. Brown. 1988. 'Law and Order Politics, Left Realism and Criminology: An Overview.' Paper presented at the annual meeting of the American Society of Criminology, Chicago

Hough, M., and P. Mayhew. 1983. *The British Crime Survey*. London: HMSO

- 1985. *Taking Account of Crime: Key Findings from the 1984 British Crime Survey*. London: HMSO

Jones, T., B. MacLean, and J. Young. 1986. *The Islington Crime Survey: Crime, Victimization and Policing in Inner-City London*. Aldershot: Gower

Kelly, L. 1988. 'How Women Define Their Experiences of Violence,' in K. Yllo and M. Bograd, eds., *Feminist Perspectives on Wife Abuse*, 114-132. Beverly Hills: Sage

Kelly, L., and J. Radford. 1987. 'The Problem of Men: Feminist Perspectives on Sexual Violence,' in P. Scraton, ed., *Law, Order and the Authoritarian State: Readings in Critical Criminology*, 237-253. Philadelphia: Open University Press

Kennedy, L., and D. Dutton. 1989. 'The Incidence of Wife Assault in Alberta.' *Canadian Journal of Behavioral Science*, 21: 40-54

King, L. 1986. 'Censorship and Law Reform: Will Changing the Laws Mean a Change for the Better,' in E. Comack and S. Brickey, eds., *The Social Basis of Law: Critical Readings in the Sociology of Law*, 197-205. Toronto: Garamond Press

Kinsey, R., J. Lea, and J. Young. 1986. *Losing the Fight against Crime*. Oxford: Basil Blackwell

LaPrairie, C. 1983. *Family Violence in Rural, Northern Communities: A Proposal for Research and Programme Development*. Ottawa: Solicitor General of Canada

Lea, J., and J. Young. 1984. *What Is to Be Done about Law and Order?* Harmondsworth: Penguin

Lowman, J., and T.S. Palys. 1991. 'Interpreting Criminal Justice System Records of

Crime,' in M.A. Jackson and C.T. Griffiths, eds., *Canadian Criminology: Perspectives on Crime and Criminality*, 349-369. Toronto: Harcourt Brace Jovanovich

Lupri, E. 1990. 'Male Violence in the Home,' in C. McKie and K. Thompson, eds., *Canadian Social Trends*, 170-172. Toronto: Thompson Educational Publishing

Lynch, M., and W.B. Groves. 1989. *A Primer in Radical Criminology*. Albany: Harrow and Heston

MacLean, B.D. 1986. 'Critical Criminology and Some Limitations of Traditional Inquiry,' in B.D. MacLean, ed., *The Political Economy of Crime: Readings for a Critical Criminology*, 1-20. Scarborough, ON: Prentice-Hall

– 1989. 'Left Realism and Police Accountability in Canada.' Paper presented at the annual meeting of the Canadian Sociology and Anthropology Association, Quebec City, June

– 1991. 'In Partial Defense of Socialist Realism: Some Theoretical and Methodological Concerns of the Local Crime Survey.' *Crime, Law and Social Change: An International Journal*, 15 (3): 213-254

MacLean, B., and W. DeKeseredy. 1990. 'Taking Working-Class Victimization Seriously: The Contribution of Left Realist Surveys,' *International Review of Modern Sociology*, 20: 211-228

MacLean, B., T. Jones, and J. Young. 1986. *The Preliminary Results of the Islington Crime Survey*. London: Borough of Islington

MacLeod, L. 1980. *Wife Battering in Canada: The Vicious Circle*. Ottawa: Advisory Council on the Status of Women

– 1987. *Battered But Not Beaten: Preventing Wife Battering in Canada*. Ottawa: Advisory Council on the Status of Women

McMullan, J. 1986. 'The "Law and Order" Problem in Socialist Criminology.' *Studies in Political Economy*, 21: 175-192

– 1987. 'Epilogue: Law, Justice and the State,' in R. Ratner and J. McMullan, eds., *State Control: Criminal Justice Politics in Canada*, 243-253. Vancouver: University of British Columbia Press

Matthews, R., and J. Young, eds. 1986. *Confronting Crime*. London: Sage

Messerschmidt, J. 1986. *Capitalism, Patriarchy, and Crime: Toward a Socialist Feminist Criminology*. Totowa, NJ: Roman and Littlefield

Michalowski, R. 1983. 'Crime Control in the 1980s: A Progressive Agenda.' *Crime and Social Justice*, 19: 13-23

Painter, K., J. Lea, T. Woodhouse, and J. Young. 1989. *Hammersmith and Fulham Crime and Policing Survey*. London: Middlesex Polytechnic, Centre for Criminology

Phipps, A. 1986. 'Radical Criminology and Criminal Victimization,' in R. Matthews and J. Young, eds., *Confronting Crime*, 97-117. London: Sage

Platt, T. 1978. 'Street Crime: A View from the Left.' *Crime and Social Justice*, 9: 26-34

– 1984. 'Criminology in the 1980s: Progressive Alternatives to Law and Order.' *Crime and Social Justice*, 21: 191-199

Quarm, D., and M. Schwartz. 1985. 'Domestic Violence in Criminal Court,' in C. Schweber and Clarice Feinman, eds., *Criminal Justice Politics and Women: The Aftermath of Legally Mandated Change*. New York: Haworth Press

Research and Statistics Group. 1984. *Canadian Urban Victimization Survey: Summary Technical Report*. Ottawa: Ministry of the Solicitor General

Russell, D. 1984. *Sexual Exploitation: Rape, Child Sexual Abuse, and Workplace Harassment*. Beverly Hills: Sage

– 1986. *The Secret Trauma: Incest in the Lives of Girls and Women*. New York: Basic Books

Saunders, D. 1989. 'Who Hits First and Who Hurts Most.' Paper presented at the annual meeting of the American Society of Criminology, Reno, Nevada

Schechter, S. 1982. *Women and Male Violence*. Boston: South End Press

Schulman, M. 1979. *A Survey of Spousal Violence against Women in Kentucky*, Study No. 792701 conducted for the Kentucky Commission on Women. Washington, DC: USGPO

Schwartz, M., and W. DeKeseredy. 1991. 'Left Realist Criminology: Strengths, Weaknesses and the Feminist Critique.' *Crime, Law and Social Change: An International Journal*, 15: 51-72

Sharp, A. 1990. *Violence against Women in Rural Outaouais: Validation of a Screening Device and of Survey Methods*. Report prepared for Conseil Regional Services Sociaux-Sante De L'Outaouais. Quebec: Conseil local des Services Communautaire Vallee-De-La Gatineau

Simpson, S. 1989. 'Feminist Theory, Crime and Justice.' *Criminology*, 27: 605-632

Smith, M. 1985. *Woman Abuse: The Case for Surveys by Telephone*. Toronto: LaMarsh Research Programme on Violence and Conflict Resolution, York University

– 1986. 'Effects of Question Format on the Reporting of Woman Abuse: A Telephone Survey Experiment.' *Victimology: An International Journal*, 11: 430-438

– 1987. 'The Incidence and Prevalence of Woman Abuse in Toronto.' *Violence and Victims*, 2: 173-187

– 1989. 'Woman Abuse: The Case for Surveys by Telephone.' *Journal of Interpersonal Violence*, 4: 308-324

– 1990a. 'Sociodemographic Risk Factors in Wife Abuse: Results from a Survey of Toronto Women.' *Canadian Journal of Sociology*, 15: 39-58

– 1990b. 'Patriarchal Ideology and Wife Beating: A Test of a Feminist Hypothesis.' *Violence and Victims*, 5: 257-273

Snider, L. 1988. 'Commercial Crime,' in Vincent Sacco, ed., *Deviance: Conformity and Control in Canadian Society*, 231-283. Scarborough, ON: Prentice-Hall

– 1990. 'The Potential of the Criminal Justice System to Promote Feminist Concerns.' *Studies in Law, Politics and Society*, 10: 141-169

Solicitor General of Canada. 1985. *Canadian Urban Victimization Survey: Female Victims of Crime*. Ottawa: Ministry of the Solicitor General

- 1987. *Canadian Urban Victimization Survey: Patterns in Violent Crime*. Ottawa: Ministry of the Solicitor General

Statistics Canada. 1985. *Canadian Crime Statistics*. Ottawa: Ministry of Supply and Services

Stets, J., and M. Straus. 1990. 'Gender Differences in Reporting Marital Violence and Its Medical and Psychological Consequences,' in M. Straus and R. Gelles, eds., *Physical Violence in American Families: Risk Factors and Adaptations to Violence in 8,145 Families*, 151-166. New Brunswick, NJ: Transaction

Straus, M. 1979. 'Measuring Intrafamily Conflict and Violence: The Conflict Tactics (CT) Scales.' *Journal of Marriage and the Family*, 41: 75-88

Straus, M., and R. Gelles. 1986. 'Societal Change and Change in Family Violence Rates from 1975 to 1985 as Revealed by Two National Surveys.' *Journal of Marriage and the Family*, 48: 465-479

Straus, M., R. Gelles, and S. Steinmetz. 1981. *Behind Closed Doors: Violence in the American Family*. New York: Anchor

Taylor, I. 1988. 'Left Realism, the Free Market Economy and the Problem of Social Order.' Paper presented at the annual meeting of the American Society of Criminology, Chicago, November

Thomas, J., and A. O'Maolchatha. 1988. 'Reassessing the Critical Metaphor: An Optimistic Revisionist View.' *Justice Quarterly*, 6: 143-172

Ursel, E.J. 1990. 'Considering the Impact of the Wife Abuse Movement on the State: The Example of Manitoba.' Paper presented at the annual meeting of the Canadian Sociology and Anthropology Association, Victoria, BC

Walklate, S. 1989. 'Appreciating the Victim: Conventional, Realist or Critical Victimology.' Paper presented at the British Criminology Conference, Bristol Polytechnic

Yllo, K., and M. Bograd, eds. 1988. *Feminist Perspectives on Wife Abuse*. Beverly Hills: Sage

Yllo, K., and M. Straus. 1981. 'Interpersonal Violence among Married and Cohabiting Couples.' *Family Relations*, 30: 339-347

Young, J. 1979. 'Left Idealism, Reformism and Beyond,' in B. Fine, R. Kinsey, J. Lea, S. Picciotto, and J. Young, eds., *Capitalism and the Rule of Law*, 11-28. London: Hutchinson

- 1986. 'The Failure of Criminology: The Need for a Radical Realism,' in R. Matthews and J. Young, eds., *Confronting Crime*, 4-30. London: Sage

- 1988a. 'Radical Criminology in Britain: The Emergence of a Competing Paradigm.' *British Journal of Criminology*, 28: 159-183

- 1988b. 'Risk of Crime and Fear of Crime: A Realist Critique of Survey-Based Assumptions,' in M. Maguire and J. Pointing, eds., *Victims of Crime: A New Deal?* 164-173. Milton Keynes: Open University Press

- 1991. 'Asking Questions of Left Realism,' in B.D. MacLean and D. Milovanovic, eds., *New Directions in Critical Criminology*, 15-18. Vancouver: Collective Press

PART FOUR
Left Realism and Victimology

14 Researching Victims of Crime: Critical Victimology

Sandra Walklate

A number of social sciences are lent a tenuous unity by their concentration upon a particular fragment of the empirical world ... David Downes once called them 'rendez-vous subjects', and they have tended to evolve around such subjects as race relations, education, prisons, crime, and, latterly, victims. It is the substance of victimization which tends to define victimology, and the discipline is correspondingly somewhat catholic. (Rock 1986: 72)

For the purposes of this essay, this catholic feature is taken to refer to the study of victims of crime. It is a feature that is not, as Rock goes on to remark, damning in itself. The discipline has, however, 'suffered' from a tendency for the 'scholarly and dispassionate' (ibid.: 74) to be intertwined with the overtly political. This intermeshing of academic questions with policy concerns has resulted in the parallel growth of both the discipline and a range of victims' movements in several different countries. This growth has not always been to the advantage of the 'forgotten victim' (as feminist work aptly illustrates) but has resulted in the setting of a contemporary stage in which criminologists as well as victimologists are focusing their attention on the victim of crime. Thus, while the 'rendezvous' nature of the discipline persists, more people are currently meeting here. As such, an opportunity is provided for assessing the characteristics of these various positions and their theoretical and empirical relevance for victimology.

Miers (1989) attempts to offer a critical appraisal of different types of victimology. He offers a twofold typology: positivist and critical victimology. For the purposes of developing a critical victimology, it is worthwhile to examine Miers's understanding of these terms. His definition of positivist victimology is not too far away from my characterization of conventional victimology (Walklate 1989a). Miers characterizes positivist victimology as having pursued three main concerns: the identification of factors that conduce to a non-random risk of victimization, a concentration on interpersonal crimes of violence, and the identification of victims who may have contributed to their own victimization. It is useful to add a fourth concern to this list since positivist victimology also reflects a tendency to concentrate on a definition of crime as it is conventionally understood; that is, it normally neglects the private as an arena of criminal victimization as well as the question of victims of 'corporate crime.' (This tendency is not tension free. The recently published collection of readings edited by Fattah [1989] contains papers on both substantive areas, but they are discussed in rather conventional terms.)

The threads identified by Miers usefully tie together to a greater or lesser extent the work of, for example, Wolfgang (1958), Amir (1971), Hindelang, Gottfredson, and Garofalo (1978), and even Sparks (1982). It could be argued that Sparks (ibid.: 33) sets the agenda for such an approach by stating that victimology is concerned with 'variations in proneness to victimization among different types of persons, places, organizations, situations, etc., where proneness in turn is defined in terms of the *a priori* probability of victimization or a crime taking place. Thus precipitation, facilitation, vulnerability, opportunity, attractiveness, and impunity all imply the probabilities of crime or victimization are higher with some situations than with others.'

This type of victimology, it should be noted, had some influence in the development of the criminal victimization survey and the concepts thought relevant for operationalization using this technique.

There are several grounds on which to criticize this positivistic victimology, from its overconcern with the culpable victim to its connections with a functionalist view of society (Walklate 1989a). Miers (1989: 3) argues that its key weakness lies in its failure to explain 'the everyday social process of identifying and responding to victimizing events.' He therefore proposes a critical victimology in which he argues that since 'the process of labelling individuals victims starts with a statement of values, it is essential to analyze how, when, and why some who sustain injury are labelled and others not.'

Drawing primarily on a social-psychological framework and more implicitly on symbolic interactionism, he argues that attention needs to be paid to the social functions of victimization, the labelling process, and the impact of the label.

Clearly Miers is drawing our attention to processes that exist and that have certainly been researched. (See, for example, the collection of papers edited by Wise and Stanley [1984]. The paper by Lee, in particular, illustrates the connections between notions of victim/evildoer, guilt and blame.) There is, however, a key weakness inherent in the definition of a critical victimology offered by Miers. This weakness, put simplistically, reflects an inability to reveal how it is that the label itself is constructed and who acquires the legitimacy of the label. This is the social construction of what Christie (1986) has called the 'ideal victim.' Neither social psychology (as traditionally formulated) nor the symbolic interactionist stance implied in the ideas of Miers have the power to cast light on the material context of the labelling process, however that context is understood. Consequently, Miers scarcely refers to work that has been informed by an understanding of the structural features of the victimization process, namely, feminist research, and, more latterly, the work of radical left realism. To construct a critical victimology, it is worth reiterating the contribution to such an endeavour made by both positions.

To construct a label 'feminist victimology' is to create a contradiction in terms. As Rock (1986: 77) states: 'Feminists have been markedly hostile, redefining "victim precipitation" as "victim blaming" and portraying victimology as a weapon of ideological oppression.' As a response to some of the work cited earlier, which emanates from positivist victimology, such hostility has been more than justified. However, the marginalization of the concerns of the feminist movement has continued despite its justified criticism of the emphasis within much mainstream (malestream) victimological work. Thus, the collection of readings, edited by Fattah (1989) and published recently in the United Kingdom (though some papers were dated), typifies a conventional victimological handling of issues about women and children. In essence, feminist research not only 'transgresses criminology' (Cain 1989: 3), but also transgresses victimology. 'Crimes, criminals, victims, courts, police officers, lawyers, social workers may be objects of investigation, but our explanations must reach beyond and encompass all of them, as the life histories and the victim studies, the continuity studies, and the ideology studies already strain to do.'

Feminists emphasize the inescapable material reality of women's (and children's) relative structural positions; both the acceptance and the resistance of this structural powerlessness contain within them a vital starting-point for a future structurally informed critical victimology. A key contribution of feminist research to a critical victimology has been the recognition of the impact of such a structural reality, in which victims and survivors are constructed in ways that we may or may not be aware of.

The development of radical left realism within criminology has made much of placing crime victims at the centre of the research gaze, making them also a valid and valuable interest for victimology. This position, which claims to have embraced the concerns of feminism (Cain 1989), aims to take 'problems as people experience them' (Young 1986: 24), simultaneously placing these experiences within a material context. This position constitutes, in part, a response to the problems inherent in 'left idealism,' but perhaps more specifically, a response to the growth of 'administrative criminology' and the more widespread adoption of the national criminal victimization survey.

National victimization surveys are considered particularly problematic for left realism since they give the impression that crime is a pretty rare occurrence, fairly evenly distributed among the population, and that the media are responsible for exaggerating the crime problem (see, for example, Kinsey, Lea, and Young 1986). The challenge to this impression is constructed through the development of geographically focused local criminal victimization surveys in which special steps are taken within the sampling process to ensure the adequate representation of women, young people, people from ethnic minorities, and the poor, since these are the groups for whom crime constitutes a problem. In the United Kingdom, the commitment to these explanatory variables has resulted in several local crime surveys: Islington (Jones, MacLean, and Young 1986; Crawford et al. 1990), Hammersmith and Fulham (Painter et al. 1989), Merseyside (Kinsey 1984), and Edinburgh (Anderson et al. 1990). These surveys, which operated with a broader remit in the questions asked of respondents than the national victimization surveys – the Second Islington Crime Survey, for instance, asked questions about child abuse and health and safety regulations at work – have done much to illustrate the extent of criminal victimization according to class location and have also achieved a higher incident report rate than have the national surveys concerning the victimization of women and people from ethnic minorities.

A call for a victimology that accounts for these empirical findings and highlights the considerable impact of structural variables on victimization rates thus would not seem unreasonable. As MacLean (1989: 28) illustrates, the local victimization survey offers a better opportunity for analysing victimization than do 'the one-sided investigations based on victim-precipitation theory.' In addition, it clearly highlights the limits of focusing all our attention on the labelling process. The question remains, however, how a victimology might be constructed that embraces the concerns of the feminist movement and incorporates the findings of radical left realism. One way into answering this question lies in a critical assessment of radical left realism.

Radical Left Realism: An Assessment

The contribution of left realism to the development of a critical victimology can be assessed in many ways. For the purposes of this essay, attention will focus on the problematic intertwining of methodological and theoretical issues – and, ultimately, on questions of philosophy – with the claim to have embraced feminism.

Edwards (1989: 18-19) states that 'the academic and theoretical separation of the issues of women and crime from those of victimization has been largely forced upon us by the intransigence of orthodox and radical criminology, the class obsession and gender-blindness of realists, and the hegemony and zealousness of some personalities within criminology. Male left realists have not integrated the needs and interests of women or the conceptual and ideological orientations into their wider concerns, and this failure reinforces their adherence to the paramountcy of male class analysis ... If left realist criminology is to be saved from the inevitable redundancy of its classical position, it must take women's issues and campaigns and the writings of radical women academics on women's issues seriously.'

In the Second Islington Crime Survey, Crawford, Jones, Woodhouse, and Young (1990) quote some of Edwards's remarks quoted above in their reply to some of the criticisms implied by her statements. Given the following passage in that same report, one might be forgiven for thinking that much feminist research had been overlooked: 'We have sought, particularly, to develop a gender-specific understanding of fear of crime which shows how gender and victimization are woven together. We have identified the cycle of violence and fear confronted by women which limits their participation in public, to the extent of virtual curfew. We have also seen how, for many women, their private, or home life, does not represent a sanctuary from fear' (ibid.: 91; note the emphasis on the 'we').

The fundamental question raised by this debate is not 'whose issue is it' as Crawford et al. imply. It is a question of whether the conceptual apparatus employed within left realism can appropriately tease out the issues of concern in feminist research.

Stanley and Wise (1987: 110-111), in discussing both feminist and non-feminist survey research on violence against women, express the problem this way:

If we wanted to 'prove' how terribly violent women's lives were, we'd go to women who live in violent places – run-down inner-city areas of large conurbations – who have actually experienced male violence and ask them about it ... However if we called this research a 'survey', then, with exemplary motives and using 'scientific means', 'the problem for those women there' could be generalized into 'the problem for all women everywhere'.

The consequence would be that we would have overestimated the amount of overt violence and actual powerlessness in the average woman's life.

Two issues are noteworthy in this passage. It implies both a necessary emphasis on women's strategies of survival and the potential for generating a 'moral panic' in the process of interpreting the results (ibid.: 112). In terms of left realism, it implies agreement with the basic stance that, if you choose an appropriate sample, it is possible to count more incidents of whatever is of concern. This of course, does not necessarily offer a 'real' picture, a totality of that individual's response to the incidents he or she is reporting. One side of the feminist equation, in particular, is missing – survival strategies. This omission raises the question of the appropriateness of local survey techniques on their own and also raises an important question concerning what aspect of (and whose) reality is being tapped by these techniques. Thus a second issue of concern here is the question of methodology.

A commitment to the local criminal victimization survey renders the empirical base of left realism subject to many of the limitations faced by any other piece of research that relies upon survey techniques in general, and the limitations associated with criminal victimization surveys in particular (see Walklate 1989b: ch. 2). As the discussion relating to feminism illustrates, despite efforts made with the nature of the samples, it means that details concerning the criminal victimization process are not accessible. As Crawford et al. (1990) are aware, there is always a need for qualitative and quantitative research. The question relating to the criminal victimization survey is, however, somewhat more fundamental than this. They state: 'The social survey is a democratic instrument; it provides an accurate appraisal of people's fear, of their experience of victimization; it enables the public to express their assessment of police and public authority effectiveness and their doubts about the extent to which the police stay within the boundaries of the rule of law. If we are to view the public as a consumer, as Sir Peter Imbert most usefully suggests, then the social survey provides a detailed picture of consumer demands and satisfaction' (1990: 153).

So that which Galtung (1967) regarded as a vice of survey research – its 'individualistic and democratic bias' – is here being reconstituted as a virtue! Galtung's point, of course, is that, although surveys give everyone an 'equal' voice, social reality is not simply the sum of these voices.

Surveys make several assumptions. They assume that consumers are in a position to know social reality, and that they accurately perceive that social reality. Ultimately, however, surveys hide the objective reality in which individuals' responses are constructed. A 'fetishism' (Cain 1986) with the survey method within left-realist work – an inevitable outcome of theoretical difficulty – is in part defended by MacLean (1989), who encourages a recognition of the sociopolitical context in which the First Islington Crime survey was formulated, that is, the local political situation and the desire to establish a social-democratic agenda on law and order.

The Second Islington Crime Survey attempts to address some difficulties implied by the above discussion. Contrasting 'objectivist' and 'subjectivist' victimology, it is argued that the former focuses on the assumption of the irrationality of human beings and the latter on the assumption of over-rationality. Left realism, it is argued, falls into the trap of neither, since it starts from 'the premise of people's actual grievances of the world' (Crawford et al. 1990: 161) in which 'the expert, the social analyst, therefore, has a vital role in contextualizing the problem of crime. First of all in mapping the problems and then putting the problems in context. In short, the analyst uncovers problems and then gives weight to their severity. This is a basis for a rational input into the system of crime control.'

It is, then, in the establishment of priorities for policy implementation that the social analyst has a key role to play. Such an agenda, however, fails to address the key methodological question being raised. Left realism still relies on the survey as if it were a democratic instrument with which to input data into this policy process, and then proceeds to deny the espoused commitment to the democracy of surveys by arguing that the social analyst gives weight, in policy terms, to the findings! Thus, the reader is left with the impression that it is a political, not a methodological, argument that is being presented.

This general difficulty reflects a theoretical tension. If the premise is to start from people's actual grievances against the world, and, simultaneously, to take seriously the material reality that frames those grievances, then the commitment to the criminal victimization survey reflects a tendency to 'reduce agents to the bearers of structures' (Outhwaite 1987: 111). Thus, although left realism espouses a commitment to the structural concepts of age, class, gender, and ethnicity, at a theoretical level it never clearly articulates how it is that these variables interconnect, though a range of empirical observations is offered concerning their effects.

These criticisms of left realism should not detract from its achievement, at an empirical level, of reminding decision makers that victimization is not evenly distributed across the population, or even within different parts of the population; moreover, distinct patterns of victimization can be identified if different inner-city areas are compared (e.g., Edinburgh in contrast to Islington). This awareness of differential distribution may also have some value for setting local policy agendas. In addition, victimology could benefit by embracing a more structurally informed platform of research. However, it is difficult at times to appreciate what the wealth of left-realist research in the United Kingdom has contributed beyond a more thoroughly documented socio–structural-ecological view of crime. It would be unfortunate if these methodological and theoretical issues were not disentangled since the development of a fuller understanding of the value of realism at a philosophical level is a precondition for useful theoretical and methodological progress for victimology.

What Constitutes the Real?

Perhaps the central weakness of the left-realist position is its poorly formulated conception of what constitutes the real. In some respects, its claims to being able to tap social reality can be met by the equally reasonable claims of other researchers who believe they, too, have tapped social reality while employing different techniques and a different theoretical emphasis. This impasse might be broken by considering the relevance of Giddens's and Bhaskar's work in setting the potential for the development of a more coherent position.

In claiming that a realist interpretation can be applied to the knowledge of social science, Bhaskar states: 'The conception I am proposing is that people, in their conscious activity, for the most part unconsciously reproduce (and occasionally transform) the structures governing their substantive activities of production. Thus people do not marry to reproduce the nuclear family or work to sustain the capitalist economy. Yet it is nevertheless the unintended consequence (and inexorable result) of, as it is also a necessary condition for, their activity' (quoted by Outhwaite 1987: 51). By developing the implications of this position – which has much in common with the work of Giddens (1984) both theoretically and methodologically – the basis for a critical victimology may be found.

The theoretical development of these ideas implies the recognition of at least four processes. First, human beings actively construct and reconstruct their daily lives. Such constructions reflect the strategies of both resistance and acceptance (the constraining and enabling effects of structure) of their social reality. (These processes, by the way, have been a key feature of feminist work.) Second, it proposes the existence of generative mechanisms (both unobserved and unobservable) that nevertheless have a real impact on individual's lives. Third, these processes have both intended and unintended consequences. Fourth, these consequences feed back into the knowledgeability of actors (their capabilities) to construct further responses to a situation. In this way, it is the duality of structure operating through time and space that becomes the theoretical framework for empirical investigation.

As Pawson (1989) illustrates, these ideas are currently fashionable within sociology. Yet, as is often the case, they mean different things to different authors. Pawson (ibid.: 168-170) states: 'For instance, Harré's [1978] interpretation of realism allows him to assert ... [a] vital generative causal mechanism in the human individual's self-direction ... In short, for "realism" here, read "ethnography-ethnomethodology,"' and goes on to say that 'the same sleight of hand is applied, albeit on a completely different plane, in Keat and Urry's [1975] version of realism ... In short, for "realism" here, read "structuralism."'

Pawson then points out that generative thinking needs to do more than assert the ontological primacy of one feature of the social world and then proceed to investigate that world in exactly the same way; it also needs to present a model of empirical investigation. The following discussion seeks to highlight the value of these ideas and assertions for a critical victimology.

Towards a Critical Victimology: Case-Studies

As previously noted, tendencies within positivistic victimology have resulted in a somewhat limited horizon for research conducted within that framework. The observation has also been made, though, that the extant alternatives have their own weaknesses in their inability to capture the full 'victimization equation.' Despite challenges to the aforementioned ideas of Giddens (1984) for their continuance of a malestream tradition (Murgatroyd 1989), they can be reworked to include issues of concern to feminists. This reworking renders explicit the way in which power – both as an unobservable generative mechanism and as a feature of interpersonal relationships (a structural property of human action) – is a key feature of the victimizing process in demarcating both the structural and the interpersonal relationship between victim and offender (respected and contempted). Two case-studies illustrate the considerable importance to victimology of identifying different kinds of power relations.

On Sunday, 2 December 1984, in Bhopal, India, at the Union Carbide Company of India (a subsidiary of the Union Carbide Corporation), water leaked into a storage tank filled with methyl-iscyanate, resulting in a chemical reaction and subsequent gas escape. Estimates on how many died that day vary from 1,754 to upwards of 5,000 people. Some sources report that two people have died every week since the accident because of exposure to that gas. The Indian government acknowledges 3,329 deaths for compensation purposes.

Pearce and Tombs's (1989) detailed analysis of the circumstances of this explosion explores the way in which expert knowledge was used in the aftermath of the event. In the competitive world of pesticides, the Bhopal plant was becoming less profitable. This fact forms a key dimension of the material reality in which those people lived and worked. This material reality not only framed the event but also contributed to the way it was subsequently managed, particularly with respect to power over knowledge and information. (See Pearce and Tombs 1989; Jones 1988; and also Tombs's 1989 work on 'disasters' in the United Kingdom.) Although it is unlikely that any of these mechanisms were actually in the minds of the participants, they certainly served to structure its direction.

This event, however, does not 'simply' sensitize us to another example of 'corporate crime.' As Geis (1973) and Box (1983) have argued, one of the 'problems' of corporate crime is 'victim-responsiveness,' on the one hand, or raising victim and public consciousness, on the other. According to Jones (1988), most people in the surrounding community seemed to know only that the factory in Bhopal was making medicine for crops. In the aftermath of Bhopal, their responsiveness has changed. Today, a range of local groups represents the interests of various sections of the community in Bhopal. In a demonstration of a greater environmental awareness, on the fifth anniversary of the event more than two hundred environmental groups from all parts of India met in Bhopal. In addition, after a small incident in the Union Carbide's West Virginia plant, there followed a rash of 'right to know' legislation in the United States (Pearce and Tombs 1989).

The second example, which illustrates the value of this theoretical starting-point, sensitizes victimology in a different way. If Bhopal was in part a product of the power of multinational corporations, then the 1987 events in Cleveland (northeastern England) reveal the powerlessness of children in the face of sexual abuse.

Through the period March to July 1987, Cleveland Social Services received 110 referrals of child sexual abuse, 90 of them during the months of May and July. By the beginning of the summer, a total of 121 suspected cases had been referred, with the average age of the child being 6.9 years. This situation contrasted sharply with that in 1986, in which there were only two confirmed cases of child sexual abuse in the area. The personalities involved in these events, the response of the various agencies, and the consequent quickly generated media interest established Cleveland as a crisis area (see Campbell 1988). An official enquiry took place, resulting in the view that 26 children from 12 families had been wrongly diagnosed.

Feminist research has established the gender base to child sexual abuse (see, for example, Russell 1984) and the capacity of women to survive such abuse. The events of Cleveland, however, highlighted the 'wall of denial' (Campbell 1987) that met these events on the part of agencies, the media, and politicians, both because of the number of cases being referred and because some of these cases involved families not normally considered social-work material.

Despite this 'wall of denial,' the aftermath of Cleveland is beginning to take some shape. Today, there is probably greater public awareness of child sexual abuse (a factor that seemed to encourage the Second Islington Crime Survey to pose questions in this area), leading to (another) evaluation of agency response to the issue. In addition, in 1985 the Criminal Injuries Compensation Board received only 12 claims pertaining to child sexual abuse, but in the first six months of 1989, it received 500 such applications (both current and retrospective).

These examples not only highlight the survival practices human actors construct for themselves daily, but also clearly illustrate the dynamic and recursive relationship that exists between agency and structure across time and space. These are processes that neither a positivist, nor a realist, nor even the critical victimology proposed by Miers, is capable of capturing.

Positivistic victimology may have the capacity to capture a snapshot of this reality at a particular moment in time and space; feminist research has revealed much about the enabling and constraining effects of the material reality on women and children; and realist victimology details the structural patterning of victimization. Yet the mechanisms that frame the reality in each of these examples and in which the survival strategies of both women and children feature (many groups formed around the Bhopal issue, for example, represent the interests of these two groups) are neither observable nor articulatable, although they feed into the (future) responses of human actors. The question remains: If such thinking were to provide the framework for a critical victimology, might it be employed to construct a research agenda?

How to Research the Real

Giddens (1984: 284-286) states that all social research has an ethnographic moment, that actors possess complex skills which make things happen, and that this takes place across space and through time. In establishing the 'facticity' of institutional conduct, Giddens proceeds to argue that the barriers between qualitative and quantitative research break down: 'each is necessary to the other if the substantive nature of the duality of structure is to be "charted" in terms of the forms of institutional articulation whereby contexts of interaction are coordinated within more embracing social systems' (ibid.: 334).

Such general comments on the nature of structurationist research have been criticized by Gregson (1989) for their lack of relevance to empirical research. In his subsequent reply, Giddens (1989: 300) becomes a little more specific. He proposes a four-item list as the basis for a program of research for a modern social science. This list, although useful and indicative of the difficulty of the task facing the social researcher in capturing the shifting relationships between agency and structure, still lacks specificity. Giddens retreats somewhat into the 'relative autonomy' of theory. Pawson (1989) offers a far more concrete agenda for a realist-informed empirical social science. The issues addressed by Pawson are of particular interest here since he primarily discusses a realist interpretation of quantitative research, though his argument does not necessarily imply that qualitative research should be ignored.

Recognizing that Bhaskar makes no recommendations with respect to the question of measurement, Pawson (1989: 323-326) offers five 'new rules of sociological measurement.' In brief, these rules are as follows:

1 Variables should not be treated as distinct entities, but rather as part of a system regulated by some generative mechanism.
2 All empirical hypotheses should pay attention to the relationship between mechanisms, regularities, and contexts. Thus, comparative and longitudinal designs are necessary to control for the potential confounding effects of other social mechanisms.
3 There is a need for networking the use of concepts at an abstract level so that they may be further tested, refined, and developed.
4 Empirical testing is an adjudicatory rather than a verification process.
5 To overcome the problems of the social nature of data collection, interviews should refer solely to institutional or mutual knowledge; interviewers should be seen as 'conceptual tutors' (but not hypothesis disclosers) and respondents should act as 'learners/informants.'

These proposals curtail the traditional way of viewing the role of quantitative research and emphasize a theoretical starting-point similar to that of Giddens.

Left realists could argue that they are already working within such a realist framework in two ways. The first link between Pawson's position and that of those favouring the local victimization survey pertains to the question of regularities, mechanisms, and contexts. The discussion of the intricate nature of 'lived realities' (Crawford et al. 1990: 163-164) reflects a concern with this question. Unfortunately, although this discussion challenges more simplistic views of the relationship between age and gender, or ethnicity and gender, for example, it merely describes that complexity. It does not reveal how, where, and when those interrelationships become more or less complex. (How much more useful it would have been, theoretically, empirically, and in policy terms, had this second survey been constituted as a panel study to come closer to one of the rules suggested by Pawson.) But perhaps more fundamental is Pawson's (1989: 302) emphasis on quantitative work focusing on mutual knowledge, as exemplified in his statement: 'I propose that the research interview should abandon attempts to ascertain directly orientations, motivations, values, worldviews, evaluations, opinions, and so forth and instead concentrate on events, happenings, actions, situations, conditions.'

Such an approach would refine and curtail the focus of both the local and the national victimization survey.

The second feature with which left realism might relate is that of the networking of concepts. It remains to be seen how well refined or developed abstract concepts may become as both national and international research programs in this area develop. Much of this, at least in funding terms, is beyond the researcher's control. A realist research strategy that is informed by these ideas would look considerably different and would surely by definition have to include and incorporate qualitative research. Giddens (1984) uses the interplay between the work of Willis (1977) (qualitative) and Gambetta (1982) (quantitative) to illustrate this point. In the context of criminal victimization, it could no longer marginalize the methodological work of feminist researchers. Although left realism could forcibly argue that it has never denied the importance of qualitative research, this position would clearly make qualitative work an integral feature of any research program.

The methodological implications of taking realism seriously are substantial. To be sure, a continued commitment to the criminal victimization survey alone would not suffice. How, then, might a research agenda sensitive to these questions be constructed?

Researching Fear of Crime

Fear of crime is an issue on the policy agenda of both administrative and realist criminology/victimology. The publication of findings from the recent International (telephone) Crime Survey has revived the Home Office view that people in England, in comparison with their European counterparts, worry about crime more than their victimization rate would suggest is necessary (Carvel 1990). As noted, a primary feature of the left-realist response was to challenge the idea that such fears are irrational. Neither the Home Office nor left realism has begun to fully explicate the dimensions of fear of crime, and it is possible to argue that this is the case chiefly because the conceptual starting point of 'crime' per se is an inappropriate one. A critical social-science discipline could perhaps more appropriately consider the underlying generative mechanism(s) that produce such fear.

Bottoms (1988) borrowed a concept from Raymond Williams in developing some themes about crime. This concept, 'mobile privatization,' is intended to convey the impact of technology on modern social life. It suggests that it is important to take seriously that we are all potentially mobile, both literally and figuratively, through the media, and yet simultaneously we have increasingly retreated into our own 'private' lives. It could be argued that this is a useful theoretical starting-point for researching fear of crime.

If the focus of our theory were to be such a mechanism, some hypotheses concerning its impact are generated: more people living in smaller groups, living private lives, not community lives; loss of confidence in public space; increase in personal anxiety; adoption of increasingly defensive strategies; the simultaneous growth in the policing of the private for some groups in society; the normalization of private life; changes in expectations of children; the growth of issue groups to support those who fall outside these processes; and so on. (Some of these features of society were commented on by Bottoms [1989] and Taylor [1990].) These hypotheses generate (at least) two key concepts: community safety (a version of which has been developed by Bright [1987]), and personal safety (Stanko 1990). These, in turn, generate several variables – ethnicity, class, age, and gender – each of which could reflect the impact of 'mobile privatization.' Thus the concepts, hypotheses, and variables become meaningfully linked with one another.

Because it attempts to offer a methodological example of generative thinking, this framework must be researched not only by employing multiple research techniques but also by using those techniques to unwrap the layers of social reality that contribute to the actors' knowledge about feeling safe. For example, the notion of community safety would need to be explored through: (1) a historical/ethnographic account of a given community (bearing some similarity to Bottoms and Wiles's [1988] notion of a community crime career) and (2) a survey of local residents, and talks with the whole range of 'agencies' and networks that operate at various levels within communities (from statutory agencies and voluntary organizations to housing associations, pre-school play-groups, and publicans).

The questions of where, when, and how people feel safe in a particular community, as well as what that notion of safety means to them, could be raised. For this information to be of value, however, it must be constituted as a comparative analysis with other types of communities and would require that time be spent looking at the changes in 'safety levels' over time. Yet even this process would not necessarily tap notions of personal safety. Although it is possible to hypothesize about connections between community safety and personal safety, it would be imperative to explore how, if at all, changes in the nature of the private relate to experiences and strategies for establishing personal safety.

Conclusion: Critical Victimology

One implication of this discussion for positivist/conventional victimology is that, if we wish to further our understanding of the processes of victimization, we must recognize that the individualistic bias of victim-precipitation research severely limits it in terms of explaining patterns of victimization. Similarly, reliance on national criminal victimization data serves only to highlight the greater problems inherent in sole reliance on police statistics. However, the success of realist victimology/criminology in using criminal victimization surveys to uncover more incidents of criminal victimization than do national surveys in specific localized areas is offset by its key weakness – a poorly formulated understanding of what constitutes the real. A critical victimology that appreciates the relevance of Bhaskar's and Giddens's ideas for the development of a critical social science could constitute a useful and valuable starting-point for building upon the empirical achievements of radical left realism and the conceptual and methodological achievements of work constructed within the feminist movement.

Such a critical victimology could even incorporate the policy agenda favoured by left realists. As both Stanley and Wise (1987) and Giddens (1982) observe: 'To regard social agents as "knowledgeable" and "capable" is not just a matter of the analysis of action; it is also an implicitly political stance. The practical consequences of natural science are "technological"; they have to do with the application of humanly attained knowledge to a world of objects that exists independently of that knowledge. Human beings, however, are not merely inert objects of knowledge, but rather agents able to – and prone to – incorporate social theory and research within their actions' (Giddens ibid.: 16).

Giddens (1989) exhorts social scientists to face a range of questions that constitute the momentous questions of our time; further, more than a hint of such momentous concern is indeed discernible in the observation made by Crawford et al. (1990: 26) that crime is now a green issue! Ultimately we must decide whether to shift the research agenda away from measuring patterns of victimization and instead more fully document and explain the deeper order that produces and changes those patterns and the strategies people use to survive them.

This article also appeared in a special issue of Social Justice, 'Feminism and The Social Control of Gender' (Vol. 17, no. 3, 1990), which is available at P.O. Box 40601, San Francisco, CA 94140.

References

Amir, M. 1971. *Patterns of Forcible Rape*. Chicago: University of Chicago Press
Anderson, S., C. Grove Smith, R. Kinsey, and J. Wood. 1990. *The Edinburgh Crime Survey: First Report*. Edinburgh: Central Research Unit Papers, Scottish Office
Bottoms, A. 1989. 'Crime, Criminals, Justice, Victims: Beyond the Barriers towards 2000 A.D.' Opening address to OICJ Conference. Bramshill, March
Bottoms, A., and P. Wiles. 1988. 'Crime and Housing Policy: A Framework for Crime

Prevention Analysis,' in T. Hope and M. Shaw, eds., *Communities and Crime Reduction*, 84-98. London: HMSO

Box, S. 1983. *Power, Crime and Mystification*. London: Tavistock

Bright, J. 1987. 'Community Safety, Crime Prevention and Local Authority,' in P. Willmott, ed., *Policing and the Community*, Policy Studies Institute Discussion Paper no. 16, 45-53. London: PSI

Cain, M. 1986. 'Realism, Feminism, Methodology, and Law.' *International Journal of the Sociology of Law*, 14: 255-267

– 1989. 'Feminists Transgress Criminology,' in M. Cain, ed., *Growing Up Good: Policing the Behaviour of Girls in Europe*, 1-18. London: Sage

Campbell, B. 1987. 'The Skeleton in the Family's Cupboard.' *New Statesman*, 31 (July): 10-12

– 1988. *Unofficial Secrets, Child Sexual Abuse: The Cleveland Case*. London: Virago

Carvel, J. 1990. '1989 International Crime Survey.' *The Guardian*, 30 March

Christie, N. 1986. 'The Ideal Victim,' in E.A. Fattah, ed., *From Crime Policy to Victim Policy*, 1-17. London: Macmillan

Crawford, A., T. Jones, T. Woodhouse, and J. Young. 1900. *Second Islington Crime Survey*. London: Middlesex Polytechnic, Centre for Criminology

Edwards, S. 1989. *Policing Domestic Violence*. London: Sage

Fattah, E., ed. 1989. *The Plight of Crime Victims in Modern Society*. London: Macmillan

Galtung, J. 1967. *Theory and Method of Social Research*. London: Allen and Unwin

Gambetta, D. 1982. 'Were They Pushed or Did They Jump?' PhD thesis, University of Cambridge

Geis, G. 1973. 'Victimization Patterns in White Collar Crime,' in I. Drapkin and E. Viano, eds., *Victimology: A New Focus*, vol. 5: *Exploiters and Exploited*, 86-106. Lexington, MA: D.C. Heath

Giddens, A. 1982. *Profiles and Critiques in Social Theory*. London: Macmillan

– 1984. *The Constitution of Society*. Cambridge: Polity Press

– 1989. 'A Reply to My Critics,' in D. Held and J.B. Thompson, eds., *Social Theory of Modern Societies: Anthony Giddens and His Critics*, 249-301. Cambridge: Cambridge University Press

Gregson, N. 1989. 'On the (Ir)relevance of Structuration Theory to Empirical Research,' in D. Held and J.B. Thompson, eds., *Social Theory of Modern Societies: Anthony Giddens and His Critics*, 235-248. Cambridge: Cambridge University Press

Harré, R. 1978. *Social Being*. Oxford: Basil Blackwell

Hindelang, M.J., M.R. Gottfredson, and J. Garofalo. 1978. *Victims of Personal Crime: An Empirical Foundation for a Theory of Personal Victimization*. Cambridge, MA: Ballinger

Jones, T. 1988. *Corporate Killing: Bhopals Will Happen*. London: Free Association Books

Jones, T., B. MacLean, and J. Young. 1986. *The Islington Crime Survey*. Aldershot: Gower

Keat, R., and J. Urry. 1975. *Social Theory as Science*. London: Routledge and Kegan Paul

Kinsey, R. 1984. *Merseyside Crime Survey: First Report*. Liverpool: Merseyside County Council

Kinsey, R., J. Lea, and J. Young. 1986. *Losing the Fight against Crime*. Oxford: Basil Blackwell

MacLean, B. 1989. 'In Partial Defence of Socialist Realism: Some Theoretical and Methodological Concerns of the Local Crime Survey.' Paper presented to the British Criminology Conference, Bristol

Miers, D. 1989. 'Positivist Victimology: A Critique' *International Review of Victimology*, 1: 3-22

Murgatroyd, L. 1989. 'Only Half the Story: Some Blinkering Effects of Malestream Sociology,' in D. Held and J.B. Thompson, eds., *Social Theory of Modern Societies: Anthony Giddens and His Critics*, 147-161. Cambridge: Cambridge University Press

Outhwaite, W. 1987. *New Philosophies of Social Science: Realism, Hermeneutics, and Critical Theory*. London: Macmillan

Painter, K., J. Lea, T. Woodhouse, and J. Young. 1989. *The Hammersmith and Fulham Crime and Policing Survey*. London: Middlesex Polytechnic, Centre for Criminology

Pawson, R. 1989. *A Measure for Measures: A Manifesto for Empirical Sociology*. London: Routledge

Pearce, F., and S. Tombs. 1989. 'Bhopal: Union Carbide and the Hubris of Capitalist Technocracy.' *Social Justice*, 16 (2): 116-145

Rock, P. 1986. *A View from the Shadows*. Oxford: Oxford University Press

Russell, D. 1984. *Sexual Exploitation*. Beverly Hills: Sage

Sparks, R. 1982. *Research on Victims of Crime: Accomplishments, Issues and New Directions*. Rockville, MD: US Department of Health and Human Services

Stanko, E. *Everyday Violence*. London: Pandora

Stanley, L., and S. Wise. 1987. *Georgie Porgie: Sexual Harassment in Everyday Life*. London: Pandora

Taylor, I. 1990. 'Crime in a Real World.' Paper presented to Department of Sociology, University of Manchester

Tombs, S. 1989. 'Learning from Disasters.' *Network: British Sociological Association Newsletter*, March: 3

Walklate, S. 1989a. 'Appreciating the Victim: Conventional, Realist or Critical Victimology.' Paper presented to the British Criminology Conference, Bristol

– 1989b. *Victimology: The Victim and the Criminal Justice Process*. London: Unwin Hyman

Willis, P. 1977. *Learning to Labour*. Farnborough: Saxon House

Wise, S., and L. Stanley. 1984. *Men and Sex: A Case Study in Sexual Politics*. Oxford: Pergamon

Wolfgang, M.E. 1958. *Patterns of Criminal Homicide*. Philadelphia: University of Pennsylvania

Young, J. 1986. 'The Failure of Criminology: The Need for a Radical Realism,' in R. Matthews and J. Young, eds., *Confronting Crime*, 4-30. London: Sage

15 The Local Crime Survey: Pitfalls and Possibilities

Ken Pease

For two reasons I should make clear the basis of experience informing this essay. First, this essay is less data driven than what I am accustomed to writing, and so the experience which underpins it is correspondingly more important. Second, that experience is incomplete: I have not yet taken a local survey through from conception to publication.

Firsthand experience of the design and analysis of a crime survey came through a supporting role in the 1984 British Crime Survey (BCS). I was involved, under the leadership of Pat Mayhew and Mike Hough, at all stages of the second sweep of the BCS. Others involved in the project included Mike Maguire, Michael Maxfield, and Tim Hope. Secondary analysis of aspects of other British crime surveys have been or will be published under my name.[1] Latterly, the Henry Fielding Centre at Manchester University has been involved in the design and execution of local surveys, and I have been particularly involved in one such survey in a massive public housing area north of Manchester, England. While this work is as yet incomplete, it is my experience in this project in comparison with that of a national survey which has given much food for thought, and has led to this essay as a first attempt to share that thought.

What Is a Local Crime Survey?

This apparently bizarre question is necessary because almost all national surveys known to the writer are also local surveys – the 'almost' is necessary because the generalization excludes telephone surveys such as van Dijk, Mayhew, and Killias (1990) – because of the economics of sampling procedures. Typically, a selection is made of a number of sampling points according to some rule of representativeness or purposive overrepresentation. For instance, in the 1982 British Crime Survey there were in excess of three hundred sampling points, with either thirty or sixty interviews being conducted at each. In effect, each of these sampling points generates a small local survey. They have not been regarded as local surveys because the number of interviews at each sampling point is insufficient to reach free-standing conclusions about that area. If a local survey needs to be large enough to enable one to draw local conclusions, it seems to follow that a local crime survey may be defined as a survey taking a subnational sampling frame such that conclusions may be reached about crime victimization suffered within the area covered, within an acceptably small range.

Defining a local survey as one which enables one to draw local conclusions about crime level is important as much for what it does not say as for what it does. It does not say that sample size is adequate to make judgments about differences, for example, according to age, gender, ethnicity, or even crime type. The point that a local crime survey which is adequate to provide a general description of victimization in the area is not adequate to enable one to make reliable statements about individual differences within an area is a crucial one and will be returned to later. The conclusion which will be drawn from my investigation is that local and national surveys are necessarily interdependent.

Motherhood, Apple Pie, and Victimization Surveys

Some of what follows may be interpreted as being critical of local surveys, and, indeed, many local surveys merit swingeing methodological criticism. However, this should in no sense be taken to suggest that the local crime survey is not an intrinsically worthwhile enterprise. It is. In essence, as MacLean (1989, 1991) has pointed out, the victim survey is an instrument of empowerment. It affords an alternative image of crime to that officially provided, one less distorted by formal and informal pressures which accompany the conversion of events into statistics. Repeated through time, it allows the determination of change independent of fluctuations in the inclination to make the events available for official processing. This is particularly important where rates of reporting incidents to the police are especially low and where increases in the recorded rates of crime may induce false pessimism, or where there is so much official investment in the idea that crime rates will change that subtle modifications in official processing can (in all honesty) generate a desired result (Bennett 1990). Data from crime surveys can also form the basis for discussions of policing practice which are not directly confrontational. The Islington Crime Survey (ICS; Jones, MacLean, and Young 1986) remains the best known of the British local surveys, and it certainly generated changes in the local political climate. It changed the discourse of victimization experience. Repeated sweeps of local surveys transform the enterprise from taking a snapshot to telling a story, thereby allowing the development of more coherent responses to crime and punishment issues.

It should be noted that many of the empowering aspects of the local survey also characterize the national survey. One of the unfortunate features of the recent past has been the tendency of criminologists favouring local surveys to deride national surveys. The national survey was pre-eminent in putting the study of victimization experience at centre stage. I will argue later that, because they throw light on different problems, local and national surveys need to complement each other.

The reason for standing back and taking a cool look at the conduct of local surveys is precisely because they are fashionable. 'Appreciate me now and avoid the rush,' proclaims the bumper sticker. Similarly, we should criticize victimization surveys now and avoid the rush which will assuredly come.

Victimization and Feelings

The basic problem with the local survey is that the number of people surveyed is small, and that, in consequence, interpretation at other than the most general level is not possible. This does not typically stop researchers from carrying on with interpretation, sometimes to the ludicrous point where a single victimized person might become as much as 20 per cent of a sample.

In an area with an average victimization rate for England and Wales, just over one interview in three would be with a crime victim, assuming a recall period of one year. I have found it difficult to explain to officials interested in commissioning a local survey that over half of the interviews will do nothing more than create a denominator for measuring levels of victimization. The pressure is intense to do something, anything, with the people who have been, at no little cost, contacted. Three kinds of 'filler' questions are obvious devices for allowing these non-victim respondents to provide information: questions concerning the evaluation of lifestyle characteristics, police services, and the fear of crime. Perhaps the first effort of imagination required of the reader – one or more such efforts is without exception demanded in victim surveys – is to recognize that none of these concerns necessarily belongs in a victimization survey. I contend that none of these properly belongs in a victimization survey, but is included (the choice is on grounds of ideology) simply because the logistics of victimization surveys require extensive filler items for the survey to appear efficient. My reservations are as follows:

a Information about lifestyle characteristics can readily develop into implicit notions of victim blame and the consequent devaluing of victim suffering.

b The evaluation of police services, valuable and necessary in its own right, when done in the context of a victimization survey links rates of victimization and judgments of adequacy of assistance in a way which may not be helpful in developing policing as a service. There are a number of reasons for this, most of which flow from the notion that, if police effectiveness is measured alongside and in terms of victimization rates, the development of policing as primarily a more general service is abraded. Make the police nothing but thief-takers and one can confidently predict that the niceties of due process will not be observed.

c The 1980s has seen crime as a problem superseded by the joint problem of crime and fear of crime. As with lifestyle characteristics and the evaluation of police services, fear of crime can perform a useful filler role to make a victimization survey more efficient. Fear of crime has taken on a life of its own in British criminal justice policy, and is regularly referred to in the speeches of Home Secretaries and officials. The next stage, evident in local initiatives in many places, is to address only the fear of crime. The commonplace finding that those most fearful of crime are those least victimized (see, for example, Maxfield 1984) is often cited as support for only examining fear of crime. There are those of us who regard that as unfortunate. We would prefer to regard fear as the product (literally, in arithmetic terms) of probability of victimization and consequences of victimization. If that is correct, a reduction in crime fear is indefensible by means other than a reduction in the rate of crime victimization. One should rather improve the social support available to those most in fear, generate systems which reduce the consequences of victimization, and reduce the rate of crime.

To restate the case simply, sample sizes in local surveys are too small to determine differences in rates and types of victimization within the group surveyed. A crime survey contains two components – determination of the rate of victimization, and 'filler' items made necessary by the urge to ask something of people not victimized. The choice of type of filler items is ideological; therefore, any observed relationship between the filler item and the experience of victimization is likely to be spurious. In this connection, it would be entertaining to choose kinds of filler items that accord with other views. Local surveys commissioned and conducted by those of the right would emphasize public perceptions of the inadequacy of police powers rather than police accountability, and ask for characteristics of known offenders in the locality. Questions about church-going would be included as fillers by those wishing to suggest a connection between religious observances and crime. Questions about diet would be asked by nutritionists – crime victims eat more fast food. Horoscope information would be required by proselytizing astrologers. It is through the shrewd use of filler items, not victimization items, that ideological messages about crime are communicated. Since the political complection of areas commissioning surveys has been predominantly of the left, the content of the filler items derives from that agenda.

There is also the issue that those competent to carry out the surveys have been educated in a leftist tradition. This matters greatly, in that those commissioning surveys with which I have been involved are prepared to delegate question content to the 'experts' far more than they should, which makes the views and values of those commissioned commensurately more important. Finally, the writings of Jock Young provide a theoretical framework for the local survey which has not been mirrored by any criminologist of the right. In short, I think that the questions which form the filler in local victimization surveys have, for a variety of reasons, been shaped by left-realist criminology.

Having outlined some of the 'pitfalls' which attend the local survey, I now describe its strengths as a way of moving towards the 'possibilities' – the argument that local and national surveys are mutually dependent. The major strength, that of local empowerment through a data base independent of official agencies, will not be repeated here.

Hard-to-Capture Crimes

One advantage which local surveys have enjoyed over national surveys has been the rate of capture of those crimes which require substantial rapport between interviewer and interviewee. Most notable among these have been sexual offences, particularly those committed against intimates. At a cost in interviewer selection, training, and time, much higher rates of victimization have been revealed in local surveys, albeit not always in the class-independent distribution that would have been the preference of the investigators. Another area in which local and national surveys do not always largely correspond is the class distribution of violence. National surveys uniformly show the lowest levels of violent victimization to be suffered by working-class people. The most common explanation for this finding is that what they regard as the hurly-burly of everyday life would be regarded as crime by other social groups, for example, as with an Asian interviewed for the first ICS who was known to have been assaulted but did not mention this (MacLean, personal communication). When challenged later, it was clear that he had not placed these assaults in a criminal frame of reference. In terms of intensity of effort, local surveys are particularly well adapted to identify particular crime types and their circumstances. Although one can overstate the poverty of national surveys in illuminating hard-to-capture crimes (Worrall and Pease 1986; Dowds and Davidoff 1990), this is clearly an area where the intensive local survey comes into its own and a national study cannot realistically hope to compete.

Local Surveys: Never Local Enough?

Local surveys complement national surveys in that they delineate local crime experience and are thus locally more informative and persuasive. Notwithstanding this, no local crime survey can ever be small enough to generate an area within which crime experience is uniform. As a general rule of thumb that has been found to work reasonably well, take any area and within it you will find 20 per cent of the units (people or places) suffering 80 per cent of the crimes. At the finest-grained level, the phenomenon is one of repeat victimization. While it has been known for some time that prior victimization is a good predictor of future victimization, the implications of this trend for the crime survey, both national and local – but particularly local – have not been fully recognized. In this respect, consider national data (chosen here simply because they are the data with which I am most familiar).

Crime incidence in an area over a specified period is a product (in the arithmetic sense) of two variables. These are prevalence (the proportion of people or places which are victimized) and the number of victimizations that each victim suffers (Trickett et al. [1990] call it 'vulnerability'). How do areas differ in the decomposed crime-incidence measures of prevalence and vulnerability? Data from the 1982 and 1984 British Crime Surveys show essentially the same thing. For purposes of illustration, let us consider the 1982 data. The total crime incidence was calculated for each sampling point.[2] Sampling points were ranked by crime incidence. To obtain numbers large enough to enable reliable conclusions, ranked areas were split into deciles, from the 10 per cent of areas with the lowest crime incidence to the 10 per cent with the next lowest, to the 10 per cent with the highest. The analysis was done for both crimes against the person (see figure 15.1) and property crimes (see figure 15.2). Three crucial points emerge. The first is the sheer scale of area differences. The worst decile of areas had twelve times the rate of property crime and thirty-five times the rate of personal crime as the lowest decile. Looking within the top decile, differences within these sampling points emerge, underlining the observation that, however small the unit of analysis, there is local variation. The second noteworthy point is that the single most dramatic variable distinguishing high and low crime areas is the prevalence of personal crime. The third point, central to the position taken here, is that the worse the crime pattern in an area, the more repeat victimization of individuals contributes to it. For instance, persons victimized will, on average, report nearly four victimizations each. The recall period for the BCS was one

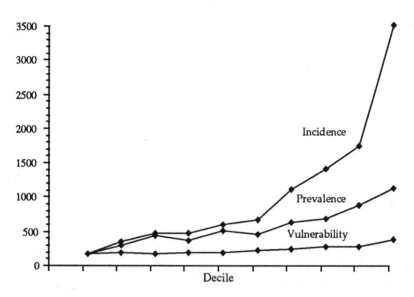

FIGURE 15.1. Personal crime: prevalence, vulnerability, and incidence by decile (all measures are set to 100 for the least crime-prone decile; data from 1982 British Crime Survey)

year, but there is a suggestion, at least for burglary and intuitively for other kinds of crime (Polvi, Looman, and Pease 1990) that the period of greatly elevated risk of repeat victimization is much shorter than this.

In conclusion, even the smallest local crime survey aggregates across areas of different crime experience. Thus, even the smallest survey does not provide a uniform basis for policing and crime-prevention activities. What is needed is the incorporation of an element in local crime surveys which draws attention to the unevenness of victimization as one basis for crime-prevention policy. One way of focusing upon the unevenness of victimization is to concentrate upon people or places who have experienced repeated victimization. This approach has a number of practical advantages for policing and for crime prevention-initiatives. Concentration on the multiple victim *ipso facto* allows concentration on types of people who suffer most without requiring direct reference to the contentious social dimensions along which victimization is ranged. A repeat victim is a repeat victim. My personal wish would be that recognition of the overwhelming importance of repeat victimization in high-crime areas would lead to the adoption of a crime-control strategy based on the prevention of repeat victimization. Further, some of the crimes which sensitive local surveys are well

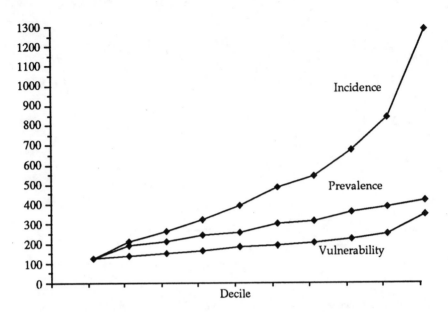

FIGURE 15.2. Property crime: prevalence, vulnerability, and incidence by decile (all measures are set to 100 for the least crime-prone decile; data from 1982 British Crime Survey)

equipped to reveal, like domestic assault, are those which will increase the prominence of multiple victimization. Unless there is a serious attempt to address the significance of repeat victimization in the local crime survey, the survey gives a spurious impression of local relevance.

The Farmer and the Cowhand Can Be Friends

The opposition between local and national surveys is largely illusory. The local survey can capture important crimes which the national survey cannot. The local survey can address special issues such as crimes by and against business. It can emphasize interviewer training more than is practicable with larger surveys. Against this, national surveys are methodologically sophisticated when it comes to sampling and analysis (see Skogan 1990). Frankly, I am worried about the technical competence of some local surveys. Twice recently I had the experience of contacting polling firms who have undertaken local crime surveys in order to obtain cost estimates for new surveys. In one case, I was told that the firm had too much work on, and in the other a price was quoted which was so much out of line with what had been the going rate a few months earlier that the only possible conclusion was that the firm wanted the business only at a price that would buy the managing director a new Porsche. The suggestion is that (at least in my part of the UK) the competent research organizations have become saturated by work. Some smaller survey commissioners may go to the local college of further education for students to do the work as a class project. The most obvious danger in these circumstances is sheer incompetence and the most obvious area in which it will be demonstrated is sampling. Earlier in this essay, I noted that a sample that is adequate to enable one to make a reasonable estimate of population characteristics is, by definition, too small to enable one to make judgments about subpopulations. This characteristic can be disguised by a judicious grossing-up of the numbers, but the survey is none the more accurate for that. One Black woman over age sixty who has been mugged may be 100 per cent of a sample group in a table, but represents no social reality beyond that. One thing that never ceases to amaze me is how quickly you run out of numbers when dividing a population, and if the original survey was kept small by cost considerations, this limitation may come as a nasty surprise. This point relates to one made earlier. Since you will run out of victims before you run out of respondents to the survey (victims + non-victims), a twilight zone will emerge in which fear of crime, lifestyle, and police behaviour will be the only show in town for the trapped surveyor, with the attendant dangers noted earlier. In fact, the optimist in me thinks that the demise of the bad local crime survey will come when the typical instance of the genre is manifestly incompetent. The pessimist in me worries that no one will notice. The wild optimist in me believes that institutes of higher education will produce enough numerate and criminologically aware graduates quickly enough to recognize the issues and translate them into defensible survey instruments and samples. But how wild can an optimist get?

I and my colleagues in Manchester are trying to bridge the gulf by using national data to inform local issues. For instance, some crimes are captured quite well by national surveys. These can be used as a baseline for local surveys – for instance, by showing how figures for a local area with a particular housing type compare with national figures for the same housing type, or how the mix of well-captured crime in similar sampling points compares with local experience. Additionally, we are, as noted above, trying to use national surveys – with their known limitations – as though they were a series of local surveys. The emphasis on repeat victimization which such analysis points up should be tested out to identify the highly victimized individuals within local surveys. The victimization survey is too useful an instrument in giving crime victims a voice for its potential to be restricted by the independent development of, and sniping between, proponents of national and local surveys.

Notes

1 See Pease (1985), Worrall and Pease (1986), Pease (1988), and Trickett et al. (1990).
2 This kind of analysis is the potential bridge between the local and the national survey, since each data point is a locality.

References

Bennett, T. 1990. *Neighbourhood Watch*. London: Heinemann

Dowds, L., and L. Davidoff. 1990. *Domestic Assault: Evidence from the British Crime Survey*, Home Office Research Bulletin no. 26, 14-22. London: HMSO

Jones, T., B. MacLean, and J. Young. 1986. *The Islington Crime Survey*. Aldershot: Gower

MacLean, B.D.S.P. 1989. 'The Islington Crime Survey, 1985: A Cross Sectional Study of Crime and Policing in the London Borough of Islington.' PhD thesis, University of London

– 1991. 'In Partial Defense of Socialist Realism: Some Theoretical and Methodological Considerations of the Local Crime Survey.' *Crime, Law and Social Change: An International Journal*, 15: 213-254

Maxfield, M.G. 1984. *Fear of Crime in England and Wales*, Home Office Research Study no. 78. London: HMSO

Pease, K. 1985. 'Obscene Telephone Calls in England and Wales.' *Howard Journal of Criminal Justice*, 24: 275-281

– 1988. *Judgements of Crime Seriousness: Evidence from the 1984 British Crime Survey*, Home Office Research and Planning Unit Paper no. 44. London: HMSO

Polvi, N., T. Looman, and K. Pease. 1990. 'Repeated Break-and-Enter Victimisation: Time Course and Crime Prevention Opportunity.' *Journal of Police Science and Administration*, 17: 8-11

Skogan, W. 1990. *Disorder and Decline*. New York: Free Press

Trickett, A., D.R. Osborn, J. Seymour, and K. Pease. 1992. 'What Is Different about High Crime Rate Areas?' *British Journal of Criminology*, 32 (1): 81-89

van Dijk, J.J.M., P. Mayhew, and M. Killias. 1990. *Experiences of Crime across the World: Key Findings of the 1989 International Crime Survey*. Deventer: Kluwer

Worrall, A., and K. Pease. 1986. 'Personal Crimes against Women: Evidence from the 1982 British Crime Survey.' *Howard Journal of Criminal Justice*, 25: 118-124

16 The Contribution of 'Left Realism' to the Study of Commercial Crime

Frank Pearce

In this essay I present some of those findings on commercial crime generated by the Second Islington Crime Survey (ICS II) conducted from the Centre of Criminology at Middlesex Polytechnic in May 1988. These findings are contextualized by a brief discussion of 'left realism' and of 'white-collar crime.' They are then used to develop some realist arguments, albeit with a somewhat different inflection.

'Left-realist criminology' has defined its task as establishing the nature, distribution, and severity of criminal and antisocial conduct within contemporary societies. It has shown that much criminal and antisocial conduct disproportionately victimizes the most vulnerable members of society and helps to undermine their community life. It has also analysed the *modus operandi* of such agencies as the police, and argued that the tasks of such agencies should be both more clearly specified and circumscribed; for example, police authorities should be made more accountable to the community. Realists have tried to develop appropriate and feasible strategies to control crime and to reform the police (Kinsey, Lea, and Young 1986). Through their analysis of the four-way interaction of victim, offender, the police (or formal control), and the community (or informal control), realists demonstrate a belief that they have successfully developed a holistic approach to the phenomenon of crime (Jones, MacLean, and Young 1986; Young 1987: 340).

Left realists have criticized many radical writers for downplaying the importance of conventional crime, particularly street crime. There has been a tendency to refuse to accept that official statistics have much utility, except as an index of changes in police practices. At the same time it is often assumed that the patterning and aetiology of street crime is self-evident. Reported working-class anxiety about crime is not taken seriously. It is argued that working-class people themselves do not view it as being as significant as some other problems, such as unemployment (Sim, Scraton, and Gordon 1987: 47) or that such fears are out of all proportion to the problem and an effect of manipulation by politicians, the media, and the police (Gilroy 1987; Chambliss 1988: 42) There is a tendency to focus on interclass crime, valorizing working-class and Black crime as forms of primitive rebellion and then treating interracial crimes by Whites, state crimes, white-collar and corporate crime as the only real forms of crime. Yet, many on the left who invoke the category of corporate crime fail to explore it in any depth; nor do they unpack it, isolate causal sequences, or specify the kinds of non-reformist reforms that could limit its occurrence now and might have a transformative potential (Gorz 1980). In truth, much of the recent empirical and theoretical work on the crimes of the powerful has been undertaken by social democrats and liberals rather than by Marxists (Clinard and Yeager 1980; Braithwaite 1984; Levi 1987; Box 1983, 1987).[1]

The left-realist strategy has been both empirical and theoretical. By using victimization surveys, attempts have been made to measure: first, the extent and patterning of street crime and the effectiveness of the police in dealing with it; second, how concerned people are with crime and other social problems and what crimes are of particular concern; third, people's experience of, and perception of police activity. This work has extended our knowledge of the distribution of crime; how particular groups, notably women, experience it; and how fear of it structures the conduct of particular groups. In addressing these issues, analysis has been extended from that of strictly criminal conduct to more general antisocial conduct. It becomes clear that the most socially disadvantaged people are often extremely worried about crime and that their fears may well be in proportion to their relative likelihood of victimization. The use of sympathetic women interviewers has uncovered many more cases of domestic violence, sexual assault, and sexual harassment than are usually acknowledged. In my view the commitment to empirical work and the belief that new research strategies can be developed to generate relevant data are major strengths of realism.

Realists have recognized the abiding importance of white-collar and corporate crime (Lea 1987: 362; Matthews 1987: 376; Young 1986: 23, 1987: 353, 355) and Lea and Young (1984) have provided a systematic examination of the relative impact of corporate crime and street crime on people's lives. In a discussion of some depth and subtlety, noting the similarities and differences between these two kinds of crime, Lea and Young argue that while both display 'the same ethos of competitiveness and individualism' (p. 74), the former 'is the most transparent of all injustices. It is a starting point for a double thrust against crime on all levels. If we concentrate on it alone, as the political right would wish, we are actively engaged in a diversion from the crimes of the powerful. If we concentrate solely on the latter, as many on the left would have us do, we are omitting what are real and pressing problems for working class people, and lose the ability to move from the immediate to encompass the more hidden, and thus demonstrate the intrinsic similarity of crime at all levels of our society' (p. 75).

Although these arguments are to be welcomed, there are a number of problems with them and other 'realist' formulations. Overall, their treatment of crime is far too voluntaristic and often overly moralistic and, of particular importance in this context, their approach to corporate and white-collar crime is often as superficial as that of 'left idealists' (cf. Young 1987: 344-346; Matthews 1987: 376-378).[2] Realism has tended to focus on the more immediate interpersonal antisocial conduct – that is, *on crimes between subjects*: 'Crime is a social relationship. It is institutionalized; it is imbued with meaning; both offenders and victims are predictable, and above all *they relate to one another*' (Young 1987: 344; emphasis added). Here, Young's characterization of the nature of crime does not adequately describe the anonymous relationship between a manufacturer and a consumer using a faulty or dangerous product. It does not capture the extent to which acts of omission are what cause harm in many such cases or in those involving dangerous pollution. Nor does it recognize that it is the failure of employers to fulfil their statutory managerial duties that lead to many workplace injuries and deaths. *Corporate crime is poorly described or understood if we stay within a conceptual framework restricted to interpersonal relations between subjects; moreover, within this framework it is equally unlikely that methods will be found to control it.* As a result, one is led to wonder if a realist analysis of murder would include an examination of the statistics for deaths caused by workplace accidents and occupationally caused diseases, as did Neil Boyd (1988) in his recent study of murder in Canada. Would a realist analysis of the violence and harassment suffered by women at work include a discussion of corporate violence and the particular forms it takes against women? In its present state of development, realism fails to engage in such analyses. Taking corporate crime, or, more generally, white-collar crime, more seriously requires a modification of realism's conceptual categories and a broadening of its field of interest. For example, as we will see, it is possible to adapt some of its research methods to explore aspects of 'commercial crime.'

The Problem of White-Collar and Commercial Crime

When it comes to white-collar crime a variety of problems of conceptualization and measurement exist. Questions can be raised about whether one is dealing with crimes, illegalities, or subjectively defined antisocial conduct. Distinctions can be drawn between white-collar and corporate crime, and occupational and organizational crime (Coleman 1989). Patterns of victimization vary by who is victimized and how. It is often difficult to know if someone has been victimized and, if so, who is responsible. Have prices and profits been elevated because of an illegal oligopolistic organization of businesses? Have people been exposed to invisible and unmonitored toxic discharges? Are workers and members of the public put at risk by the careless practices of foremen or bosun, and, if so, are such functionaries really responsible for these practices? Do the official statistics of prosecutions for consumer fraud, for health and safety violations, or for environmental pollution tell us anything worth knowing? Are there other ways of measuring white-collar crime? There are no general answers to these questions. Responses depend upon the specific uses to which one is putting the concept of white-collar crime. I want to answer some of these questions in the context of the development of the research strategy used in ICS II.

First, let us briefly address general issues characterizing the field of study. In defining 'white-collar crime' as 'a crime committed by a person of respectability and high social status in the course of his occupation,' Sutherland (1949: 7) challenged the view that the criminal was typically working class. Powerful 'business and professional men' also routinely commit crimes. Criminal acts are not restricted to those dealt with in criminal courts. A crime exists when there is a 'legal description of [the] act as socially injurious and legal provision of a penalty for the act' (Sutherland 1945, cited in Geis 1968: 354). Many laws enforced by administrative bodies through the civil courts also regulate actions which cause injuries to specific individuals or undermine social institutions, and they also routinely impose punitive sanctions. Moreover, it is not true that such acts are merely 'technical violations and involve no moral culpability'; in fact they are 'distributed along a continuum in which the *mala in se* are at one extreme and the *mala prohibita* at the other' (ibid.: 363). The content of laws and such legal distinctions are themselves social products (ibid.; Palmer 1976).

Contra Sutherland, Tappan (1947) argued for a restrictive definition of crime and criminology: 'Crime is an intentional act in violation of the criminal law (statutory and case law) committed without defense or excuse, and penalized by the state as a felony or misdemeanor. In studying the offender there can be no presumption that arrested, arraigned, indicted, or prosecuted persons are criminals unless they also be held guilty beyond a reasonable doubt of a particular offense (cited in Geis 1968: 370). He elaborates his argument with a particularly telling rhetorical question:

Who should be considered the white-collar criminal? Is it the merchant who, out of greed, business acumen, or competitive motivations, breaches a trust with his consumer by 'puffing his wares' beyond their merits, by pricing them beyond their value, or by ordinary advertising? Is it he who breaks trust with his employees in order to keep wages down, refusing to permit labor organization or to bargain collectively, and who is found guilty by a labor relations board of an unfair labor practice? May it be the white-collar worker who breaches trust with his employers by inefficient performance at work, by sympathetic strike or secondary boycott? Or is it the merchandiser who violates ethics by undercutting the prices of his fellow merchants? In general these acts do not violate the criminal law. All are within the framework of normal business practice.' (Ibid.: 369)

The argument that such 'regulatory offences' are inherently different from criminal offences is not, of course, restricted to Tappan. More recently Hawkins (1984: 11) has argued that regulatory violations differ from 'traditional' or 'consensual' crimes in that the former are 'morally problematic.' For Jamieson (1985: 30) they lack 'self-evident moral blameworthiness' and for Hutter (1988: 10-11) they are characterized by 'moral ambivalence.'

Tappan was correct to criticize the looseness with which the category of criminal is sometimes extended to those who, if they were subject to the due process of the law, would not be found guilty of any offence beyond a reasonable doubt. This observation is of relevance in the area of victim studies where individual perception of criminal injury is too easily accepted as a legally adequate description of what has occurred. Nevertheless, he is only partially correct. His perspective does not logically entail the conclusion that there are no acts which, while currently unknown, would not lead to a successful prosecution if the relevant facts were known. In other words, there can be such thing as an undiscovered murder, or more generally, a 'dark figure of crime.'

In fact the law is by no means consistent about what differentiates a crime from other offences, nor about what constitutes due process (Sutherland 1945, cited in Geis, 1968: 358). Further there is a problem of how and, indeed, whether 'due process' is achieved (Blumberg 1967; Feeley 1979; McBarnett 1981). Whether they are successful professional criminals or respectable prosperous citizens, wealthy defendants are best placed to concretely realize their formal right to due process (Chapman 1968; Mann 1985). Sutherland (1945) demonstrated the contingent nature of the distinction between criminal and other offences by tracing the genealogy of the laws regulating false advertising, infringements of copyrights, labour relations, and antitrust (cited in Geis 1968: 354). More recently, Blum-West and Carter (1983: 550) have shown that many illegalities can be pursued as either crimes or torts: 'crimes against the person may also be dealt with as torts of assault, battery, and negligence. Property crimes, both theft and destruction of property, may be pursued in civil suits charging trespass. Libel may be both a criminal and a civil offense. Fraud and crimes of false pretense may also be remedied through the tort of deception. Even acts of embezzlement can be heard under civil suits of wrongful conversion.' Maiming and killing at work *could* easily be defined as offences under the Canadian Criminal Code (Glasbeek and Rowland 1979). In Britain, health and safety violations already come under the Criminal Code and this is one of the areas where, as in the United States, issues concerning corporate homicide are beginning to be recognized (Coleman 1989). Further, the same logic used in the criminalization of British road traffic offences *could* be applied to British health and safety offences (Pearce and Tombs 1990). In all of these areas, incidentally, as in much consumer legislation involving criminal law, many offences are based upon strict liability. This is also true of much private law, particularly in relationship to consumer affairs, and hence, yet another alleged distinction between criminal and other kinds of offences can be seen not to hold.

At this point there are two different ways of proceeding. One strategy is to argue that most or all illegalities should be treated as crimes. Doing so could pre-empt the argument put forward by the powerful that their illegalities are merely 'regulatory offences,' merely *mala prohibita*. The other strategy is to argue that crimes should be viewed merely as illegalities subject to specific administrative procedures, but which, like all such procedures, have important effects. Under British legislation companies are tried in the criminal courts for health and safety offences – if they are indicted for specific violations the Crown must demonstrate both a *mens rea* and an *actus reus*, but if a company is charged with failing to discharge its general duties the burden falls on the company, as defendant, to demonstrate that it has fulfilled them, but only on the balance of probabilities.

The distinction between different kinds of illegalities has consequences. It *matters* ideologically whether something is defined as a crime or a civil offence. It matters practically what penalties are applied. It matters procedurally, as we have seen, but it also matters in that any changes in procedure tend to be generalized to other kinds of offences. This problem arises with Box's (1987) suggestion that jury trials should be abandoned and the rule of evidence changed for certain corporate crimes. (Incidentally, Glasbeek and Rowland [1979] specifically identify this problem.)

Sutherland did not go far enough – not just state-initiated actions but any kind of demonstrable wrongs should be treated as if they are crimes. Any of them, if *generalized*, would undermine community. We should focus upon 'illegalities' – i.e., actionable infringements on the right of others (singly or collectively) or failure to perform one's duties. We should move from criminology to the study of the sociology of law.

But what is law? Is it the command of the sovereign? Is it the codification of the values backed by sanction of the community? Is it a system of rules produced in a rule-guided way and backed by a sovereign, itself bound by rules, as Hart

(1961) argues? Or is it equivalent to what the state enunciates as law and claims governs its own conduct, although in fact only certain aspects of its activity are rule-governed or constrained by the rule of law. In other words, as Pashukhanis (1978) argues, has the state a dual logic or hidden agenda – one involved with the reproduction of class relations and class inequalities, sometimes secured lawfully and sometimes unlawfully?

We can bracket away some of these issues if we use the definition proffered by Roger Cotterell (1984: 45): 'Law is a body of doctrine – social rules importing certain cognitive and evaluative principles and concepts.' Law requires an institutional base within the state, a body of lawyers, a mechanism for the closure of meaning. It defines what is lawful conduct – it prohibits, enjoins, and facilitates behaviours; it can constitute entities, such as a corporation, as a legal person; it can empower. It requires a sanctioning apparatus to achieve all of these goals. Thus legal regulations can command, constitute, and empower, but they are always backed up by sanctions (Pearce 1989). Law in turn must be understood as itself requiring explanation. Very often, the offence calls forth the law, but, of course, it may not.

The advantage, in relation to ICS II, of making a strategic decision to call such illegalities crimes is clear. While some of the illegalities studied are crimes by any definition – they involve fraud and theft – others are less straightforward. Some offences are covered by the Health and Safety at Work Act, 1974, and its regulations, and yet others are covered by such acts as the Housing Act, 1961; Protection from Eviction Act, 1977; Trade Descriptions Act, 1968; Sale of Goods Act, 1979; and Supply of Goods and Services Act, 1982; and by the common law.

The term white-collar crime is itself problematic. It refers to quite heterogeneous actions and situations of different relations of power between criminals and their victims (Sutherland 1940, cited in Geis 1968: 48). The victims *vary* – workers, consumers, other businesses, one's own business, a business's shareholders, and so forth. The *consequences* of the illegality vary – they may be trivial or may damage life and limb. The *modus operandi* varies – an illegality may be undertaken alone, or in concert. The goal varies – it may be *primarily* for personal gain or in the interest of an organization. The capacity to avoid detection and responsibility varies, as do the consequences of detection.

One solution has been to redefine such crimes as 'economic crimes' (Edelhertz 1970), a category which is so wide that it includes both those who run Medicaid scams and those who cheat on social security. A more adequate and useful redefinition is that provided by Laureen Snider's (1988) concept of 'commercial crime.' Such crime involves a 'violation of the law committed by a person or group of persons of an otherwise respected and legitimate occupation or financial activity' (p. 232). The activities of companies, shopkeepers, and tradespeople would be included in this definition.

Let us then turn to the more general question of measuring commercial crime. One strategy is to make use of the official statistics. In the case of health and safety violations, for example, it is now possible in Britain to obtain information on the number of successful and unsuccessful prosecutions, and on improvement and prohibition notices. Nevertheless, what usually remains missing is any record of the number of observed offences – even if not formally acted upon – how these are distributed, and attempts to assess their likely prevalence in industry as a whole. One of the rare exceptions is Carson's early work (1970) in which he found that every one of the two hundred firms he visited in the course of his research violated health and safety laws on average eighteen times and at least twice. It is also necessary to estimate the broader 'dark figure' of these crimes. One method developed by the British Factory Inspectorate is to investigate the circumstances surrounding fatalities and then to generalize from these for the industrial sector as a whole. As a result, in their reports over a number of years, they have been able to state quite categorically that, since it routinely failed to fulfil its somewhat weak, statutory duties to employees, *management* bears legal responsibility for over 60 per cent of deaths in general manufacturing, the chemical industry, farming, and the construction industry (Pearce and Tombs 1992). It is useful and legitimate, then, to view accident rates and, particularly, fatalities as, indices, or non-obtrusive measures, of the degree of compliance and non-compliance with the law. In the ICS II we asked individuals about (non-fatal) accidents at work and also whether any remedial measures had been taken subsequently at the workplace. We also asked more general questions on what was done at a person's workplace to deal with safety. I should add here that there exist a range of other non-obtrusive measures which can be used to measure victimization. In the case of pollution, for example, it is often possible and not necessarily prohibitively expensive to independently monitor toxic discharges. It is also possible to use a combination of public records and epidemiological information to estimate the effects of exposure to toxic substances, regardless of whether such exposure is exposure legal or illegal.

If we turn to consumer affairs we find a somewhat similar situation. In their prosecutorial role, consumer-protection department officers make use of computer listings of all relevant offences in the UK under such categories as 'illegal trading practices.' Such listings, then, are a potential source of information on prosecutions and convictions. The agencies uncover a significant amount of illegalities. While Cranston (1979) found that the majority of prosecutions by consumer agencies are the result of complaints, agency personnel still proactively seek out offenders and, by the very public patrolling of shops and other businesses, try to deter other potential offenders (Hutter 1986), particularly in instances of violations of environmental health standards and the accuracy of weights and measures. Such inspections reveal many dangerous and legally sanctionable situations – for example, the unhygienic state of many restaurants – about which the consumer is unlikely to have much knowledge (McLaughlin 1989). But their effectiveness is limited by three major factors: first, like most inspectorates they are understaffed; second, they tend to work with a compliance orientation (Hutter 1988); third, while it gives them considerable powers, the legal framework in which they work is often not facilitating enough (Cranston 1985).

In addition to the activities of these enforcement agencies, motoring and other consumer organizations and newspapers have played a key role in uncovering various consumer frauds, e.g., the incompetent work of many garages which has revealed so many of their proprietors to be knaves or fools (Leonard and Weber 1970). These exposés could not rely upon the unaided activities of individual consumers, although many certainly complain about auto repairs (Cranston 1985: 38). In order to get a more complete picture, such investigative techniques need to be supplemented by victimization surveys. The ICS II showed, for example, that motor vehicle owners were significantly overrepresented among those dissatisfied with goods and services (30 per cent of those who owned motor vehicles, compared to 22 per cent of those who did not). More generally, as we will see, it uncovered a high level of infractions which never come to the notice of any of these organizations. It is essential that victimization studies be extended to include the crimes of the respectable. It is of no little significance that in a major recent British collection of writings, *Victims of Crime: A New Deal?* (Maguire and Pointing 1988), there was no discussion of corporate or commercial crime. The ICS II has begun the task of addressing this area of crime.

The Second Islington Crime Survey and Commercial Crime

The ICS II, conducted in 1988, involved a target sample of 2,160 households, with respondents aged sixteen years and over. In all, 1,621 questionnaires were completed, 76.5 per cent of the target sample. A subset of 889 individuals was asked a series of questions concerning commercial crime, including questions about workplace safety, unlawful trading practices, and the victimization of housing tenants.[3] All reported incidents occurred in the year immediately preceding the survey.

In Britain every year some 600 people are killed, and some 12,000 seriously injured because of accidents at work. In the period from 1987 to 1988, the non-fatal accident rate was just over 90 per 100,000 workers (*Observer*, 6 May 1990).

Moreover, after a long period of decline in the numbers injured at work in Britain, the 1980s have seen dramatic increases in major injuries in certain industrial sectors (HSE 1987). About 750 people die each year from occupational diseases, though a royal commission has estimated that prescribed occupationally related illnesses may account for just 20 per cent of actual occupational-related illness (Royal Commission on Civil Liability 1978). Trades unions have estimated that 20,000 people die each year partly as a result of work-related ill-health (Work Hazards Group 1987). Employers have a general statutory duty to take all reasonably practicable measures to ensure the safety of their work force, and in addition, there are more specific obligations. We were interested in uncovering how dangerous were our respondents' workplaces and how committed were their employers to safety at work. Fifty-eight per cent of respondents had been in paid employment during the previous twelve months. Of those individuals who had worked during the previous twelve months, 5 per cent had been injured in an accident there. At least half of these accidents were reportable under the 1985 Reporting of Injuries, Diseases and Dangerous Occurrences Regulations (RIDDOR). This translates into an accident rate per 100,000 workers nearly 30 times the national average.

This high accident rate may be related to the number of respondents who work in the garment trade or in construction – at that time there was no shortage of either kind of work in or around Islington. Both small textile firms and small construction firms are notorious for their poor safety practices and, particularly in the case of the latter, for their high accident rate. Thus, in a recent proactive initiative on small textile firms, the factory inspectorate issued enforcement notices at a rate of 7 per cent of visits (the average is 0.03 per cent of visits) and took out prosecutions on 0.7 per cent of visits (as opposed to the average of 0.005 per cent of visits); 191 of the 300 premises inspected were not even registered (*Health and Safety at Work*, April 1985). Similarly, in summer 1987, the inspectorate concentrated on construction sites. The result of inspecting the work of about 4,500 contractors was 868 prohibition notices; thus work on approximately one in five building sites visited had to be stopped (*Occupational Safety and Health*, December 1987). In a 1987 survey of work conditions in Islington, it was found that, of the population in full- or part-time work within the borough, a mean of 18 per cent (varying between 7 and 28 per cent) experienced bad working conditions. Such conditions were defined as a work environment where three or more of the following were experienced: dust, polluted air, moisture or dampness, noise, vibration, heavy lifting, high temperature, low temperature, bad lifting, unguarded machines (MORI 1987).

In a majority (56 per cent) of the cases where accidents had occurred, our respondents believed that their employers had taken no measures to see that such accidents did not happen again. As far as respondents knew, in 34 per cent of places where they worked there was no safety representative, and in 49 per cent no safety committee. Establishments with five or more employees are required by law to have a safety plan, entailing, but by no means restricted to, the display of safety information. Yet, in some 14 per cent of such workplaces, no safety information was displayed. These figures are interesting because they show that many serious accidents go unrecorded and that a significant minority of employers do not even show a gestural concern for safety. By contrast, we found that the more that safety is taken seriously in the workplace, the less likely are accidents. Those workplaces that had safety representatives or safety committees, and/or displayed safety information were all significantly less likely to have accidents than were those who showed no such concern (2.8 versus 7.0 per cent, 2.9 versus 6.2 per cent, and 3.8 versus 7.3 per cent, respectively). It is of no little interest that 79 per cent of respondents agreed strongly with the view that the public have a right to know all information about health and safety violations by individual companies.[4]

Victimization of Individuals as Consumers

To place commercial crime in perspective, it is useful to look at the victimization figures generated by the survey for some conventional crimes. Six per cent of respondents had their houses broken into or burglarized; 4 per cent had a vehicle stolen (anything from a car to a bicycle); 6 per cent had something stolen from their vehicle; 9 per cent had their vehicle deliberately damaged; 6 per cent suffered theft or attempted theft from the person; 7 per cent had been assaulted; 3 per cent had been sexually assaulted. Now, let us turn to our respondents' experiences as consumers.

The Consumer Credit Act (1974) was passed, in part, because of an awareness that consumers were often coerced into making transactions on credit by sales pressure when they were not clear on the terms of the arrangement and when they might not be able to undertake repayment responsibilities (Cranston 1985: 195). Recently, accompanying the ever-increasing pressure to consume, there has been a credit explosion. Some individuals are both deemed credit worthy and are able in practice to pay their debts. Others were never seen to be credit worthy or, if they were, soon ran up crippling debts. Such individuals, no doubt, were included in the twenty-two respondents, who borrowed money or arranged credit with a moneylender other than a building society, a bank, or a credit card company. In the transactions involving these twenty-two people, eleven separate violations of the act were identified. This bears out the suspicion of the local consumer protection agency that these kinds of credit arrangements are routinely exploitative.

Let us turn to some other consumer offences. Nine per cent of respondents believed that they had been given misleading information about goods or services. As a result, 45 per cent of these complained, and of these 49 per cent received some kind of compensation. Nineteen per cent of respondents believed that they had been deliberately overcharged for goods or services. Of these, 68 per cent complained, of whom 67 per cent received some kind of compensation. Twenty-five per cent believed that they had paid for goods or work which turned out to be defective. (Of these, 74 per cent complained, of whom 72 per cent received some kind of compensation.) In examining these figures, it is important to be clear that all reported incidents involved crimes, regulatory offences, or actionable deeds. Research in the United States in the 1960s reported a victimization rate of 121 per 10,000 persons for consumer fraud (Geis 1973: 100), and, although many of the cases reported here would not be consumer fraud, strictly defined, it seems unlikely that only one in fifty would fulfil such criteria. It would appear that the estimates of this kind of victimization constructed by the ICS II are much higher than those constructed by the US study.

These figures are more in line with, but defined in a somewhat more legalistic way and span a shorter time period than, McGuire and Edelhertz's research (1980) on the consumer abuse of the elderly. In surveys in 1977 and 1978, they found evidence of widespread consumer abuse in the preceding two years. In Flint, Michigan, 35 per cent and in Seattle, Washington, 55 per cent of respondents had been victimized. Whereas victimization patterns seemed to be unaffected by age, older people (55 and older) were significantly less likely to complain to consumer organizations than were other age groups. Our findings are somewhat different: virtually no one in our sample, whatever his or her age, complained to consumer organizations; in the three major areas of consumer abuse that we explored, the elderly consistently had the lowest victimization rates. If, as Edelhertz (1970) points out, poverty is the greatest prophylactic against consumer fraud, then it seems likely that it is this, rather than superior skills and resources, that could explain such relatively low victimization rates.

More comparable to McGuire and Edelhertz's work are our data on the experience of those in rental accommodation. Nationally, 40 per cent of people live in rental accommodation, compared to 66 per cent of our sample who had done so at some time during the preceding twelve months. We found some evidence of criminal activities by landlords – harassment, illegal evictions, unlawfully keeping deposits – but all of these together affected approximately only 3 per cent of those paying rent. But, the major and massive complaint was the failure of landlords to undertake essential repairs. Although this was not always a legally actionable offence, it certainly made life unnecessarily difficult for many people living in Islington. Seventy-two per cent of tenants were or had been in local-authority accommodation and 25 per cent of these complained that the local authority had failed to carry out essential repairs; 19 per cent rented from private landlords, and of these 22 per cent were similarly dissatisfied; 13 per cent were in housing co-ops, and 21 per cent of these were similarly dissatisfied.[5] In all three cases, inefficiency must have played some role, but so did a shortage of funds. In the case of the council, this was a direct result of central government policies. Three years earlier, in 1985, 'public expenditure restrictions' had already 'resulted in 84 per cent of LA houses, in England alone, requiring repairs averaging £4,900 each' (Hudson and Williams 1989: 72). There is no reason to believe that the situation changed for the better in the subsequent three years. When placed in context, then, Islington Council was relatively efficient in repairing its housing stock. In the case of the co-ops – and, no doubt, for some landlords – this poor performance was related, in part, to high London property prices. Undoubtedly, too, some landlords were simply making very high profits by cutting back on maintenance costs. In all cases, though, there is clear evidence of a failure of housing policies and the victimization of many individuals and families. Where the responsibility lies for this is, of course, contentious, but the policies of the central government have clearly played an important role. Here is clear evidence of the failure of housing policies and of the victimization of many individuals and families.

Policing Consumer Offences

In all of the offences that we examined, few people consulted the police, consumer protection services, citizens' advice bureaux, or lawyers. This raises intriguing questions about the way that the law works. Does it mean that commercial relations are self-adjusting? To the extent that this is true is it because of goodwill? This seems unlikely – particularly in a society in which the maxim *caveat emptor* holds such sway. But, enlightened self-interest may well play a role in the generally accommodating reaction to complaints. After all, the continued custom of a disgruntled person is made more likely if his or her complaints are treated with consideration. Some businesses build their reputation, in part, on their customer service. Furthermore, consumer complaints are used by some retailers and producers to monitor quality control and as a way of assessing design adequacy (Cranston 1985). But, and this is a very important qualification, most of these transactions took place in the anonymous market-places of a large city. There is relatively little interdependence between suppliers and consumers.

In fact, the reaction is far more likely to be conciliatory if the complaint of the customer is backed up by potential legal sanctions and by the knowledge that there are different forms of agencies that can be called upon if litigation were to take place. This situation is particularly telling if other businesses are known to be subject to similar constraints (Pearce 1990). Ross Cranston (1985) has provided a detailed and persuasive argument that the more the legal framework furthers the interests of consumers – by imposing duties which constrain the suppliers of goods and services and by assigning rights which empower the consumer – the better service they will receive. Law, after all, has a number of different functions – it can sanction, empower, and constitute (Pearce 1989).

Unemployment

The ICS II also uncovered evidence of considerable *concern about* unemployment and considerable *evidence of* unemployment, particularly among young people, Black people, and males. Of 1,621 respondents, unemployment was seen as one of the most serious problems in the borough, in terms of race, by 59 per cent of Blacks and by 38 per cent of Whites; in terms of gender, by 42 per cent of men and by 37 per cent of women; and in terms of age group, by 45 per cent 16-44, 44 per cent 25-44, and 35 per cent over 45.

Only 48 per cent of the sample were in full-time employment. Many were in part-time work (10 per cent), in full-time higher education (4 per cent), or receiving pensions (18 per cent), unemployment or social security benefits. All except those in full-time employment, and even some of these, were quite likely to live in poverty. Further, we can, somewhat speculatively, estimate unemployment rates by treating as potential workers those on social security or unemployment benefit (15 per cent) or on government job training/creation schemes (1 per cent). The circumstances of this last group, after all, represent a form of concealed unemployment (actually there were only seven people on such schemes in the whole survey), which means excluding all those who said that they were in full-time or part-time work (although the latter might prefer a full-time job), in full-time education, or receiving a pension. It is true that some people may not be able to work because they are sick, but some of them would be receiving a disability pension. Furthermore, young people, age sixteen to eighteen, are no longer eligible for any form of state benefit. Some people, particularly women, who are more likely to be responsible for care of children than are men, may be involved in child care. Hence, we tend to view the figures for men as providing a better estimate of unemployment. The figures, then, for young men under the age of thirty-five are quite stunning (see table 16.1). And this was true, note, at the height of the recent 'Thatcher boom.'

Although there is consensus on little else, and although there is no consensus on why it is so, all who write about crime accept a correlation between a relatively high participation in street crime and being male, sixteen to twenty-four years of

TABLE 16.1

Estimated unemployment rates in per cent by age

	16-24	25-34	35-44	45-54	55-64
Women	22	35	25	59	50
Men	24	34	20	22	23
White men	19	38	19	20	24
Black men	37	21	21	25	20

age, unemployed, and living in large cities. Yet these figures suggest that just such a criminogenic population has been produced in Islington. That this is so and why, has, in my view, been most convincingly explored by Box (1987) and how meaningful employment leads to a reduction in the tendency to engage in these crimes has been well documented by Currie (1985). It is to the more general crime picture that we now return.

Crime and Victimization

Eighty-one per cent of respondents viewed crime as a major problem, 78 per cent mentioned vandalism, 76 per cent dirty streets, 74 per cent unemployment, and 67 per cent poor housing. By 'crime,' respondents meant various forms of theft and different kinds of interpersonal violence, including sexual assaults on women and children. They thought that the police should spend more time dealing with these offences. They did not prioritize white-collar crime. However, the questions asked in the survey about what the police's priorities should be use only company fraud and embezzlement (ranked 13) and cheating tradesmen and shopkeepers (ranked 16) as examples of white-collar crime. Not mentioned are those guilty of the kinds of safety violations that lead to disasters. In the aftermath of the Zeebrugge disaster and the King's Cross fire, there might have been quite different results if they had. After all, when, in another part of the survey, questions were asked about the public right to know about 'regulatory issues,' 88 per cent strongly endorsed the view that the public had a right to know all evidence presented at public enquiries relating to public disasters, and King's Cross was cited as an example.[6]

Further analysis of the data shows that people in Islington are criminally victimized to a very considerable degree – indeed, even more than they realize. During the survey year, 29 per cent of respondents had been victims of at least one of the six conventional criminal offences (their house broken into or burglarized; their vehicle stolen; something stolen from their vehicle; their vehicle deliberately damaged; theft or attempted theft from the person; assault). Twenty-seven per cent of this group (8 per cent of the overall sample) experienced multiple victimizations. Although their overall victimization rate was similar, women differed from men in that, whereas 21 per cent of the victimized men were multiple victims (5 per cent of the overall sample), 32 per cent of victimized women were multiple victims (9 per cent of the overall sample). Again, the 3 per cent of the sample who had been sexually assaulted were almost exclusively women. Indeed, 19 per cent of women aged sixteen to twenty-four had been sexually assaulted.

At least 39 per cent of the overall sample suffered from deliberate overcharging or faulty goods and services and/or their misrepresentation, and 28 per cent of these were multiple victims (11 per cent of the overall sample). The victimization of individuals as consumers, tenants (with 24 per cent suffering from inadequate repairs), and workers (with 30 times the average national accident rate) was also extensive.

If we examine the overall victimization pattern for the six street crimes, sexual assault, and the three main commercial crimes, the figures become even more horrifying. Fifty-five per cent of individuals were criminally victimized in one way or another, and 42 per cent of these (22 per cent of the overall sample) were multiple victims. This was all in one year.

The figures on criminal victimization, on unemployment, on inadequate housing conditions – and, we might add, on poor local transport, dirty streets, and so on – suggest a very Hobbesian world indeed. To, undoubtedly, overdramatize, Islington seems like a large-scale version of Hazel Genn's (1988) 'Bleak House,' a tower block on a run-down housing estate in North London. There social deprivation is so general and so pervasively subversive of any genuine community that everybody seems to be a victim of wider social forces, and many of each other's predatory activities. What makes this analogy even more telling is the extent to which so many people are not simply subject to the predatory illegal activities of others, but also face inadequate housing conditions and experience poverty and the reality or threat of unemployment.

The Impact of Crime and Other Offences

At this point I should make clear that, as I was writing this essay, and as I began to engage in a more detailed analysis of the data generated by the crime survey, I was stunned by what it revealed about both the level of individual deprivation and the extent to which this inner-city environment has become increasingly inhospitable. Crime and a very rational fear of crime play a very important role in downgrading the quality of people's lives and in severely restricting their options. In the recently published general summary of the ICS II it becomes clear how the lives of women in particular are affected. I underestimated the degree to which street crime is a massive problem. Yet also, and to an extraordinary and generally unrecognized degree, we have shown that the quality of life is also under attack from commercial crime. And we have shown this despite the fact that, in the confines of this survey, it was not possible to investigate many examples of the illegal and antisocial conduct engaged in by commercial enterprises. For example, we did not explore such dangerous and illegal practices as the sale of unhealthy food, or air pollution, although we did discover that the latter was of serious concern to many respondents (it ranked sixth, after poor housing, as a neighbourhood problem). The survey pointed to the concern of individuals with the state of public transportation and the health service. The survey shows that Islington has become, in many ways, a dangerous and unpleasant place to live, and it is by no means the most deprived London borough. What, then must be the quality of life in Hackney or Harringey?

By definition, commercial crimes are not committed by people while they are unemployed. They are offences committed by respectable people who supply goods and services to the public. They may be self-employed tradespeople, small shopkeepers, the owners or managers of businesses or their employees. Undoubtedly some of the crimes are occupational crimes, committed exclusively for the personal gain of individuals. Others will be organizational crimes that are facilitated by or encouraged by the 'dominant coalition' within an organization and benefit it as well as the individual (Ellis 1987; Coleman 1989). One example, given by two consumer protection officers whom I interviewed, was a large retailing butcher's chain. By using their powers of inspection on a number of occasions these officers, and others, had established that, in a number of its branches, short weight had been often given for meat. True, they did not prosecute counter hands, but rather local managers. Yet, they did so believing that the real responsibility lay with the senior management of this chain. The company was thought to routinely employ relatively immature local managers and to pay them low wages, but to give them large mortgages at a preferential rate (in North American terms, the infamous 'golden handcuffs'). They were expected to make high profits in each shop whatever the commercial environment in which it operated. If this proved difficult, the heavily mortgaged managers interfered with the shop scales, encouraged in the knowledge that senior management did not regularly check them. Because of the 1972 Tesco judgment (*Tesco Supermarkets Ltd.* v. *Nattrass*) it is both easy to prosecute the manager and very difficult to bring a case against the company or its senior executives. A classic criminogenic organizational structure, with senior management engaging in willful blindness (Wilson 1979), then, is positively encouraged by a legal framework which only punishes more junior employees (Cranston 1985: 271). Even some relatively prosperous individuals may, on occasion, be subject to strong pressures to engage in criminal acts – calling them 'egoistic' may have only a limited explanatory value (Box 1987).

If our findings do not allow us to discriminate between these different kinds of acts, they do show that the crimes of the respectable are commonplace. They also show some of the dangers of colluding in the scapegoating of particular kinds of individuals as the source of criminal conduct. The term 'scapegoating' is used here in a particular sense. It is not that the innocent are forced to bear the burden of everybody's misdeeds, but, rather, that those who are really only as guilty as many others are treated as if they are the only guilty ones (Girard 1977, 1989). Furthermore, it is generally assumed that their victims are the very embodiment of innocence. Yet, how many of those who have been burglarized have approved of unsafe working practices, short-changed others, completed shoddy repairs, or routinely driven when they are drunk? And this is equally true of many of those who condemn the street criminal and weep over his or her victim. This is not a plea to ignore the plight of the victim, but to stop reserving compassion for the victim and vindictiveness for the criminal. Most of us have been, and are, both victim and criminal. Many working-class people understand this very well. They want criminals to be caught, but they do not want their punishment to be permanently disabling. They see the need to establish the relationship between 'crime, shame and reintegration,' to borrow the title of John Braithwaite's recent (1989) book.

We must accept that a certain level of crime is inevitable; all but the saintly have engaged in criminal or victimizing activities. To be able to follow a rule is to be able to deviate from it, and we all have occasions when it makes compelling sense to violate the law (Durkheim 1938; Pearce 1987). But the specific level of crime is an expression not so much of human capacities and random exigencies as of the ways in which societies are organized. In that sense, for any set of social conditions there is a normal level of crime. But to accept this Durkheimian proposition is not to counsel inaction. Rather, it means that if we wish to change the level of crime it is imperative to change those social conditions. Currently, in Britain, the dominant ideology is egoistic, inequalities are increasing, and resources are distributed according to the wealth of individuals in a way that pays scant regard to the needs of the less wealthy. There has been a removal of many of the collective supports of social life. There has been a localization and ghettoization of poverty, particularly within large cities. Further, if the comments in this essay have been gender and colour blind, it is only because the findings on commercial crime show no particular pattern in relationship to men and women, Whites and Blacks. Many other inequalities, injustices, and forms of deprivation clearly do (Sim, Scraton, and Gordon 1987; Field 1989; Hudson and Williams 1989). If we wish to deal with crime, we have to deal with the variety of social conditions that generate different kinds of crime. What these are, and how we deal with them, are issues where, to some extent, I part company with left realists. This is not, however, an appropriate place to develop these arguments. I have begun to do so elsewhere (Pearce 1989; Pearce and Tombs 1992). Here, let me once again stress where left realism's strengths lie: in the empirical data it has generated on the pattern of criminal victimization and on the *modus operandi* and effectiveness of the police and on community attitudes towards both.

Conclusion

In the first part of this essay I explored the question of how best to conceptualize and measure what is loosely termed white-collar crime. I argued that it covered such heterogeneous phenomena and had been developed to make such a range of theoretical and political points that its use and development were inevitably dependent upon the pragmatic uses to which it was being put. I then addressed the problem of identifying and measuring some of the acts that came under its purview. The major focus was on health and safety violations and various ways in which consumers are victimized. This discussion provided the framework for exploring the incidence of some commercial crime in Islington and assessing its significance by comparing it to the incidence of some street crimes. It became clear that a proper understanding of its significance depended upon relating commercial crime and street crime to the many other forms of victimization experienced by the residents of this inner-London borough. Left realists have demanded that we take street crime seriously. I was forced by the brute facts uncovered while working on the data generated by the Second Islington Crime Survey to do just that. Yet it is also necessary to contextualize these in relation to other kinds of victimizers and other forms of victimization. Finally, we must make sociological sense of this phenomenon and not collapse into moralistic and individualistic positions.

I am grateful to Tom Woodhouse for his role in collecting and transmitting data, to Bob Arnold for explaining the vagaries of SPSSX, and above all to Linda Vieregge. Any errors are my responsibility alone.

Notes

1 For some exceptions see Snider (1988, 1992); Barnett (1982); Pearce and Tombs (1989, 1990, 1992).
2 For a critical commentary see Pearce (1989) and Pearce and Tombs (1992).

3 A further subset of these, 454 individuals, were asked about the public's right to know about dangers associated with industrial activity.
4 Some relatively comparable data has just been generated by the recent survey on patterns of criminal victimization in Canada (Sacco and Johnson 1990).
5 Figures for tenancies exceed 100 per cent because individuals may have been tenants of more than one kind of accommodation in the previous twelve months.
6 Also unequivocally endorsed were *complete* public access to information on food additives, 83 per cent; on chemicals added to the water supply, 85 per cent; on air pollution, 84 per cent; and on nuclear leaks, no matter how small, 87 per cent.

References

Barnett, H. 1982. 'The Production of Corporate Crime in Corporate Capitalism,' in P. Wickman and T. Dailey, eds., *White Collar and Economic Crime*, 157-170. Lexington, MA: Lexington Books
Blumberg, A. 1967. *Criminal Justice*. Chicago: Quadrangle Books
Blum-West, S., and T.J. Carter. 1983. 'Bringing White-Collar Crime Back In: An Examination of Crimes and Torts.' *Social Problems*, 30 (5): 545-554
Box, S. 1983. *Power, Crime and Mystification*. London: Tavistock
– 1987. *Recession, Crime and Punishment*. London: Tavistock
Boyd, N. 1988. *The Last Dance: Murder in Canada*. Scarborough, ON: Prentice-Hall
Braithwaite, J. 1984. *Corporate Crime in the Pharmaceutical Industry*. London: Routledge and Kegan Paul
– 1989. *Crime, Shame and Reintegration*. Cambridge: Cambridge University Press
Carson, W.G. 1970. 'White-Collar Crime and the Enforcement of Factory Legislation.' *British Journal of Criminology*, 10: 383-398
Chambliss, W. 1988. *Exploring Criminology*. New York: Macmillan
Chapman, D. 1968. *Sociology and the Stereotype of the Criminal*. London: Tavistock
Clinard, M.B., and P.C. Yeager. 1980. *Corporate Crime*. New York: Free Press
Coleman, J.W. 1989. *The Criminal Elite*. New York: St Martin's Press
Cotterell, R. 1984. *The Sociology of Law: An Introduction*. London: Butterworths
Cranston, R. 1979. *Regulating Business: Law and Consumer Agencies*. London: Macmillan
– 1985. *Consumers and the Law*. London: Butterworths
Currie, E. 1985. *Confronting Crime*. New York: Pantheon
Durkheim, E. 1938. *The Rules of Sociological Method*. New York: Free Press
Edelhertz, H. 1970. *The Nature, Impact and Prosecution of White-Collar Crime*. Washington, DC: National Institute for Law Enforcement and Criminal Justice, Department of Justice

Ellis, D. 1987. *The Wrong Stuff*. Toronto: Macmillan

Feeley, M. 1979. *The Process Is the Punishment*. New York: Russell Sage Foundation

Field, F. 1989. *Losing Out*. Oxford: Basil Blackwell

Geis, G. 1968. *White Collar Criminal: The Offender in Business and the Professions*. New York: Atherton Press

‒ 1973. 'Victimization Patterns in White Collar Crime,' in I. Drapkin and E. Viano, eds., *Victimology: A New Focus*, vol. 5: *Exploiters and Exploited*, 86-106. Lexington, MA: D.C. Heath

Genn, H. 1988. 'Multiple Victimization,' in M. Maguire and J. Pointing, eds., *Victims of Crime: A New Deal?*, 90-100. Milton Keynes: Open University Press

Gilroy, P. 1987. 'The Myth of Black Criminality,' in P. Scraton, ed., *Law, Order and the Authoritarian State*, 107-120. Milton Keynes: Open University Press

Girard, R. 1977. *Violence and the Sacred*. Baltimore, MD: Johns Hopkins University Press

‒ 1989. *The Scapegoat*. Baltimore, MD: Johns Hopkins University Press

Glasbeek, H.J., and J. Rowland. 1979. 'Are Injuring and Killing at Work Crimes.' *Osgoode Hall Law Journal*, 17: 507-594

Gorz, A. 1980. *Ecology as Politics*. London: Pluto

Hart, H.L.A. 1961. *The Concept of Law*. Oxford: Oxford University Press

Hawkins, K. 1984. *Environment and Enforcement*. Oxford: Clarendon Press

Health and Safety Executive. 1987. *Statistics 1984-5*. London: HMSO

Hudson, R., and A.M. Williams. 1989. *Britain Divided*. London: Belhaven Press

Hutter, B. 1986. 'An Inspector Calls.' *British Journal of Criminology*, 26 (2): 114-128

‒ 1988. *The Reasonable Arm of the Law?* Oxford: Clarendon Press

Jamieson, M. 1985. 'Persuasion or Punishment: The Enforcement of Health and Safety at Work Legislation by the British Factory Inspectorate.' MPhil thesis, Oxford University

Jones, T., B. MacLean, and J. Young. 1986. *The Islington Crime Survey*. Aldershot: Gower

Kinsey, R., J. Lea, and J. Young. 1986. *Losing the Fight against Crime*. Oxford: Basil Blackwell

Lea, J. 1987. 'Left Realism: A Defence.' *Contemporary Crises*, 11 (4): 357-370

Lea, J., and J. Young. 1984. *What Is to Be Done about Law and Order?* Harmondsworth: Penguin

Leonard, W.N., and M.G. Weber. 1970. 'Automakers and Dealers: A Study of Criminogenic Market Forces.' *Law and Society Review*, 4 (February): 407-424

Levi, M. 1987. *Regulating Fraud*. London: Tavistock

McBarnett, D. 1981. *Conviction*. London: Macmillan

Mcguire, M.V., and H. Edelhertz. 1980. 'Consumer Abuse of Older Americans: Victimization and Remedial Action in Two Metropolitan Areas,' in G. Geis and E. Stotland, eds., *White-Collar Crime: Theory and Research*, 226-296. Lexington, MA: Lexington Books

McLaughlin, J. 1989. 'On Patrol with the Food Police.' *New Statesman and Society*, 3 March: 28-29

Maguire, M., and J. Pointing. 1988. *Victims of Crime: A New Deal?* Milton Keynes: Open University Press

Mann, K. 1985. *Defending White-Collar Crime*. New Haven, NJ: Yale University Press

Matthews, R. 1987. 'Taking Realist Criminology Seriously.' *Contemporary Crises*, 11 (4): 371-401

MORI. 1987. *Service Provision and Living Standards in Islington*. London: MORI

Palmer, J. 1976. 'Evils Merely Prohibited.' *British Journal of Law and Society*, 3 (1): 1-16

Pashukhanis, E. 1978. *Law and Marxism*. London: Inklinks

Pearce, F. 1987. 'Review of R. Matthews and J. Young, *Confronting Crime*.' *Sociology*, 21 (3): 490-491

– 1989. *The Radical Durkheim*. London: Unwin Hyman

– 1990. '"Responsible Corporations" and Regulatory Agencies.' *The Political Quarterly*, 61 (4): 415-430

Pearce, F., and S. Tombs. 1989. 'Union Carbide, Bhopal, and the Hubris of a Capitalist Technocracy.' *Crime and Justice*, 16 (2): 116-145

– 1990. 'Ideology, Hegemony and Empiricism: Compliance Theories of Regulation.' *British Journal of Criminology*, 30 (4): 423-443

– 1992. 'Realism and Corporate Crime,' in R. Matthews and J. Young, eds., *Issues in Realist Criminology*, 70-101. London: Sage

Royal Commission on Civil Liability. 1978. *Report*. London: HMSO

Sacco, V. and H. Johnson. 1990. *Patterns of Criminal Victimization in Canada*. Ottawa: Statistics Canada

Scraton, P., ed. 1987. *Law, Order and the Authoritarian State*. Milton Keynes: Open University Press

Selwyn, N.M. 1985. *Law of Employment*. London: Butterworths

Sim, J., P. Scraton, and P. Gordon. 1987. 'Crime, the State and Critical Analysis,' in P. Scraton, ed., *Law, Order and the Authoritarian State*, 1-70. Milton Keynes: Open University Press

Smith, P.F. 1985. *Evans: The Law of Landlord and Tenant*, 2d ed. London: Butterworths

Snider, L. 1988. 'Commercial Crime,' in Vincent Sacco, ed., *Deviance: Conformity and Control in Canadian Society*, 231-283. Scarborough, ON: Prentice-Hall

– 1992. 'Models to Control Corporate Crime: Decriminalization, Recriminalization and Deterrence,' in F. Pearce and M. Woodiwiss, eds., *Global Crime Connections*, 212-239. London: Macmillan

Sutherland, E. 1940. 'White-Collar Criminality.' *American Sociological Review*, 5 (February): 1-12
- 1945. 'Is "White Collar Crime" Crime?' *American Sociological Review*, 10 (April): 132-129
- 1949. *White Collar Crime*. New York: Dryden Press
Tappan, P. 1947. 'Who Is the Criminal?' *American Sociological Review*, 12 (February): 96-102
Wilson, L. 1979. 'The Doctrine of Willful Blindness.' *University of New Brunswick Law Journal*, 28: 175-194
Work Hazards Group. 1987. *Death at Work*. London: WEA
Young, J. 'The Failure of Criminology: The Need for a Radical Realism,' in R. Matthews and J. Young, eds., *Confronting Crime*, 4-30. London: Sage
- 1987. 'The Tasks Facing a Realist Criminology.' *Contemporary Crises*, 11 (4): 337-356

17 A Program of Local Crime Survey Research for Canada

Brian D. MacLean

In developing their approach to the study of inner-city street crime, left realists proceed from the observation that the historical emergence and use of official criminal statistics to a large extent have been politically based. In the United States, the introduction of the Uniform Crime Reports (UCRs) represented a scheme employed by police managers to monitor the activities of the rank and file and to manage, to some extent, public perceptions about crime and policing (MacLean 1989; Maltz 1977; Phipps 1987). The dangers of police agencies collecting and reporting criminal statistical information were both noted and expressed by the Wickersham Committee (National Commission on Law Observance and Law Enforcement 1931), whose observations went largely unnoticed. While criminal statistics may not accurately reflect patterns of criminal victimization, the tendency in criminology has been increasingly to draw upon these statistics as measures for the frequency and distribution of crime. Such a dependency on criminal statistical indicators has resulted in theorizations which are one-sided, class biased, and correctionalist in nature (MacLean and Milovanovic 1991).

The phenomenological revolution of the 1960s, however, spearheaded an assault upon positivist-oriented criminology, while the scientific utility of criminal statistics was increasingly called into question.[1] At the same time, social constructionism argued that criminal statistics were the product of a set of definitional and institutionalized practices which provide greater insight into the processes by which the data were constructed than they did about the frequency and distribution of crime (Kitsuse and Cicourel 1963; Downes and Rock 1982/4; MacLean 1989). In response to the increasing dissatisfaction with criminal statistics, other measures of the frequency and distribution of crime have begun to emerge, the most historically important of which is the victimization survey.

In this essay, I examine both the emergence and the evolution of crime survey technology. Because this technology emerged in response to the noted limitations of criminal statistics,[2] it is necessary to assess its ability to measure crime and policing processes accurately. Left-realist surveys in Britain have been funded by local labour councils who have required sets of survey data which can be publicly defended in order to meet their political objectives (MacLean 1991). While the utility of left-realist survey data has been hotly debated, both within this volume and elsewhere, it is necessary to evaluate their usefulness in relation to data generated by other crime surveys.

The central argument advanced in this essay is that, while the victimization survey provides the potential for documenting the patterns of certain kinds of victimization, describing the relations among these patterns and other social variables, and explaining these observed relationships, the thrust of such surveys has been primarily political rather than academic. I begin by distinguishing victimology from victimization surveys. It is argued that, while they have common origins, their objectives differ, and it is the victimization survey that is of central concern here. I proceed to examine the evolution of the crime survey through three distinct phases. It is argued that the first two genres of crime survey are characterized by a number of methodological and theoretical deficiencies which the third-phase surveys must address. Because left-realist surveys can be seen as occurring within the third phase, such critique is necessary to defend their methodological basis. Finally, having reviewed the weaknesses, deficiencies, and strengths of local crime surveys advanced in earlier essays and elsewhere, I propose that the left-realist commitment to local crime survey research has important enough potential to consider adopting a program of such research in Canada. Briefly, I conclude with a proposal for such a program.

Victimology

In addressing the potential of victimization surveys to assess the impact of crime upon society, whether in terms that are crudely monetary or in terms of changed attitudes and behaviours, Sparks suggests that 'questions of this kind belong, I suppose, to "victimology" assuming (what I am personally not prepared to concede) that there really is such a science. It is in fact questionable how far "victimology" – and its political arm, the victim-compensation movement – have influenced victimization surveying. It is clear, however, that victimization surveys can provide much valuable information relevant to compensation and restitution schemes, service delivery to victims and the like' (1981: 47). Thus, for Sparks, a distinction between victimology[3] and victimization surveys is not only conceptually important but necessary, since the they have quite different objectives. Nevertheless, these objectives are not incompatible, and Sparks

(1981) suggests that the surveys can provide some direction to victimology, although it is doubtful if such a relation is reciprocal. For purposes of this essay, such a distinction will be made between victimology and victimization surveys, despite their common origins. The former has sought to build a scientific discipline with the crime victim as its object (Birkbeck 1983; Schneider 1975) and 'although victimology began by studying all victims, most of its output and history has stressed crime victims. Thus it has mostly defined itself scientifically as the study of crime victims. Despite those boundaries, it has still considered many issues that criminology has traditionally ignored' (Elias 1986: 21).

Victimology encompasses a wide range of activities and research methods which seek to build both an empirical description of victimization processes and a conceptual framework for explaining patterns which emerge from that description. Victimological research might involve ethnographic accounts of victims' experiences (Schecter 1982) or of the development of state agencies charged with the responsibility of policy-oriented research on crime victims (Rock 1986).[4] Some victimology research evaluates services provided for victims of crime by victim support schemes (Maguire and Corbett 1987).[5] There has been a considerable amount of research which identifies victims of particular kinds of crimes from police records and later interviews the victims on a variety of issues (Evans and Leger 1979; Sparks 1976).[6] For example, Chambers and Millar (1984) examined the way in which victims of rape were affected by police investigations, while Wolfgang (1958) used police records to establish the degree of affiliation between the homicide victim and offender. Still another direction of research has been the examination of the relation between fear of crime and victimization for populations such as the elderly (Brillon 1987) and women (Dutton and Kennedy 1987; Gordon and Riger 1979; Hanmer and Saunders 1984; Horton and Kennedy 1985; Smith 1990, 1989, 1987; Stanko 1983).

Despite its relatively recent debut, victimology has rapidly been gaining momentum; however, while the scope of victimological research is wide and varied, the predominant thrust has been to discover the degree to which the victim has precipitated his or her misfortune (Phipps 1987). In his pioneering work *The Criminal and His Victim*, Von Hentig (1948) advances the theory that victims play a role in their own plight:

Experience tells us that ... the relationships between perpetrator and victim are much more intricate than the rough distinctions of criminal law. Here are two human beings. As soon as they draw near to one another, male or female, young or old, rich or poor, ugly or attractive – a wide range of interactions, repulsions as well as attractions, is set in motion. What the law does is to watch the one who acts and the one who is acted upon.

By this external criterion, subject and object, a perpetrator and a victim are distinguished. In sociological and psychological quality the situation may be completely different. It may happen that the two distinct categories merge. There are cases in which they are reversed and in the long chain of causative forces the victim assumes the role of determinant. (1948: 383-384)

The relationship which Von Hentig addresses above has been referred to as 'The Duet Frame of Crime' (Sparks 1982: 19), and in all fairness to Von Hentig, his work should not be viewed as crude victim-precipitation theory. Rather, the empirical evidence for his theoretical formulation consisted of a wide variety of data which illustrated that victims and perpetrators were often familiar with each other. His work is both sociological and dynamic because he was interested in exploring the relationship between victim and offender as a factor in determining crime. On that basis, most would argue that his contribution to criminology cannot be denied (Schafer 1968).

Despite Von Hentig's complexity of thought, numerous writers have since vulgarized his ideas, and have attempted to classify victims into typologies which are based upon the degree to which they precipitate their own misfortune.[7] For example, Wolfgang (1958), Sellin and Wolfgang (1964), Fattah (1967), Reckless, (1967), Schafer (1968), and Silverman (1974) have produced typologies which distinguish different kinds of victims. However, such conceptions of the victim are one-sided in nature, risking degeneration into theories that 'blame the victim' (Ryan 1976) or victim precipitation. For this reason, a number of writers highlight the need for a victimology which is more theoretically sophisticated (Phipps 1986; Young 1986), attentive to the empirical basis for the needs of victims without being paternalistic (Maguire 1984a), and non-opportunistic politically (Elias 1986).

Victimization Surveys

In contrast to the discipline of victimology, victimization surveys were conceived as a method for estimating the frequency and distribution of unreported crime (Bottomley and Pease 1986; Chambers 1984; Hood and Sparks 1970; Hough and Mayhew 1983; O'Brien 1985; Maguire 1984b; MacLean 1989, 1991; Sparks 1982). If victimology is a recent phenomenon, the victimization survey is even more so. During the 1960s, positivist criminology was under attack, including its main empirical base – official crime data. It is not surprising, then, that positivistic criminologists seized the opportunity in the suggestion offered by Inkeri Anttila in 1964 that the general population could be an untapped store of information which might be used to estimate the frequency and distribution of crime. Clearly, the development of victimization surveys offered an opportunity for positivist criminology to recover from the interactionist assault which threatened its domination of the discipline. The recognition of such a 'window of opportunity' is reflected in the rapid evolution of the victimization survey. This evolution can be characterized as embracing three discrete moments, outlined briefly below.

First-Generation Surveys

The aim of the first-generation surveys was twofold. While surveys would initially produce an estimate of the extent of unrecorded crime, they would also serve as exploratory studies through which the technology might be refined. For example, because of the measured infrequency of serious crime, and in the absence of any reliable estimates for the 'dark figure' of unreported crime, it would be necessary to establish from these surveys what proportion of crime remains unreported so that effective sampling strategies could be developed for future research. Skogan describes the problem as follows:

The infrequency of serious crime in the general population has important consequences for victimization surveys. This was a major concern when the Crime Commission first considered conducting a victimization survey. Official statistics for the mid 1960s suggested, for example, that there were 180 robberies of all kinds ... for every 100,000 persons in the population. Given, the apparently low frequency of such incidents, very large samples would be required ... if victimization rates are relatively low, sampling error may lead to very substantial variations in estimates of those rates ... Those who favoured the surveys were convinced that the 'dark figure' of unreported crime was large enough that a national sample of 10,000 households would uncover enough victims for analysis. The truth lay somewhere in between. (1981: 2)

Thus, these surveys were exploratory in nature, with the objectives of estimating unreported crime, both in terms of refining measures and for informing methodological questions in future research. While most of these studies were carried out in the United States, exploratory studies relevant to left-realist surveys were also conducted in England.

United States. While Anttila (1964) is generally credited with conducting the first victimization survey (by mail in Finland), the primary initiative for the development of victimization surveys came in the United States from the President's Commission on Law Enforcement and Administration of Justice appointed by President Johnson in 1967. This major research undertaking included a number of local victimization surveys in different US cities such as Washington, DC (Biderman et al. 1967; Reiss 1967), Boston and Chicago (Reiss 1967), and a national survey (Ennis 1967). Because these surveys were novel, the technology employed required refinement, and according to O'Brien (1985), a number of further pilot studies followed during the early 1970s. The US Bureau of the Census piloted surveys in Baltimore (1970a) and Washington, DC (1970b); the Law Enforcement Assistance Administration (LEAA) piloted surveys in San Jose (Turner 1972; Kalish 1974); Dodge and Turner (1971) piloted a survey in Cleveland and Akron; and in combination with the Quarterly Household Survey of the US Bureau of the Census, Dodge and Turner (1971) piloted a national survey (O'Brien 1985).

In his review of the findings from these studies, Sparks (1980) suggests that, while the frequency of violent crime is rare, that of unreported crime remains rather high and varies by offence. Furthermore, these surveys established that crime tended to be spatially and socially clustered rather than randomly distributed (Sparks 1982). For example, two-thirds of the reported robberies in the United States were concentrated in thirty-two cities which housed only 16 per cent of the US population (Skogan 1979). Moreover, the variation in crime frequencies *between* cities was observed to be less than the variation *within* cities (Skogan 1981), and as Skogan concludes: 'The relatively extreme spatial concentration of victims, especially victims of violent crime, presents a challenge to samplers ... If crime is clustered on the basis of demographic, economic, and physical features of individuals and neighbourhoods and is disproportionately concentrated in certain small areas, probability samples reflecting only the distribution of people in the population across space will very often miss the mark' (ibid.: 4). Thus the first-generation surveys in the United States helped to establish that the distribution of unrecorded crime had serious implications for sampling designs. If measures of unreported crime were to be accurate, it was established that sampling designs would command a high level of expenditure in terms of the sheer size necessary to capture sufficient cases of victimization for reliable estimates to be calculated. The implications of these early findings for the sampling designs of the third-generation surveys are important and are discussed below.

Britain. The first major local victimization survey[8] carried out in England included 545 in-depth interviews with residents of the three London boroughs of Hackney, Brixton, and Kensington (Sparks, Genn, and Dodd 1977). This study falls within the category of first-generation survey because 'the study is more of a study of the *measurement* of criminal victimization than of the phenomenon itself' (Phipps 1987: 344; emphasis in original).

According to Sparks (1982), some questions on victimization were included in the General Household Surveys of 1972 and 1973, and that an even earlier attempt was made by Durant, Thomas, and Willock (1972) to measure some aspects of victimization on the survey conducted by the Royal Commission on the Penal System in 1966. Nevertheless, the Sparks, Genn, and Dodd study (1977), conducted in 1973, represents the first serious attempt in England to explore systematically patterns of victimization and their implications for future research. In this study, a rate of unrecorded crime of eleven times that published in the 1972 police statistics was estimated for the crimes investigated, indicating that unreported crime was not just a North American phenomenon.[9] More importantly, however, a rigorous set of analyses were performed on these data for future design purposes. Sparks (1976) reports that, first, there were more victims of multiple victimization and more cases of non-victims than would be expected by chance for both violent and property offences. This corroborated the findings of Reynolds et al. (1973), Aromaa (1971), Wolf and Hauge (1975), and various findings from the National Crime Panel (NCP). Sparks (1976) concludes that these data suggest that *further research on the factors which propel some individuals into being victimized, while others are not, is needed.* The implications of this conclusion lead to theories of victim precipitation, so that future studies would be designed to collect as much personal information as possible from respondents.

A second analysis of these data which Sparks (1976) employed involves the use of reverse record checks to establish the degree of non-sampling error associated with memory fading and loss. The results of this procedure indicated that rather than questionnaire design or wording of questions producing a strong degree of error, 'simple memory failure, operating in a more or less random fashion among different kinds of respondent' (p. 50) had the greatest impact on error. This finding has important implications for the bounding procedures later adopted in the second-generation surveys.

Critique. In their totality, the first-generation surveys made two important contributions. First, they illustrated that only 30 to 50 per cent of the crimes they measured were recorded in the UCRs (O'Brien 1985). Second, and perhaps of greater importance, the surveys provided considerable insight into the methodological problems associated with such research (Garofalo and Hindelang 1977). Together, these two outcomes provided the incentive to pursue victimization survey research more rigorously. Researchers hoped that data derived from victimization surveys would serve to produce reliable and valid estimates of the frequency and distribution of crime. Criticisms about the weaknesses of the empirical referent for positivist criminology – police-generated crime statistics

– are now more easily rebutted, since victimization survey data are increasingly used by positivist criminologists for estimates of norm-violation rates. Statistics derived from survey data are 'closer to the crime' than police statistics. In this way the opposition expressed by the Wickersham Commission (1931) to the production of statistics by the police would be no longer valid. Finally, because this research was both funded and used politically, governments, police, and agencies of justice probably recognized that these surveys would help to bring them back into control of the debate on policing and law and order.

While the positivist nature of the new developments meant that they inherited many of the limitations characteristic of earlier research, victimization surveys differed from earlier research as well. Specifically, the new positivism moved away from crimes known to the police, focusing on the victim as the source of information about the frequency and distribution of crime. For this reason, I have applied the term 'neopositivism' to a criminology which uses crude victimization surveys as its empirical referent. However, it is probably more important to recognize that the combination of cost considerations, the repeated observation that multiple victimization was a frequent occurrence, and the need to collect as much personal information as possible to justify the expenditure practically and theoretically produced an emphasis on the individual victim. Thus, the second-generation surveys advanced victim-precipitation theory, which eclipsed the processes of law enforcement and the social construction of the social reality of crime.

Second-Generation Surveys

Once it was established that the victimization survey could be a useful political and academic tool for the investigation of crime, control of crime, and management of public perceptions about crime, governments in many Western nations committed huge sums of money to such research; '[surveys of this nature] were widely and enthusiastically accepted by much of the criminal justice community shortly after their initial appearance' (Hindelang 1976: 40). Thus, once the findings from the exploratory research, reviewed above, were analysed, a new wave of victimization studies with an entirely different set of objectives began to emerge. These second-generation surveys differed from the first-generation surveys in two significant ways. First, the methods of investigation for these surveys were much more sophisticated because a wealth of information derived from the earlier research about the patterns of victimization and the methodological nuances for their measurement was available to researchers. Thus, while the design of the original surveys was more exploratory/descriptive, the designs of the latter were more descriptive/explanatory. Second, the theoretical thrust was much better developed than that of the earlier surveys. The theoretical frame-work for many of these surveys can be identified as victim precipitation. In short, by attempting to answer the question 'what are the characteristics of a person who is victimized?' an ontological shift can be observed from the earlier dominant theoretical framework of criminology which attempted to answer the question 'what are the characteristics of a person who violates norms?' In this section, I briefly review the major second-generation surveys in order to point out the political and financial commitments dedicated to them in Britain and North America. In this way, the political advantages involved in shifting the responsibility for documenting the epidemiology of crime from the police to large departments of justice located in the central governments will be illus-trated.

United States. In the United States, the National Crime Surveys were initiated in two distinct ways.[10] City samples which surveyed twenty-six large cities (thir-teen of these twice per year) (US Department of Justice 1975, 1976a, 1976b) commenced in 1972 and were discontinued in 1975 (O'Brien 1985). The second type of survey was the National Crime Panel (NCP) (Sparks 1982). Whereas the city sample interviewed 22,000 people from 10,000 households in each of the cities (ibid.), the national sample included 136,000 interviews conducted in 72,000 households (ibid.). As a panel study, households were divided into six subsamples of 12,000 each, one of which was visited in its entirety every month, and each of which was visited in its entirety twice per year. The logic behind this strategy was to set a period of optimal recall of six months and to establish a time period of recall for the respondents which was bounded by the actual interviews. Because the first interview does not have an initial boundary, data from all first interviews were not included in the data set. In this way, each of the 136,000 respondents were interviewed twice per year for three years – a total of seven interviews, from which only the last six were included (ibid.).[11] Each of the subsamples was rotated out of the panel every six months, and replaced with a new one. The panel portion of the project spanned five years and was temporarily discontinued in 1977 (ibid.).

One of the major characteristics of this design was the theoretical ability to reduce non-sampling errors resulting from forward and reverse telescoping. Figure 17.1 presents the magnitude of telescoping identified from the reverse record check method on the San Jose pretest from the National Institute of Law Enforcement and Criminal Justice study of 1972.

From figure 17.1 it can be seen that, for the San Jose data, the degree of telescoping (both forward and backward), or error in recall, increases with the time elapsed since the incident being recalled. Sparks, Genn, and Dodd (1977)

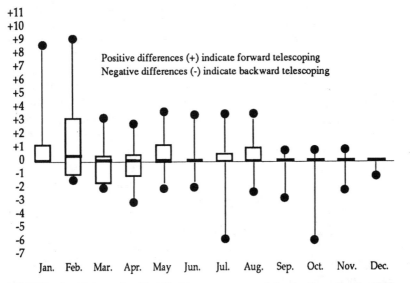

FIGURE 17.1. Telescoping identified by reverse record checks (from Sparks 1982: 75; month of incident according to police records)

found a similar pattern of telescoping in their London study, as did Gottfredson and Hindelang (1977) in their analysis of the NCP data. Of considerable interest, however, is that the effects of forward and backward telescoping are not identical. The box and whisker plot in figure 17.1 suggests that more error in recall is attributable to forward telescoping, indicating that, if anything, survey estimates will in the long run err on the positive side, even when a bounding procedure is included. Sparks (1982) concludes from these data: 'It may be that, like recall on an all-or-nothing basis, [telescoping] can to some extent be controlled by optimum interviewing strategies, within acceptable limits. If so, then the expensive procedure of 'bounding' now being used in the NCP national panel may need to be reconsidered. At present, this practice results in about 15% of the data collected simply being wasted so far as estimation purposes are concerned' (1982: 76). The implications of this finding are that bounding the time frame for the respondent in the interview may be all that is necessary for improving accuracy, although the effects of reverse telescoping probably do not equal the effects of forward telescoping in the long run. Formulated in this way, however, the problem of telescoping does raise important considerations for multiple victims and victims of series incidents. Thus data from the NCP has served to reinforce the study of victim characteristics, particularly for multiple victims. In this way, both theoretically and methodologically, victim-precipitation theory has been reinforced.

Such large-scale data collection and methodological experimentation has been expensive. During the years 1972 to 1977, the National Crime Surveys cost a total of $53 million US (US House of Representatives 1977). Sparks (1982) suggests that this estimate is conservative because it does not include the costs of the exploratory research required to develop the technology. The exorbitance of the National Crime Surveys not only led Wood (1984) to label these efforts an industry rather than a survey, but also underscored the termination of the program by the then LEAA (Sparks 1982). However, reaction against this decision to terminate the National Crime Survey resulted in hearings before the Subcommittee on Crime of the Committee on the Judiciary, in the House of Representatives, where this decision was eventually reversed (ibid.). Apparently, a considerable number of academics, criminal justice practitioners, and politicians recognized that the political advantages of the program outweighed the exorbitant costs, and it might be argued that, as is the case with crime statistics, the use of survey estimates serve more of a useful political than measurement function.

Canada. Second-generation surveys have been conducted in other countries as well. After a testing program consisting of smaller studies in Vancouver, Edmonton, and Hamilton (Catlin and Murray 1979; Evans and Leger 1979), the Ministry of the Solicitor General conducted the Canadian Urban Victimization Survey in 1982.[12] Data were collected from a total of 60,000 households in seven major Canadian cities, using a random digit dialing sampling procedure to reduce the costs of the research (Canada, Ministry of the Solicitor General, Programs Branch 1983). Although Rock (1986) documents that the original purpose of the survey was crime prevention, by 1982 there was a shift in the officially stated purposes: 'To be sure, crime prevention work is designed to reduce the number of victims. But there may be detected a steady shift of emphasis away from crime prevention and towards the provision of services to victims. The meaning and purposes of the survey were not stable. They evolved as the experiences of officials changed and as the social organization of expertise and knowledge began to develop' (1986: 138). Despite this fluidity of the perceived goals of the survey between 1977 – when the program was initiated with an allocation of $200,000[13] – and 1982 – when the survey was completed – Rock (1986) observes that there were no concomitant changes to the research design or methods. The survey was finally carried out with an overall cost in excess of $1 million (Hepworth 1987). Evidence suggests that the way in which the findings from this study were reported stressed previous policy decisions made by the ministry (DeKeseredy and MacLean 1991; MacLean and DeKeseredy 1990). Thus, as a well pre-tested survey and despite rhetoric which locates the purpose of the survey, the CUVS was employed primarily for political purposes, and now that these have been realized, the entire crime survey research program at the Ministry of the Solicitor General has been slashed (Hepworth 1987).

Britain. In the United Kingdom, a second-generation national survey was initiated in 1981 (Hough and Mayhew 1983) and repeated in 1983 (Hough and Mayhew 1985) and 1987 (Mayhew, Elliott, and Dowds 1989). In the first sweep, some 11,000 interviews were carried out in England and Wales (Hough and Mayhew 1983) with an additional 5,000 households in Scotland (Chambers and Tombs 1983) for a total cost in excess of £250,000 (Wood 1984). The second sweep (which did not cover Scotland), collected data on some 11,000 households in England and Wales. In the third sweep, methods of data collection were strongly influenced by those employed by left realists in conducting a barrage of local crime surveys. Findings from the British Crime Survey (BCS) are particularly relevant to the current discussion.

On the first sweep, the BCS employed a multistage cluster sample that produced national estimates of criminal victimization (Hough and Mayhew 1983). The second sweep employed a stratified sampling design in which the Acorn classifications were used for stratification of the samples. These designs are characterized by a conservative bias which has important implications for the future of crime survey research (MacLean 1991).

Findings from the BCS data suggest that there is considerable variation in victimization patterns *between* the Acorn classifications. The results are not dissimilar from the NCP findings in which there are high levels of unreported and unrecorded crime that vary by offence, by region, and by population.

According to Bottomley and Pease (1986), in addition to the National Survey there has been one local study in England which can be properly classified as second generation: that of Farrington and Dowds (1983) conducted in Nottinghamshire, Leicestershire, and Staffordshire.[14] Although this study restricts itself to three local areas, the purpose of the research was not so much to map out the characteristics of those victimized by crime as to explain the comparatively high rate of recorded crime in Nottinghamshire. These authors conclude that three-quarters of the observed differences in recorded crime are explained by different police recording practices and one-quarter by a higher actual crime rate in Nottinghamshire than Leicestershire. For Nottinghamshire and Staffordshire, the figures are two-thirds and one-third, respectively. This research illustrates the effect of police recording practices on recorded crime but, in order to determine this impact, the authors were required to study the actual behaviours of the police at work. Nevertheless, although the differences in recording practices occur *between* jurisdictions rather than *within* jurisdictions, it may be possible to estimate the effect of police recording practices on public reporting rates and recorded rates *within* a local jurisdiction by studying police practice vicariously, i.e., through the eyes of local residents.

Critique. These second-generation surveys have produced sufficient quantitative data to keep the criminological community actively engaged for years with their analyses. The monetary costs of victimization surveys are well documented. The cost to the criminological community, however, has been an expensive one-sided investigation into victim precipitation. The second-generation survey can be differentiated from its ancestor not only because of its methodological sophistication; as Maguire (1984b) notes: 'Once it was established empirically what everyone knew already in theory – that there was much more crime than reflected in the official statistics – crime surveys were no longer fun to carry out. So everyone busied themselves with creating measures about the victims lifestyle, the social and geographic patterns of crime, the effect of the police, public attitudes, the impact of the crime and the needs of the victims.'[15] The second-generation survey also differs from the earlier survey by expanding the scope of inquiry from a mere estimation of the frequency of crime to an investigation of a variety of other personal and social variables associated with the experience of victimization. The victimization survey becomes a crime survey by examining a variety of factors associated with crime. The result has been the identification of characteristics of those persons in the high-risk populations with an implicit focus on 'what sorts of persons would have this happen to them.' Crime prevention initiatives that stem from this line of inquiry result in attempts to 'rehabilitate the victim,' including alteration in their lifestyle. In short, the tendency has been towards victim-precipitation theory, drawing upon the previously noted 'themes' of Von Hentig and Mendelsohn.

Another difficulty with the second-generation survey is that, more often than not, it has been used nationally. The result is that, while it provides national estimates of victimization patterns, these estimates are of little use to local authorities. Crime patterns vary both *between* jurisdictions and *within* jurisdictions, as the foregoing discussion has illustrated. While the national survey can identify variations *between* jurisdictions, it cannot so readily measure variation *within* jurisdictions to the same extent that a local in-depth study can. Clearly, it is the variation within jurisdictions that is the most valuable for an effective law enforcement and crime prevention initiative, since local areas are policed by local law enforcement agencies.

Finally, these surveys are expensive to conduct. In order to capture enough cases of victimization to allow for statistical comparisons, many interviews must be conducted, and these are costly. The difficulty is that local authorities do not generally have the funds necessary to finance such projects, and the result has been excessive use of the national crime surveys.

As early as 1970, Hood and Sparks correctly observed of the crime survey that 'this kind of research is of great potential value and likely to be used by other investigations in the future' (1970: 5). Therefore, despite the obvious limitations to the crime survey, there are a number of potential benefits that might be derived from its use:

1 Crime surveys offer the potential to provide estimates of unrecorded crime.
2 Crime surveys have the potential for identifying the reasons why victims do not report crimes to the police.
3 Crime surveys can produce both qualitative and quantitative measures of crime.
4 Crime surveys can provide valuable information on the impact of crime upon victims.
5 Crime surveys have the potential of being explanatory rather than purely descriptive and can, therefore, facilitate the identification of risk populations and the aetiology of crime.
6 Crime surveys offer a source of data necessary for the formation of policy across a number of dimensions, such as law enforcement, victim support, crime prevention, and sentencing.
7 Crime surveys can facilitate the evaluation of community/police relations, focused policing methods, and estimates of police misbehaviour.

While the second-generation survey has been successful in achieving only some of these potentials to some degree, it has been fully successful in conveying its political importance to politicians at the highest levels who are ultimately responsible for assigning the research funds to such endeavours. If the local and central governments shared similar political perspectives in relation to law and order, then it might be very likely that the second-generation survey would be transformed into more of a localized in-depth crime survey jointly undertaken by local and central governments. Such an idea is of particular significance in England where the Home Office has openly encouraged studies at the local level. The difference in political perspectives on law and order in England has to a large extent been the most acute between local and central government, particularly when the locale is the inner-city dominated by radical labour governments committed to the movement for police accountability. It is of little wonder, therefore, that some of these councils have been interested in deriving the same kind of political mileage from a ready source of information on crime and policing trends that central governments have enjoyed.

The needs of these councils as clients and the sociological concerns represented in academic criminology are not incompatible. Rather, as the left-realist framework began to develop, it was as much influenced by the needs of the local London councils as these councils were influenced by left realism (Currie, DeKeseredy, and MacLean 1990). This set of circumstances represented the intellectual, political, and material circumstances for a new stage in the evolution of the crime survey – third-generation crime surveys.

Third-Generation Surveys

Different moments in criminological history have been characterized by one-sided investigations into different moments in the crime process (MacLean and Milovanovic 1991). The focus of 'neopositivist' criminology has been the victim, but the victim in isolation from the process of crime. Second-generation surveys do not realize their potential (as noted above) because of the positivist framework within which they are employed. Thus the questions of differential definition are not satisfactorily resolved, and the role of the police in the crime process has been left uninvestigated by these surveys. The result has been another set of formal definitional processes that organize people's experiences into a legalistic set of categories. Figure 17.2 depicts the process by which survey estimates of crime are socially constructed and should be considered in comparison with the model for the social construction of crime statistics advanced by Sparks (1981).

Figure 17.2 illustrates that the set of processes involved in the construction of survey estimates of victimization are similar to those involved in the construction of official statistics, but with two distinct differences. First, for survey estimates the respondent must recall the incident, whereas in official estimates such a recall problem is unlikely to occur. Sparks (1982) suggests that there is as yet very little known about the psychological processes of recall in the interview situation as it pertains to victimization. The process of telescoping is involved here, but, as already noted, it might be that both problems are better addressed by methods other than bounding. The second difference is that, in a survey, the respondent is being probed to recall an incident, whereas such probing does not generally occur in the construction of crime statistics. This second difference generally accounts for the construction of higher estimates by the crime survey.

Seen in this way, the crime survey provides not a measure of crime trends so much as a socially constructed estimate based on different processes. This differential method of estimate construction offers a great potential; however, since the crime survey estimates have to a large extent been carried out by criminal justice agencies, the crime survey might also be viewed as a broken promise. The crime survey promised to provide more accurate measures of the

**Incident involving crime
against respondent**

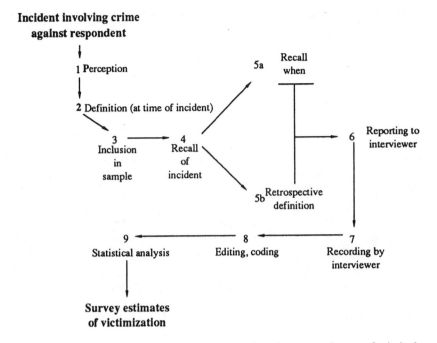

FIGURE 17.2. Processes involved in the construction of survey estimates of criminal victimization (from Sparks 1982: 66)

frequency and distribution of crime; instead, it reproduced the very categories and conceptual biases of the data-collection system upon which it sought to improve. Instead of addressing the political processes of data collection and reporting, the crime survey helped to make them more obscure. While the responsibility for the collection of crime survey data was placed with departments of justice and not the police, it still rested with agents of formal social control. Thus crime survey data are still politically biased and are still used politically in the law-and-order debate. It is doubtful that such difficulties can ever be overcome, and criminologists will probably just have to learn to accept such biases. While methodological craftsmanship can serve to greatly improve the accuracy of these estimates and reduce such limitations, the method of investigation itself will always create limitations, and the wise criminologist will interpret findings within these limitations.

In summary, a close examination of crime survey data in their current context reveals that they have the limitations that are associated with police statistics, with one major exception: because departments of justice and not the police are responsible for their production and use, their political basis is veiled by apparent social-scientific objectivity. Thus the crime survey served to rescue the law-and-order lobby from the assault of left-wing criminology and allowed the control over crime and policing knowledge to pass from the police to their employers.

Left-realist discourse has advanced the use of crime survey technology for the independent collection of criminal victimization data that will also be used politically; however, since the data collection is carried out independently, the information generated can serve to provide yet another independent estimate of victimization rates that may improve upon the limitations of the second-generation surveys. Despite the alleged differences between left-realist surveys and second-generation surveys, the methodological difficulties faced are similar (MacLean 1991), and it is probably an overestimate of the importance of left realism to suggest that it exclusively governs third-generation surveys.

It has been argued in this section that the third-generation surveys developed as an attempt by local authorities in combination with academics to overcome the biases of police statistics, the political domination of crime and policing knowledge by central governments, one-sided investigations into victim precipitation, and the lacuna of measures for police and community practices in relation to crime and policing. The third-generation survey can have great potential for local authorities and, therefore, by definition these surveys must be localized studies. If this new wave of crime survey research is to realize the potential described above, then surveys must employ highly complex and crafted sampling designs aimed at reducing costs; they must pay the same attention to non-sampling and sampling error; they must attempt to be holistic by measuring policing and community practices; and they must make the provisions to reduce the inherent conservative and sexist biases characteristic of the second-generation surveys. For the present, proxy interviewing might provide a cheaper way of generating larger subsamples of victims, while the use of random-digit dialing and telephone interviewing techniques should be reserved until further methodological research on representativeness justifies their use (MacLean 1991).

Left-realist surveys have paid considerable attention to each of these ideas in a conscientious manner, and as such should be seen as a pioneering effort that can be viewed as third-generation surveys. Currie, DeKeseredy, and MacLean observe that 'where and how this technology is likely to develop depends upon a number of key political and academic questions. For example, how likely is it that local authorities will undertake such research initiatives independently? ... Can a defensible, relatively accurate, alternative source of information be generated by such technology that will assist local councils and local police in resolving their crime and policing differences to the extent that they exist? To what extent can the descriptive statistics provided by these surveys be of use in explaining crime and policing trends? Finally, can these surveys provide a less politically biased account of crime and policing than other measures of crime?' (1990: 49-50; emphasis in original).

These questions are practical and can only be resolved practically. The third-generation local crime survey is an attempt to map out specific variations of the patterns produced by various crime-related processes. The identification of locally specific patterns such as these can be quite useful in developing successful interventionist strategies, of whatever political ilk. For this reason, I advocate the use of the local crime survey in Canadian criminological research. What follows is an agenda for such a research program, which the sceptical reader should comprehend not as a *panacea* imported from abroad, but as an attempt to construct *our own tradition with its own specificities*, the data from which should be *interpreted and used within the limitations of the method employed.*

A Program of Local Crime Survey Research for Canada

From the foregoing discussion and essays, it is evident that, despite expressed criticism and reservation, left realism has made a significant advance in the crime and policing debates. In this book, Young, Matthews, and Elliott Currie have advanced the notion that realism has a considerable potential to impact progressively upon crime and policing practice. Carlen, Dawn Currie, Ahluwalia, and DeKeseredy agree that, while realism has broken ground in terms of investigating feminist criminological concerns, it must make a more concerted effort to incorporate a feminist analysis of gender relations into its discourse. Such will be the empirical test for the utility of realism for feminist concerns. Walklate's major criticisms of realism are that (1) as a survey technology it makes certain assumptions, (2) that realism does not document the ways in which survivors cope with their higher rates of victimization, and (3) that in the realist conception of the community inheres negative implications for civil liberties and so forth. These criticisms, while 'true,' ring fairly hollow. In regards to the first criticism, it is a truism that all methods of investigation, indeed all social practices, involve assumptions. The main point is that researchers should be aware of these assumptions and draw their conclusions accordingly. Walklate's second criticism seems to confuse victimology with victimization surveys. While the coping strategies of victims is clearly within the domain of victimological research, it does not necessarily follow that such a concern is relevant to victimization research. Surveys have their limitations. Finally, the realist conception of community is as a *variable* not as a *constant*. The nature of 'the community' varies from time to time, place to place, and culture to culture. The aim of realist research is to begin to map out the characteristics of the particular community being investigated, not to impose a particular ideal conception of how that community should appear. The only way that such categories can be developed is through preparatory research in the community. In virtually every realist survey done to date, a considerable qualitative preparatory study precedes the actual quantitative survey investigation.

Pearce points out that a weakness of left realism is in its fixation on street crime at the expense of commercial crime. In part, this limitation characterizes survey research generally. The second sweep of the Islington Crime Survey (ICS II; Crawford et al. 1990) makes some pioneering attempts to measure the frequency and distribution of commercial crime; however, as a pioneering effort, there are still certain limitations because any attempt to measure any form of victimization is limited to incidents about which the respondent is conscious. Since most forms of commercial crime occur against unwitting victims, it may well be that survey technology is inappropriate, and that completely different methods of investigation need to be developed. Meanwhile, the lack of attention to such forms of victimization is a limitation imposed more by the method than by the theoretical tenets of realism, and more concerted efforts to document the extent of commercial victimization should continue to be a component of local crime survey research.

The balance of the essays in this book make specific criticisms of specific areas in which it is argued that the weaknesses of realism are specifically theoretical. None of the authors claims that left-realist crime surveys have been unimportant. Indeed, Pease recognizes the potential of local crime surveys to provide a wealth of information useful to criminologists and local governments, but cautions us that, as these surveys have proceeded in England, the thrust towards cost-effectiveness has resulted in a decrease in competence combined with a host of data from filler questions, the utility of which are increasingly questionable.

Given all of these considerations, I believe it is clear that the Canadian criminological community, and the community in general, can benefit from a program of local crime survey research. However, in order for such a program to have merit, it must adopt a number of principles.

Surveys Must Be Local Not National

If the goals of crime survey research remained those pursued by second-generation surveys, then a national survey would serve the purpose. However, in the attempt to overcome the deficiencies of second-generation surveys, third-generation surveys focus on all moments of the crime process: victim, offender, community, and state (MacLean 1991). Public attitudes towards all aspects of crime and policing, and public-police encounters are central to these surveys. Thus policing is one key area in which the third-generation surveys eclipse the second-generation surveys. For the most part, policing is a jurisdictional phenomenon, i.e., police institutions are organized and derive their authority locally. Thus, the characteristics and quality of the 'crime problem' in Vancouver may be quite different from those in Halifax. Vancouver city police are not really affected by the specificities of crime and policing in Halifax. Similarly, public perceptions and concerns with the 'crime problem' in Vancouver are directly linked to the specificities of crime there and the way in which the specific policing practices serve to shape those patterns. While it may be true that there are commonalities among different cities, those commonalities are expressed as local specificities.

In order for the crime survey to assist in the documentation of local policing practices, the monitoring of community-police relations, the measurement of the specific patterns of victimization relevant to the community, and the monitoring of the success of various crime control and prevention strategies, in-depth surveys at the local level are required.

For the present, there is not a single department of justice in the Western world that disagrees that local crime survey initiatives will provide useful crime-related information; however, the tendency seems to be the desire to build a national survey based on numerous local studies. Such a program would simply add up to a national survey with much larger samples drawn from the same geographic sampling frames. In this sense, the specificity of the locality could be lost because the tendency might be to impose the same categories on specific communities in order to allow for the analysis of between-group variations. By contrast, local studies would be committed to the purpose of identifying within-group variations. The importance of maintaining this specificity is discussed below. For now, it may be useful to conceptualize a program of local studies which includes some measures that can be compared between jurisdictions as well as within jurisdictions.

Surveys Must Be Based on Preparatory Research

In order for the local crime survey to be specific, and to document the specificities of the communities it studies, a program of local in-depth study must precede the survey. This component of the study is central to the process of documenting the concerns of the local people. In some communities prostitution may be the central concern, in others drug trafficking.

By including a preparatory component of qualitative investigation, research-

ers are able to tap into the appropriate domains within the community. Once these
have been established, the role of the survey is to measure the relative frequency
and distribution of the elements within these domains. In this way, the study is
not only total and relevant to the community, but also offers the advantage of
large-scale measurements which help to identify the risk populations and
facilitate an explanatory design.

Surveys Must Be Longitudinal

While cross-sectional surveys are useful in providing a 'snapshot' of social
reality, that snapshot is immediately out of date. As processual phenomena,
crime and policing processes occur through time and are not bounded by the
artificial time-limits of the survey. Longitudinal research is necessary to establish the nature of these processes over time. Of particular importance is the ability
to evaluate the impact of particular policing practices and crime control and
crime prevention strategies, and how these impact upon public perceptions and
experiences with crime. Only a longitudinal research design is capable of
providing such insight. Some national surveys have been longitudinal in nature
– the NCP is a panel study, and the BCS is conducted biannually – however, most
are not. The time dimension is crucial to pertinent policy questions such as 'is
crime increasing?'

Surveys Must Be Independent

History demonstrates that the state measurement of crime has been more a
political process aimed at shaping public perceptions about crime and policing
than an academic process attempting to identify criminogenesis. Maltz (1977)
illustrates that the adoption of a standardized record-keeping system by the FBI
in the United States was for political purposes, not crime control. MacLean and
DeKeseredy (1990) argue that the findings of the CUVS were, in part, a product
of policy initiatives established by the Ministry of the Solicitor General prior to
the analysis of the survey data. In short, governments and their agencies such as
police departments and departments of justice have certain vested interests in
controlling public perceptions about crime and policing, and surveys have been
useful in helping these agencies to maintain a degree of control of these
perceptions.

In one example, the Saskatoon Community Crime Survey (Ruby and McDowell 1986), police were employed to collect data by distributing questionnaires to
neighbourhood watch coordinators. Clearly, the local police have already
established a positive relationship with neighbourhood watch groups sympathetic to their interests. Of the approximately 60 neighbourhood watch areas

surveyed, more than 33 per cent reported responses rates in excess of 100 per cent (Anderson 1988). A joint venture between the local police and the Ministry of the Solicitor General, the survey demonstrated that the public were satisfied with the police. While the local police were happy with such findings, the Ministry of the Solicitor General was concerned about the methodological flaws. Only forty copies of the report were printed, and their location was virtually impossible to determine.

Such problems are easily avoided by contracting academic researchers to conduct these surveys. Police should do policing, and researchers should do research. Independent academics contracted to carry out a program of local crime survey research are in a better position to do reliable and valid research than are police or department of justice personnel, who tend to be more influenced by the official policies of their specific workplaces. If the purpose of the surveys is to conceptually grasp the 'real' as opposed to the 'apparent' problems, then it is only through more distanced research that such objectives can be met. In this way the research can be much more meaningful and useful.

Surveys Must Be Funded in Partnership

If a program of local crime research is undertaken that follows the guidelines described above, then it is clear the expense involved is too great for most local councils to finance. Encountered in Britain, this problem was partially resolved by the Home Office providing partnership funding to those councils interested in committing funds to a local crime survey.

If Pease (this volume) is correct in his observation, then the problem develops in which the emphasis on cost-effectiveness ultimately impacts upon the quality and utility of the research. Funding for such surveys needs to be adequate, and if local governments are unable to meet these financial demands, then a form of partnership funding should be devised which includes all three levels of government. Some sceptical criminologists, such as Brickey (1989), argue that contract research necessarily leads to the compromise of the researchers. Perhaps, when the 'contractor' is the central government, there are times when client 'interests' impact heavily upon the findings and analysis of the researcher; perhaps, there are times when they do not. In any event, partnership funding from the three levels of government will help to ensure that a variety of concerns and interests are included.

Surveys Must Be Sensitive to the Experiences of the Disenfranchised

Perhaps, the most fundamental criticism advanced against realism by the contributing authors in this book is that it fails to deliver on its promise to document the injustices experienced by women, racial minorities, gays and lesbians, working-class people, and other disenfranchised groups. Such concerns must be central to any program of local crime research if it is to remain balanced in its perspective. How, then, is the centrality of such concerns to be ensured? The use of independent researchers, combined with a component of preparatory research, should help to ensure that variations of the problems of criminal justice administration are well documented. In this way, the conservative bias of previous crime survey research (MacLean 1991) should be reduced.

Conclusion

I began this essay from the premise that the major contribution of left realism has been its commitment to the development of the local crime survey. From this starting-point, I argued that, while victimization survey research might be located within the domain of victimology, the scope of research interests investigated by the victimization survey have had a much broader orientation than the purely victimological. In order to prove this assertion as well as to assess the weaknesses and potential of crime survey research, I provided a brief history of the emergence and development of the victimization survey.

The result of this investigation for this writer suggests that the method of left realism, *viz.* the local crime survey, is important to a Canadian criminological research agenda, and I proceeded to lay out some guidelines for such a program of research.

Having said this, I must also admit that I am sensitive to the almost xenophobic rigour with which some members of the Canadian critical criminological community reject all ideas foreign. Admittedly, such scepticism has a history and is linked to the expansion of post-secondary education in 1960s Canada (MacLean 1992), the study of criminology being no exception. As a young academic tradition, Canadian criminology was polluted with US and UK criminological categories imported as discursive baggage by the newly immigrated British and American criminologists employed to fill the faculty positions of the expanded academy. In many ways, the dominance of these discourses in Canadian literature has impeded the development of our own tradition. However, the adoption of left-realist method should not be seen as just another example of the importation of foreign discourses that are not applicable to Canadian society. Rather, with the emphasis upon the local community as the target of investigation, a program of local crime survey research based upon realist method should be beneficial to the development of our own theoretical tradition in three important ways.

First, the in-depth data pertaining to local crime and policing processes and the richness of such data will undoubtedly be a boon to the Canadian criminological establishment. Such data will be one basis upon which a distinct Canadian tradition can emerge. Second, with our efforts focused upon local communities, we will be in a much better position to advocate changes that are both progressive and resistant to dominant discourses which are not really relevant to the Canadian milieu. Finally, because of the political nature of both the crime and policing processes and those processes by which they are studied, by endorsing such a program, Canadian critical criminologists will undoubtedly find themselves engaged in the practical political struggle. After all, is this not what distinguishes critical criminology from its more conservative academic predecessors?

I would like to thank Dawn Currie, Walter DeKeseredy, John Lowman, Ken Pease, Paul Rock, and Gerald Rose for their helpful suggestions on earlier versions of this essay.

Notes

1 While the literature on this subject is too vast to refer to in its entirety, some seminal pieces would include Bell (1962) and Kitsuse and Cicourel (1963). For reviews of this literature, see MacLean (1986, 1989) and Phipps (1987).

2 Virtually every large-scale victimization survey in the Western world has been conducted under the justification of assessing the so-called dark figure of unreported crime.

3 The origins of victimology can be traced to Von Hentig (1948) and Mendelsohn (1963). While generally Von Hentig is given the credit for developing a victimological orientation, Mendelsohn first coined the term 'victimology.' Schafer (1968: 41) argues that 'Mendelsohn claims that he originated the idea. He refers to his article, published a decade before Von Hentig's study, which, though not a study of the victim, led him to his "gradual evolution towards the conception of victimology."'

4 Rock (1986) provides a detailed account of the origins and development of the Justice for Victims of Crime initiative in the Ministry of the Solicitor General in Canada.

5 Maguire and Corbett (1987) conducted an evaluative study of the National Association of Victim Support Schemes (NAVSS) in England.

6 Evans and Leger (1979) and Sparks (1976) both carry out reverse record checks, although for different reasons. Evans and Leger (1979) are concerned with evaluating differential survey disclosure rates between telephone and in-person interviews, while Sparks (1976) is concerned with establishing the magnitude of non-sampling error attributable to forward and backward telescoping. Both of these issues will be discussed below.

7 Levine (1978) is critical of such typifications which ultimately serve to vulgarize what Sparks (1982) identifies as a rich complexity of thought in Von Hentig's work.

8 Other minor studies in England during this phase of development include Durant, Thomas, and Willock (1972), Genn (1976), Mawby (1979), Sparks (1976).

9 This study also demonstrated that police statistics and victim survey data showed different patterns of the spatial distribution of victimization patterns.

10 According to Sparks (1982) there were four levels: (a) the National Crime Panel, (b) the National Commercial Survey, (c) the City Sample, and (d) the City Commercial Sample. I shall deal with only the first two.

11 Respondents were actually interviewed seven times, but because of the bounding procedure employed to reduce the effects of telescoping, only data from the final six interviews were recorded. In effect, this means that 1/7, or 14.28 per cent, of the total interviews are scrapped in the NCP studies.

12 Prior to the preliminary studies undertaken by the Ministry of the Solicitor General, there are only two small studies in Canada. See Koenig (1977), Waller (1976), Waller and Okihiro (1978).

13 This figure is cited in Rock (1986: 135).

14 Other crime surveys in the UK are discussed in the sections on first- and third-generation surveys in this essay.

15 Reconstructed from my field notes of an oral presentation to the AGM of the Islington Victim Support Scheme, November 1984, by Mike Maguire.

References

Anderson, D. 1988. 'A Critical Analysis of the Saskatoon Area Crime Survey.' MA thesis, University of Saskatchewan, Saskatoon

Anttila, I. 1964. 'The Criminological Significance of Unregistered Criminality.' *Excerpta Criminologica*, 4: 411-414

Aromaa, K. 1971. *Everyday Violence in Finland*. Helsinki: Kriminologinen Tutkimoslaitos, Series M (11)

Bell, D. 1962. 'The Myth of Crime Waves,' in D. Bell, ed., *The End of Ideology: On the Exhaustion of Political Ideas in the Fifties*, 137-158. New York: Free Press

Biderman, A., L. Johnson, J. McIntyre, and A. Weir. 1967. *Report on a Pilot Study in the District of Columbia on Victimization and Attitudes towards Law Enforcement*, U.S. President's Commission on Law Enforcement and the Administration of Justice, Field Survey I. Washington: USGPO

Birkbeck, C. 1983. 'Victimology Is What Victimologists Do, But What Should They Do?' *Victimology: An International Journal*, 8 (3/4): 270-275

Bottomley, K., and K. Pease. 1986. *Crime and Punishment: Interpreting the Data*. Milton Keynes: Open University Press

Brickey, S. 1989. 'Criminology as Social Control Science.' *Journal of Human Justice*, 1 (1): 43-62

Brillon, Yves. 1987. *Victimization and Fear of Crime in the Elderly*. Toronto: Butterworths

Canada, Ministry of the Solicitor General, Programs Branch. 1983. *Canadian Urban Victimization Survey 1982, Summary Technical Report*. Ottawa

Catlin, G., and S. Murray. 1972. *Report of Canadian Victimization Survey Methodological Pretests*. Ottawa: Statistics Canada

Chambers, G. 1984. 'Findings from the British Crime Survey Scotland.' Paper presented to the Edinburgh Survey Methodology Group conference on crime surveys, Edinburgh, December

Chambers, G., and A. Millar. 1984. *Investigating Sexual Assault*. Edinburgh: HMSO

Chambers, G., and J. Toombs. 1983. *The British Crime Survey Scotland*. Edinburgh: HMSO

Crawford, A., T. Jones, T. Woodhouse, and J. Young. 1990. *Second Islington Crime Survey*. London: Middlesex Polytechnic, Centre for Criminology

Currie, D., W. DeKeseredy, and B.D. MacLean. 1990. 'Reconstituting Social Order and Social Control: Police Accountability in Canada.' *Journal of Human Justice*, 2 (1): 29-54

DeKeseredy, W.S., and B.D. MacLean. 1991. 'Exploring the Gender, Race and Class Dimensions of Victimization: A Left Realist Critique of the Canadian Urban Victimization Survey.' *International Journal of Offender Therapy and Comparative Criminology*, 35: 143-161

Dodge, R., and A. Turner. 1971. *Methodological Foundations for Establishing a National Survey of Victimization*. Fort Collins: American Statistical Association, Social Statistics Division

Downes, D., and P. Rock. 1982/4. *Understanding Deviance*. Oxford: Clarendon Press

Durant, M., M. Thomas, and H. Willock. 1972. *Crime, Criminals and the Law*. London: HMSO

Dutton, D. and L. Kennedy. 1987. *The Incidence of Wife Abuse in Alberta*, Edmonton Area Series Report no. 53. Edmonton: University of Alberta, Population Research Laboratory

Elias, R. 1986. *The Politics of Victimization: Victims, Victimology and Human Rights*. New York: Oxford

Ennis, P. 1967. *Criminal Victimization in The United States: A Report of a National Survey*, U.S. President's Commission on Law Enforcement and the Administration of Justice, Field Survey II. Washington DC: USGPO

Evans, J., and G. Leger. 1979. 'Canadian Victimization Surveys.' *Canadian Journal of Criminology*, 21 (2): 166-183

Farrington, D., and E. Dowds. 1983. *Explaining the High Nottinghamshire Crime Rate*,

Final Report to the Nottinghamshire County Council. Cambridge: Institute of Criminology

Fattah, E. 1967. 'Toward a Criminologic Classification of Victims.' *International Criminal Police Review*, 22: 163-169

Garafalo, J., and M. Hindelang. 1977. *An Introduction to the National Crime Survey*. Washington, DC: US Department of Justice

Genn, H. 1976. 'Some Findings of a Pilot Survey of Victimization in England.' *Victimology: An International Journal*, 1 (2): 253-262

Gordon, M., and S. Riger. 1979. 'Fear and Avoidance: A Link between Attitudes and Behaviour.' *Victimology: An International Journal*, 4 (4): 395-402

Gottfredson, M., and M. Hindelang. 'A Consideration of Telescoping and Memory Decay Biases in Victimization Surveys.' *Journal of Criminal Justice*, 5: 205-216

Hanmer, J., and S. Saunders. 1984. *Well Founded Fear: A Community Study of Violence to Women*. London: Hutchinson

Hepworth, D. 1987. 'Canadian Urban Victimization Survey.' Paper presented to the American Society of Criminology annual meetings, Montreal, November

Hindelang, M. 1976. *Criminal Victimization in Eight American Cities*. Cambridge: Ballinger

Hood, R., and R. Sparks. 1970. *Key Issues in Criminology*. London: Weidenfeld and Nicholson

Horton, J., and L. Kennedy. 1985. 'Coping with the Fear of Crime.' Paper presented at Canadian Research Institute for the Advancement of Women annual conference, Saskatoon

Hough, M., and P. Mayhew. 1983. *The British Crime Survey*. London: HMSO

- 1985. *Taking Account of Crime: Key Findings from the 1984 British Crime Survey*. London: HMSO

Kalish, C. 1974. *Crimes and Victims: A Report on the Dayton–San Jose Pilot Survey of Victimization*. Washington, DC: National Criminal Justice Information and Statistics Service

Kitsuse, J. and A. Cicourel. 1963. 'A Note on the Use of Official Statistics.' *Social Problems*, 11: 131-139

Koeing, D. 1977. 'Correlates of Self-Reported Victimization and Perceptions of Neighbourhood Safety,' in D. Brucegard and L. Hewitt, eds., *Social Indicators in Canada*, 77-90. Edmonton: Government of Alberta

Levine, K. 1978. 'Empiricism in Victimological Research: A Critique.' *Victimology: An International Journal*, 3 (1/2): 77-90

MacLean, B.D. 1986. 'Critical Criminology and Some Limitations of Traditional Inquiry,' in B.D. MacLean, ed., *The Political Economy of Crime*, 1-20. Scarborough, ON: Prentice-Hall

- 1989. 'The Islington Crime Survey 1985: A Cross Sectional Study of Crime and Policing in the London Borough of Islington.' PhD thesis, University of London
- 1991. 'In Partial Defense of Socialist Realism: Some Theoretical and Methodological Concerns of the Local Crime Survey.' *Crime, Law and Social Change*, 15 (3): 213-254
- 1992. 'The Emergence of Critical Justice Studies in Canada.' *Humanity and Society*, 16 (3): 414-426

MacLean, B.D., and W. DeKeseredy. 1990. 'Taking Working-Class Victimization Seriously: The Contribution of Left Realist Surveys,' *International Review of Modern Sociology*, 20: 211-228

MacLean, B.D. and D. Milovanovic. 1991. 'On Critical Criminology,' in B.D. MacLean and D. Milovanovic, eds., *New Directions in Critical Criminology: Left Realism, Feminism, Peacemaking, and Postmodernism*, 1-8. Vancouver: Collective Press

Maguire, M. 1984a. 'Victims' Needs and Victim Services.' Paper presented to the Third International Institute on Victimology, Lisbon, November
- 1984b. 'A National Study of Victim Support Schemes.' Paper presented to the Islington Victims Support Scheme Annual General Meeting, November

Maguire, M., and C. Corbett. 1987. *The Effects of Crime and the Work of Victims Support Schemes*. Aldershot: Gower

Maltz, M. 1977. 'Crime Statistics: A Historical Perspective.' *Crime and Delinquency*, January: 32-40

Mawby, R. 1979. *Policing the City*. Farnborough: Saxon House

Mayhew, P., D. Elliott, and L. Dowds. 1989. *The British Crime Survey*, Home Office Research Study no. 111. London: HMSO

Mendelsohn, B. 1963. 'The Origin of the Doctrine of Victimology.' *Excerpta Criminologica*, 3 (3): 239-244

National Commission on Law Observance and Law Enforcement. 1931. *Report on Criminal Statistics*, Report no. 3. Washington, DC: USGPO

O'Brien, R. 1985. *Crime and Victimization Data*. Beverly Hills: Sage

Phipps, A. 1986. 'Radical Criminology and Criminal Victimization,' in R. Matthews and J. Young, eds., *Confronting Crime*, 97-117. London: Sage
- 1987. 'Criminal Victimization, Crime Control and Political Action.' PhD thesis, Middlesex Polytechnic

Reckless, W. 1967. *The Crime Problem*. New York: Appleton-Century Crofts

Reiss, A. 1967. *Studies in Crime and Law Enforcement in Major Metropolitan Areas*, vol. 1: U.S. President's Commission on Law Enforcement and the Administration of Justice, Field Survey III. Washington, DC: USGPO

Reynolds, P., D. Blyth, J. Vincent, and T. Bouchard. 1973. *Victimization in a Metropolitan Region: Comparison of a Central City Area and a Suburban Region*. Minneapolis: Minnesota Center for Sociological Research

Rock, P. 1986. *A View from the Shadows: The Ministry of the Solicitor General Canada and the Justice for Victims of Crime Initiative.* Oxford: Clarendon Press

Ruby, L., and K. McDowell. 1986. *Saskatoon Community Crime Survey.* Saskatoon: Ministry of the Solicitor General of Canada, Consultation Centre, Prairies

Ryan, W. 1976. *Blaming the Victim.* New York: Vintage

Schafer, S. 1968. *The Victim and His Criminal.* New York: Random House

Schecter, S. 1982. *Women and Male Violence: The Visions and Struggles for the Battered Woman's Movement.* Boston: South End Press

Schneider, H. 1975. *Victimology: Science of Crime Victimology.* Tubingen: Mohr

Sellin, T., and M. Wolfgang. 1964. *The Measurement of Delinquency.* New York: Wiley

Silverman, R. 1974. 'Victim Typologies: Overview, Critique, and Reformulation,' in I. Drapkin and E. Viano, eds., *Victimology: A New Focus*, 55-66. Lexington, MA: D.C. Heath

Skogan, W. 1979. 'Crime in Contemporary America,' in H.D. Graham and T. Gurr, eds., *Violence in America*, 2d ed., 375-392. Beverly Hills: Sage

– 1981. *Issues in the Measurement of Victimization.* Washington, DC: USGPO

Smith, M. 1987. 'The Incidence and Prevalence of Woman Abuse in Toronto.' *Violence and Victims*, 2: 173-187

– 1989. 'Woman Abuse: The Case for Surveys by Telephone.' *Journal of Interpersonal Violence*, 4: 308-324

– 1990. 'Patriarchal Ideology and Wife Beating: A Test of a Feminist Hypothesis.' *Violence and Victims*, 5: 257-273

Sparks, R. 1976. 'Crimes and Victims in London,' in W. Skogan, ed., *Sample Surveys of Victims of Crime*, 43-71. Cambridge: Ballinger

– 1980. *Studying the Victims of Crime: Problems and Perspectives*, Crime and Delinquencies Issues Monograph, National Institute of Mental Health. Washington, DC: USGPO

– 1981. 'Surveys of Victimization – An Optimistic Assessment,' in M. Tonry and N. Morris, eds., *Crime and Justice: An Annual Review*, 1-60. Chicago: University of Chicago Press

– 1982. *Research on Victims of Crime: Accomplishments, Issues and New Directions.* Rockville, MD: US Department of Health and Social Services

Sparks, R., H. Genn, and D. Dodd. 1977. *Surveying Victims.* Chicester: Wiley

Stanko, B. 1983. 'Hidden Fears.' *The Guardian*, 5 September

Turner, A. 1972. *The San Jose Methods Test of Known Crime Victims*, National Criminal Justice Information and Statistics Service, Law Enforcement Assistance Administration. Washington, DC: USGPO

US Bureau of the Census. 1970a. *Household Survey of Victims of Crime: Second Pre-test (Baltimore).* Washington, DC: Bureau of the Census, Demographic Surveys Division

- 1970b. *Victim Recall Pre-Test (Washington)*. Washington, DC: Bureau of the Census, Demographic Surveys Division

US Department of Justice. 1975. *Criminal Victimization Surveys in 13 American Cities*. Washington, DC: USGPO

- 1976a. *Criminal Victimization Surveys in Chicago, Detroit, Los Angeles, New York, Philadelphia*. Washington, DC: USGPO
- 1976b. *Criminal Victimization in Eight American Cities*. Washington, DC: USGPO

US House of Representatives. 1977. *Suspension of the National Crime Survey*. Washington, DC: USGPO

Von Hentig, H. 1948. *The Criminal and His Victim*. New Haven, NJ: Yale University Press

Waller, I. 1976. 'Victim Research, Public Policy and Criminal Justice.' *Victimology: An International Journal*, 1 (2): 240-262

Waller, I., and N. Okihiro. 1978. *Burglary and the Public*. Toronto: University of Toronto Press

Wolf, P., and R. Hauge. *Scandinavian Studies in Criminology*, vol. 5: *Criminal Violence in Three Scandinavian Countries*. London: Tavistock

Wolfgang, M. 1958. *Patterns in Criminal Homicide*. Philadelphia: University of Pennsylvania Press

Wood, D. 1984. 'Sources of Non-Sampling Error in the British Crime Survey.' Paper delivered to the Edinburgh Survey Methodology Group Conference on Crime Surveys, Edinburgh, December

Young, J. 1986. 'The Failure of Criminology: The Need for a Radical Realism,' in R. Matthews and J. Young, eds., *Confronting Crime*, 4-30. London: Sage

Contributors

Seema Ahluwalia is a member of the South Asian Women's Action Network (SAWAN) in Vancouver, BC. She is an active member in community struggles against racism and sexism. Currently she is teaching sociology on the Richmond campus of Kwantlen College in Vancouver, and is working towards the completion of her PhD at the London School of Economics.

Pat Carlen is Professor and Director of the Centre for Criminology, University of Keele. Her many publications include *Radical Issues in Criminology* (co-edited with Mike Collison 1981); *Women's Imprisonment* (1983); *Criminal Women* (with C. Hicks, J. O'Dwyer, and C. Tchaikowsky 1985); *Gender, Crime and Justice* (with A. Worrall 1987); *Women, Crime and Poverty* (1988); and *Alternatives to Women's Imprisonment* (1990).

Dawn H. Currie received her doctorate from the London School of Economics. She is Assistant Professor in Sociology and Women's Studies at the University of British Columbia. Her major publications include *The Administration of Justice* (1986) and *Rethinking the Administration of Justice* (1992), both co-edited with Brian MacLean; she was editor of *From the Margins to the Centre* (1988); and was co-editor, with Valerie Raoul, of *The Anatomy of Gender* (1991). She is currently researching courtroom interpretations of testimonies received from feminist expert witnesses.

Elliott Currie teaches legal studies at the University of California, Berkeley. He is a critic of conservative approaches to criminal justice and a leading voice on the liberal-democratic Left of US criminology. His many publications include the seminal *Confronting Crime: An American Challenge* (1985).

Walter S. DeKeseredy is Associate Professor in Sociology at Carleton University. He has published numerous articles on both woman abuse and left realism. He is author of *Woman Abuse in Dating Relationships* (1989) and, with Ron Hinch, co-author of *Woman Abuse: Sociological Perspectives* (1991).

Paul Havemann began his academic career in 1972 at North East London Polytechnic, developing the law degree and a diploma for advice workers. He was involved with Legal Action Group and Newham Rights Centre. From 1977 to 1988 he worked to establish the School of Human Justice at the University of Regina, where he was Director (1980-7). In 1988 he joined the Department of Legal Studies, La Trobe University, and assisted in establishing the National Centre for Socio-Legal Studies. Since 1991, he has been foundation Professor of Law at the new Law School of Waikato University in New Zealand. His publications include articles in the special issues of *Social Justice* for Canada and Australia, and he is co-author of *Law and Order for Canada's Indigenous Peoples*.

John Lowman is Professor of Criminology at Simon Fraser University. He is co-editor of *Regulating Sex* (with Margaret Jackson, Ted Palys, and Shelley Gavigan 1986), *Transcarceration* (with Bob Menzies and Ted Palys 1987), and *Gambling in Canada* (with Colin Cambell 1989). He is author of *The Vancouver Field Study of Prostitution* (1984) and *Street Prostitution: Assessing the Impact of the Law* (1989).

Brian D. MacLean studied at the University of Saskatchewan and the London School of Economics. He is the editor of *The Political Economy of Crime* (1986); with Dawn Currie, co-editor of *The Administration of Justice* (1986) and *Re Thinking the Administration of Justice* (1992); with Dragan Milovanovic, co-editor of *Racism, Empiricism and Criminal Justice* (1990) and *New Directions in Critical Criminology* (1991). He is co-author with Trevor Jones and Jock Young of *The Islington Crime Survey* (1986), and is currently the founding editor of *The Journal of Human Justice*; production editor of *The Journal of Prisoners on Prisons*; and, with Walter DeKeseredy and Bernard Headley, co-editor of *The Critical Criminologist*. Currently, he teaches criminology on the Richmond campus of Kwantlen College in Vancouver, Canada, and he is Associate Research Fellow, Centre for Criminology, Middlesex Polytechnic.

Rob McQueen is Senior Lecturer in the Department of Legal Studies at La Trobe University, where he teaches criminology and business regulation. In various Australian journals he has published numerous articles on legal history and theories of business regulation. He has just completed a monograph on the history of company law in England and Australia, 1856-1914.

Roger Matthews is a Lecturer in Criminology at the Centre for the Study of Public Order at the University of Leicester, where he is also the course director

for the MA in Criminology. He gained his PhD from the University of Essex in 1983. He is currently engaged in research on penal reform.

Robert Menzies is an associate professor in the School of Criminology at Simon Fraser University. He is currently researching the social organization of Canadian criminology, crime and corruption among Canadian political élites, and the history of psychiatric treatment and control in British Columbia. His books include *Survival of the Sanest* (1989) and *Transcarceration* (co-edited with John Lowman and Ted Palys 1987).

Raymond Michalowski is currently Professor of Criminal Justice and Adjunct Professor of Sociology at Northern Arizona University. Because he is wholly incapable of focusing on only one aspect of the problems of law, crime, and justice, his works have covered topics such as vehicular homicide, corporate crime, criminological theory, the political economy of imprisonment, computer crime, and, most recently, the character of socialist law and socialist justice in Cuba.

Frank Pearce is Professor of Sociology at Queen's University. From 1987 to 1988 he was senior visiting Research Fellow at Middlesex Polytechnic where he worked on the second Islington Crime Survey. He is the author of *Crimes of the Powerful* (1976) and *The Radical Durkheim* (1989) and co-editor of *Global Crime Connections* (with Mike Woodiwiss 1992). He is currently writing a book with Steve Tombs, 'Crimes of Capital.'

Ken Pease is Professor of Criminology at the University of Manchester and holds an appointment with the Correctional Service of Canada. He also currently acts as consultant to the United Nations Drug Control Programme. He has published widely in penology and more recently in crime prevention.

Paul Rock studied at the London School of Economics and Oxford University. He is Professor of Sociology at the London School of Economics, Director of the Mannheim Centre for Criminology and Criminal Justice, and editor of *The British Journal of Sociology*. He has written and edited a number of books and articles on criminology and the sociology of deviance, including *Making People Pay* (1973); (with David Downes) *Understanding Deviance* (1982/1988) and *Deviant Interpretations* (1979); *A View from the Shadows: The Ministry of the Solicitor General of Canada and the Justice for Victims Initiative* (1986); and *Helping Victims of Crime: The Home Office and the Rise of Victim Support in England and Wales* (1990). An ethnographic study of a London Crown Court will be published by Oxford University Press as *The Social World of an English Crown Court: Witnesses and Professionals in the Crown Court Centre at Wood Green.*

Sandra Walklate is currently lecturer in Sociology at the University of Salford, England. She is co-author of *Introducing Police Work* (with Mike Brogden and Tony Jefferson 1988), author of *Victimology: The Victim and the Criminal Justice Process* (1989), and co-author of *Critical Victimology: The Victim in International Perspective* (with Rob Mawby, forthcoming with Sage Publications).

Jock Young is Professor of Sociology and Head of the Centre for Criminology, Middlesex University. He was educated at the London School of Economics. His many publications include *The Drugtakers* (1971); *The New Criminology* (with Ian Taylor and Paul Walton 1973); *The Manufacture of News* (co-edited with Stan Cohen 1981); *Losing the Fight against Crime* (with Richard Kinsey and John Lea 1986); *The Islington Crime Survey* (with Trevor Jones and Brian MacLean 1986); and *Issues in Realist Criminology* and *Rethinking Criminology* (both co-edited with Roger Matthews 1992). He has recently completed the revised edition of *What Is to Be Done about Law and Order?* (with John Lea) and *Crime in the Inner City* (with Adam Crawford and Frank Pearce).